LIFE AMONG
the CANNIBALS

ALSO BY SENATOR ARLEN SPECTER

Never Give In: Battling Cancer in the Senate

Passion for Truth: From Finding JFK's Single Bullet to Questioning Anita Hill to Impeaching Clinton

LIFE AMONG
the CANNIBALS

A Political Career,

a Tea Party Uprising,

and the

End of Governing

As We Know It

SENATOR ARLEN SPECTER
with CHARLES ROBBINS

Thomas Dunne Books
St. Martin's Press ❧ New York

B
Specter

THOMAS DUNNE BOOKS.
An imprint of St. Martin's Press.

LIFE AMONG THE CANNIBALS. Copyright © 2012 by
Senator Arlen Specter with Charles Robbins. All rights reserved.
Printed in the United States of America. For information, address
St. Martin's Press, 175 Fifth Avenue,
New York, N.Y. 10010.

www.thomasdunnebooks.com
www.stmartins.com

ISBN 978-1-250-00368-3

First Edition: April 2012

10 9 8 7 6 5 4 3 2 1

My dedication is to my family: those who have nurtured, inspired, and supported my lifetime of opportunities and adventures.

Central is my wife, Joan, a sixty-year plus partner, whom I loved at first sight when I met her at eighteen and she was fourteen.

My parents, Russian immigrants, instilled values, motivation and confidence. My father, who experienced the Czar's wrath, taught me the importance of government in providing opportunity. The youngest of four siblings, my mother saturated me with confidence that I could be anything I wanted to be.

Our two sons taught me perhaps even more than I taught them. The matriarchy of an extraordinary daughter-in-law and four beautiful, talented Specter girls project a future of generations sharing my parents' genes.

This and my earlier books tell where we Americans came from and where we have the capacity to go.

Contents

Preface

The United States has provided worldwide negative leadership in amassing gigantic annual deficits and a staggering national debt, resulting in the emergence of the Tea Party, which produced gridlock and a dysfunctional government. European nations followed the U.S. lead in spending more than taxpayers were willing to pay, producing economic crises in Ireland, Spain, Portugal, Italy, and riots in Greece.

Occupations, protests, demonstrations, riots, and violence dominated 2011. The "Arab Spring" changed governments in Tunisia, Egypt, and Libya, and threatens authoritarian regimes in Syria and Yemen. Suicide bombings and insurgent attacks may topple fledgling democracies in Iraq and Afghanistan.

All eyes are now on the United States to see how we will cope with the politics of deficit and debt. The 2012 elections provide an opportunity for the voters to speak to these issues. The occupation of Wall Street, replicated in many other cities, projects a message of desperation, disgust, and despair. Wall Street provides the prime target because huge profits have been amassed with criminal insider trading; unethical, if not illegal, bundling of overvalued mortgages with bankers simultaneously betting against them; and banks speculating in commercial ventures with government bailouts.

The populist causes that projected strong voices to succeed in the civil-rights movement and in opposing the Vietnam War will have a hard, if not impossible, time being heard over the billions to be anonymously spent in 2012 by corporations and the ultrarich as authorized by the Supreme Court in *Citizens United*. In ignoring 100,000 pages of Congressional fact-finding on the corrupting influences of large campaign expenditures, the Court overturned a 100-year-old law.

The Court left a narrow opening for Congress to require disclosure. That was rejected by the U.S. Senate when fifty-nine members on one side of the aisle voted to proceed with legislation requiring disclosure, but not one Republican would provide the sixtieth vote to cut off the filibuster, notwithstanding the fact that at least eight Republican senators were on record favoring such action. In the face of Tea Party intimidation threatening heavily financed primary opposition, there is no longer a moderate Republican in the United States Senate.

This book provides a unique perspective from someone who has recently been in both Republican and Democratic Senate caucuses. It is one man's view of how we got here and some insights on where to go.

I thank Thomas Dunne and others at St. Martin's Press, with special appreciation to my long-standing colleague, Charles Robbins, who can turn hours of conversing with a microphone into a coherent text. I urge my grandchildren and their grandchildren and others to join the political fight to produce a better America.

LIFE AMONG
the CANNIBALS

ONE

THE NEW SUPER
TUESDAY

On May 18, 2010, which the media had dubbed "the New Super Tuesday," CNN anchor T. J. Holmes opened the network's 9 a.m. newscast from Atlanta:

We've got a test going on today of the nation's anti-incumbent fever. . . . It is a big deal for the country and it could change the balance of power down the road. These primaries we're talking about today are going to measure something much larger. A nationwide uprising of anger and disgust with Washington . . .

Candy Crowley, CNN's chief political correspondent, burst onto the screen from Philadelphia's Independence Mall. Over her left shoulder, Independence Hall, where the founders had adopted the Declaration of Independence and the Constitution, glowed through a gray mist. "Here in Pennsylvania, Arlen Specter—he has been in the Senate thirty years," she intoned. "That is a lot of power, that's a lot of seniority, that's a lot of sway." President Obama's agenda was also at stake, Crowley said.[1]

Across town in East Falls, I walked alongside my wife through a cold morning rain to my polling place at Alden Park Manor, a historic complex of apartments and gardens. Behind the Jacobean revival building, seven television trucks and vans clogged Schoolhouse Lane and the nearby greenery, their tires gouging the soggy soil.

In a day the press was billing as a referendum on the president's power, the Tea Party, incumbency, and the political center, my Pennsylvania Democratic Senate primary was the marquee contest. Reporters from the *New York Times*, *USA Today*, the *Washington Post*, and a slew of other major papers had descended on Philadelphia. MSNBC was broadcasting live from the Loews Hotel. Even Qatar-based Al Jazeera TV sent a camera crew to Pennsylvania.

The worst was happening, as predicted. Whatever chance I had hinged on heavy voting in the African American wards. The rain, which had been pelting Philadelphia all morning, could snuff that turnout.

Just inside the polling place door, a battery of TV cameras idled. I was eighty; this might be my last primary, either way. I used to joke about beating Strom Thurmond's record: the former Dixiecrat served in the Senate until age one hundred. But another run at eighty-six seemed speculative at best.

I shrugged out of my tan topcoat, presenting myself in basic Senate dress uniform of navy suit over white shirt and red tie. My wife slipped off her black military-style raincoat. Joan, a former four-term Philadelphia city councilwoman, was a prime political adviser. She also softened my prosecutor image. This guy can't be all bad if he has a nice wife like that, critics have said over the years. Joan and I had begun dating as teenagers in the late 1940s, when I was a University of Pennsylvania sophomore and she was a stunning blonde with a mouth full of braces. We had campaigned for each other. I once took a bullhorn to an Eagles game for her. Most people had never seen a sitting U.S. senator working the Veterans Stadium aisles. "Joan Specter for city council," I called. "Support Joan Specter. I do." At a recent fund-raising event, I announced that Joan and I had just celebrated fifty years of happily married life. When the applause ebbed, I said, "Not too bad, out of fifty-seven years of marriage."

We waded into the media mass. I usually tried to count the cameras, but there were too many and the lights were too bright. This was the first Democratic primary ballot I would cast since 1965. For the forty-five years between those elections, I'd been a Republican. But I was the guy *Time* magazine had featured as "the Contrarian" in the leadoff profile of a Ten Best Senators package, someone who had never hewn to orthodoxy—of either party. Who had, the *Washington Post* wrote, turned blurring political lines into an art form.[2]

When I had arrived in the Senate in 1981, that independence—making judgments and decisions as each vote and issue arose—had placed me snugly within a cabal of centrists. Those moderate senators made the deals that kept the country moving—on highways, health care, domestic violence, and a slew of other issues over the years.

But over the decades, the rise of extremists—in both parties—replaced tolerance with purity tests. For several years, the fringes had been purging centrists, applying screens in which the old Ivory Soap standard of 99 44/100 percent pure wasn't pure enough. Senators began actively campaigning against members of their own caucuses. And they did it with relish, like cannibals devouring colleagues with condiments. "Extremism" was no longer sufficiently extreme to describe what was going on. The quest for ideological purity was destroying comity and compromise and bringing government to a standstill.

With the rise of the intolerant right and the incompetent left, centrists became an endangered species, especially in the GOP. The moderate Republican Wednesday Lunch Club, once nearly two dozen strong, shrank over the years to "the gals from Maine"—Senators Olympia Snowe and Susan Collins—and me. Our lunches moved to my small Capitol "hideaway" office and we became known as "the Mod Squad," a takeoff on the Vietnam-era counterculture TV series.

Still, coming into the cycle for this race, I had a clear shot at re-election to a sixth term. Former congressman Pat Toomey, who had nearly unseated me in a 2004 Republican primary, had announced a bid for governor. Then, in February 2009, Obama's $787 billion stimulus bill came up for a vote. The stimulus, I became convinced, offered our only chance of averting a 1930s-style depression. I had lived through the Great Depression and was determined not to see it happen again. I took the Republican lead in negotiations, and wound up one of only three Republicans in the entire Congress to vote for the stimulus, and the only one of that trio facing re-election. That was the margin of passage.

As the Republican furor swelled, political pundit Chris Matthews cataloged the demise of GOP moderates and told me, "Now you're almost the last of the Mohicans, you and Senators Snowe and Collins. Has the party got to change?"

"I believe there has to be more accommodation to different points of view," I replied, "and not to assert a philosophy which says we're not going to yield even in the face of enormous problems."[3]

But those changes didn't come. And the backlash to my stimulus vote raged, fed by Tea Party vitriol and my other apostasies from Republican orthodoxy over the years, such as torpedoing Robert Bork's nomination to the Supreme Court, championing stem cell research, and pressing to increase the minimum wage and extend unemployment compensation. Toomey abandoned his gubernatorial campaign to run against me. My poll numbers looked bleak.

I wasn't going to put my twenty-nine-year career in front of that jury, in a closed Pennsylvania Republican primary. I had edged Toomey in 2004, but since then 200,000 moderate Pennsylvania Republicans had become Democrats. I decided in April 2009 to join them. That left only Snowe and Collins as GOP moderates, but they no longer acted consistently centrist; they couldn't afford to. The Republican center had died. The Democratic center was healthier, but no longer had a common meeting ground.

I had arguably been the Senate's last Republican independent. Now I awaited another verdict on my career, this time from Democratic voters whose party I had opposed for half a century.

As Joan and I voted and fielded questions from the press, my chief of staff, Scott Hoeflich, and two other aides worked BlackBerrys, tracking the weather across Pennsylvania and the national news. They scrolled for updates on a hotly contested Arkansas primary in which fellow centrist Democrat Blanche Lincoln was fending off a union-funded challenge. Throughout the day, Hoeflich was also swapping data with state and national poohbahs, including Pennsylvania governor Ed Rendell, a former Democratic National Committee chair and one of my deputies when I was Philadelphia district attorney. Rendell had barnstormed the state with me the past few days and was deploying what *Politico* called "one of the most storied political operations in the country" to re-elect me.[4] My aides weaved through the polling place, coiled to spring at any news, danger, or summons.

My stimulus vote, which had set off this latest round of trouble, was one of ten thousand Senate votes I'd cast and one of countless acts of defiant independence. I'd done it my way successfully for decades, and I thought I could succeed again. But that vote was the straw that broke the camel's back. It landed atop a mound of other troubles I'd invited over the years. My former law partner Mark Klugheit once said I'd be remembered for believing in a theory that most people doubted when I developed the Single Bullet Conclusion as a young lawyer on the Warren Commission, and for doubting a woman most people believed in my questioning of Anita Hill at Justice Clarence Thomas's confirmation hearings. I'd added to that legacy by killing Bork's nomination and voting "Not Proven" on President Clinton's impeachment, among other acts that alienated sizable slabs of the electorate.

Several weeks earlier, I had enjoyed a double-digit lead among Democrats, before my challenger, Congressman Joe Sestak, began running TV ads. The former three-star admiral advanced steadily as he first aired a biographical spot and followed it with a slashing, negative ad. The final major polls all showed the race too close to call, with Sestak and me tied or within the margin of error. My own tracking polls showed me ahead 43–41. My approval rating had recently hit 65 percent and my favorability rating 56 percent, dazzling numbers, especially in a throw-the-bums-out climate. Still, undecided voters break mostly for the challenger. If they hadn't embraced Pennsylvania's longest-serving senator by Election Day, they probably wouldn't. An endangered species might become extinct that day.

If I won, pulling out another tight victory in a nine-lives career, I'd be hailed as a genius, but there wouldn't be much news. If I lost, the headlines would be huge.

At Alden Park Manor, Andrea Mitchell, the veteran MSNBC reporter who had cut her journalistic teeth in Philadelphia when I was district attorney, opened the fusillade of questions. "Joan, how do you feel this morning?" "Senator, aren't the polls running against you?" "Can you possibly withstand Sestak's surge in the face of that devastating commercial label-ing you unprincipled, opportunistic, and closely tied to Bush, Roberts, and Alito?"

Over the years, I'd learned to smile through the slings and arrows. An older Philadelphia lawyer and mentor, Mort Witkin, had once admonished, "Never let your face show how hard your ass is being kicked." Witkin's other pearl was: "The higher the monkey climbs a flagpole, the more his ass shows." In other words, the higher you rise, the bigger a target you become.

In a sense, I was not the only monkey on that Primary Day flagpole. Alongside me, or perhaps even higher up, was Obama, who had promised me his full backing. When a reporter shouted, "Why didn't the president come to Philadelphia for you in the last few days before the election?" he probed an open wound. Some argued that the president had thrown me under the bus, suggesting that Obama thought our prospects weren't good.

I replied, "He was in Philly every few minutes on TV stations."

That figurative flagpole also carried incumbency and the political center. Some nine months earlier, at town meetings throughout Pennsylvania, I had taken the first burst of Tea Party fire against incumbents. Constituents had shouted at me: "You're a socialist, fascist pig." "Shut up and get out of the way." One man hollered, "God's going to stand before you and he's going to judge you." He seemed to have an inflated view of a senator's importance.

So I smiled and answered the reporters' questions. I felt good, I said. I cracked a few jokes.

We voted at 9 a.m., breaking a 7 a.m. routine set with my first DA race, so I could squeeze in two drive-time radio interviews first. I had left my house at 6:30 a.m., as rain dimmed the dawn, for a five-minute ride to radio station WIP across the Schuylkill River in Bala Cynwood.

For a decade, at 6:45 every Monday morning, I had phoned Angelo Cataldi, a *Philadelphia Inquirer* sportswriter turned sports radio anchor with a manic following. Cataldi thrived on controversy. On his show, then-candidate Obama had made news by describing his grandmother as "a typical white person."[5] My rapport with Cataldi had begun in 2000, when I detailed my Warren Commission work in my book *Passion for Truth*, and learned that Cataldi was a Single Bullet Conclusion skeptic. As a Phillies and Eagles fan who devoured the sports pages, it was easy for me to find more material. Our on-air chats developed into a mutual admiration society. During one re-election campaign, Cataldi read with unusual gusto a paid ad supporting my candidacy. Studio officials found that excessive, and we went back to the regular political spots for WIP for the next cycle. An in-person visit to Cataldi seemed a must for this tight primary. We exchanged praise and I stressed the importance of every vote and urged my supporters to come out for me.

In the same building, Michael Smerconish, a nationally syndicated radio host, newspaper columnist, and MSNBC personality, broadcast over WPHT, the Big Talker. I had known Smerconish for three decades, through his friendship with my elder son, Shanin. Smerconish was an unabashed supporter, but he was candid about our relationship and never crossed the fine line of objective journalism. After another pitch on Smerconish's show, we headed to vote.

A photograph of Joan and me at the polling place would run on the front page of the *New York Times* the next day. Joan radiated grace and poise and dressed as though she had just stepped out of *Vogue*. We hit two more Philadelphia polling places, at Simon Recreation Center and Finley Playground, where more TV cameras were waiting. The voters were warm. "Good luck today, Senator," they called. "Hey, I voted for you, Senator." But they were sparse. And the rain pounded.

Along the way, I later learned, Hoeflich told John Gillespie, one of my senior aides, to e-mail Andrea Mitchell about protocol for a live interview Gillespie had scheduled for me later that day. Hoeflich, who had served earlier as my press secretary, wanted to avoid a repeat of an interview Mitchell had done with me in Washington the previous week.

Mitchell had begun that May 12 interview in the Russell Senate Building rotunda by asking me, "Senator, this is a lot tighter than anyone ever thought it would be. What do you think is going on here? Are you having a hard time selling yourself to Democrats as a newly converted Democrat?" She then asked, in turn, whether an abortion-rights group's endorsement of Sestak was "a big setback" for me, whether Elena Kagan's recent nomination for the Supreme Court would force me to defend my earlier vote against Kagan for solicitor general, and why the president wasn't making more appearances for me. "Is he trying to avoid being tied to someone who he's not sure is going to win?"

Then Mitchell showed Sestak's devastating TV attack ad, with my comments about party switching taken out of context, and a clip of my misspeaking at an Allegheny County Democratic event, calling attendees Allegheny County Republicans.

"Does that make it harder to say you're a true-blue although newly minted Democrat?" she asked. She let me make my case, and then thanked me for the interview. I said, "Always a pleasure, Andrea."

As we hit the polling places in the morning, Shanin did something he had never done before: he grabbed a street list, went up to North Philadelphia, and knocked on doors for a couple of hours, to get people to come out to vote. "As I was doing it," he recalled later, "I was saying to myself, 'You know, I think this is the last time I'm ever going to have a chance to do this for my dad. So I'm just going to go up there and do that.' For me, it was therapeutic."

Shanin had helped run a lot of campaigns for public office, for me and for other candidates, but he usually spent his mornings downtown, where he was a founding partner in the Philadelphia region's leading plaintiff's law firm. In the African American neighborhood that day, a lot of people wondered what he was doing there. "Anybody who wondered out loud, I told them. People were very nice."

In the car a few minutes after noon, Hoeflich worked his BlackBerry and turned to me. "Senator, I want to update you." Physically, Hoeflich was a middleweight, but he pulsated energy, even at rest, and could focus his intense blue eyes in a searing stare. Organizing for America (OFA), an extension of the White House political arm, had just e-mailed him its first exit-poll analysis of the day. The report showed a host of demographic and geographic cross-tabs, and looked like a side-effect guide for an experimental diuretic. Based on OFA's polling and a model they were using, we were up one point overall.

I asked Hoeflich about the poll's methodology, but he was more intent on clinging to good news. "It means absolutely nothing at all, but it means everything," he would recall later. "You still have the lead; you're not trailing. Spirits are up."

That May 2010 primary marked my twentieth appearance on a ballot. Sometimes I can't believe how old I've grown. Jon Stewart asked me on *The Daily Show* how old I was. I said, "I forget." A friend and squash partner had advised me, "Why let a little thing like your date of birth bother you? It happened so long ago."

For years, I said my squash game was the most important thing I did every day. After a while, I modified it to say it was really the only important thing I did every day. Those workouts were essentially deposits in the health bank against my increasing withdrawals. In the past two decades, I'd survived two brain tumors, a heart bypass, and two bouts with cancer, among other challenges. Since my second round with Hodgkin's lymphoma and chemotherapy in 2008, sleep and exercise had become crucial. I'd been grinding through an hour-long regimen with a trainer at the gym, including a vigorous treadmill run, a series of lower- and upper-body machine exercises, and then "the Plank," a form of torture in which you brace on your elbows and lift off the deck for one and then two minutes at a time. My Senate colleague John Kerry, after trying the Plank for twenty seconds, said it was too vigorous for somebody his age.

We arrived at the Loews Hotel just in time for Mitchell's interview. She had become a celebrity in her own right, her status enhanced by her marriage to former Fed chairman Alan Greenspan. MSNBC was broadcasting from a corner fishbowl with picture windows and piped-out sound that let passersby watch and listen. Some gawkers dressed and hollered like hockey fans, maybe gearing up for that night's Flyers playoff game. The Phillies were also playing at home that night, with their ace, Roy Halladay, on the mound, which didn't bode well for voter turnout.

Mitchell began: "What do you say to those who say your time has come, you did great service, but they want a change?"

I rattled off a list of those who wanted me to stick around, including the Democratic State Committee, the black clergy, and the AFL-CIO. I said the key was who could beat Republican nominee Toomey in the fall, with the GOP threatening to take America back to the eighteenth century.

Mitchell fired her next shot. "Isn't the White House signaling that it thinks that Sestak would actually be a stronger candidate—younger, more vigorous—that's the campaign he's running—against Pat Toomey than you? The president has done a lot for you—robocalls, commercials—but he isn't here now. He wasn't here to close it. He didn't try to do a big rally, you know, in Philadelphia yesterday, turn out that vote."

"Andrea, he's on every few minutes on all the TV stations," I said. "You can't live on the planet Earth and not see Barack Obama for Arlen Specter. But when you talk about Sestak being more vigorous, you must be smoking Dutch Cleanser. Did you see us on the debate?"

The blogosphere erupted over my Dutch Cleanser line. The *Huffington Post* ran an item: "Oh, great. So, Arlen Specter, seeking to combat the perception that he is [not] still 'vigorous,' cites an old-timey saying about an old-timey product which cannot be found anywhere on the Internet, but maybe you can pick some up at a 'dollar store.'"[6]

Mitchell fired her next question: "Are you a true-blue Democrat? Now, you're not going to switch again on us?"

I laughed.

In closing, Mitchell said she had just been talking to some Democratic Party activists, who reported anemic turnout. "So the rain is not doing you any favors today."

After the MSNBC interview, we drove to the Famous Fourth Street Delicatessen, where I'd been campaigning since the 1960s. Photos lined the walls, and traditional Jewish deli fare such as corned beef, pastrami, and tongue sandwiches, stuffed cabbage, and matzo ball soup covered the tables, fortifying diners who had packed in against the cold rain.

As *Roll Call* reported: "The former Republican shook hands and was greeted as though he'd been a Democrat all his life, with a brief chant of 'Arlen, Arlen, Arlen' breaking out among those in attendance."[7]

Hoeflich recalled: "Everyone's clamoring to be with him, everyone's standing to shake his hand, the media is all over him—still photographers, TV cameras. So the boss is working the room—'Senator, you've got to meet this one, you gotta meet that one,' people are throwing themselves in front of him to get attention. I'm like, 'We gotta go! Let's go, let's go, let's go, let's go.' Push, push, push, push, push. Five minutes. Grab the lunch for Joan, get in the car, let's move, let's move, let's move, let's move, let's move. You can't. You can't. There's so many people there, dying to shake his hand."

I learned later that among the hands I shook was Sestak media consultant Neil Oxman's. Oxman had also represented some of my earlier opponents, and was quoted in November 2006 after I beat Hodgkin's for the second time: "When I think of Arlen, I think of those horror movies where you think the guy is dead and in the coffin, and then the last scene is a shot of a hand coming up through the casket. That's Arlen's political career."[8] Maybe that thought hit Oxman again at the Famous Deli.

Shortly after we left the deli, Senator Lincoln flamed into the blogosphere over a polling-place snag in Little Rock. She had arrived to vote, only to be turned away by election officials who found that she had already requested an absentee ballot. Critics who questioned Lincoln's commitment to Arkansas had been deriding her $2 million Virginia home, where the absentee ballot was sent. Reports circulated about the staff snafu of the century. Lincoln wound up showing her driver's license and filling out a provisional ballot that might be counted after the other returns were tallied. Not the ideal Election Day photo. "This is not only embarrassing, it could prove politically fatal," the *Los Angeles Times* cried.[9]

A candidate can run a disciplined, scientific campaign for months or years, only to get tangled by the caprices of man or nature—a rogue absentee ballot or a rainy forty-five-degree day in the middle of May. My father used to quote a Yiddish proverb, *Mensch tracht, un Gott lacht.* Man plans and God laughs.

As we arrived an hour late for a lunch Shanin had arranged at Smith and Wollensky, OFA's 2 p.m. update flashed. Turnout was approaching early predictions of 1.3 million. My lead had shrunk to one-tenth of a percent.

I took a place at a big round table, among a lot of old friends from a lot of campaigns and a lot of years. As Shanin later recalled, "I think everybody at the table felt that the day was going to be uphill for us. Nobody really said it. . . . He came in—and he was very positive, very talkative. But he didn't know, with precision, what was going to happen. Nobody did."

Right after lunch, our crews in Pittsburgh and Harrisburg phoned in breathless reports that the clouds were breaking, the sun was coming out, turnout was up, we're good.

Time for the most important part of the day. We drove to the squash court for a session with Pop Shenian, one of my regular partners and a longtime supporter. Shenian ran a commercial real estate company, had a black belt in karate, and played an intense squash game.

Along the way, Hoeflich asked me, "What are we going to do about the lucky tie? When are we going to go shopping?" Every Election Day, I bought a tie. The previous election, in 2004, I had chosen a purple-and-white number with white Burberry emblems. An earlier campaign tie from Brooks Brothers had red hoops sewn on a blue field. After the election, I put them into my regular rotation.

We stopped at Burberry in the downtown shopping district, where I had bought the 2004 tie. On that trip, an associate had greeted us, saying, "I've been waiting for you all day; I've got a whole selection for you." My chief of staff now hunted for the same clerk, but he wasn't there.

I told Hoeflich, "Scrap it, let's go."

"What about the lucky tie?" he insisted. *We need this,* he was thinking; *this is part of the formula for victory.*

Hoeflich had his own Election Day ritual. "I was wearing my lucky suit," he remembered later. "Navy blue suit, windowpane, like a faint white windowpane, brown belt, brown shoes, Canali. I had worn it for all our big campaign events, like when the president came, I wore it. . . . My father had bought it for me. Things go well when I'm wearing this one."

"All right," I said. "Tell Pop we'll be there in five minutes. Let's go do this."

We pulled into the Bellevue Hotel parking lot, trotted inside, dropped off our squash gear, and headed back to the stores. The rain had ebbed, and the sunlight now bounced off the puddles.

"It was fun to see him shopping for the tie," Hoeflich would recall. "There was this sense of purpose and urgency and need. It was like a cook searching for the right ingredient to make it come out well."

We walked into Polo. None of the ties appealed to me. We stepped into Brooks Brothers. Nothing grabbed me there, either. Then Barney's. All new-age trend, not my style. Back to Burberry. I looked hard, but just couldn't find a winner. I told Hoeflich, "All right, let's walk back to Brooks Brothers. I'll pick the best tie I can find."

Back at Brooks Brothers, an exuberant salesman rushed to greet us. "Senator, welcome in! I voted today, I voted for you. I'm so happy you're here today. This made my day; I can't wait to tell my wife."

"Did your wife vote?" I asked.

"No, but I'll call her right now, make sure she votes."

Within minutes, I found The One: small white sailboats on an ocean-blue field, all divided by diagonal magenta and light blue stripes. "Okay," I told Hoeflich. "Let's get it. Meet me back at the squash club."

My aides gave Shenian, a squash partner of nine years, a cold assessment of the primary, based on the latest reports. "When I played him that day," Shenian later recalled, "I took a little off the gas, accelerator—just because I thought it would lighten the mood a little bit." Shenian had played with me during my two rounds of chemo. "He was so gaunt at the time, I was afraid he wasn't going to make it," he said. "He thought it was extraordinarily important to fight through it. I just saw such bravery from him—he wanted no pity whatsoever. I pushed him very hard. If he ever sensed I would go easy on the court, he would fire off at me—he wouldn't put up with it."

But on Primary Day, Shenian thought he was being artful, that I wouldn't detect his easing off. I won the best-of-three match. As soon as the final point ended, I told Shenian, "You gave me a salesman's game," that is, the kind of soft game a salesman gives a customer.

"I just looked at him," Shenian later recalled. "I was just very surprised he was able to pick up on it. Because I wasn't blatant about it. I wanted to put him in a better frame of mind."

After squash, I put on the new tie, which complemented the navy suit and white shirt. But then, what wouldn't?

The 4 p.m. OFA update hit. We'd lost the lead and were now down by three-tenths of a point. Voting was running ahead of projections. The new model predicted turnout at over 1.5 million people. But I didn't find out any of this until later. "I didn't tell the boss," Hoeflich said later. "I didn't have the heart in me to give him bad news."

Back at MSNBC's Loews Hotel field studio, I eased into a chair for Chris Matthews's *Hardball*. Outside the fishbowl, my supporters and Sestak's pressed up to the glass, jockeying for a camera's attention. Our crew included several burly International Brotherhood of Electrical Workers volunteers, who waved "Jobs" signs and squeezed Sestak's bantamweights out of the way.

Matthews, a Philadelphia native, began, "Senator, I was over at the Famous Deli where you were today, and everybody says you by a couple of points; that close." He asked a few tough questions worthy of the *Hardball* moniker, then closed by saying, "I think you're the first guy I ever voted for."

The next stop was IBEW Local 98's hall at Seventeenth and Spring Garden Streets, where the union had lent us space for our campaign headquarters. Signs plastered the front doors: "Specter = Union Jobs" and "Sen. Specter and the Flyers—Both Great for Phila." The IBEW was by far the biggest-spending political committee in the state.[10] I got a tour of the command center, a converted meeting room where the brain trust was working cutting-edge hardware and software to direct get-out-the-vote efforts, file legal challenges, and monitor precincts. The place looked like mission control for a space launch, with consoles in tiered circles around a giant screen in the center well.

Brad Koplinski, our statewide political director, briefed me, explaining how this color on the map showed high turnout, while that one showed low turnout. They brought up satellite video of neighborhoods and told me we'd completed 90 percent of our "turf package," the houses of likely voters we needed to canvass based on performance in previous elections.

Thousands of volunteers, bolstered by OFA staff and paid workers—"Arlen's Army"—had been going door to door, sometimes making two or more tours to complete a given street. Most of Pennsylvania's 4.3 million registered Democrats lived in the Philadelphia area.

After fifteen or twenty minutes, somebody passed me a note. My briefing was keeping volunteers from making get-out-the-vote phone calls. "Hoeflich is telling me to leave you alone and get the hell back to work," I said with a smile. "So get back to work."

As we headed for the Philadelphia Center City Sheraton, where we would hold our Primary Night party, the 6 p.m. OFA numbers hit. We had regained the lead. We were now up half a point. But Hoeflich had stopped sharing the updates with me. "He's not asking, I'm not telling."

The Center City Sheraton was the same hotel where I had celebrated my first Senate election victory in 1980. That night, thirty years earlier, the hotel had been new, and so had I.

After Joan and I checked in, I did a quick gaggle with reporters who had gathered in the Independence Ballroom, already laced with streamers. They asked how I felt about my primary prospects. If we got the turnout the experts in the green eyeshades said we needed, I told them, we would win.

"Rendell wants to meet with you," Hoeflich whispered. "He's on the way over. Can I bring him up to the room at 7:15?"

Sure, I told him. Around 6:30 p.m., I went to my room to take a nap. Understandably, I couldn't sleep, thinking about the tight polls and the morning rain that might have doused my winning margin. My four defeats, for mayor, district attorney, senator, and governor, before winning my Senate seat in 1980, moved to the front of my mind. I phoned Hoeflich around 7 p.m. and told him I was heading downstairs now to work the crowd, because I wanted to be back upstairs at eight o'clock watching the returns.

"All right," Hoeflich said, "but Rendell's on the way."

"Ah, he's always late." I had given Ed Rendell his first job out of law school in 1967 as an assistant district attorney. We had become not just friends, but neighbors, living a few doors apart on Warden Drive in Philadelphia. Rendell had a reputation for always being late, which he'd earned. Just the night before, stuck in traffic, he had missed headlining my final rally outside the Phillies' stadium. Rendell often recounted an episode when he had arrived twelve minutes late for a meeting at the DA's office, and I "excoriated" him for making eleven people wait, prorated their salaries, and told him that he had wasted $4,872.

The 7 p.m. OFA report showed our lead had expanded. We were now up by seven-tenths of a point. We'd gained a full point in two hours. The gurus continued to estimate turnout at a high 1.5 million voters. High turnout was key for me.

Rendell arrived at the Sheraton more or less on time, and we worked the ballroom. We had half an hour until the polls closed at 8 p.m., and I wanted to prod every voter I could who hadn't yet cast a ballot. Supporters weren't scheduled to arrive until eight, so the crowd was sparse, but cameras and reporters had already set up on a riser in the rear.

"Isn't it sad that people worry about a few raindrops?" one reporter asked, suggesting a depressed turnout that would hurt me. "I mean, they go out in rain for everything else. This is important stuff here. As Joe Biden would say, 'This is a big deal.'"

"I never heard him say that little in one sentence," I replied. "Joe Biden having a five-word sentence? I don't think you're right about that."

Another reporter asked, "Anything you wish you'd done differently over the course of the last year?"

"No regrets, no regrets, no regrets." I told them the stimulus vote was the single most important vote of ten thousand that I had cast, and it excommunicated me from the Republican Party. And then I provided the sixtieth vote on comprehensive health care reform. "I wasn't sent to Washington to play it safe. . . . So I have something to show for what I've done."

"Senator, you seem—and I may be reading you wrong—but you seem remarkably mellow," CNN's Crowley told me. "Sort of at peace."

We bantered, but the talk soon grew serious. "We are seeing the Republican Party move far, far to the right," I said. "We're about to see some fundamental institutions in our society challenged. It could be a different world. We could be back in the eighteenth century if the Tea Party people do what they want to do."

A reporter asked, "Senator, do you remember another year when the voters have seemed so angry and so upset at incumbents?"

"No," I said. "This is an all-time record. And I understand it. The gridlock in Washington is fierce. You can't pass anything." I'd been fighting that gridlock, consorting with the enemy, as many Republicans saw it. "I've crossed the aisle perhaps once too often. That's a laugh line, guys."

Another reporter asked, "Is there as much anger on the left as there was on the right in terms of people sort of trying to purify ranks?"

"I think Joe Lieberman would tell you yes. I think there has been a lot of anger there. In all quarters." Lieberman, a centrist and a friend, had lost a Connecticut Democratic primary in 2006, retaining his seat by winning the general election as an independent. He planned to retire at the end of 2012.

Paul Kane of the *Washington Post* asked why I was running on my seniority and my record of delivering for Pennsylvania, given the virulent anti-incumbent climate.

"Remember Popeye, who used to say, 'I am what I am'?" I replied. "I don't think anyone could dress me in different attire. I am what I am."

Channel 10 wanted to go live. "Right now," I said, ready to go. No, the reporter said, at 8 p.m. "Not a chance," I said. The hit wouldn't do any good once the polls had closed.

Around 7:40 p.m., we rode up to our suite on the twenty-fourth floor so Joan and I could grab a quick dinner. That's when I had the first debate of the evening. I wanted to watch some news channels, to get the latest on Blanche Lincoln and other developments. Joan wanted to watch a movie. We settled on Fox. By 8 p.m., room service brought salad and club sandwiches. Down the hall, Hoeflich was working a TV and his BlackBerry.

On CNN's 8 p.m. report, anchor Campbell Brown was saying:

Tonight's breaking news, the elections that could set the national political agenda. The voters' choices in a handful of states matter to all of us, including President Obama. The backlash threatening incumbents could also deliver a blow to moderates, sending Congress running for the extremes left and right, and spelling a whole new level of gridlock.[11]

Soon the networks broke to Rand Paul, an optometrist and Tea Party activist who had just won a Republican Senate primary in Kentucky, where the polls had closed at 7 p.m. Paul had run on a limited-government platform, arguing that federal civil rights laws should not bar businesses from engaging in racial discrimination.

"I have a message, a message from the Tea Party," Paul exulted. "A message that is loud and clear and does not mince words. We have come to take our government back!"

From the other room, Hoeflich called, "The returns are starting to come in!" With 2 percent reporting, I was ahead 65 percent to 35 percent. But those were Philadelphia precincts, where I needed a massive lead to offset other areas.

I stepped toward a window and looked out. For some minutes, I gazed down at Philadelphia from the twenty-fourth floor, just ruminating about the view.

Toward 8:30 p.m., I headed downstairs to the "war room," a chamber off the ballroom with a separate entrance. In the ballroom, Rat Pack songs were playing, including Dean Martin's "Ain't That a Kick in the Head?" and "Return to Me," and Frank Sinatra's "High Hopes." Guests devoured prime rib, shrimp cocktail, and bacon-wrapped scallops. They sipped themed drinks, including one that staffers had named an "Arlentini," after my Beefeater and vermouth martini, heavy with olives. In the windowless bunker, staff and experts were tracking the results. More high-tech screens, lights, and audio feeds.

At this point, I could only watch as my fate was decided.

TWO

THE KID FROM KANSAS

At the height of the Great Depression in 1935, when I was five, my father installed wooden posts in his pickup truck, stretched a tarpaulin, and packed up the family for a cross-country trek from Wichita to Philadelphia, where his sister Chaika and brother Joe lived. My father routinely rose before dawn and worked past dusk, peddling blankets in the winter and cantaloupes in the summer, and doing any other work he could find. But it was no longer enough to feed our family.

My sisters Shirley, eight, and Hilda, thirteen, and I rode in the back of the pickup. We had nothing to cushion us from the steel truck bed. My brother, Morton, the eldest child, rode up front with our parents and did some of the driving. The trip took four days. The first night, we had free lodging with my grandmother in St. Joseph, Missouri. The second night, we stayed with my mother's older sister Anne in Chicago. We spent the third night on our own. In Philadelphia, we moved in with Chaika; her husband, Ben Greenberg; and their three children in an area inaptly called Strawberry Mansion. For nine months, we shared cramped quarters on Columbia Avenue near Thirty-Third Street, and I attended half a year of kindergarten.

With my pennies, I bought rubber balls to throw and catch against buildings. When a ball got past me, it rolled into Columbia Avenue and onto the streetcar tracks, and more than once a trolley ran over one, slicing it in half. When a big snow struck, a bunch of us built an igloo. A dog went inside and wagged its tail, knocking it down.

It was a typical Depression situation, moving in with relatives to survive. For years, I've been called a "survivor." That was my first training. I wasn't going to see those times repeated.

My father, Harry Specter, was born in the Ukrainian village of Batch-kurina and lived in one room with his parents and eight siblings. He never got any formal education. They were the village's only Jews, and convenient targets when Cossacks galloped through the streets looking for sport. At eighteen, my father determined to escape the czar's heel and avoid conscription in Siberia. He scraped together a few rubles and walked across Europe, alone, to sail steerage to America. He settled briefly in Philadelphia, saved his earnings working in a tailor's sweatshop, bought a Model T Ford, and drove west to learn English and see America. When buying blankets and dry goods at a store in St. Joseph, Missouri, he struck up a conversation with a widow named Freida Shanin, and wound up courting her eldest daughter, Lillie, a beautiful redhead. Lillie, then sixteen, had quit school after eighth grade to support her mother and six siblings.

World War I soon interrupted Harry Specter's romance with Lillie Shanin. My father joined the American Expeditionary Force. Thirty days after he enlisted at Camp Funston, Kansas, he disembarked in France and took a place on the front lines in the Argonne Forest. Essentially, they sent him to France with a big bull's-eye on his back. Harry Specter was too proud to realize he was cannon fodder. One hundred days after he shipped out, he was seriously wounded in action, leaving him with shrapnel in his legs and a permanent limp. He convalesced and returned to St. Joe to marry the slender redhead who would become my mother.

My parents played roles in the great American drama of pilgrims, immigrants, and westward-bound settlers who made this country. Over the next forty-five years, they would move back and forth between the East Coast and the Midwest, searching for ways to support the family. My father often said, *"Schver tsu machen a lebn,"* Yiddish for "It's hard to make a living." That was certainly true for him.

In 1930, my parents learned that a fourth child was on the way—me. My mother was initially distraught, but my father seemed content, saying, "There'll be another set of feet on the floor." My unplanned arrival may account for my view on abortion, which is that I'm personally opposed, but don't think it's a matter for the government to decide.

In 1932, the family was living in Wichita when legions of my father's fellow combat veterans, many with their families, massed in Washington to press the federal government for payment of their promised $500 bonuses. They called themselves the "Bonus Expeditionary Force" and set up camp, building shacks, staking tents, and moving into half-razed warehouses and market stalls. My father, in the depth of the Depression with four young children, didn't have the money to join them. A standoff escalated, and President Hoover eventually ordered his Army chief of staff, Douglas MacArthur, to clear the vets. Cavalry, infantry, and tanks chased the unarmed veterans and burned their makeshift villages, injuring hundreds and killing two infants by tear gas suffocation.

I can only imagine my father's anguish when his comrades-in-arms, who had survived enemy fire in the French forest, were cut down by U.S. troops on the main boulevard of America's capital. In a figurative sense, I've been on my way to Washington ever since to collect my father's bonus—to push government to treat its citizens, the millions of hardworking Harry Specters, justly.

After our Philadelphia sojourn we returned to Wichita, where my boyhood home rang with my father's constant talk of government and politics. He called prospective presidential candidates "presidential timber." He often told of going to the Wichita railroad station when Governor Al Smith of New York, the 1928 Democratic presidential nominee, came by for a whistle-stop or perhaps a rally, and shaking Smith's hand. I can picture my father standing among a crowd to touch the candidate. But I'm sure he wasn't one of those who vowed never to wash his hand after touching the great man. My father, who grew up in a cramped, dirt-floored hut, had a fetish about washing his hands at virtually every opportunity. That's one of his many habits I inherited.

Herbert Hoover was our villain. Hoover talked about a car in every garage and a chicken in every pot, but he led the country into the Great Depression and routed the Bonus Army. When Franklin Roosevelt launched the New Deal to help America's little guys, he became the savior and hero in our household, and my parents became FDR Democrats.

My dad was a great believer in the power of government. He came by that from brutal firsthand experience with the czar's regime. He believed in the American government, and was proud to be a veteran. He hobbled back from France on crutches and said, "My country right or wrong, my country." My aunt Anne Shanin later told me my father had aspired for me to be a senator, but I don't recall his ever saying that. To my mind, satisfying my father required becoming president.

I became an avid sports fan in 1938, at age eight, when the Chicago Cubs won the pennant. I picked the Cubs as my team because of our 1935 Chicago visit to Aunt Anne, whom I greatly admired because she was a scholar. She went to Palestine in 1937 and brought me back a wooden camel that was also an inkwell, and a metallic pen.

When I was eleven, my aunt Rose arranged a job for me as a bicycle messenger, delivering bills of lading for the grain company where she was the president's secretary. In the basement of the building where the company had its offices—at eight stories, it seemed a skyscraper to me—they had a pool hall with ticker tape that reported baseball games. I watched them work the ticker tape and the scoreboard and then went home, and at 3 p.m. every day, KFH Radio aired a baseball game with announcer Larry Stanley. Stanley had the most wonderful delivery. "Good afternoon, ladies and gentlemen, welcome to Wrigley Field for the rubber game in the series between the Chicago Cubs and the Boston Bees."

One day, I came home to hear Stanley doing the play-by-play of a game that I'd seen on the ticker board, and which was over. *What's going on?* I went to see Stanley at the radio station. Bald and fat, he sat in a small, windowless room. Ticker tape spun out, "On a 3–2 pitch, Mize walked." And Stanley effused, "And here he is, kicks high in the air, it's a three-two count, then he comes in, low and out-side! Ball four." Stanley was making it all up. It was re-creation, and fabrication. My first career ambition was born—to be a broadcaster.

When I was twelve, we moved to Russell, Kansas, a town of five thousand on the western plains. Another future senator, Bob Dole, also grew up in Russell. When my father opened a scrapyard, he weighed his junk on Dole's father's scale. I went to Russell High School, where I got my best formal education. Russell had hired a new debate coach, twenty-two-year-old Ada Mae Gressinger, who was determined to win the state championship. She put each of us through two practice debates a day, one at debate class at 9 a.m. and the second at either 4, 5, 7, or 8 p.m., which she personally critiqued. Debate was the best education conceivable: it taught us how to speak fluently, think on our feet, organize extemporaneously, do research, and deal with public-policy questions. We won the state championship, but along the way we learned how to take defeats as well as victories. I still recall, vividly and visccrally, bitter losses at high school debate tournaments, ferocious competitions waged with the passion and energy of youth, when I was a consummately invested sophomore. I didn't lose many debates as a junior and senior.

After graduation, I enrolled at the University of Oklahoma, but I transferred after a year to the University of Pennsylvania, partly to be closer to my parents, who had moved to Philadelphia. At the time, Penn had no speech department, so I put down prelaw. I continued debating. My ambition— and the ambition of all serious scholastic debaters—was to win a national championship. I won one with Marv Katz in February 1951, the Boston University National Invitational Debate Tournament. But I sorely wanted to win the West Point National Invitational. I competed at West Point three times, and the closest I got was the quarterfinals in the spring of 1949.

At my last try in the spring of 1951, General Dwight Eisenhower's son John, who was teaching at West Point, was one of the judges. The topic was "Resolved that the noncommunist nations should form a new international organization." I proposed an international immigration organization, which technically fit the title. I argued that the noncommunist nations had already formed an international organization by moving into Korea through a United Nations operation. History has vindicated me on that. For the judges, it was too far-out, a harbinger of the popular reaction nearly fifty years later to my "Not Proven" vote on President Clinton's impeachment.

After graduation, I served two years as a lieutenant in the Air Force Office of Special Investigations, conducting background investigations on applicants for top-secret security clearances and investigating crimes and procurement fraud. The character references alone took me from West Virginia taprooms to the Center City office of Grace Kelly's father, John Kelly Sr. I had a government Chevrolet with nontraceable plates, so I parked where I wanted. It was my first experience at not complying.

After my discharge, I spent three years at Yale Law School, serving as a law review editor. Upon graduation in 1956, I joined Barnes, Dechert, Price, Myers & Rhoads, becoming the first Jew to crack a white-shoe Philadelphia law firm. Philadelphia then was an entrenched community controlled by the WASP Main Line establishment.

Our offices had wall-to-wall carpet, newly in vogue, and I knew what it meant: the wall-to-wall life, the big law firm's equivalent of cradle-to-grave, law school graduation to the farm on retirement. I had always been more interested in working in the public sector, especially in elective office, than in the private world. The public sector delivers a greater intensity of interest and a greater sense of accomplishment.

Despite my parents' FDR fervor, I didn't have any key political alliances. I hadn't joined a Democratic club in either college or law school, though I wrote a supportive letter in 1952 to Democratic presidential nominee Adlai Stevenson. Still, in 1956, I knew I was a Democrat, largely because of my father's influence.

I had thoughts at the outset of becoming an assistant district attorney, to gain trial skills and work into the political system. Because the Democrats had tight patronage control, I began as a Democratic committeeman in Center City, Philadelphia. My job was to get residents to register Democratic and then to vote. Twice I climbed four flights in a row house on the 1700 block of Spruce Street to urge a man to register. Finally, I climbed the stairs a third time and dragged him out. Annoyed, he registered Republican.

Working the primary election of 1959, I got to know my ward leader, Ben Donolow, a lawyer and state senator. Short and slight, Donolow wore sharp suits and combed over his thinning black hair. I took Donolow to lunch at the Yale Club, which was a little snooty for his taste. He ordered a simple egg salad sandwich.

In October 1959, I decided to leave Dechert's wall-to-wall life to become an assistant district attorney. Owen Rhoads, a name partner at the firm, warned me that I was throwing away a bright future at Dechert and would be miserable. Donolow also wasn't supportive, except for wanting to keep me working as a committeeman.

Attorney General Nicholas Katzenbach would soon say that in Philadelphia in those days, "half the people are on the take." Under District Attorney Vic Blanc, you had to have a political patron to get a job in the office. I had Bob Dechert, another senior partner at my firm, who had gone to law school with Blanc.

Blanc didn't ask about my record, or why a Phi Beta Kappa Ivy Leaguer from a top firm would take a 40 percent pay cut to become one of his assistants. All he needed to know was that he was doing somebody a favor. He hired me.

I got my first big chance prosecuting Philadelphia Teamsters Local 107, a corruption case built by Robert F. Kennedy, then chief counsel for the Senate Select Committee on Improper Activities in Labor and Management known the McClellan committee. Blanc had sat on the case until the pressure grew too great. The International Brotherhood of Teamsters, under Jimmy Hoffa, was the largest, richest, and mightiest labor union in the nation. Teamsters Local 107 was the biggest labor union in the Delaware Valley, and could choke the city's food supply within hours by striking. The McClellan committee report warned that Hoffa threatened the nation's survival. Left unchecked, the senators wrote, Hoffa would destroy the decent U.S. labor movement and place the underworld in a position to dominate American economic life.

My first day on the job, as the only unassigned assistant in the DA's office, I was immediately drafted for legal research on the Teamsters case. The same Philadelphia politicians who would give Senator Jack Kennedy a decisive majority in the 1960 presidential race were whitewashing corruption that the Kennedy brothers had uncovered among Hoffa's lieutenants running the Philadelphia Teamsters. Blanc charged the Teamsters leaders with conspiracy to cheat and defraud a union of its money, goods, and property.

The top gun in the Teamsters' legal battery, Morton Witkin, was Philadelphia's finest defense lawyer. No other lawyer could match his experience, shrewdness, and competitive drive. Witkin, then sixty-eight, had been trying cases for more than forty years. He was equally accomplished in the political wars. He had been the first Jewish minority leader of the Pennsylvania State House of Representatives. Afterward, he ran a meticulously honest county commissioner's office. At five feet four with dull features, Witkin looked like a gnome. But when he spoke, he took on a dancer's grace.

Until 1962, the Teamsters' legal strategy of stalling and delaying had worked perfectly, except for one detail: the Kennedy brothers had risen to national power. Jack Kennedy was president and Robert Kennedy was attorney general, and he had not forgotten the Philadelphia Teamster leaders' insults. I saw the determination in Robert Kennedy's eyes when we discussed the Teamster case in August 1962 at the District Attorneys' National Convention in Philadelphia. He seemed to distrust the entire Philadelphia scene. When our exchange ended, he said, "We'll be in touch." It was clear he meant, "We'll be watching you."

I had been serving as chief of the appeals division since October 1960. I had fallen heir to the Teamsters 107 case, which none of the other assistants wanted. Finally, I would lead the kind of courtroom battle that had drawn me to the DA's office.

On March 25, 1963, the case came to trial. When we lined up for the opening day, nine defense lawyers sat on one side and I sat on the other, prompting one reporter to write that it appeared the courtroom might tilt to one side. The defense lawyers were superb. Any one of them handling the case alone might have won it. Together, though, they were bumping into each other.

The trial lasted seventy-one days. The jury deliberated two hours, and convicted each labor leader. We had scored the first convictions of labor leaders targeted by the McClellan committee's massive two-year investigation.

The next day, Robert Kennedy invited me to Washington. In his Justice Department office, amid his children's chocolate milk bottles and drawings, the attorney general asked me to join the Justice Department team prosecuting Jimmy Hoffa. I declined, saying I wanted to stay in Philadelphia for personal and professional reasons. After my meeting with Kennedy, his deputy Howard Willens, one of my law school classmates, pressed me again.

A few months later, on New Year's Eve, Willens phoned me with another offer: a position as assistant counsel on a presidential commission to investigate the assassination of President Kennedy. It was another wrenching decision. I'd have to leave my two young sons, and probably abandon a state senate run that I was preparing. But I had great admiration for John F. Kennedy as our nation's vibrant young leader, and for Jackie and their two small children, close in age to mine. I was caught up in the swell of Camelot, like so many Americans. I finally accepted.

The commission had divided the investigation into six major areas and had hired a team of lawyers from around the country, accomplished but with limited courtroom and investigative experience. The commission deliberately chose a geographically diverse team with limited government connections to avoid any appearance of a whitewash.

When I arrived on January 13, 1964, senior lawyers had been assigned to areas, but the younger ones had not. That essentially let me choose my focus. I wound up in Area 1, which covered President Kennedy's activities from his departure by helicopter from the White House lawn on November 21, 1963, to his body's return to the White House the morning of November 23 after the autopsy. It seemed the most compelling. I had no idea at that point of the turns the medical evidence would take or where Area 1 would lead.

The senior lawyer in Area 1 was Francis W. H. Adams, a former New York City police commissioner who was then a senior partner at a major New York firm. Early on, the *New York Post* quoted Adams as calling the

Kennedy assassination "just another first-degree murder case." Adams told me right off that he had to begin a major antitrust case five weeks after the commission convened.

From the start, Frank Adams appeared only sporadically at commission headquarters at the Veterans of Foreign Wars Building, and only briefly when he did. By mid-March, Adams rarely showed at the commission. On March 16, the autopsy surgeons arrived to testify, and I introduced each in turn to the chief justice. Frank Adams walked in during those introductions, just a few moments late. "Good afternoon, Doctor," Warren said to Adams. That was the last we saw of Frank Adams.

As for my own distractions from the investigation, it turned out I would not have to juggle a run for the Pennsylvania State Senate with the commission's work. The Democratic ward leaders voted 3–2 to nominate my opponent, Louis Johanson, who went on to win the seat. In 1980, Johanson, then a Philadelphia city councilman, would be arrested in the ABSCAM sting, in which FBI operatives posed as intermediaries for a fictitious Saudi sheikh trying to buy favors on winning U.S. asylum and moving funds. He would be convicted and jailed.

I wound up working closely with the Area 2 team, Joe Ball and David Belin, which covered the assassin's identity. The team would treat it as an open question, despite Lee Harvey Oswald's arrest. The line between our areas had never been clearly drawn. We decided that the bullet in flight was our dividing point. Before the bullet left the rifle barrel, it was the responsibility of Ball and Belin. After striking the president, it was my responsibility.

I wound up questioning Texas governor John Connally; his wife, Nellie; the trauma surgeons; the autopsy surgeons; the Secret Service agents; Senator Ralph Yarborough, the Texas Democrat who had been riding in the follow-up car with then–vice president Lyndon Johnson; and Jack Ruby, who shot Oswald. I also sifted through countless files, reports, and tests.

I have been credited—or condemned—as the author of the Single Bullet Theory. I now call it the Single Bullet Conclusion. It began as a theory, but when a theory is established by the facts, it deserves to be called a conclusion. The conclusion holds that a single bullet fired from Oswald's

Mannlicher-Carcano rifle passed through two large strap muscles in the back of Kennedy's neck, exited the front of his neck, nicking his tie, then entered Connally's back, exited under the Texas governor's right nipple, tumbled through Connally's wrist, and lodged in his thigh. Sometimes truth is stranger than fiction. The theory appeared intact in the final, official Warren Commission Report, submitted to President Johnson on September 28, 1964.

While I put the pieces together, the chief autopsy surgeon, Dr. James J. Humes, laid them out, even if he did not think the bullet went through Connally's wrist. I've always been willing to take on the mantle of authorship that an early Warren Commission critic first thrust on me, mostly because I've always been confident that the Single Bullet Conclusion is correct. Advances in technology have allowed computer simulations, most notably by ABC News, that seem to prove the Single Bullet Conclusion definitively. Still, fifty years later, it remains hard to accept that a lone warped gunman could bring down the most powerful man in the world and shatter the nation's idyllic dream of Camelot. Kennedy was erudite, charming, lucky. At a gut level, it all feels wrong.

After completing work on the Warren Commission, I made a brief trip to Kansas to visit my brother, Morton, and flew to Philadelphia. Joan met me at the gate at 10:30 p.m. to tell me that the chancellor of the Philadelphia Bar Association wanted me to call him back, no matter how late. Within days, I had accepted an offer to run a full investigation of Philadelphia's magistrates, serving as chief counsel with the rank of special assistant state attorney general.

Inspired by an ongoing *Philadelphia Inquirer* series, Governor William W. Scranton, a blue-blooded centrist Republican, and state attorney general Walter Alessandroni were leading the charge. Philadelphia's magistrates, mostly former ward leaders, presided over the city's minor criminal and civil courts. Only nine of the twenty-eight had graduated high school. Only one was an attorney. They dealt with far more Philadelphians than any other court, and when people saw corruption in the only court system they knew, they inevitably thought all government was just as corrupt. Such cynicism weakens a community's moral fiber.

I didn't think anything about taking a key position in a Republican administration. But a lot of Democrats were unhappy about my probe because the magisterial system was a key cog in Philadelphia's political machine. From the outset, I knew it would be tough to convict magistrates or to change the system. Payoffs greased the machine, and magistrates were the most powerful politicians in the state.

Ben Donolow, my former ward leader, was incensed at the upstart who had won a prosecutor's job over his objections. He took the state senate floor to denounce me and my probe, calling me the "kid from Kansas." Donolow was doing me a favor: his assault lent credibility to our efforts.

We forged ahead, even when previously promised subpoena power was denied. Eventually, Payola Palace, as city Democratic headquarters was known, began to quake. Ultimately, we disclosed more than forty cases of payoffs demanded to fix criminal cases. We documented the magistrate-constable corruption racket. We identified thousands of technical violations showing magistrates' incompetence and indifference. We produced the first admissible proof of outright corruption in the 274-year history of the Philadelphia magisterial system. We put it all in a 515-page report. That document is the best work I have done in my years of public service. The grand jury returned hundreds of indictments against magistrates, bondsmen, constables, lawyers, and ward leaders.

In early January 1965, as the magistrates probe was raging, U.S. senator Joseph Clark wrote a letter to the Democratic City Committee that was published in the *Sunday Philadelphia Bulletin* listing five potential district attorney candidates for the coming elections whom he preferred to the Democratic machine's slate. The second name on Clark's list was mine. Clark seemed like the last guardian of good government, a white knight reformer. I went to see him.

"Senator, will you help me?" I asked him. "Will you help me raise money?" I figured a primary run for DA would cost $250,000.

"No, no, I wouldn't do that," Clark said.

"Well, would you come out and publicly support me?"

"No, no, I can't do that," the senator said. "I have to run for re-election in three years myself." But he added, "I will vote for you in the Democratic primary." Clark meant that he would support me publicly if the party followed his recommendation and slated me, but not if I was running against the party choice.

For years I had thought of running for district attorney. At a Phillies game, I confided my ambition to my close friend Marv Katz, who was an extraordinary lawyer. He said that I'd never do it, that it was just a pipe dream. In retrospect, Marv was right. My run was idiotic.

I pitched my candidacy to the chairman of the Democratic City Committee. He wasn't interested. "We don't need another Tom Dewey," he told me. In other words, the machine wanted a DA it could control.

Shortly after my session with the Democratic chairman, the Philadelphia Republican leader, Billy Meehan, approached me about running for district attorney on the GOP line. I had met Meehan through Morton Witkin, the former statehouse Republican leader I had battled in the Teamsters case. Witkin and I had become friends during the trial and he had grown into a sort of father figure to me. On Saturday nights Witkin and I used to go out to dinner with our wives, often at the Vesper Club, a Center City restaurant established in 1901 as a private club to circumvent the old Quaker blue laws restricting alcohol.

Meehan had been the Republican leader only since 1961, taking over from his father. His fondest ambition was to win the mayoralty. Witkin hosted strategy sessions at his large apartment at South Rittenhouse Square, where he and Meehan pressed me to make the run. The sessions were an evolving process, like a seduction. But my suitors were also desperate. They'd been unable to find another candidate for what seemed a suicide run. So they were willing to make concessions.

I walked into Billy Meehan's political life, and it was as if he opened up the windows to let in fresh air, and a hurricane blew in. But Bill Meehan could somehow get everybody to do whatever he wanted. He was one of a kind.

They didn't do me any favors in offering me the nomination, because it wasn't worth much. I wouldn't claim to have done them any favors in being their candidate. They never pressed me about my decision to remain a registered Democrat while running on the Republican line. Maybe they even saw it as an advantage. Philadelphia was a Democratic town, and they may have figured my registration would encourage Democrats to vote for me, hoping I would stay in the party after the election. My registration also lent the appearance of a fusion ticket, which had even wider appeal. I was the first Republican candidate to win backing from Americans for Democratic Action.

I insisted to Meehan and Witkin that there would be no strings attached and no obligations for patronage. We never discussed that they would raise all the money, but that was understood. At one point a wearying Witkin lectured me on patronage: "If they give you a round peg for a round hole, take it. If they give you a square peg for a square hole, take it. If they give you a square peg for a round hole, don't take it." Witkin liked to give advice but made it clear he would give his advice only to those who took it, which wasn't always me.

I was apprehensive about running on the Republican ticket, which was almost like changing my religion. The decision was even tougher because I couldn't consult my father, my lifelong adviser. A few months earlier, my parents had set off to visit Israel, fulfilling a lifelong dream. My father got so excited on his arrival that he overexerted himself, dashing to too many places too fast to see the marvels of the young country. He suffered a massive heart attack and landed in a Tel Aviv hospital. On November 2, 1964, he died.

I consulted my sister Hilda, the family matriarch, who as a politically attuned Wichita College student had engaged my father in long discussions about history and politics. She gave me forceful advice: Do it!

I was doing what nobody else was brave—or foolish—enough to do: trying to unseat a party-backed Democratic incumbent in a Democratic town, while running as a Republican. Republicans had not won a DA's race since 1947. I was also fighting an accusation of betrayal, which I would hear again forty-five years later. Democrats shouted, "Benedict Arlen!" and "Judas!" But I had never taken an oath to the Democratic Party—I had taken one to the people of Philadelphia. I believed that my former boss, DA Jim Crumlish, who had succeeded Blanc, had shirked his responsibilities as the city's top law-enforcement officer, failing to crack down on

crime and corruption. I knew that Philadelphia needed tough law enforcement, and I thought I could deliver it.

Meehan dominated our strategy sessions at the Bellevue Hotel. Physically, Bill was unimposing: short, slight, and asthmatic. But he was tough
and shrewd. Every once in a while I would bring up public policy, and
Meehan would say, "Cut it out, Specter. We don't want to know what you're
going to do; we want to win this election." We always ate at Kugler's, a
patriotic-themed restaurant on Chestnut Street near the Bellevue. One
day I told Meehan we ought to eat someplace else. "We didn't run you to
eat, Specter," he said. "We ran you to win this election." We continued to
eat at Kugler's.

I knocked on doors all over Philadelphia and shook countless hands,
on trains, in stores, on streets, and anywhere else I found them. I held street-
corner rallies, standing on a flatbed truck at a busy intersection and urging passing pedestrians to support us.

The May 20 Republican primary was a breeze. I was unopposed. It was
hard enough for the Republicans to find someone to run at all, let alone
someone to oppose the party choice.

Gradually, the campaign's momentum grew. At street corners, eyes that
had once stared into shopping bags were making contact. Crumlish ran
his campaign out of his DA office, relying on a stable of part-time public
relations men and Payola Palace regulars. A month before the election,
polls finally showed me turning the corner. The Saturday before the election,
when I was in Cheltenham at the north edge of the city, I heard that Senator Joe Clark wanted to talk to me. I found a phone booth and called the
white knight.

"Arlen," the senator said, "I think you're going to win the election.
Before you do anything after the election, come see me." I knew he meant
a possible change in registration. I agreed to talk to him first.

Clark had promised his vote, but nothing more. Billy Meehan had
strained himself and never asked for anything. Meehan had financed my
entire campaign, raising $550,000.

When the votes were counted, I beat Crumlish 52.5 to 47.5 percent.
"Specter Breaks Machine's Hold at Hall," the *Philadelphia Bulletin* blared

in a banner headline. Shortly afterward, I went to see Clark. "I really admire what you've done," the senator said. "I just hope you don't become a Republican."

"Senator Clark," I said, "up to this minute I hadn't made up my mind. But now I have."

Even so, the decision remained traumatic, largely for what I thought my father would have said about it. In December, after getting the okay from my sister Hilda, I officially changed my party registration to Republican. It wasn't out of any philosophical love or affinity for the GOP cause. Ideology doesn't drive city government. According to New York mayor Fiorello La Guardia's dictum, there's no Democratic or Republican way to clean the streets. Or to prosecute criminals. Clark, Payola Palace, Meehan, and Witkin all played roles in the decision. I also wanted to bring back a second major party to Philadelphia. The city needed it.

It was the most wonderful feeling, at 8:30 a.m. on January 3, 1966, walking into the district attorney's office—in my mind's eye, I can still see the route and the detective I passed—and taking over, the orderly transition in a democracy. I thought how much different it would be in a dictatorship, where you had to shoot your way in.

I brought a sense of outrage and urgency to the DA's office. Of Crumlish's fifty-one assistants, I kept a third, fired a third immediately, and kept another third through a transition. Many of Crumlish's assistants eventually became state court judges. The common pleas courts were a refuge for politically connected lawyers.

I hired bright, ambitious young talent, recruiting at the nation's top law schools and at the best city schools. I raided top Philadelphia firms. I reached out to the African American bar and recruited women. Many of my assistants went far in the office and even further after they left. Three of my assistants became district attorneys: Lynn Abraham; Ron Castille, later Pennsylvania Supreme Court chief justice; and Ed Rendell, later mayor, governor, and chairman of the Democratic National Committee. Oscar Goodman is mayor of Las Vegas. Paul Michel rose to chief judge of the U.S. Court of Appeals for the Federal Circuit. Three became U.S.

attorneys. Two became university presidents. Legions of my former prosecutors became top private attorneys.

I hired on merit. No more clearance from ward leaders for jobs. In fact, no questions about political affiliation. Rendell would recall my asking him in December 1973, when I was leaving the DA's office and he was my chief of homicide, what he planned to do next. Rendell replied that he planned to open his own practice. "I'm also going to try to get active in politics."

"Great, I think you're a natural for politics," I would tell the future governor. "I'd be happy to give Billy Meehan a call for you."

"Thanks very much, Arlen," Rendell said. "But there's only one problem: I'm a Democrat." Rendell recalled, "I had served for seven years for the man, held one of the six or seven most important positions in the DA's office, and he never knew what party I was registered in. Never knew."[1]

Under the new regime, the Philadelphia district attorney's office became professional, with a vision of government as an engine of social justice, buzzing with optimism and hope, and buoyed by the Great Society and by Supreme Court rulings expanding individual rights. Our office was at the forefront of criminal justice reform, which was at the nexus of social change. In short, we created the modern prosecutor's office.

I had been district attorney for less than a year when in the fall of 1966 Meehan asked me to run for mayor in the next city election. I resisted. I was thirty-six and having a banner first year as DA, doing a job I loved. I knew it would look opportunistic to run for mayor so soon.

The Greater Philadelphia Movement, the community leaders known as the "Movers and Shakers," also weighed in. The civic and business crowds were eager to eject Mayor James H. J. Tate. An April 1967 poll showed me with a 70–30 lead over Tate, who had a 26 percent approval rating. It was treated as a race that couldn't be lost. Meehan, again, would raise all the money, about $1 million this time.

Shortly before the Democratic primary, Tate ordered his police department to raid unruly taprooms owned by Democratic ward leaders, to bring the pols to their knees to exact their support. On the night of Tate's primary victory, Police Commissioner Edward Bell resigned in protest of Tate's tactics. That provided the mayor with an opportunity to promote Frank Rizzo, a tough street cop turned deputy police commissioner, who provided a powerful general election asset.

Two issues proved pivotal: my refusal to commit to reappoint Rizzo as police commissioner, and my opposition to a bill to give state aid to Pennsylvania's parochial schools. I said House Bill 1136, which the state legislature was debating, was unconstitutional and that we shouldn't divert funds from public schools. Eventually, the legislature passed HB 1136, and the U.S. Supreme Court ruled that it was unconstitutional. But the ruling came too late for my campaign. The Sunday before the election, Tate's campaign brochures hit every church pew, noting that I opposed aid to parochial schools. That night on the 11 p.m. news, John Facenda, a Philadelphia radio personality and observant Catholic who would later win national fame as "the Voice of God" for his NFL Films narration, came down hard against me.

In the end, Tate edged me by fewer than 11,000 votes of some 700,000 cast, 1.5 percent, the closest margin in a citywide race in Philadelphia history. Exit polls showed that 3 percent of the voters cast ballots for Tate to keep me as their district attorney. The biggest cost of the mayoral race was tarnishing my "white-knight-on-a-charger" image. It had been too soon to run again, and that made me look too political.

Nevertheless, I won re-election as DA in 1969, by more than 100,000 votes. I wanted to run for governor in 1970. Philadelphia was key to Pennsylvania statewide elections. If you could carry Philadelphia by 100,000 votes, you could carry the state handily. Coming off a 101,000-vote landslide, I might have been the only Republican who could beat Milton Shapp, the Democratic frontrunner. A September 1969 statewide poll by Meehan's pollster showed me leading the prospective Republican field, with 26 percent support among the entire electorate, Democrat and Republican.

But party leaders wouldn't back me. Meehan was saving me for the junior prom, the 1971 mayor's race. I flatly wouldn't do that. But I continued doing the party's bidding. I chaired the 1972 Pennsylvania Committee to Reelect President Nixon, CREEP. In 1973, Meehan again pressed me to run for an office I did not want—a third term as DA.

The DA election, as it turned out, came only days after the Saturday Night Massacre, in which then–solicitor general Robert Bork fired Watergate special prosecutor Archibald Cox, after Attorney General Elliot Richardson and his deputy, William Ruckelshaus, resigned rather than obey Nixon's fire-Cox order. My CREEP chairmanship proved decisive. I lost to F. Emmett Fitzpatrick, who had been Vic Blanc's first assistant, by 28,000 votes.

I was still by far the best Republican candidate to run statewide, because of my popularity in southeastern Pennsylvania. I wanted to run for governor in 1974. But party leaders had somebody else in mind. So again I was a good team player, and backed Andrew "Drew" Lewis, who would later serve as Ronald Reagan's transportation secretary.

In 1976, I wanted to run for Senate, and again the party wouldn't back me. They supported then–congressman John Heinz of Pittsburgh, scion of the Heinz global food empire. When the race began, federal law restricted a Senate candidate from Pennsylvania from spending more than $35,000 of his own money. Then the Supreme Court changed all that with its decision in *Buckley v. Valeo*, and Heinz spent what it took to win by 26,000 votes out of 1 million cast.

In 1978, I ran for governor, again without the party's backing. In the primary, I finished second to former assistant U.S. attorney general Dick Thornburgh after two other candidates joined in: Bob Butera, the Speaker of the Pennsylvania House of Representatives, and David Marston, who had gained extensive notoriety as a U.S. attorney prosecuting corrupt Philadelphia politicians. Butera, Marston, and I were all from southeast Pennsylvania, so in the perennial east-west battle, I had to divide the east while Thornburgh had a monopoly on the west.

In 1980, when the other Senate seat came up with Dick Schweiker's retirement, only one person thought I should run: me. The family was embarrassed. Again, the Republican Party actively opposed me. Governor Thornburgh and Senators Heinz and Schweiker all supported Bud Haabestad, the state Republican chairman and a former Princeton basketball star.

I went it alone, like Shapp campaigning for governor in 1966 and 1970 as "Man Against Machine." The establishment's anointment could be a

mixed blessing. Thornburgh had offended a lot of people. I beat Haabestad 36–33 in the primary. I won because I was against them all.

In the general election, I created the 67 Club, hitting all 67 Pennsylvania counties, and outworking former Pittsburgh mayor Pete Flaherty. I
wore them out, and beat Flaherty 50.5 to 48 percent. As Richard Fenno
wrote in a study of my early Senate career, "His election to the Senate was
a triumph of one man's persistence."[2]

Unlike nearly all the other fifteen Republicans elected to the Senate in
1980, I did not fly in on Reagan's coattails as part of "the Reagan Revolution," but in some ways in spite of it. Our election patterns were completely different. Reagan lost Philadelphia by 225,000 votes, while I won
Philadelphia by 14,000. Reagan carried the Pittsburgh area, while I lost
badly there, as my opponent had been that city's mayor. I didn't feel I
owed Reagan anything. And I certainly didn't owe the Republican Party
much.

As I told Fenno shortly after my first Senate victory:

> I felt strongly that I had been given short shrift by the Republican
> Party. I was once a Democrat, as you know. And the party was very
> willing to use that fact, to use my connections in liberal circles, in
> the Jewish community, in the black community and let me run for
> mayor of Philadelphia. They were willing to use me to pull all those
> groups in. But when it came to the choice plums, they reserved
> them for [others]. . . . Even though I campaigned my heart out for
> [Governor] Scranton and Sens. Schweiker and Scott and others on
> the ticket. Dick Schweiker said it best in 1970. He said I ought to
> be promoted—"promoted" was the way he put it—to governor.[3]

My pattern of independence continued ever after. In 1993, newly elected
president Bill Clinton addressed the Republican Senate caucus at a Tuesday lunch in the LBJ Room, an ornate chamber originally built as the
Senate library, before Majority Leader Johnson claimed it in 1959. Clinton
worked the room, shaking hands with every Republican senator, exchang-
ing greetings and making comments, in a manner that signaled he was

not in a hurry. When he extended his hand to me, he said, "Senator, you ran a really fine campaign."

"So did you, Mr. President," I said.

"Well, yeah," he said. "You and I got a lot of the same votes."

Those demographics would continue until ultimately, thirty years later, they would help drive a cataclysmic move.

THREE

RUB-A-DUB-DUB,
TWO MEN IN A TUB

I was in the whirlpool at the Senate gym in 2008, recovering from Hodgkin's, when Ted Kennedy came over and climbed into the bath. Kennedy was one of the Senate's giants, in many ways. It was as though a gigantic walrus had plunged into the sea, causing the level to swell.

I'd never seen two men in the whirlpool before, but the tub was big enough for two or more. There was a sign that you had to shower before entering. I hadn't checked that out with Kennedy, but I had neither an objection nor compunction about his coming into the bath. We chatted.

Kennedy and I had bonded over opposing Bork's Supreme Court nomination, and that bond was strengthened by my sponsoring Kennedy's 1997 hate-crimes legislation, alone among Republicans. Those were difficult times, with gays held in low esteem. The hate-crimes bill came to be named after two victims of grisly murders: Matthew Shepard, a gay university student whom thugs beat to death in Wyoming; and James Byrd, a black man whom racists chained to a truck and dragged to death in Texas.

Surprisingly, the *Washington Post* panned the bill, opining, "The victim of bias-motivated stabbing is no more dead than someone stabbed during a mugging. Ultimately, we prosecute crimes, not feelings."[1] Kennedy and

I wrote a rebuttal, arguing that "hate crimes are uniquely destructive and divisive because they injure not only the immediate victim, but the community and sometimes the nation," and that the *Post*'s metaphor about equally dead victims "suggests a distressing misunderstanding of hate crimes." Eventually, through my lead, we enlisted seventeen Republicans, enough to pass the bill.

My rapport with Kennedy spawned decades of collaborations. When I was first elected in 1980, the Senate was "a bipartisan liberal institution," as described by Senate historian Donald Ritchie. As George Packer noted in a masterful portrait of the Senate in the *New Yorker*: "Every major initiative—voting rights, open housing, environmental law, campaign reform—enjoyed bipartisan support. In the rare event of a filibuster, the motion to end debate was often filed jointly by leaders of both parties."[2]

In my early years, senators regularly reached across the aisle. In that era, Howard Baker and Lloyd Bentsen worked together. Bob Dole and Russell Long reached accommodation on tax issues. Bill Cohen and Henry "Scoop" Jackson found compromises on the Armed Services Committee. The Nunn-Lugar threat-reduction initiatives on nuclear and biological weapons were legendary. Dan Inouye and Ted Stevens perfected bipartisanship on the Appropriations Committee.

Baker, a superb Senate leader, deserves some of the credit. He maintained civility across party lines while also racking up legislative wins. He ran the Senate with an iron hand, but still let a certain lightness and humor pervade. He earned the sobriquet "the Great Conciliator," the twentieth-century version of "the Great Compromiser," the epithet of Henry Clay.

I was presiding over the Senate one day in November 1983, as freshmen were supposed to do, on the way to earning a Golden Gavel Award for chairing one hundred hours, when Baker walked in to gush about nearly beating President Reagan to make the Tailors' Council of America's list of the ten best-dressed men in government.

"I want to say I have absolutely no taste in clothes, that I am so bad that my wife will not let me out of the house in the morning without first standing for inspection," Baker said. "During the Watergate hearings, I was flooded with gifts of clothing because people were ashamed to see me representing the forces of light and reason in my chosen attire. I am a slob."[3]

Later, when I began doing stand-up comedy, mostly at clubs' political and celebrity nights, I sometimes noted Baker's skills. In a 2007 routine at the D.C. Improv, I said Baker had been lecturing the caucus about negotiating and told us that the greatest negotiator of all time was Moses. But even Moses slipped up now and then. For example, Baker told us, when Moses came down from Mount Sinai, he announced, "There's good news and there's bad news: we got the number down to ten, but adultery's still there."

Baker worked us all night fairly often. One night at 11:45, we faced sixty-three pending amendments on a tax bill, with lobbyists and staff hovering outside the chamber like bees at a hive. Baker said, "Amendments are like mushrooms; they grow overnight." He wanted us to finish the bill by morning, to avoid facing more amendments the next day. And we did.

Today, the Senate is a vastly different place. Following postwar prosperity and 1950s conformity, the Senate's modern, fractious era grew from the upheaval of the 1960s and 1970s. In 1964, Lyndon Johnson trounced conservative Arizona senator Barry Goldwater for president, but southern whites began shifting from Democrat to Republican. In his 1969 inaugural address, President Nixon urged civility, as the Vietnam War and the counterculture revolution raged: "We cannot learn from one another until we stop shouting at one another." The new president's call to end inflated, angry, and bombastic rhetoric went largely unheeded, at least in Washington.

During Jimmy Carter's troubled presidency, conservative hard-liners, mostly southern religious leaders, formed what would become powerful groups and blocs with strong ties to the GOP: Paul Weyrich's Free Congress Research and Education Foundation in 1977; James Dobson's Focus on the Family in 1978; and Jerry Falwell's Moral Majority in 1979. In following years other groups would join, including the Family Research Council in 1983, and Pat Robertson's Christian Coalition in 1989. These leaders' mission was "to save the nation's soul through its political institutions, using civil law to impose religious law," wrote Christine Todd

Whitman, the moderate Republican New Jersey governor and EPA director. "Jerry Falwell captured their goal when he proclaimed, 'I have a Divine Mandate to go into the halls of Congress and fight for laws that will save America.'"[4]

These groups' hot issues included prayer in schools, reciting the Pledge of Allegiance, and elevating creationism above evolution. But their main crusade was outlawing abortion. They sought to impose litmus tests on candidates and nominees, and to purge the party. Still, when Carter turned over the White House to Reagan in January 1981, the ideological chasm between the political parties had not yet opened. There were enough progressive Northeastern Republicans and conservative southern Democrats to keep the parties closer on the issues.

At a 1981 party at a majestic art gallery near the White House to welcome newly elected senators, Mark Hatfield spoke proudly of being a "liberal." That was the first and last time I heard a Republican senator identify himself as a liberal. When straying from conservatism, most GOP members used the label "moderate," while I preferred "centrist."

That night, a nearby branch of the Riggs Bank set the tone with its large sign: "The most important bank in the most important city in the world." Self-importance infects Washington, D.C. Republicans, who had taken control of the Senate for the first time since 1954, saw their ascension as momentous. Even before the Reagan Revolution took its name, Republicans gloried in a feeling of *We've made it*.

Reagan worked to hold together the moderate and conservative wings of the fracturing GOP. He practiced what he called the Eleventh Commandment: "Thou shalt not speak ill of thy fellow Republicans." As early as the 1977 Conservative Political Action Conference, Reagan had said:

Let me say this about our friends who are now Republicans but who do not identify themselves as conservatives: I want the record to show that I do not view the new revitalized Republican Party as one based on a principle of exclusion. After all, you do not get to be a majority party by searching for groups you won't associate or work with.

When Reagan, others, and I arrived in Washington in January 1981, the Senate had just begun its decline. Packer traced the slide to 1978:

> The Senate's modern decline began in 1978, with the election of a new wave of anti-government conservatives, and accelerated as Republicans became the majority in 1981. . . . Liberal Republicans began to disappear, and as Southern Democrats died out they were replaced by conservative Republicans. Bipartisan coalitions on both wings of the Senate vanished.[5]

One of the liberal Republicans who disappeared was Jacob Javits, the New York icon, who lost a 1980 Republican primary to conservative Alfonse D'Amato, and then ran futilely on the Liberal line in the general election, siphoning liberal and Jewish votes and spoiling the race for the Democratic nominee, Congresswoman Elizabeth Holtzman. Javits had talked about developing a liberal wing of the party. He came to speak at a dinner for me in Philadelphia, which produced a photo of him with two of my close friends that still hangs in my study.

After Javits's departure, I wound up sitting in Appropriations Committee meetings between D'Amato and Warren Rudman, who both smoked at the conference table. D'Amato was a colorful character who provided some fodder for my comedy routines. At my October 2007 DC Improv gig, I said I was riding the Acela from Washington, going to Philadelphia, and Al D'Amato was with me, and he was going on to New York. A steward came by and said, "What will you have?"

And Senator D'Amato said, "I'll have a manhattan."

The steward asked me, "What will you have?"

I said, "I'll have a martini."

Then the steward came to the next man, who had his back to him, and asked, "What will you have, sir, scotch, rye, or whiskey?"

The man turned around, and he was a man of the cloth—he had a collar on. He said, "Scotch, rye, or whiskey! I'd commit adultery first!"

And D'Amato jumped up and said, "I didn't know that was an option."

I recruited four Javits staffers, my largest bloc. I was Jewish and perhaps in the Javits mold, a liberal, to use an unfashionable term. But at that point I was hardly the last moderate standing. "You wouldn't think that Specter was taking up the mantle," said Sylvia Nolde, a Javits veteran who signed on as my scheduler and stayed with me, in various roles, till nearly the end. "It was a very large group of moderate Republican senators."[6]

The Republican Party has changed the most ideologically from the days when the steering committee, led by Jesse Helms, represented the conservatives, and the moderate Wednesday Lunch Club founded by Javits in the 1970s was almost as big, with Mark Hatfield, Charles "Mac" Mathias, Lowell Weicker, Nancy Kassebaum, John Danforth, Charles Percy, Bob Stafford, John Heinz, John Chafee, Bob Packwood, Alan Simpson, John Warner, Warren Rudman, and Slade Gorton, in addition to Baker, Dole, Stevens, and Cohen. After the 2008 election, the moderates had shrunk to Snowe, Collins, and me. We could have met in a phone booth.

On the Democratic side, the early 1980s centrist cabal included Scoop Jackson, Dan Inouye, Joe Biden, Daniel Patrick Moynihan, Pat Leahy, Gary Hart, and Bill Bradley.

Every year, Moynihan and his wife gave me a large jar of honey from their upstate New York farm. But bipartisanship did not preclude sharp elbows—or tongues. Moynihan dismissed a Republican senator from a western state whom he considered uninformed about a foreign-policy bill, saying that when the senator "puts his feet in the ocean of foreign policy, he's in over his head." Moynihan's own credentials were stellar. He had formulated the War on Poverty in the Kennedy and Johnson administrations and then produced a series of profound policy memos in the Nixon White House. He later served as ambassador to India and to the United Nations, and wrote some thirty books. If some have reduced my career to the phrase "Single Bullet Theory," others unfairly distilled Moynihan's to "benign neglect." He wrote in a 1970 memo to Nixon, hoping to cool the fervor over the civil rights movement, "The issue of race could benefit from a period of 'benign neglect.' The subject has been too much talked about. . . . We may need a period in which Negro progress continues and racial rhetoric fades."

I was generally out of sync with the social conservative movement, though we found occasional common ground, on opposing flag burning and partial-birth abortion, which Moynihan rightly likened to infanticide. I often infuriated the fringe, though never more deeply than with what Bork handler Tom Korologos called my "game-winning RBI" against Bork in 1987.

Steve Goldstein, who covered me for years for the *Philadelphia Inquirer*, wrote:

> Specter's record inspires fear—and loathing—on the right. . . . Specter, 74, is the one Republican whom conservatives love to hate. Since he was elected in 1980, the iconoclastic former Philadelphia district attorney has practiced a stubbornly independent form of politics that has bedeviled right-leaning Republicans.[7]

I cemented a reputation as a centrist, or a maverick, in 1985, when I took on William Bradford Reynolds, Reagan's nominee for associate attorney general. Reynolds was then assistant attorney general for the Civil Rights Division. We found out that he had misrepresented some facts to the Judiciary Committee at his first confirmation, and Mathias and I joined the eight Democrats on the committee to defeat him. The Reagan administration pushed for a vote before the full Senate, but couldn't get enough support and withdrew Reynolds's nomination.

A year later, U.S. Attorney Jeff Sessions was defeated for a district court judgeship in Alabama. At Sessions's confirmation hearings, four Department of Justice lawyers testified that he had made racist remarks. On June 5, 1986, the committee voted 10–8 against Sessions's nomination, with Mathias and me joining the Democrats. That was the Senate's first rejection of a Reagan judicial nominee.

Sessions would win election to the Senate in 1996 and ultimately succeed me as senior Republican on the Judiciary Committee. I have since publicly acknowledged that my opposition was a mistake. It also remains one of my biggest regrets, based on what I later got to know about Jeff Sessions. He was not a bigot. We would go on to enjoy a cordial relationship, both before and after my party switch.

Straying from the party line brought increasing heat. During my first term, a fellow freshman Republican, Jeremiah Denton of Alabama, arrived late for a vote to find that all the other fifty-three Republicans had voted aye and that I alone had voted nay. Denton looked at me and asked, "Are we permitted to vote no?" The question seemed especially ironic coming from a former Navy admiral and Vietnamese prisoner of war renowned for his courage and resistance, who had blinked "T-O-R-T-U-R-E" in Morse code when his captors put him on a propaganda video.

The GOP's rightward shift made me uncomfortable, and even more independent. Almost from the beginning, Democrats courted me, sometimes passionately. For twenty-eight years, then-senator Biden and I shared weekly train rides from Washington to Delaware and Pennsylvania. Biden would essentially say, "You'd be a lot more comfortable as a Democrat, Arlen." He maintained that I had registered as a Republican but was really a Democrat. Occasionally I got to say something, but usually not until the train left Wilmington.

Amtrak staged my first meeting with Biden. One Friday in early 1981, the week's final vote began at 5:52 p.m., which didn't leave me enough time to catch the 6 p.m. train for Philadelphia. I called Sylvia Nolde, the Javits veteran, and she said she could hold the train for five minutes.

Meanwhile, Biden hustled the three blocks to Union Station, dodging pedestrians, to arrive by 5:59 p.m. As he raced onto the platform, the conductor shouted, "Slow down, bud, there's a senator coming!" When an exasperated Biden found me on the train, he demanded to know how I knew how to hold the train. "You've been in the Senate eight days and I've been here eight years." After that bumpy start, we became best friends.

Biden would get his Amtrak revenge in December 2010, when we arranged to travel home together from Washington on a 4 p.m. train at the end of the 111th Congress. Biden was vice president at that point, and was presiding that afternoon over the Senate as we considered START, the key U.S.-Russian arms reduction treaty.

The vote ended at 3:45 p.m., leaving barely enough time to get from the Capitol to Union Station and the train. I rushed over, only to be kept waiting on the platform fifteen minutes as a sprawling security detail cleared a route for the vice president. I walked the distance of a long train to find

Biden in the first-class section. We renewed our pattern of nonstop talking to Wilmington.

For three decades, Biden and I had worked closely together, senators from neighboring states with similar interests and philosophical approaches. We supported increased Amtrak funding and economic development to produce jobs for the Delaware Valley. We took similar positions on the Judiciary Committee, including opposing Bork. We cosponsored legislation on violence against women, among other bills. When I was chairman of the Judiciary Committee, I put Biden's name first on the violence against women reauthorization bill, which was unheard of. The party in power goes first, especially if you're the chairman.

In 1984, I cut a TV ad for Biden, crossing the aisle. At the time, Biden thought he was in trouble. His Republican opponent, former Delaware House majority leader John Burris, was making an issue of Biden's Senate attendance record, and Reagan, atop the Republican ticket, was cruising to an overwhelming re-election victory over former vice president Walter Mondale. On camera, I attested to Biden's character. The issue was character, not competency. At the time, the spot seemed an acceptable thing to do. In retrospect, with all the polarization, it was conclusively inappropriate. Biden put my ad in the proverbial can, and never ran it. He went on to beat Burris by 20 points. Biden invoked these efforts in repeatedly urging me to return to the Democratic Party.

Joining the chorus were Ed Rendell and Senate Majority Leader Harry Reid. I had known Rendell since he was a Villanova Law student. When I was DA, I made him chief of my homicide division. With five hundred homicides a year, he got his name in the Philadelphia papers every day, sometimes twice a day. Rendell was on his way. When he became DA, he followed my policies, and our approaches to government were similar. During my time in the Senate, Rendell came to me constantly for funding for Philadelphia and then for Pennsylvania. He repeatedly urged me to return to my roots, arguing that I would be much happier as a full-time Democrat.

For about a decade, Reid had tried to recruit me. Senate Democratic leaders were always trolling for Republican converts, and even had a term for their efforts: "missionary work." Reid said, "I'd like you to change, become a Democrat." I said, "Harry, I'm able to do more here as a Republican than I would be as a Democrat." I said it was essential to have a two-party system and a moderate wing of the two-party system.

Reid did succeed in 2001 in engineering the switch of Jim Jeffords, who had long showed signs of unease in the Republican ranks. Jeffords and I had cast the deciding votes to cut $2.5 billion from President Bush's $1.7 trillion 2001 tax cut. The Vermonter chafed a being ignored as chairman of the Health, Education, Labor, and Pension Committee, as the administration worked instead with second-ranking Republican Judd Gregg of New Hampshire, and a being rebuffed in his efforts to increase education funding. A highly publicized snub added sting, when Jeffords was excluded from a White House meeting on education.

After a late-night vote in June 2001, an irate Jeffords told Snowe that he was considering changing parties. That threw the Senate into a tizzy because Republican control rested on a 50–50 split with Democrats, with Vice President Cheney casting the decisive vote. A series of charged, emotional meetings followed. Among many other Republicans, I urged Jeffords not to switch. Chuck Grassley cried when complaining that Jeffords's switch would cost him the Finance Committee chairmanship, which Grassley had worked more than twenty years to attain.

The Republican Party had treated Jeffords unfairly, and lost him. Jeffords changed parties after then–Democratic whip Reid offered him the chairmanship of the Environment and Public Works Committee, for which Reid was in line. I confronted Reid on PBS's *The News Hour with Jim Lehrer*:

> But Senator Reid didn't quite deal with the specifics as to whether there is an arrangement for Senator Jeffords to become chairman of the Environment and Public Works Committee, which is a position which would customarily go to Senator Reid and the word is that Senator Reid is going to step aside. Senator Reid used the term "quid pro quo." I'm not saying that Senator Jeffords did switch because he is getting the chairmanship. . . . But one of the reasons may well be this chairmanship and we'll fight about that . . . in due course if we don't this evening.[8]

Still, Senate bipartisanship endured. For more than a decade, Tom Harkin and I carried on a seamless change of the gavel, alternating as chairman and ranking member of the Appropriations subcommittee that oversaw all federal health-care spending. We nearly tripled the National Institutes of Health budget, from $12 billion to $30 billion. I arranged for another $10 billion for the NIH through the 2009 stimulus bill. I took the lead on advancing research on stem cells, which can become any type of cell in the human body, promising a virtual fountain of youth.

When I was Judiciary chairman, I worked closely with Pat Leahy, the committee's ranking Democrat, on the John Roberts and Samuel Alito Supreme Court confirmations. I went out of my way at the start to show Leahy extra consideration. For our first meeting, I went to his office. Customarily, the Judiciary chairman escorts a Supreme Court nominee to the hearing room. For Roberts's hearing, we stopped by Leahy's office on the way to the Russell Caucus Room, to allow the top Democrat special deference, the three of us walking in together so that Leahy was at our side for the TV cameras. I went far out of my way to accommodate Leahy on scheduling. On the Roberts hearing, I even gave Leahy an equal number of character witnesses, which was not done; it was always a 2–1 split. I was following my father's advice: "When in a partnership, give 60 percent, because it will look like 50 percent to the other guy. If you give 50 percent, it will look like 40 percent."

Time magazine wrote, "With Patrick Leahy, the ranking Democrat on the Judiciary Committee, [Senator Specter] turned what could have been colossal battles over the Supreme Court nominations of John Roberts and Samuel Alito into disciplined and respectful hearings."[9]

Renowned partisan warriors on the committee, both Democrats and Republicans, thanked me for my fairness in giving both sides what Chuck Schumer called "a full opportunity to ask questions."[10] Tom Coburn, a conservative Oklahoma Republican, told me later, "What I saw was fairness, and it didn't have anything to do with the fact that you were a Republican. . . . It meant that when something actually went onto the floor, you didn't

Sens. Specter and Ted Kennedy during the confirmation hearing for Justice Samuel Alito. Kennedy and Specter conferred about obtaining records concerning Alito's alleged membership in Concerned Alumni of Princeton, a group of Princeton graduates that advocated views widely seen as discriminatory. (CORBIS/REUTERS)

have anybody wanting to try to kill it, saying they didn't get into it. . . . What came to the floor *did* have a consensus."[11] That was nice to hear.

In May 2006, CNN anchor Jack Cafferty said, "We better all hope nothing happens to Arlen Specter, the Republican head of the Senate Judiciary Committee, because he might be all that is standing between us and a full-blown dictatorship in this country."[12] Cafferty was referring to my vow to question phone company executives about their providing tens of millions of citizens' telephone records to the National Security Agency, as part of the fight against terrorism. Schumer and I had introduced the Telephone Records and Privacy Protection Act, signed into law in January 2007, which carried a penalty of up to ten years in prison for the fraudulent acquisition or the unauthorized disclosure or transfer of telephone records. But I'd like to think Cafferty was also talking generally about an open, bipartisan approach.

In 2006, during my whirlwind Judiciary chairmanship, Trent Lott approached me and said, "Arlen, I want to make a suggestion to you: Slow down, you're making the rest of us look bad."

In my final years in the Senate, I got to know a Democratic neighbor down the hall in the Hart Senate Building, whose former office now bears an embossed bronze plaque stating when he occupied it. A conversation with then-senator Obama in the early spring of 2008 provided a vignette that I could use in my 2010 primary campaign, bringing laughs and illustrating my rapport with the president.

During the 2008 presidential campaign, Obama walked over to my chair on the Senate floor and said, "Arlen, I'd like some political advice."

I was a little surprised that a Democrat would come to me for political advice, but I was collegial. "Be glad to respond, Barack. What do you want to know?"

He then popped the question: "If a Jewish kid from Kansas can carry Pennsylvania, how can a black kid from Kansas carry Pennsylvania?"

I knew Obama had Kansas connections. His mother had lived during her youth in Wichita and later in El Dorado, a little town forty miles east. I advised him to go to small towns, not just population centers. Such visits would do three things: impress people in that small town, impress people in other small towns, and impress people in cities. *That guy goes everywhere.*

Obama later said he followed that advice. He held Hillary Clinton, who had been a heavy favorite in the Pennsylvania primary, to a net win of only nine delegates.

In my speeches, I would say, "Well, I gave him some advice"—pause— "and now he's president of the United States. I'm not saying my advice was determinative, but now he's president of the United States. That's a true story, and you don't get many true stories out of Washington."

Actually, what I told him was solid advice. It's like the teacher who said, "Johnny, what are two and two?" Johnny said, "Four." The teacher said, "Very good, Johnny." Johnny said, "Hell, teach, that's perfect."

I worked that roiling Democratic presidential primary into my comedy routines: There was a vicious argument in the Democratic cloakroom— and you might imagine who the arguers were: Hillary, Barack, and Joe Biden. Finally, Biden got tired and he said, "Listen, I had a dream last night—and the Lord came to me, and he said, 'Joe, I hereby designate you as the Democratic nominee.'"

Obama scowled and said, "Listen, that's nothing, because I had a dream last night. And the Lord came to me and said, 'Senator Obama'—a lot of respect for Senator Obama—'you will not only be the Democratic nominee, but you will be the next president of the United States.'"

Hillary frowned and said, "Listen, guys, I had a dream last night myself—and I didn't say anything to either of you."

My first six years in the Senate passed in the blink of an eye. As Richard Fenno wrote:

> There was never much doubt that Arlen Specter would run for re-election. The Senate had been his lifelong ambition, and no one had worked harder than he to get there. In every sense, he had made a huge investment in a Senate career. Every utterance I heard . . . bespoke immense career satisfaction.[12]

But that first re-election hit a snag when Governor Thornburgh announced interest in challenging me for the Senate in 1986. A poll showed him winning 52–40. My vote against William Bradford Reynolds had created a hell of a stir. Thornburgh invited me to visit him in the governor's mansion. He told me there was nothing personal in what he was doing. I replied that I took it very personally that he wanted my job.

Thornburgh remained bitter over my criticizing him during the 1980 primary. What did he expect? He had run Bud Haabestad and lined up both senators behind his surrogate. For his 1986 Senate run, Thornburgh began building support, including some of my backers. Then at a Republican

State Committee gathering in late 1985, he abruptly dropped his effort. As Peter DeCoursey of the *Harrisburg Patriot-News* would write years later:

> So the roughly 20 GOP State Committee bigwigs shivered, feeling exposed to the famous wrath of Specter, who built his reputation tenaciously prosecuting political hacks in Philadelphia.
>
> But Specter's reaction to his eastern betrayal set the stage for the rest of his career.
>
> Instead of rage, which you'd expect from someone whom the Republican State Committee had defeated and spurned in 1976 and 1978, and tried to beat in 1980, Specter wooed those who had thwarted him for a decade all over again.
>
> Even the eastern leaders who'd promised him support in 1985, only to back Thornburgh when pushed to the wall, were welcomed back. And having won them, Specter kept most of them ever since.[14]

Thornburgh gave no reason for abandoning a run, but he probably yielded to Heinz's repeated public criticism of his proposed candidacy and to concern about getting blamed for losing a Republican seat by forcing a primary fight.

In the 1986 general election, I faced Congressman Bob Edgar, an ordained Methodist minister and six-term House veteran from suburban Philadelphia. Smart, skilled, and good-looking, Edgar was, in George Will's words, "an unreconstructed, undiluted liberal."[15] Edgar's campaign, as the *New York Times* put it, "appear[ed] more like a social movement than a conventional electoral contest."[16]

In 1985, as the race was heating up, a *New York Times* reporter informed me that the White House said if I did not vote to fund the MX missile, President Reagan would not come to Pennsylvania to raise $1 million for my campaign. Reagan had been pressing publicly for the MX, calling the missile a key bargaining tool in arms-reduction negotiations with the Soviets. I instantly replied, "He's not invited."

Shortly afterward, Reagan came to a Tuesday Republican senators' lunch. I was still seething at the challenge to my integrity, the implication that I could be bought. In front of some fifty senators, I told the president so. A photo of that confrontation shows other senators looking in various directions, some at the floor, all mortified.

I decided to vote for the MX, which I had been inclined to do, but announced I would not have the president raise money for me. In 1986, even without the White House money, I was able to defeat Edgar 56–43. But Republicans lost seven seats and control of the Senate. Republican senators had been pressed to walk the plank on a host of unpopular party-line votes, such as cutting Social Security.

Amid the battles, I had many pleasant contacts with Ronald Reagan. Contrary to his image, he was a hands-on chief executive. At one point, I had trouble getting hold of Reagan's chief of staff, Don Regan, who wouldn't answer my calls. I asked Reagan to get Regan to call me. He was glad to do it.

Sometimes Reagan's hands-on approach got ahead of him. I got a letter from him about a situation involving the Sandinistas in Nicaragua, followed soon by a call from the president. Over the phone, in a very conversational manner, Reagan read the letter verbatim. He got his signals crossed.

I had heard Reagan say on a couple of occasions that the Strategic Defense Initiative, also known as Star Wars, would not upset the balance on mutual assured destruction, because once we had developed the technology for the system, we'd give it to the Soviets. He repeated it in a presidential debate with Democratic nominee Walter Mondale.

I had a concern about Reagan's plan, and I broached it with him while we were riding from the Philadelphia airport to Independence Hall on September 17, 1987, to commemorate the two hundredth anniversary of the signing of the Constitution. We were alone in the cabin of his limousine, sitting opposite each other. "Mr. President, there are a couple of problems with that proposal," I said. "One, you won't be president by the time we develop SDI. And two, the president can't do that unilaterally. It's the property of the country, and only Congress can do that, with the president's approval or override." The thought weighed on my mind that there might be some conceivable exercise of executive power to justify Reagan's plan, but I didn't think so. Besides, Star Wars wouldn't be developed until well into the twenty-first century.

I got a blank look from Reagan. Not quite like eyes glazing over, but sort of a blank expression. Then, after a long pause, he said, "Did you hear the one about our sending condoms to the Soviets, sixteen inches long"— pause—"marked 'Medium'?"

I wondered whether some phallic symbol had brought that kind of a response from him. I have since wondered whether Reagan was in an early stage of developing Alzheimer's at that time.

I included Reagan's line in an early draft of *Passion for Truth*, but deleted it from the published version because of a concern that the book's release might coincide with Reagan's death, and it would be embarrassing. But I think it's a significant comment which ought to be in the public sphere.

In 1986, Reagan hosted Soviet leader Mikhail Gorbachev at the White House. I was there because I wanted to see the Russian's arrival. Gorbachev had gotten rave reviews during a 1984 trip to England. I had urged Dole, then the majority leader, to invite Gorbachev to the Senate. A vote to do so in the Republican caucus came out a 22–22 tie. At the White House, Gorbachev stepped out of a magnificent limousine, wearing a gray and black jacket and gray slacks, expertly tailored, angled just so from the tops of his shoes to the back of his heels. He looked like the great leader of a great country.

Shortly thereafter, at one of Reagan's periodic meetings with the "Sweet Sixteen," the Republican senators who had arrived with Reagan in the landmark 1980 election, the president recounted a conversation with Gorbachev during that 1986 summit, in which he had conveyed what it's like to enjoy freedom of speech in the United States, contrasted with the intolerance of a closed society. Reagan recalled:

Mikhail and I were standing, looking out the window, in a northerly direction, at Lafayette Square, and I said, "Mikhail, anybody can go into Lafayette Square and bring with him a tall ladder, right across Pennsylvania Avenue, and stand at the top of that ladder with a bullhorn, where the sound would carry over to the White House, and shout at the top of his lungs, 'Ronald Reagan is no good—he's a terrible person, he's a bum, and he ought to be thrown out of office.'"

And while I was embellishing the way any American could criticize the president of the United States, Mikhail Gorbachev stood passively taking it all in. After I finished the description of how critical anyone could be of the president, Gorbachev paused, very poised, and he responded. He said, "I've listened to you very carefully, Mr. President, and all I can say is that anyone can go into Red Square, right opposite the Kremlin, and can also bring a ladder, and can also bring a bullhorn, and can also stand at the top of the ladder and shout into the bullhorn, 'Ronald Reagan is no good. . . .'"

As the eighties advanced into the nineties, the number of Republican Senate moderates shrank. Mathias, Stafford, Danforth, Nancy Kassebaum, Cohen, Simpson, and Hatfield all retired, and Packwood resigned rather than being ousted over a harassment scandal. Weicker and Percy lost re-election bids. Heinz and Chafee died. By 2000, the Wednesday Lunch Club had only five members: Jeffords; Snowe; Collins; John Chafee's son and successor, Linc; and me.

Moderates fared even worse in the House than in the Senate. Ascendant Speaker Newt Gingrich led a Republican takeover in 1994. A group of brash young conservative freshmen formed the Gang of Seven and advanced their "revolution" with little regard for congressional courtesy. They forced the release of raw data on all House members who had used the House Credit Union, even those who hadn't run overdrafts.

Redistricting redrew House seats as safe for red or blue, making primaries the key contests, and leaving centrist Democrats to fend off attacks from the left, and centrist Republicans from the right. "House moderates today are outnumbered and intimidated," Juliet Eilperin, who covered the House for the *Washington Post*, wrote in 2006. "There is no room for middle ground anymore."[17]

The House shifts directly affected the Senate. As Eilperin noted: "More

House ideologues have been winning Senate seats in recent years. . . . In such a small chamber, the influx of a few committed partisans can make an enormous difference . . . and they brought polarization along with them to the upper chamber."[18] In the early 1990s, on both sides of the Capitol, the Republican move to the right sprang off the issues of health care and crime.

In 1991, Thornburgh, now U.S. attorney general in the George H. W. Bush administration, pondered another Senate run, this time in a special election to replace Heinz, who had been killed in a plane crash in April. During this time, I was in the White House talking to Chief of Staff John Sununu, who was emphatic that it was solely up to Thornburgh to stay on as attorney general or run for the Senate. I wondered whether the White House really preferred for Thornburgh to leave, because a U.S. attorney general just doesn't run for a Senate seat. But I concluded there was no reason for their wanting him to leave. And Sununu's view jibed with the classic Bush 41 view of a lot of people: he'd let them do what they wanted, and not get involved.

On a trip to Philadelphia with the first President Bush and his wife, Barbara, we passed the Navy Yard, and Barbara Bush commented on how she had visited her future husband in 1942 when he was stationed there. Her mother had sent a chaperone. On our trip, the issue came up about who should be seated in the presidential limousine. The president said he preferred to have someone else decide. He didn't want to be bothered, or to decide.

Thornburgh won the Republican nomination for Pennsylvania's Senate seat, and resigned as attorney general to face appointed incumbent Harris Wofford in the special election. I assured Thornburgh that I would support him, despite our earlier friction, and I worked hard for him in that election.

I thought Thornburgh was a sure winner. Initial polls showed him up by 45 points. But the state and the country had slid into a deep recession, and Wofford—not the former two-term governor and attorney general— was seen as the candidate of change. And Thornburgh's line in his announcement speech about being effective in "the corridors of power," amplified by Wofford's campaign team, alienated voters.

The health-care debate also came into full bloom during that race. Wofford, brandishing a pocket copy of the Constitution at their debate, said, "If the Constitution guarantees criminals the right to a lawyer, shouldn't it guarantee working Americans their right to a doctor as well?" Wofford's campaign, led by then-unknowns James Carville and Paul Begala, hammered that message, creating the strongest ad sound bite I have ever heard as Wofford joined a sick patient by a hospital bed and said, "If criminals have the right to a lawyer, I think working Americans should have the right to a doctor." Wofford won an upset 55–45. As *Washington Post* columnist Charles Krauthammer wrote, "One way to view the Wofford victory is that if you campaign in an economically depressed state and promise to pay everybody's doctor bills, you are likely to win."[19]

In the twenty years since that election, Thornburgh and I have had a very cordial relationship. I took the lead in introducing a bill to rename the Pittsburgh courthouse after him. That effort hit resistance, on general concern about naming a courthouse for somebody living, who might practice law there and have an advantage.

Today's gridlock rose largely from rancor among senators who have built fewer and weaker relationships within "the world's most exclusive club." It's much harder to demonize a colleague with whom you've dined or cheered at a ball game. But developing those friendships has grown tougher as fewer members bring their families to live in Washington, partly because travel has become easier and partly because politicians have taken to damning D.C. So the Georgetown salon and the dinner party died, along with the friendly beer, and with them prime chances to build rapport.

Coburn, first elected to the Senate in 2004, told me that I'd had an advantage. "You served in the Senate when we had better relationships and we spent more time together. . . . It's when you get to know people and work with them, you can work through these things."[20] Coburn, who drew right-wing ire for voting for the 2010 bipartisan budget commission's draconian proposals, has consorted with a variety of Democrats.

"I think we've not built relationships like we need to," Republican Sam Brownback, who left the Senate in 2011 to become governor of Kansas, told me recently, also wistful for a warmer Senate era. "And then I think we question each other's heart." Brownback said a much older senator advised him early on, "Friendship first, business second." He added, "If you have a relationship, it's easier to start a conversation. But so many people are dug in so hard, just dug in so hard."[21]

Brownback, a staunch conservative, was able to find common ground with Ted Kennedy, a champion of the Special Olympics and the disabled, on a bill to create an adoption registry for Down syndrome babies, who are usually aborted. Brownback also collaborated with Paul Wellstone, a fiery liberal from Minnesota, on the first human-trafficking bill. That effort grew from Wellstone's wife's seeing Ukrainian women, who had been shipped to Minnesota brothels, at shelters where she worked. "So they came at it from that side, I came at it from the right," Brownback said. "Great guys to work with."[22]

Brownback and I had sparred over the years, most heatedly about stem cell research, which he fiercely opposed. But he still swung by my office a month after my 2010 primary loss to chat, and implicitly to offer condolences. "You fight hard, but you fight fair," he told me. "And also, I think the core of it is, you never question somebody else's principles."[23]

The modern Senate climate, by some measures, seemed relatively healthy. As I was waiting in the wings in 1995 for my first appearance on Bill Maher's television show *Politically Incorrect*, a man emerged and said, "And now, Bill's going to come out, and I want to have a big round of applause here." Maher came out and the man whooped it up, boosted by an enormous neon sign, sparking raucous applause.

On the set, Maher told me I was supposed to be a pretty good guy, and asked, How do you get along being in the Senate, the United States Congress, with all those phonies? They're as phony as three-dollar bills.

I said, "Coming from the Senate, where we've already been accused, convicted without a hearing or trial, I'll be able to go back to the chamber and tell my colleagues how to do things with real integrity. For example, this applause sign." I pointed to the giant illuminated sign, and the camera panned. The audience broke up. Maher laughed. The segment later made "Politically Incorrect's Greatest Hits" and a *60 Minutes* feature on Maher and his show.

I was on Maher's show several times. He later gave me a compliment that encouraged my stand-up sideline. "He's a pretty funny guy, especially for a senator," Maher said of me. "He is rather candid and self-deprecating, which I appreciate."[24]

I saw how far right the GOP had veered while weighing a run for the 1996 Republican presidential nomination, for a shot at unseating Bill Clinton in the general election. In Des Moines in June 1994, when I mentioned the constitutional doctrine of separation of church and state before an Iowa Republican group, they booed me. That wasn't Arlen Specter's doctrine. That was Thomas Jefferson's. That got me going. I launched exploratory travels in November 1994 and announced my candidacy in March 1995. I was also inspired to run because my father so admired the presidents. He bestowed a prized tag, "presidential timber," on those he deemed White House prospects.

Roger Stone, the flamboyant Republican operative, observed that I had some solid conservative credentials, including my presses for a balanced-budget amendment; a line-item veto; the death penalty, which I'd long believed an effective deterrent; arms control; and a strong national defense. I had gotten involved with Stone when he sponsored a group to moderate the GOP.

In 1996, a right-wing Republican had no chance to win the White House. I said in my announcement speech that a candidate from the intolerant right would only produce a president from the incompetent left. My campaign catchphrase evolved into "We need to eliminate the intolerant right to avoid the incompetent left." But the timing was awful. Republicans had just recaptured the House and the Senate in the November 1994 elections, for the first time in forty years, and didn't want any ants at their picnic.

We drew some support, and attracted some major leaguers. Congressman Tom Campbell, a Stanford Law professor turned House star, served as my California chairman. Howard Stern, the shock jock and cult personality, made loud and repeated endorsements. "If Senator Specter manages to stay in the primaries until he gets into one of the markets I'm heard in, we'll make sure he wins," Stern wrote in his 1995 book, *Miss America*.

The strategy was to capture the moderate vote, leaving the other candidates to split the conservatives. I spent fourteen months in thirty-two states. At a forum in Manchester, New Hampshire, we nine candidates faced the question: Would you commit to eliminating the Department of Education? Everybody said yes except me. Everybody was pro-life except me.

I didn't like Clinton's Health Security Act, a 1,342-page plan to redraw the nation's health-care system. I was amazed at its complex bureaucracy and structure. The day in October 1993 that I was reviewing the administration's statement on the bill, heavy rains forced me to drive from Harrisburg to Washington instead of flying, and during the drive I noted the various bureaus involved in the new bureaucracy. I asked my health-care policy aide, Sharon Helfant, to make a list of all the agencies, boards, and commissions. Instead, she sat at her dining-room table with a straight edge and a pen and taped together ten pieces of paper into a chart, showing how the system worked, from the new National Health Board atop the chart all the way down to the offices that would deal with the average citizen somewhere down at the bottom. Her chart looked like a microchip circuit diagram, showing 105 new federal agencies in red and 47 existing agencies, boards, and commissions that were given new responsibilities in green.

During my presidential campaign, I toted a thirty-by-forty-inch foam-board-backed version of the chart across the country. Bob Woodward of the *Washington Post* called it the decisive factor in defeating Clinton's plan.

When Clinton gave his State of the Union address in January 1994, Bob Dole, then Senate minority leader, used my chart to reply. The *Washington Post* reported, "The chart, even more than Dole, was the star of Tuesday night's official Republican response." Even Clinton presidential counselor David Gergen publicly called it "effective."[25] More than two thousand callers jammed my office phones asking for copies of the chart.

After Dole won the nomination, he asked to use a giant blow-up of my chart, nearly ten feet high. Dole's enlargement was a perfect replica except for one detail: my name was omitted.

That fifty-square-foot Clinton health-care chart hung for years over the doorway in my two-story Hart Building conference room. Shortly after I became a Democrat, my legislative director urged me, "You've got to take that chart down."

I said, "I'm not going to take it down." I knew some of the reaction the chart was drawing. A couple of times in caucus, Barbara Boxer had piped up. "Arlen's chart defeated health care during the Clinton administration."

My legislative director told me how many Democrats were offended by the chart. He noted, especially, Nancy DeParle, Obama's "health czar," who had served during the Clinton administration as the Office of Management and Budget's representative on health-care reform, and then as director of the Health Care Financing Administration. DeParle had told me how painful that chart was to their efforts in 1992. She had told one of my staffers that every time she came into my conference room and saw that chart, she cringed.

When word came that then-senator Hillary Clinton would attend a meeting in my conference room, I later learned, my staff went through contortions to program her movements. They wanted to escort her into the room through its main entrance, rather than through the door from my adjoining private office that my colleagues generally used, and to seat her directly under the chart with her back to it. That way, they hoped, she might not notice it. The meeting never came off.

In July 2010, the Republican Joint Economic Committee would produce a crammed chart titled "Your New Health Care System" to mock Obama's recently passed health-care plan. As *USA Today* would report, "It's Republicans' take on Obama's new system, and it reminds The Oval of the devastating chart Sen. Arlen Specter used in 1994 to attack the Clintons' proposed health care overhaul."[26]

In an apparent miscommunication in 2010, my conference-room chart would come down. DeParle was elated.

For several months in late 1995, former Joint Chiefs chairman Colin

Powell dangled the prospect of launching a presidential bid, sucking up the oxygen from my already wheezing fund-raising. Many of my donor letters came back marked "Waiting for Powell" or with similar messages. Was Powell just posturing to sell books? Rather than go into debt, I suspended my campaign on November 22, 1995.

My campaign served as a warning, clear and present danger, to any centrist—and certainly any pro-choice centrist—who would set foot in the wilds of Republican presidential politics. It wasn't a shot across the bow; it was a shot into the bow.

In the wake of my failed White House run, pundits and politicians thought my odds weak to win re-election to the Senate in 1998. By the 1996 Republican national convention in San Diego, the vultures were circling low, with Tom Corbett, then Pennsylvania's attorney general and later governor, and State Senator Melissa Hart traveling the state exploring primary runs.

But I knew, despite the polls and pundits, that I had a lot of residual strength from my years of work and travel throughout Pennsylvania. I built my war chest. The story of the 1998 primary was our care in finding issues of common ground with the social conservatives, such as pressing legislation to combat religious persecution worldwide, promoting abstinence, and decrying partial-birth abortion. Republican challengers dropped out. Leading Democrats also demurred. State Representative Bill Lloyd of Somerset County, a Navy veteran and Harvard Law graduate, won the Democratic nomination. But Lloyd never raised enough money to air radio or television ads, and his statewide name recognition barely hit double digits.

Democrats at all levels came out for me. Senator Bob Kerrey of Nebraska, then chairman of the Democratic Senate Campaign Committee, spoke at my annual issues forum in Washington, Citizens for Arlen Specter Day. From a podium at the Capitol Hyatt, the head of the Democrats' Senate political arm lauded my record before a gathering of Pennsylvania political players and media. By that point, Kerrey and I had been friends for years, since I had chaired the Intelligence Committee in 1995–96 and he was vice chair.

Ted Kennedy, appearing opposite his conservative comrade Orrin Hatch, and Joe Biden also made CAS Day speeches. Compelling as they were, they didn't draw as big a response as James Carville had at my 1993 CAS Day, fresh from managing newly elected President Clinton's 1992 campaign. Carville, who had won initial fame managing Wofford's 1991 Senate victory over Thornburgh, had famously said, "Pennsylvania is Philadelphia and Pittsburgh with Alabama in between."

Carville seemed to figure I was a good guy, not a rabid partisan. And he seemed to get along with some Republicans, marrying Mary Matalin. Carville arrived at my office wearing a white T-shirt with a pack of cigarettes rolled up in the short sleeve, stretching and gathering the fabric and exposing his bare shoulder. At our event, he told my guests that the new president had just carpeted his bathroom in Little Rock, and was so pleased he was going to run the carpet all the way to the main house.

As the twenty-first century dawned, Senate Republican centrists looked forward to a new day in the sun. There was some thinking that centrists would hold the balance of power in a 50–50 Senate. As we awaited the Supreme Court's decision in *Bush v. Gore* in late 2000, Dick Cheney, poised to ascend to the vice presidency, accepted my invitation to join the Wednesday Lunch Club in my hideaway. CNN filmed live as Cheney strode down the carpeted corridor to my Capitol office.

We enjoyed the lunch with Cheney, whom most of us had known since his time in the House and as defense secretary. His casual, down-to-earth approach impressed us. I worried when he ordered fried chicken, after just suffering his fourth heart attack. But he devoured the bird, even dropping a piece that left a permanent stain on the white carpet.

I voted with the Democrats more often on big issues than with the Republicans. The Capitol Hill newspaper *The Hill* editorialized:

> And in strict partisan rather than ideological terms, conservatives are wary of Specter's willingness to make deals with the Democrats. . . . What Specter's many critics are learning is that the problem with a dealmaker—that he makes deals—is also what

makes him an asset. Specter compromises not only with liberals but also with conservatives. . . . We suspect that many doubters to his right would willingly concede today that the dealmaking that is one of his hallmarks has worked to their advantage at least as much as it has aided their opponents."[27]

As Republicans moved right, Democrats moved left as hard-line liberals filled their caucus. Bernie Sanders of Vermont, a registered independent and self-described socialist who caucused with the Democrats, constantly argued in caucus that Democratic senators shouldn't seek Republican votes, which would water down efforts to reform campaign finance and Wall Street. Democrats also took hard left turns on national defense and abortion, and on welfare and other social-services issues.

Conservative Democratic senator Zell Miller, in his 2003 book *A National Party No More—The Conscience of a Conservative Democrat*, wrote:

> All left turns may work on the racetrack, but it is pulling our party in a dangerous direction. . . . I began to refer to the Tuesday [Senate Democratic Caucus] meetings as the "TUMS-days" lunches as the ideology moved further and further to the left and the oratory was turned up to a decibel level that got so shrill for my old ears that I needed Tylenol to go along with my antacid.[28]

But the Democratic center remained at least viable in the Senate, if not what it had once been. Today, Democrats and Republicans are literally on different wavelengths. The party caucuses send separate closed-circuit TV feeds of floor action to their members' offices, sometimes indicating how to vote.

At the end of 2010, Evan Bayh of Indiana, a second-generation senator, decamped in frustration. In announcing he would not run for another term, Bayh said, "There is too much partisanship and not enough progress—too much narrow ideology and not enough practical problem-solving. Even at a time of enormous challenge, the people's business is not being done." Bayh elaborated in an interview with the *New York Times:*

Mr. Bayh said he was startled at how much the Senate had changed since he arrived in 1998, and even more since his father, Birch Bayh, served in the Senate, from 1963 to 1981.

. . . "It wasn't perfect; they had politics back then, too. But there was much more friendship across the aisles, and there was a greater willingness to put politics aside for the welfare of the country. I just don't see that now."[29]

The abortion issue continues to drive Senate polarization and paralysis. Some Democratic senators will not support a pro-life nominee, and some Republican senators will not support a pro-choice nominee. "Extremist" often serves as code for pro-choice or pro-life.

For me, the Senate gym, with its baths and massages and machines, offered a haven and a forum. I spent increasing hours in that Russell Building sanctum as I worked through rigorous rehab regimens for Hodgkin's and other ailments. Chemotherapy, especially after my second bout with Hodgkin's, left my muscles weaker, most dramatically in my legs, and skewed my balance. For years, when constituents or activists groused about Senate perks, I'd reply, "You wouldn't say that if you had to see Ted Kennedy naked in the gym."

Neuropathy occasionally caused my feet to go numb and my eyes to tear. My eyes were tearing so much during Justice Sonia Sotomayor's 2009 Supreme Court confirmation hearing that I made a comment that the waterworks were because of chemo. Philadelphia's WPVI-TV misinterpreted my comment and announced that I was suffering from a recurrence of Hodgkin's.

I put an extraordinary amount of time and effort into physical recovery. Tom Coburn, a doctor turned senator who is also a two-time cancer survivor, called me "absolutely the toughest man I've ever met in my life" for grinding through extensive chemo while maintaining my Senate rigors. I appreciated his generous sentiment.

In the old days, the Senate gym had three massage tables going. They were often jammed for hours, and you had to wait. Few senators get massages anymore. Today, two tables operate, and you get right on. I also often used the steam room, where I'd almost always find somebody to talk to. Today, the Senate steam room is empty. For all the mania about health and exercise, senators just don't frequent the gym the way they used to, or don't linger.

In my early Senate days, West Virginia Democrat Jennings Randolph would sprawl across three massage tables side by side by side. We were there to relax, but Jennings was on the phone constantly. He and fellow West Virginian Robert Byrd were elected at the same time, in 1958, Randolph through a special election to fill a vacancy. I don't know how Jennings figured to be senior, but he was. Maybe because of his House tenure, having been first elected to Congress in 1932.

Ted Stevens, Sam Nunn, John Warner, Dale Bumpers, and Ernest "Fritz" Hollings were also all big massage guys. Hollings served forty years as South Carolina's junior senator while Strom Thurmond set longevity records. Hollings said his 1984 presidential campaign didn't get off the ground because people thought he was a German moving company, Fritz's Haulings. Part of his problem, Hollings said, was that "Peachy [his wife] and I are in love with the same man."

Sometimes courtesy and camaraderie waned, even in the gym. Once, during lengthy waits for massages while we used a temporary gym in the Dirksen Building, I was walking undressed to the last table. Another senator, also naked, walked briskly, perhaps at a slight run, and slipped in ahead of me. That was something that senators just don't do.

Bumpers could keep you in the steam room with his storytelling and southern humor. One of his most raucous tales was about a traveling salesman tooling along an Arkansas dirt road in a convertible with the top down when a giant wasp landed right where you can imagine, with a long penetrating stinger, causing the area to swell instantly and enormously.

Trying to relieve the pressure, the man loosened his pants and drove as fast as he could to the nearest town. Unable to find a doctor, he went to a drugstore. Behind the counter was an elderly woman. Holding this protuberance in both hands, enormously swollen, he said in a plaintive tone, "What will you give me for this?"

The woman looked at it and said, "I'll have to consult with my twin sister, who's in the back." They came out, and after a short huddle one said to the man, "Would $1,000 and a half interest in the drugstore be sufficient?"

I urged Bumpers to run for president in 1984. He was the last of the rambunctious orators. Ted Kennedy was still there, but, as Bumpers said, it took Kennedy five minutes to clear his throat. Bumpers had a back-row seat and a long mic cord, which allowed him to wander the Senate floor when he orated. He had a lot of good ideas and would enliven the process. He was a Democrat, so I wasn't going to support him. But I thought he ought to get in the mix. But Bumpers would have nothing to do with a presidential run because he didn't want to take up residence in Holiday Inns across the country. He must have gotten enough of rough quarters as a Marine noncom during World War II.

Bumpers was the exception. An old gag holds that every senator looks in the mirror and sees a president. In the 1996 cycle, four of us ran for the Republican nomination: Dole, Phil Gramm, Dick Lugar, and me. In the last presidential cycle, in 2008, six senators ran, including both eventual nominees and one running mate: Obama, McCain, and Biden.

In 1985, the Senate voted on Bumpers's budget resolution amendment to add $7 million for child immunizations. I recalled my roots, the polio scare of the 1930s, and my family's limited budget. I sided with Bumpers, alone among the GOP. I always had my father in mind when I cast those votes. Even so, I expected Bumpers to notice. When he didn't, I told him about it. And for the next fourteen years, until he retired in 1999, whenever Bumpers asked me to vote for some interest he had, I always joshed him. "Why should I? You don't even notice it when I vote for you."

My approach, even my style, drew some support. *Time* profiled me in April 2006 as "the Contrarian" in its Ten Best Senators package:

Republican Arlen Specter of Pennsylvania is known for being blunt, not sparing even members of his own party. . . . Specter's principled contrarianism fits in the tradition of lawmakers Senate historian Richard Baker described as the conscience of the institution, men and women who "stand up and say, 'Hold on a minute.'"

The *Economist* wrote in May 2010:

He is a moderate in a country where the loudest voices applaud immoderation. When Republicans had a majority, he nonetheless urged his party's leaders not to change Senate rules to disempower the minority. He pushed for a more welcoming immigration policy. And if he is rude, so what? Someone needed to tell Joe Biden to pipe down.[30]

The *Philadelphia Inquirer*, often a scold, went overboard in November 2007, editorializing, "Sen. Arlen Specter (R-Pa.) has more clout than some sovereign nations."

That kind of recognition helped offset voices from the fringe, such as the conservative *National Review*, which ran a September 2003 cover story calling me the "Worst Republican Senator."

For years, and especially as Judiciary chairman, I pressed to curb executive branch excesses and outright power grabs—no matter which party held the presidency—and to try to restore balance to our system of checks and balances. I fought incursions on congressional oversight of the White House and federal agencies and pressed for greater judicial review of executive actions. The biggest battle played out over George W. Bush's warrantless wiretapping program, which the NSA had essentially been using since 9/11 to spy on Americans. The Foreign Intelligence Surveillance Act (FISA), enacted in 1978 in the wake of Cold War and Nixon administration surveillance abuses, required the federal government to obtain warrants from a special secret court before conducting electronic surveillance of suspected terrorists or spies.[31] I was also convinced that President Bush's failure to notify Congress of the secret program violated the National Security Act of 1947.

After the *New York Times* disclosed the warrantless wiretapping in a story headlined "Bush Lets US Spy on Callers Without Courts," I held multiple hearings on what the administration was calling the Terrorist Surveillance Program. At a hearing on February 6, 2006, Attorney General Alberto Gonzales testified that the eavesdropping program was authorized by the Constitution's Article II passages on presidential powers, and that Congress gave specific authority with a sweeping resolution shortly after 9/11, and that nothing in FISA was meant to block the program.[32] Gonzales insisted that the program was essential in the war against terror. I told him that federal law prohibited any electronic surveillance without a court order. Our exchange escalated:

SPECTER: I don't think you can use principle of avoiding a tough constitutional conflict by disagreeing with the plain words of the statute. Attorney General Gonzales, when members of Congress heard about your contention that the resolution authorizing the use of force amended the Foreign Intelligence Surveillance Act, there was general shock.

GONZALES: We've never asserted that FISA has been amended. We've always asserted that our interpretation of FISA, which contemplates another statute and we have that here in the authorization to use force, those complement each other. This is not a situation where FISA has been overwritten or FISA has been amended. That's never been our position.

SPECTER: That just defies logic and plain English.

I pressed to subject the wiretap program to judicial review. After talking to the hierarchy of Justice Department officials, I met with the president in July 2006. Bush said his deputies opposed the deal, but I got him to agree to submit his program to the FISA court's review, which I thought was an enormous accomplishment.

The press also seemed to think so. In a front-page story, the *New York*

Sens. Specter, Patrick Leahy, and Ted Kennedy confer at a hearing on warrantless wiretaps at which Attorney General Alberto Gonzales denied habeas corpus was in the Constitution. (CORBIS/REUTERS)

Times would write: "After months of resistance, the White House agreed Thursday to allow a secret intelligence court to review the legality of the National Security Agency's program to conduct wiretaps without warrants on Americans suspected of having ties to terrorists. . . . The plan, brokered over the last three weeks in negotiations between Senator Arlen Specter and senior White House officials, including President Bush himself . . ."[33]

I didn't tell the press corps waiting outside the meeting, which was the way it was usually done, deciding instead to present the issue at the Judiciary Committee's executive session the following Thursday. The Democrats were ho-hum. They had Bush on the run on the issue, and wanted to keep him on the run. They weren't interested in settling the matter, getting judicial review, and getting a determination as to whether Congress and FISA governed under Article I of the Constitution, or the commander in chief under Article II.

At a hearing a few days later, on July 18, I summarized my deal with the president and said, "If there is a better way to obtain judicial review, I, for one, would be anxious to hear about it."

Leahy, the committee's ranking Democrat, huffed:

Last week we learned in closed-door negotiations with Senator Specter the administration made a conditional offer to submit one of its domestic spying programs to secret review by a single FISA judge. As I understand the administration's offer, Congress must first agree to completely gut FISA and deprive American citizens of the right to challenge domestic wiretapping in open court, which seems nothing more than a ratification of the administration's actions after the fact, even if they had acted illegally.

So when the President tells this committee he's agreeable to judicial review of that program and his other actions, I hope you'll understand why some of us are a bit wary.[34]

I introduced a FISA reform bill, which the Judiciary Committee approved on September 13, 2006, on a 10–8 party-line vote. The Democrats appeared to be in no hurry for compromise. A final vote on the Senate floor never came because the House settled on a different approach to the Terrorist Surveillance Program that did not authorize court review of the spying.

Meanwhile, I fought other White House excesses, such as the administration's treatment of detainees in the war on terror. In a stern rebuke of executive overreaching, Justice Sandra Day O'Connor, a Reagan appointee, declared in a June 2004 opinion in *Hamdi et al. v. Rumsfeld*, "We have long since made clear that a state of war is not a blank check for the President when it comes to the rights of the nation's citizens."

Instead of accepting the Court's decisions, Congress responded with legislation that eliminated detainees' right to habeas corpus review, the centuries-old method of challenging one's detention, on grounds that foreign terrorist suspects did not have the same rights as others in U.S. custody.

On January 18, 2007, Gonzales testified before the Judiciary Committee that proposals to restore habeas corpus, such as a bill Leahy and I had introduced, were "ill-advised and frankly defy common sense." He said, "There is no expressed grant of habeas in the Constitution. There's a prohibition against taking it away."

I was astounded. "Wait a minute," I said. "The Constitution says you can't take it away except in case of rebellion or invasion. Doesn't that mean you have the right of habeas corpus unless there's an invasion or rebellion?"

"I meant by that comment," Gonzales said, "the Constitution doesn't say every individual in the United States or every citizen is hereby granted or assured the right to habeas. Doesn't say that. . . ."

I replied, "You may be treading on your interdiction and violating common sense, Mr. Attorney General."

Gonzales's performance and his rationales continued to decay. At a July 2007 public hearing, I told him, "I do not find your testimony credible, candidly. The committee's going to review your testimony very carefully to see if your credibility has been breached to the point of being actionable." I renewed the suggestion that I had first made a month earlier, in June 2007: "I think the Attorney General has not done the job and that the Department of Justice would be better off without him."

I took a lead in holding Gonzales accountable and, ultimately, forcing his resignation over the wiretapping in violation of FISA, contrived rationales to justify torture of prisoners, and the allegedly politicized firings of several U.S. attorneys. Syndicated *Washington Post* columnist E. J. Dionne Jr. wrote in August 2007, "Gonzales was forced to go not because of Democratic opposition, but because many in Bush's own party—notably and honorably Sen. Arlen Specter, the ranking Republican on the Judiciary Committee—were appalled by his performance."[35]

It was left to the Supreme Court to beat back the encroachment of executive power, which it finally did on June 12, 2008, in *Boumediene v. Bush,* upholding Guantánamo detainees' right to habeas corpus.

On the U.S. attorneys, I spearheaded the Bicameral Judiciary Committee's investigation into the requests for resignations of nine U.S. attorneys and allegations that George W. Bush's Department of Justice had been politicized. Evidence showed that presidential adviser Karl Rove was involved in at least one firing. John Conyers, the Michigan Democrat who chaired the House Judiciary Committee, said, "Karl Rove and his cohorts at the Bush White House were the driving force behind several of these firings, which were done for improper reasons."[36]

I didn't think it was any grand plot on Rove's part, or the Republican administration's. Citing executive privilege, the White House resisted surrendering documents, and Rove and White House Chief of Staff Josh Bolten refused to testify before Congress. Negotiations followed. I tried hard to structure Rove's testimony in a way that would satisfy the White House on its executive-privilege claim and still give the committee significant information. Rove didn't want to be under oath, wanted the session to be informal, and didn't want to appear before both the House and the Senate.

I agreed to all his conditions, except I insisted on having a transcript. Otherwise, conflicting claims would arise on what Rove had said, and his testimony would generate more heat than light. Leahy would never agree to just a transcript, but that's what I wanted.

I recognized it was unproductive to initiate proceedings that began with subpoenas and would eventuate with contempt citations because of executive-privilege assertions. That process, including litigation, would take longer than the Bush administration would last, becoming moot. Technically, though, I thought subpoenas were appropriate. I regretted that some would infer that Bolten's conduct was being questioned, since he was being subpoenaed solely in his capacity as custodian of the records, keeping the papers in his office. He wasn't substantively involved in the matter.

I knew and respected Bolten, and had socialized with him in 2007 when he invited me to a Phillies-Nationals game at Washington's old RFK Stadium. When I arrived at the ballpark and walked down the aisle toward the seats in the first row along the third-base line, I saw that Bolten wasn't there. Understandably, he had been detained at the White House. As I approached our seats, I saw a bearded man in scruffy blue jeans, a baseball cap obscuring most of his face. He looked like a hobo.

Up close, I recognized Ben Bernanke, chairman of the Federal Reserve Board. I had recently gotten to know Bernanke from impromptu morning chats on the tough issues of the day. For years, I had been playing squash at Fed headquarters in downtown Washington, finishing shortly after 8 a.m., as Bernanke was arriving. But that evening, our discussion focused on baseball, not finance.

Bolten arrived, and the three of us watched the game together. Bernanke turned out to be a real student of baseball lore. During the game, a batter swung at a third strike, which got past the catcher, and the batter took first base. Bolten asked whether we thought such a scenario had ever played out before. Bernanke and I then jointly regaled him with the story of the 1941 World Series between the Brooklyn Dodgers and the New York Yankees. In Game 4, with two out in the ninth, no runners on base, and Brooklyn leading 4–3, on the verge of tying the Series at two games each, Yankee slugger Tommy Heinrich whiffed on a pitch, but Dodger catcher Mickey Owen dropped the ball. The Yankees rallied for four runs in the inning and went on to win the game and the Series.

Some months after our evening at RFK Stadium, in December 2007, I supported contempt of Congress charges against Rove and Bolten for refusing to testify or to turn over documents in the firings of several U.S. attorneys. I've come to regard that vote as a mistake, and to regret my vote to subpoena Rove and Bolten. I hadn't wanted the issue to be viewed in a partisan context, but considering the futility of taking the first step on a long litigation process, with no substantive purpose, it would have been preferable to drop the issue.

In June 2010, Obama's Justice Department declared that the Bush Justice Department's actions had been inappropriately political, but not criminal, in firing a U.S. attorney in 2006. It closed a two-year investigation without filing charges.

Although I also knew, respected, and liked Bernanke, I felt I should vote against his nomination for a second term when he came up for confirmation in January 2010. Bernanke had scoffed at the real estate bubble, which helped create the financial crisis that brought about the worst recession in eighty years and nearly caused another depression. Bernanke, then chairman of President George W. Bush's Council of Economic Advisers, testified in October 2005 before Congress's Joint Economic Committee that the 25 percent rise in housing prices over the previous two years "largely reflect[s] strong economic fundamentals," such as strong growth in jobs, incomes, and the number of new households.[37] The *New York Times* wrote, "By any serious measure, houses in much of this country had become overvalued. . . . More than a few people—economists, journalists, even some Fed officials—noticed this phenomenon. It wasn't that hard, if you were willing to look at economic fundamentals. Instead, Bernanke missed the biggest bubble of our time." As late as May 2007, Bernanke said that Fed officials "do not expect significant spillovers from the subprime market to the rest of the economy."[38]

Charles Ferguson's masterful 2010 documentary *Inside Job* captures the combination of arrogance, inertia, and raw conflict of interest that led a bevy of the nation's top financial officials and thinkers, in an era of deregulation, to propagate the lending and investing process that created the housing bubble. The film also notes that many of those running the country's financial superstructure during the Obama administration had been playing major roles for years across various administrations, in some cases both Democratic and Republican, including Bernanke; his predecessor as Fed chairman, Alan Greenspan; and former treasury secretary Lawrence Summers. The film's villains evoke Claude Rains's line from *Casablanca*, "Round up the usual suspects."

I knew that Bernanke would win confirmation, but I felt compelled to cast a protest vote. The full Senate confirmed Bernanke 70–30, the closest margin for any Fed chief. For personal reasons, I would have preferred to vote for him, but I thought it more important to vote for accountability, since his actions had been key to such financial calamity.

My vote against Bernanke would cause ripples I had not imagined. Days before my Senate tenure ended in January 2011, my aide David DeBruyn, who regularly accompanied me to my morning squash sessions, went to Fed headquarters to drop off his building-access badge, which was about to expire. The Fed employee who took DeBruyn's badge asked him whether he planned to clean out my locker. "And my question in response was, well, is that a question on your part or is that a suggestion?" DeBruyn later recalled. "And they said it was a suggestion." DeBruyn did me a favor and collected my gear, not knowing whether we'd get another chance.[39]

DeBruyn wasn't surprised at the Fed employee's attitude. When I voted against Bernanke's confirmation, DeBruyn said, various Fed staffers, and even the manager of the sundry shop who refrigerated the Gatorade I guzzled to combat the effects of chemotherapy, seemed surprised to see me back at the Fed. "Word travels."

Shortly after the vote, DeBruyn told me, when he tried to renew our access badges for 2010, lower-level Fed officials turned him down, and he wound up appealing to the Fed's chief of staff, Stephen Malphrus. Malphrus told DeBruyn that I was welcome to come back to the Fed to play squash as long as I liked.

The reaction over my vote against Bernanke that apparently swept the Fed's lower echelons may not have reached the top. DeBruyn gathered some intelligence while getting his hair cut in the Fed's basement shop by the same barber who coiffed Bernanke. "He asked Bernanke one time when he was cutting his hair, 'Is Senator Specter's vote against you going to change whether or not he's allowed to play . . . squash at the Fed?'" DeBruyn recalled. "And Bernanke's response was—he kind of shrugged his shoulders as though he really didn't care one way or the other."[40] Perhaps Bernanke felt differently but wasn't going to advertise it.

DeBruyn's account suggests that the Fed officials who barred me from the building knew they were dealing with a touchy situation with a sitting senator. They may have felt they had to tolerate me while I remained in office.

FOUR

BATTLE FOR THE SOUL OF THE REPUBLICAN PARTY

The morning after the 2002 election, I went to my Washington campaign office and phoned more than ninety supporters we had identified of the Lehigh Valley's newly re-elected congressman, Pat Toomey.

Toomey had been talking about running against me two years from then. A staunch conservative first elected in 1998, Toomey had pledged to serve only three terms in the House, which would end his stint just in time for the 2004 Senate race. A few years earlier, Toomey had signed on to my re-election committee, even serving from 2000 to 2001 as my fundraising co-chair. That was a good sign, but I wasn't relying on it. I was preparing very carefully.

In each phone call to Toomey's people, I asked for support for my 2004 re-election bid. All but two agreed. One was noncommittal, and one said he was for Toomey. That number would quickly erode, as I expected. But I was moving instantly. I knew my 2004 race was going to be tough.

With the calls, I was also sending a signal to Toomey, a technique I had learned on the Russell High School gridiron. I heard our coach tell a defensive guard, "The first thing you do when the ball is snapped by the center, is just ram right into him." The point was to make the center apprehensive, knowing he would take a wallop every time a play began, so he might botch a snap. I built that advice into my approach to life and politics, to demonstrate tenacity, toughness, and immediacy. I used the expression "Put our foot on his neck, and don't let up." That was the signal I wanted to send to Pat Toomey.

Over the years, I had made a number of joint appearances with Toomey, including one event in his district on the day his first child was born. Toomey didn't show that day, which I understood. I phoned the hospital and sent flowers, to show respect for the occasion.

Toomey was smart and stayed on message. He opposed earmarks, any earmarks, and wouldn't pursue federal funding even for vital local projects. But he would come to my events in his district when I had arranged an earmark and get his picture and name in the paper. When I got more than $5 million in federal funding for a bridge that collapsed into a sinkhole in his district, he attended the announcement and stepped up to speak and take credit, moving my press secretary to challenge him as a gate-crasher.

An Eagle Scout and a licensed pilot, Toomey had grown up working-class in East Providence, Rhode Island, the son of a union-member electric company cable layer and a church secretary. The *New Yorker* magazine offered a fair description of him:

> Pat Toomey is a conservative Republican of rigorous doctrinal purity: anti-abortion, anti-taxes, anti-spending (except for defense); a fiscal hawk, appalled by big deficits, a crusader for school choice, tort reform, Social Security privatization, and a smaller federal government. . . . He is forty-two, a Catholic, the son of working-class Democrats and also a Harvard man, blond, meticulously groomed, with unnervingly white teeth and scrubbed pink skin. He has a tightly wound but forthright manner. . . . If Toomey has a sense of humor, he is careful not to flaunt it.[1]

Toomey had a 97 percent American Conservative Union rating, dwarfing even Pennsylvania senator Rick Santorum's 87 percent rating, and

President George W. Bush and Sen. Specter carry their 2004 re-election campaigns to Pittsburgh. (GETTY)

Santorum was a staunch conservative. Christine Todd Whitman called Toomey "an archconservative Republican congressman who could be a poster child for the ideological zealots who are trying to exclude from the party those who don't share their views."[2] But Toomey also projected a measured mien that hid his zealotry. As *Harrisburg Patriot-News* writer Peter DeCoursey told CNN: "Toomey is an odd conservative in that he votes like Santorum, but he has a very businesslike manner. He comes across very matter-of-fact, very reasonable. And so he seems a good deal less conservative than he is. And that's how he got elected to Congress."[3]

Toomey had also earned a reputation as being, foremost, out for himself. In his second term, he had raised $450,000 from Republican colleagues and campaign committees, partly from late pleas for help against a Democratic challenger for his House seat. Toomey would ultimately keep the money and transfer it to his Senate campaign account to try to unseat a fellow Republican—me. Pennsylvania congressman Phil English, who pressed Toomey to return the funds, told the media, "Pat is not known as a team player."[4]

As 2004 approached, Toomey took on a strident campaign tone, arguing that my positions on various issues were dangerously liberal, though he had been able to support me and even help run my fund-raising only a couple of years earlier. Toomey enlisted with the Club for Growth, a nascent cabal of wealthy, fiscally conservative bankers and businessmen that wanted to purge moderate Republicans to remake and control the party. The Club had helped elect Toomey to the House.

I enlisted the White House to send Toomey an even stronger signal. On February 24, 2003, the day before Toomey was scheduled to announce his Senate candidacy, White House Chief of Staff Andrew Card stood beside me in a banquet room at the Holiday Inn in Bethlehem, in Toomey's district, and endorsed me. We raised $100,000 at the event. We had fourteen months until the Republican primary, scheduled for April 27, 2004. "It's unusual for the White House to take interest in a campaign this early," Card told the media.

Toomey launched his bid. The *New York Times* wrote that Toomey's challenge was being "engineered" by the Club for Growth. I called Toomey's campaign a wholly owned subsidiary of the Club for Growth, the "Club for Toomey."

In 2004, I was the only sitting senator to face a primary. The Club, which targeted elected officials they considered RINOs, or Republicans in name only, saw unseating me as a ticket to legitimacy and stature. Club founder and president Stephen Moore told *Time* magazine, "If we're going to be a major political force, we have to defeat one of the incumbent RINOs."[5] He told another reporter: "We won't fully arrive as an organization until we have a major scalp on the wall."[6] Moore effused about how taking me out would advance the Club and its agenda:

For us, it will be huge in the sense that it basically would make the Club a force to be contended with in races around the country. This race would not only rid the Senate of a prominent RINO, it would put the fear of God in the 15 or 20 other RINOs in the Senate. You would see a dramatic change in the way the Republicans vote because now they would say, "We don't want to go through this."[7]

Moore told the *National Journal*, in a piece headlined "All Eyes on Pennsylvania," that the Club's efforts had attracted almost universal political attention. "Even House members are watching this race very closely. . . . If we were able to beat a four-term incumbent senator, then you can really make a credible challenge against piddly House members."[8]

Moore's ambition threatened not only those he deemed Republican outliers, but also the GOP establishment. He told the *New York Times* that the Republican Party was jealous or resentful of the Club: "They think we're replacing the party, and that is our goal. We want to take over the party's fund-raising. We want it to be, in ten years, that no one can win a Senate or a House seat without the support of the Club for Growth."[9]

Moore helped found the Club for Growth in 1999 as a nationwide political membership organization dedicated to cutting taxes and limiting government. The Club would advance its agenda by electing like-minded Republicans. In the 2000 cycle, the Club spent $2.4 million and its PAC helped elect ten new Republicans to Congress. By the 2004 cycle, the Club had grown tenfold. Its Web site boasted, "We are now #1 in funds for Republican candidates outside the Republican Party itself!" The Club was by then the nation's fifth-largest 527 corporation, a designation named for a federal tax code provision that granted tax-exempt status to political advocacy groups that run issue—not candidate—ads. The Club was capitalizing on a loophole in the McCain-Feingold campaign finance reform act that limited the amount of soft money a party could spend on behalf of a candidate, offering another channel for those funds.

By 2004, Moore and the Club didn't seem content to merely cow "wayward" centrist Republicans. They craved trophies. Moore gushed to the *New York Times*, "If we can take out a four-term incumbent, the other

moderates in Congress will start behaving themselves, for fear of suffering the same death experience." He added, "If we beat Specter . . . it serves
notice to Chafee, Snowe, Voinovich and others who have been problem
children that they will be next."[10]

Moore billed my primary against Toomey as a "battle for the soul of
the Republican Party." The national media seemed to concur. With no
Republican presidential primary, our race became the marquee contest
and a national cause célèbre. *U.S. News & World Report* wrote:

> The Keystone State primary has become a proxy fight over whether
> there is still a role for moderates in the increasingly conservative
> GOP. . . . "There is going to have to be room, because if there isn't
> room, they won't have a party," says Specter."[11]

Steve Moore made an unlikely firebrand. The *New York Times* described
him as "a nerdy 43-year-old economist with an affable, self-mocking laugh."[12]
Behind oval, metal-framed glasses and a vigorous head of brown hair,
Moore always seemed to be thinking, or plotting. He was a "scholar" at the
libertarian Cato Institute and a former Republican aide on Capitol Hill.
But for all his fiery rhetoric, Moore's approach was essentially cold and
bloodless. By his calculus, the candidates he courted and carried seemed so
many chess pawns. He dismissed politicians as "loathsome" and "cowards"
and crowed about scaring them into submission. The economist pursued
the bottom line, measured in dollars or Senate seats. The humanity behind
those numbers didn't seem to interest him. As the *New York Times* put it, the
Club was "agnostic" on social issues, to the point that Moore had banned the
word "abortion" from Club meetings.[13]

Moore spewed an endless flow of molten vitriol. He told the *Philadelphia Inquirer*, "The only reason God put Republicans on this earth is to cut
taxes. We want to improve the party's gene pool." He called me a Republican traitor for voting against the first Bush tax cut in 2001, reviving the
old Philadelphia Democratic moniker "Benedict Arlen."[14]

Republicans implored Moore and the Club to ease off, warning that
I would make a far stronger general-election candidate than the extremist

Toomey, and that the Club might succeed only in handing the Senate seat to the Democrats. That was okay with the Club. They'd rather purify the party than win elections. Six years later, in the 2010 cycle, the Tea Party would take the same approach and hand at least three Senate seats to the Democrats.

Dick Armey, the former Republican House majority leader turned de facto Tea Party national chairman, would trace the Tea Party's birth to my 2004 race against Toomey. He would say at a Philadelphia event in October 2010, "Its moment of conception was six years ago when the Republican President George W. Bush endorsed Arlen Specter over Pat Toomey."[15]

By 2004, Pennsylvania politics had already shifted enough to make me vulnerable to a primary challenge from the right. Experts figured any primary opponent began with a baseline of 35 percent support, given my centrist, pro-choice views in heavily Catholic and Christian fundamentalist, socially conservative Pennsylvania. As the *Los Angeles Times* wrote, "Though Pennsylvania has a history of electing centrist Republicans, such as former Gov. Tom Ridge and the late Sen. John Heinz, that is changing. The state's GOP—like the national party—has been increasingly influenced by more ideological conservatives."[16]

I ran on my record, my seniority, and my independence under the slogan "Courage, clout, conviction." I was two seats from Appropriations chairman and in line to chair Judiciary when Hatch had to step down because of GOP-imposed term limits. I had also delivered Pennsylvania's fair share of federal resources. I joked that when Byrd was chairman of Appropriations, he paved half of West Virginia, and that when I became Appropriations chairman, I'd pave all of Pennsylvania. A local news reporter buttonholed my press secretary after a town hall meeting and asked, quavering, whether I was really going to pave over the entire state. "He's just using a little poetry to make a point," my aide assured her. I had brought home so much of what some considered bacon—but which others considered vital infrastructure and defense projects—that Citizens Against Government Waste named me its 2003 Porker of the Year.

As for my bipartisanship, I told the *New Yorker*, when Joe Biden needed a co-sponsor, he came to Arlen Specter. "That kind of balance is really important for the country. It's more than the soul of the Republican Party; it's to have some balance within the Party and within the two-party system."

About Toomey, I said he wasn't far right, he was far out. My challenger had voted by himself—and against the other eleven Republican members of the Pennsylvania House delegation—seventy-six times. None of his fellow House Republicans endorsed him. The *Philadelphia Daily News*, in endorsing me, wrote, "Heaven help the United States of America if Pat Toomey ever does represent 'the mainstream of the Republican Party,' as he claims to do now."

Toomey, for his part, branded me a "liberal," chanting the word like a mantra. One of his ads carried the tagline "Arlen Specter—Three decades of liberalism is enough." That seemed a play on Oliver Wendell Holmes's infamous opinion in *Buck v. Bell*, a 1927 forced-sterilization case, in which the usually brilliant justice wrote, "Three generations of imbeciles are enough."

Toomey called himself the "real Republican." He said I represented the Ted Kennedy wing of the Republican Party, but he represented the Republican wing of the Republican Party.[17] Toomey seemed untroubled by facts and unconcerned with consistency. The press reported, "Toomey seems to have a deft touch for having it both ways. His campaign bio boasts that 'his father was a union worker,' while his Web site faults Specter for having too much union support."[18]

The race got ugly, fast. Toomey opened his air assault nearly a year before Primary Day, launching TV and radio ads in June 2003. Our air war became so loud and pervasive that Pennsylvania Republican chairman Alan Novak wrote to both campaigns urging us to halt all TV and radio advertising until after the November 2003 elections, to keep the focus on those races. Toomey soon broke the truce, and we fired back. He vowed to stay on TV from January 8, 2004, when he launched a thirty-second spot twisting statistics to blast me as a liberal, through the primary. Another Toomey ad showed me as a grinning jack-in-the-box. When Toomey went off the air, the Club for Growth continued the barrage. The Club and

Toomey were clearly coordinating, which was illegal. I filed a Federal Election Commission complaint.

At a news conference, I challenged Toomey to declare what federal spending in Pennsylvania he considered wasteful. For most of the day, as reporters pressed, Toomey stalled. Then, near 5 p.m., his campaign identified an $800,000 outhouse at a national park—built ten years earlier.

Our early ads, including a "Where's Pat?" series, showed Toomey constituents grousing about their do-nothing congressman whose antipork extremism prompted him to vote against projects in their district, while other Pennsylvanians testified about my effectiveness. We also made an issue of upright Toomey's interest in a shabby local nightclub.

The Club for Growth's press for Toomey drew the centrist Republican establishment, such as it was, to my side. The Republican Pro-Choice Coalition spent a reported $450,000 on my effort, including 200,000 mailings to moderate Republicans. The group targeted an estimated 30,000 "Rendellicans" or "Rendellocrats"—Republicans who had become Democrats to vote for Ed Rendell in the 2002 primary—to get them back to the GOP to vote for me.

The Republican Main Street Partnership, which included sixty-three members of Congress, set up phone banks to urge 175,000 moderate Republicans to vote for me. They brought home 19,000 Rendellocrats. The Partnership ran TV, radio, and newspaper ads in conservative markets. They also smacked Toomey for changing his position on abortion, from his pro-choice stance in his first race, when he found himself running against multiple pro-life candidates. In 1998, Toomey had even cashed a $500 contribution from Republicans for Choice.[19]

Toomey bristled, and the *Philadelphia Inquirer* eventually weighed in: "Here is the gist of it: Toomey started his career declining to discuss the issue, then he supported abortion rights during the early stages of pregnancy, then he came out against the procedure except in cases of rape, incest, or endangerment to the mother."[20]

The Partnership had qualms about the campaign's tone. Its executive director, Sarah Chamberlain Resnick, told *Congress Daily*, "Main Street does not like to go negative. The only reason I was allowed to do that was because Toomey was so brutally attacking Specter."[21]

The Club for Growth and the Republican Main Street Partnership, also a 527 corporation, made enough noise that the *Hotline* ran a piece in April 2004 headlined "Pennsylvania: Battle of the Superfriends . . . Main Street vs. the Club."

I got heavy support from the entire Republican establishment, beginning with President George W. Bush. I had developed a good relationship with Bush, going back to 1999, when I had jetted down to Florida at his request to run a news conference and provide other help during the 2000 presidential recount. Bush would come to Pennsylvania twenty-seven times during my 2004 primary cycle. Vice President Cheney, Senate Majority Leader Bill Frist, Senate Republican whip Mitch McConnell, Republican Senatorial Committee chairman George Allen, a bevy of cabinet secretaries, and other top Republicans would also come to the state to campaign for me. Even First Lady Laura Bush came. Santorum, a former Republican Senatorial Committee chairman, proved vital, lending his conservative credibility in ads and appearances. Rudy Giuliani, "America's Mayor," headlined events in Philadelphia and Pittsburgh and cut radio spots. "We can be a broad party, a party that represents the full range of opinions in the United States," Giuliani said. Cheney, headlining a fund-raising luncheon at the Crowne Plaza in Harrisburg, told the crowd of three hundred, "We are absolutely united in our determination to see Arlen Specter re-elected to the United States Senate."

My establishment support both frustrated and tantalized the Club for Growth, which now also had a chance to vanquish the party by bagging its RINO. And Toomey could make history. The last time a candidate embraced by the Pennsylvania Republican organization lost a statewide primary was in 1980, when I beat Haabestad for the Senate.

The battle escalated. On January 16, the White House sent Toomey a letter ordering him to cease and desist from using images of the president in his advertising. Toomey had sent flyers showing photos of himself next to Bush, both smiling, with the caption "Bringing our traditional Republican values to the U.S. Senate." The Toomey campaign pulled the photos from its Web site but said the flyers had already been distributed.

Bush came to Pennsylvania forty-four times in all between 2001 and 2004, when both he and I were running, and he always invited me along. Whenever I traveled on Air Force One, he invited me up to the cabin right away. He liked to talk. And he was also a good listener. We had a lot of talks in his plane and his car during the forty-five-minute flights from Andrews Air Force Base to Pennsylvania and the thirty-minute limo rides to our destinations.

We talked about Senate filibusters of his judicial nominees, and I told him about the historical value of the Senate in cooling the temper of the times. I described at some length the impeachment proceedings against Justice Samuel Chase and President Andrew Johnson. I repeatedly urged Bush to take an activist role in brokering an Israeli-Syrian peace treaty. I also urged him to engage Iran in a dialogue to try to defuse its threat of developing a nuclear weapon. I told the president of my numerous trips to Syria to meet with Hafez al-Assad and his son Bashar al-Assad. I also spoke of my efforts to arrange an exchange between members of the U.S. Congress and the Iranian parliament, known as the Majlis. Our delegations came very close to meeting in Geneva in 2001, but it fell through because of a highly publicized U.S.-Iranian disagreement shortly before the scheduled confab.

I always found it interesting, even stimulating, to try to persuade the president to advance dialogue with Syria and Iran. He always listened patiently and then always said no. But Bush was easy to talk to, and we lightened the heavy discourse with banter. One day I said, "Mr. President, after our extensive discussions, I've come to the conclusion that you're less disinclined to deal with Syria than with Iran."

He looked at me a little quizzically and said, "Would you run that by me again?"

I said, "Sure." And then I slowly said, "I guess you're less disinclined to deal with Syria than with Iran."

He smiled and said, "Arlen, you've got it about right."

On one airplane trip, Bush had a bowl of fruit on his desk. I ate a banana, and finished it to find myself holding a rotting peel. I looked all around for a wastebasket, but couldn't find one. Then a hand reached across the table. It was the president's. He said, "Give me that." Bush took the peel from me. He had a wastebasket on his side.

During a ride from the Pittsburgh airport to the downtown area, when Santorum was with us, we got into an extended discussion about stem cell research. The vote was 2–1 against me, although under Abraham Lincoln's rule, Bush didn't need a majority. Lincoln had polled his cabinet on an issue, found himself universally opposed, and announced, "Seven nays and one aye; the ayes have it." I thought from our discussion—though I couldn't cite anything specifically—that the president was not enthusiastic about the rule prohibiting federal funds for embryonic stem cell research. He had, in fact, issued an executive order in August 2001, not long after taking office, allowing federal funds for research on already existing lines. Bush wasn't as doctrinaire as his policies suggested. He was like his father, to the extent that some thought 43 was really pro-choice.

During our trip, Bush was almost affectionate, wrapping his arm around my shoulder repeatedly as we worked reception lines after landing and giving me long, enthusiastic introductions at events. Bush touted my reputation for independence when he talked me up. On a March 2004 trip to Ardmore, Pennsylvania, in Montgomery County, to speak about affordable housing, he told the crowd, "I consider Arlen Specter an ally and a friend. Oh, he doesn't do everything you ask him to do all the time, but when you need him . . . when you need him, he's there. He's an independent voice for the great state of Pennsylvania and he's doing a fine job as a United States senator."

Bush's graciousness sometimes came at a cost. During an early 2004 trip to Scranton, we landed in a drizzle, and the president invited me to join him for the walk down the Air Force One stairway, the first time he had done that. He was wearing an immaculate blue overcoat, and I slipped on a scruffy raincoat.

"Arlen, Arlen, we're going to have to upgrade your wardrobe," the president told me.

I told Shanin that story, and he bought me a more presentable coat. But I hadn't heard the last of the old raincoat. Months later, at my April

Pittsburgh rally, Bush told a crowd of two thousand about scolding me about the "ratty coat" I had worn. Even so, the president said, "He's earned another term in the United States Senate."

Certainly, the White House saw some self-interest in helping me. Pennsylvania—which Bush had lost to Gore by 200,000 votes in 2000—was a key state for the president in 2004, and the White House thought I could attract the moderate and independent voters it needed, and also help keep the Senate under Republican control.

The dynamic reminded me of my 1971 visit with Nixon in the Oval Office. Nixon spent almost an hour with me talking about a wide range of subjects, with emphasis on law enforcement, since I was DA at the time. Attorney General John Mitchell joined us, and Nixon asked me about the Supreme Court's interference with the White House drive for law and order. I told the president about the problems with habeas corpus, and he looked over at Mitchell and said, "John, get hold of Burger, get that straightened out," as though the chief justice were at the attorney general's beck and call, and a word from Mitchell would resolve the issue.

Nixon thought I might be helpful with young people, blacks, Jews, and liberals. More than thirty years later, President Bush and his advisers seemed to think so too. I told reporters, "I think I can help the president hold down the margin in Philadelphia. I think I can help him win the suburban counties."

"Bush and Specter are joined at the hip," G. Terry Madonna, Pennsylvania's premier political seer and director of Franklin and Marshall's Center for Politics and Public Affairs, told the *Los Angeles Times*.[22]

Moderates came out strong for me, some bridling at Moore's warnings about the Club for Growth's hunt for scalps to mount on its walls. Arnold Schwarzenegger, six months before being elected California governor, headlined an event at a Capitol Hill hotel. The former bodybuilding champ and action-movie hero began the day testifying on the value of after-school programs before the Appropriations subcommittee I chaired. "Next time there is a hearing to save after-school program funding," he vowed, hitting his signature line as the Terminator, "I'll be back."

That evening at the Citizens for Arlen Specter fund-raiser, Schwar-zenegger held court, a garrulous, big-time Hollywood star. Afterward, a couple of women complained that he had pinched their rear ends.

I tried to convert Jews, who generally registered Democratic, to the GOP, to help the president as well as me. The *Pittsburgh City Paper* ran a story on my efforts headlined "Let My People Go Republican."

And I drew Democratic and union support. The AFL-CIO and vari-ous unions endorsed me, citing my long and solid relationship with orga-nized labor. The Transportation Communications International Union even urged its Democratic members in Pennsylvania to switch their regis-tration to vote for me in the primary. Labor gave me nearly twice as much money as any other Republican in the 2004 primary cycle, $72,250. In all, I had raised $187,750 from unions since my 1998 campaign.[23]

I even got some key conservative support. David Keene, chairman of the American Conservative Union, wrote in a column in *The Hill*, "Arlen Specter is what we used to call a standup guy. . . . He isn't always with us, but when he is, you can take his word to the bank. . . . That should count in a world where most elected officials don't have the courage to disagree with anybody."[24]

Conservatives' support for me set off battles within their movement. Some publicly questioned whether Grover Norquist could remain an ef-fective conservative leader after his group, Americans for Tax Reform, gave me its "Hero of the Taxpayer Award."[25] I had met the group's 85 percent voting threshold, so the award, in a sense, was not discretionary. But Norquist also said conservatives' fire would be better directed at Demo-crats than against me, drawing more rebuke.

Madonna and Berwood Yost, the political observers, gushed:

His greatest weakness is also his greatest strength. Specter is just as popular among Democrats as he is among Republicans. . . . His job performance ratings are higher among Democrats than among Republicans. . . . Specter looks like he is in better position to win a general election than to win a primary, particularly if conservative turnout is high. Little wonder the Republican leadership is lining up behind him. . . . Over time, Arlen Specter has demonstrated his skills as Pennsylvania's best electoral politician. His campaigns are the stuff that textbooks are written about.[26]

Even so, we had to overcome a fierce fight from the right wing. National conservatives ultimately funneled $2 million in contributions and attack ads into Pennsylvania to help Toomey.[27] I had been able to reduce that sum a bit. I spoke in New York at the Monday Meeting, a gathering of the conservative financial and intellectual elite, to rebut Toomey's earlier appearance. One member of the Club for Growth's board told the press, "He froze a lot of money that was going to go to Toomey."[28]

In all, my campaign spent $10 million on the primary, outspending Toomey and his handlers two to one. But that bottom line didn't count the ink that right-wingers spilled on Toomey's behalf.

James Dobson, the evangelical Christian radio and newspaper personality who ran Focus on the Family, wrote to his flock: "The defeat of Arlen Specter would send a mighty signal that the days of waffling, devious, anti-family Republicans who are liberals in disguise is finally over." Dobson also recorded endorsement radio spots for Toomey.

Led by Dobson, a legion of pro-life activists descended on Pennsylvania to denounce me. They saw a second Bush term as a chance to tilt the court with justices who would overturn *Roe v. Wade*, capping their thirty-year crusade. Despite my support for all of Bush's first-term nominees, they worried that I would oppose pro-life nominees to the high court.

Magazine publisher and failed presidential candidate Steve Forbes lamented in a column that solid conservative legislation was passing in the House but that, "unfortunately, the legislation then proceeds to 'the graveyard of good ideas' in the Senate, where a few liberal Republicans, led by Arlen Specter, too often side with Democrats to thwart these important efforts."[29]

The *Pittsburgh Tribune-Review*, a rabid conservative rag with no pretense of objectivity, maintained a drumbeat against me. Its headlines during the primary included: "Pat Toomey Undaunted in Bid to Defang Snarlin' Arlen," "Specter's Slime Machine: There He Goes Again," "Specter's Sad

Ploy: Desperate Coward," and "Specter Dives for Reagan's Coattails: Can the Philly Liberal Fall Any Lower?"

The *Tribune-Review* was owned and published by Richard Mellon Scaife, an heir to the Andrew Mellon fortune whom the *Washington Post* described as "the most generous donor to conservative causes in American history," and whom friends and relatives described as a "gutter drunk" and an intellectual lightweight.[30] Scaife had been expelled from Yale during his freshman year for rolling a keg of beer down a flight of stairs and breaking a classmate's legs.[31] More recently, Scaife's messy divorce made national headlines over allegations of alcoholism, motel trysts with a woman who had been arrested for prostitution, and dognapping.[32]

Over the decades, Scaife had given hundreds of millions of dollars to conservative causes. A 1999 *Washington Post* study found, "His biggest contribution has been to help fund the creation of the modern conservative movement in America."[33] Scaife ranked among the Club for Growth's top ten contributors. He and his wife also each gave Toomey the maximum $2,000 then allowed by law.[34]

Scaife had had a vendetta against me for aeons. One of his former confidants told the *Post*, "When he gets a hate on for somebody he tends to pursue it to substantial length."[35] But Scaife never had the guts to say anything adverse to me face-to-face. His newspaper's editorial board refused to meet with me.

I first met Scaife at a 1967 district attorneys' convention in San Francisco. He was there with his friend Allegheny County DA Bob Duggan, who had introduced young Scaife to conservative Republican politics while dating Scaife's sister Cordelia.[36]

In 1969, Elsie Hillman, the grand dame of Pennsylvania Republican politics, pressed me to talk to Duggan about running a grand jury investigation. At the time, I was running a massive investigation into corruption in Philadelphia land development and urban renewal. Our probe would ultimately indict a slew of city power brokers and convict the head of the Philadelphia Housing Authority for steering $5 million to his brother's redevelopment firm and to a bank where he was a director and a shareholder. Hillman thought a similar grand jury in Pittsburgh would tip the scales against Democratic corruption in that city and help elect John Tabor, an attractive young lawyer who was running for mayor against the discredited Pittsburgh political machine. I made the suggestion to Duggan. It went in one ear and out the other. The Pittsburgh Republicans' plans were thwarted by a young reformer, city councilman Pete Flaherty, who beat the Democratic machine's candidate in a primary and went on to trounce Tabor in the general election.

A few years later, the IRS and then–U.S. attorney Thornburgh investigated Duggan's sources of income and criminal connections. On March 5, 1974, the day Thornburgh's tax-fraud indictment against Duggan was returned, Duggan was found dead on his farm in Ligonier, Pennsylvania, a shotgun wound to the chest. Cordelia Scaife, who had secretly married Duggan in Nevada, decided that her brother was somehow involved. They stopped speaking. Ultimately, she decided that Duggan had committed suicide, and she and her brother reconciled.[37]

I met Scaife again, with his wife, around 1986. At the time, they were both pro-choice. Scaife also went to a Hillman fund-raiser and contributed $500.

Scaife's animus began, maybe, with his distaste for my politics. James Whelan, who edited the *Sacramento Union* when Scaife owned it, said, "In general he sees certain villains in American life and society and thinks he should do everything he can to attack them and bring them down."[38] Whelan added, "If you're not my friend, you're my enemy—he lives by that kind of code."[39] If there was a single event that set off Scaife, it was my appointing Terry Slease to my judicial nominations panel in the 1980s. Slease had been Scaife's top aide and legal adviser, and they'd had a falling-out.

Scaife could be as generous to his friends as he was vengeful to his enemies. In 1972, he gave $1 million to Richard Nixon's re-election campaign. But after Nixon's troubles, Scaife turned to supporting causes and ideas rather than candidates. In the mid-1990s, he gave $2.3 million to the *American Spectator* magazine to unearth dirt on President Clinton, and donated to a host of other anti-Clinton efforts. Hillary Clinton called Scaife the central figure in the "vast right-wing conspiracy" against her husband.[40] He sank millions every year into the money-draining *Tribune-Review*, which steadily attacked us perceived villains.

The *National Review*, the conservative canon, also took up Toomey's cause, running two cover stories on the race. The first cover, on September 1, 2003, was a photo of me with the headline "The Worst Republican Senator." The article declared, "Specter may not be the most unreliable GOP senator—he faces strong competition in that category from Lincoln Chafee of Rhode Island—but he is almost certainly the most harmful, because he is smart, ruthless and influential."

National Review president Richard Rhodes was a big Toomey backer, and also gave $5,000 to the Club for Growth, an insidious network, if not a vast right-wing conspiracy.[41] The *National Review* made a bogus charge that I had demanded that then–majority leader Lott attend two fundraisers in Pennsylvania in exchange for my supporting an appropriations bill. I produced a letter signed by all four living Republican majority leaders—Dole, Lott, Baker, and Frist—asserting:

> Senator Trent Lott has confirmed that the *National Review* story is false in accusing Senator Specter of signing off on an Appropriations bill in exchange for Senator Lott's attending two fund-raisers in Pennsylvania. Nothing like that ever happened. . . . As the *National Review* concedes, quoting an unnamed former Senate staffer: "If there is a tough debate going on, you definitely want Specter on your side."

The second *National Review* cover story, in March 2004, carried a head shot of Toomey with the headline "The Right Choice" and the subhead "Conservative Pat Toomey challenges Sen. Arlen Specter in a battle for the GOP's future."

Toomey's campaign even recruited Robert Bork for an endorsement in early 2004. The judge expressed alarm that I was poised to become chairman of the Senate Judiciary Committee. "He has a record of supporting quite liberal judges," Bork told a gathering Toomey arranged. "He thinks the judges should be making up the Constitution, in many respects."[42]

The *Allentown Morning Call* reported, "Bork said his main concern was that Specter would use the chairmanship to block judicial candidates who believe—as Bork does—that cases should be decided based on the original intent of those who wrote the Constitution."[43]

Around that time, I ran into Bork at a big black-tie social event in the grand ballroom of the Washington Hilton, the hotel where Reagan had been shot in March 1981. I could see the bitterness in his eyes. I said, "Hello, Judge Bork." He turned away.

Despite it all, I thrived on the race. When my finance director, Todd Averette, announced at a March 2004 campaign team dinner, "Only twenty-nine days to go," I said not to look at it that way, that these were exciting times, great fun. I drew a few odd looks.

Until six weeks out, I was significantly ahead, mostly because voters hadn't heard of Toomey. Even if enough conservatives were ready to replace me, they didn't know enough about Toomey to vote for him. Then the race tightened. I had a 23-point lead in January, a 15-point one on April 7, and a 5-point lead on April 20, a week before the primary.[44] Conservatives, some said, were coming home. The Quinnipiac University Polling Institute found "a majority of likely primary voters now agree Specter is too liberal."

A week before the election, in a conference call with reporters, Toomey predicted he would win, even calling his tally to a tenth of a percentage point, 51.7 percent of the vote.[45]

The president's detractors were using my candidacy to attack Bush. I was unhappy with our advertising, and personally advanced an idea for an ad. I insisted, over the hesitancy of my key advisers, that the language be blunt: This election is not between Arlen Specter and Pat Toomey, it's between President George Bush and Pat Toomey. I designed the final TV spot. We used footage from a Pittsburgh event the week before, with Bush saying, "I'm here to say it as plainly as I can . . . Arlen Specter is the right man for the United States Senate. . . . I can count on this man. . . . He's a firm ally when it matters."

Toomey, in making his precise victory prediction, had also promised prompt poll results and an early evening. Instead, the night wore on, an emotional whipsaw for my team at the Bellevue Hotel, where I had announced my first run for office, for district attorney, nearly forty years earlier.

Sensing the returns would be extremely close, I did something I had never done before. Around 6 p.m., two hours before the polls closed, I went from camera to camera in the hotel ballroom, where the media were readying for the results. The tactic would fail six years later, but in April 2004, several television stations agreed to carry my final comments. I was especially emphatic in an extended live interview on KYW Radio urging listeners to go out and vote if they wanted to keep me in office, because it looked very tight.

The early tallies were better than we had expected, or even dreamed. It turned out that a ninety-five-thousand-vote error from Bucks County, which somehow was not immediately detected, had given me a reported 59–41 edge, sending our troops into elation. Corrected, the margin shrank immediately to 51–49, and then to a reported 50–50 tie by 11 p.m. The tally was never actually that close, though, and the margin was never less than 2 points, we would later learn. Other reporting errors had skewed the later numbers.

But the conventional wisdom held that the late returns, from rural counties using paper ballots, represented pockets of Toomey's strength. The question was whether I could do well enough in those outposts to maintain my narrow margin.

Toward midnight, one Philadelphia network affiliate was showing a split screen of my event and Toomey's. Toomey's camp bustled as they seemed to smell their prize. At the Bellevue, depression and lassitude appeared to overtake my minions as many left for their rooms or stepped outside, and those remaining slumped around the perimeter, waiting for periodic updates and hoping to hold on. Some of my crew, sure of defeat, launched into emotional farewells with co-workers.

The late-voting theory also proved faulty, as some final returns came from odd precincts from the southeast and other redoubts of my strength. In the end, we held on. The final tally showed 50.8 percent for me to 49.2 percent for Toomey. I had won by some seventeen thousand votes out of more than a million cast.

Toomey conceded around 1 a.m., phoning me to offer a gracious—if brief—congratulations, and then delivering a gracious—if long—concession speech from his headquarters, which we watched from the Bellevue TV monitors.

Several of my supporters chanted for Toomey to wrap up and let me make a victory speech. When my turn came, I complimented Toomey on a hard-fought campaign and spoke of settling "a family disagreement in the Republican Party." I urged Republican unity heading toward November. I had won the battle for the soul of the Republican Party, at least for the moment.

To some, my victory, by any margin, was a miracle. The day after the primary, John Baer wrote in the *Philadelphia Daily News*:

> And the extraordinary thing about this win, all his wins, is this: on paper, he shouldn't be elected in Pennsylvania. He's a Jewish Republican Ivy League lawyer from Philadelphia in a rural state where Democrats hold a 473,000 registration edge, where Philadelphia lawyers are as popular as Dutch Elm Disease and where a majority of the population thinks the Ivy League is minor league baseball.[46]

The Club for Growth had sent its message, even if it hadn't collected its scalp. E. J. Dionne wrote a *Washington Post* column headlined "The GOP's Vanishing Breed": "Mamas, don't let your babies grow up to be moderate Republicans. There's not much room for them in this political world."

Within days of the election, Steve Moore endorsed me, reasoning that I would come closer to advancing his agenda than my Democratic opponent,

Congressman Joe Hoeffel. As for Toomey, Moore said, "The Number One thing is that a star was born. This guy is now maybe the second most important Republican in the state. . . . I think we feel this was a smart investment."[47]

Moore might soon have had second thoughts about that investment. That December, the Club for Growth board ousted Moore as president and replaced him with Toomey. Moore's partisans claimed that Toomey wanted the Club post mainly to tap its donors as he prepared for future political runs. Moore and some loyalists formed a rival conservative fund-raising group, the Free Enterprise Fund, and tried to poach Club members. The Club, in turn, threatened lawsuits against Moore's new group for stealing the Club's donor lists. Moore eventually landed as an editorial writer at the *Wall Street Journal*.

After the 2004 election, I spent a lot of time trying to cultivate conservatives. David Keene told me that Moore wanted to meet with me. Moore and I had a couple of lunches in the Senate Dining Room. He was smart, cordial, and friendly, breathing none of his campaign fire.

In the 2004 primary aftermath, members of my campaign team met with conservative movement leaders and some of Toomey's people. "We sat down and broke bread with them," my campaign manager, Chris Nicholas, recalled. "Specter, he wants to meet with everybody: How can we work together now? And one of the things that became apparent was, one way for us to have a peace offering with them was to make a major contribution to Jim DeMint." At the time, DeMint was a conservative congressman from South Carolina making a first Senate run.

That summer, I made the largest contribution we could to DeMint, $5,000 through my Big Tent PAC. "So they were all happy with that," Nicholas said.

In the general election, Joe Hoeffel veered as far left as Toomey had veered right. In July, Hoeffel blocked the doorway of the Sudanese embassy in Washington to protest human rights violations, getting himself arrested, replete with handcuffs, on charges of disorderly conduct and unlawful assembly. Despite Hoeffel's near-perfect rating with the AFL-CIO, we won the union's endorsement with around 70 percent support. In November, I beat Hoeffel by 700,000 votes, winning 53–42, with 4 percent going to a Constitution Party candidate supported mostly by Toomey loyalists. My nearly 3 million votes was the largest raw vote total any Republican had ever gotten in Pennsylvania. Bush lost Pennsylvania to Kerry, but still won a second term.

After Hoeffel conceded that night in November 2004, I took the stage at Philadelphia's Four Seasons Hotel ballroom as the *Rocky* theme blared. I had beaten back a challenge from the far right and then from the far left. Over supporters' manic cheers, I called, "This victory tonight is a symbol for the moderate wing of the Republican Party."

But I was about to wade into an even tougher fight.

FIVE

THE TOUGHEST
FIGHT

Around 11:30 a.m. the day after the 2004 election, I held a news conference at Philadelphia's Four Seasons Hotel, in a wide foyer just outside the ballroom where we had celebrated victory some ten hours earlier. I'd survived another tough campaign and a tough year. And there seemed no question that I would inherit the Judiciary Committee gavel, a dream for decades, and take the chair once occupied by Martin Van Buren, "Big Jim" Eastland, Ted Kennedy, and Joe Biden. A day-after news conference was traditional for election wins.

I was still euphoric as reporters peppered me with questions about Chief Justice William Rehnquist's failing health and the ongoing battles over judicial nominations. I let the news conference go on too long. A reporter asked, "Mr. Bush, he just won the election, even with the popular vote as well. If he wants antiabortion judges up there, you are caught in the middle of it, what are you going to do?" I replied:

When you talk about judges who would change the right of a woman to choose, overturn *Roe v. Wade*, I think that is unlikely. . . . Nobody can be confirmed today who didn't agree with *Brown v. Board of Education* on integration, and I believe that while you traditionally do not ask a nominee how they're going to decide a specific case, there's a doctrine and a fancy label term, *stare decisis*—precedent—which I think protects that issue. That is my view, now, before, and always.

The reporter continued: "You are saying the president should not bother or make the move to send somebody up there who is clearly anti-abortion?" I said:

I don't want to prejudge what the president is going to do. But the president is well aware of what happened when a number of his nominees were sent up, with the filibuster, and the president has said he is not going to impose a litmus test. He faced that issue squarely in the third debate, and I would not expect the president—I would expect the president to be mindful of the considerations that I mentioned.

The words seemed innocuous. They were statements of fact. But they would soon set off what CNN called a raging conservative campaign against me.[1] The next day, the Associated Press posted a story headlined "Likely New Senate Judiciary Chairman Warns Bush Against Nominating Anti-abortion Judges," which ran in the *Washington Post* and across the country.

Santorum tracked me down between flights in Chicago to tell me the problems the story was making for him. Santorum's support and assurances to conservatives, along with President Bush's, had given a vital boost in my beating Toomey.

I promptly issued a statement that I didn't have a litmus test against pro-life judicial nominees. I noted that I had voted to confirm Chief Justice Rehnquist and Justices O'Connor, Scalia, and Kennedy and had led the fight to confirm Justice Thomas. I had, in fact, voted for all of Bush's judicial nominees, and for other vocal pro-life nominees, and had gone to the Senate floor seventeen times to argue against Democrats' filibusters.

But we couldn't stop the frenzy. Democratic filibusters of President

Bush's nominees threatened to derail the Senate. The issue had played big in Bush's race against Kerry and in my primary against Toomey, especially among hard-line conservatives. During my primary, Toomey had said, "The most palpable fear among Republicans is what would happen if Arlen Specter is re-elected and becomes the next chairman of the Judiciary Committee. It's a frightening prospect."

Social conservatives joined the chant. A Family Research Council leader warned, "You put a person like that in charge of the Judiciary Committee, and we won't see many of President Bush's nominees get through. With regard to social issues, he is a poster child of NARAL and NOW."[2] Some spun my day-after comment to claim I was warning the president not to nominate pro-life judges, in an act of defiance, ingratitude, and self-assertion.

Economic conservatives piled on. FreedomWorks, Dick Armey's limited-government group, which would later join forces with the Tea Party, led the charge, issuing a news release blasting some of my votes on proposed tax cuts and concluding, "And when it comes to curbing lawsuit abuse, well, Sen. Specter has received the endorsement of the American Trial Lawyer Association in every election he has run. Enough said."

The right-wing machinery that had been pounding me and grinding up Kerry was still in high gear, and here was some fresh meat. The media waded into the maelstrom. On November 5, the day after my clarifying statement, headlines carried my assurances, such as the *Washington Post*'s "Specter Denies Warning Bush over Court Nominees" and Reuters's "Key Senator Denies Warning Bush on Abortion Issue." But other headlines fanned the fringe's ire, such as the *Los Angeles Times*'s "Dobson Blasts Senator Specter's 'Arrogant Grandstanding'; Focus Action Founder Says Republican Is Wrong to Threaten Bush over Nominees." The *Philadelphia Inquirer* captured my plight with a story headlined "Specter: His Abortion Remark Puts Panel Leadership at Risk."

I had strutted into a minefield. On judicial nominations, up-or-down votes left little room for compromise, and both sides had increasingly dug in on their key issues—principally abortion. In February 2002, I had said on the Senate floor:

> There is an element expressed by some members of the Judiciary Committee on the so-called litmus test, with some people believing that unless a judicial nominee is willing to endorse *Roe v. Wade* on a woman's right to choose, that individual should not be confirmed to the Supreme Court—really, an effort to place *Roe v. Wade* on a level with *Brown v. Board of Education.*

Some senators had explicitly endorsed litmus tests on abortion. As his presidential campaign was heating up, Kerry said, "I am prepared to filibuster, if necessary, any Supreme Court nominee who would turn back the clock on a woman's right to choose or the constitutional right to privacy, on civil rights and individual liberties, and on the laws protecting workers and the environment."[3]

During a November 2003 "Justice for Judges Marathon"—or talkathon—that Republicans staged to draw attention to Democratic filibusters, Orrin Hatch complained: "They [Democrats] do not want anybody on the circuit courts of appeals who may be pro-life. That is what this is all about. It is about abortion."[4] Hatch laced into Democratic colleagues for "not having the guts" to stand up to pro-choice, inside-the-Beltway interest groups.[5]

Some abortion-rights advocates had gone even further. Dawn Johnsen, NARAL's legal director, filed a Supreme Court brief in 1989 elevating *Roe* to *Brown*'s level by equating a woman's carrying a child against her will to slavery. Johnsen would reappear two decades later as Obama's failed nominee to head the Office of Legal Counsel, and her pregnancy-as-slavery argument would draw no Senate defenders.

Democrats and Republicans shared the blame for the partisan gridlock. Both parties put qualified nominees in the deep freeze of Senate procedure. The party out of power bottled up nominees in committee or omitted them from the agenda for floor action if that party controlled the Senate, or through the filibuster if it did not. Among blocked nominees for lower-court judgeships were future Supreme Court justices John Roberts and Elena Kagan.

The payback theory operated at full force, with each party retaliating as it gained control, escalating the feud. As I said on the Senate floor in February 2002, before the issue took on national prominence:

> Regrettably, there is a great deal of partisan politics in the way judges are confirmed by the Senate. Regrettably, that is a practice regardless of which party is in control of the White House and which party has control of the Senate.
>
> . . . We ought to declare this truce and ought to sign this armistice so we take partisan politics out of the confirmation process of federal judges. It is high time we did that.

In mid-2003, I would have to cast a deciding vote on a circuit court nominee who would spark a national furor over religion and further escalate the nominations war. Alabama attorney general William Pryor looked boyish and scrubbed at forty-one under a mane of brown hair. He was, by any measure, a staunch social conservative. Pryor had defended student-led prayer in public schools and called *Roe v. Wade* "the worst abomination of constitutional law in our history." He warned in a brief that if the Supreme Court overturned a Texas law banning gay sex, the decision would result in legalized "prostitution, necrophilia, bestiality, and possession of child pornography." The high court overturned the law.[6] Senator Chuck Schumer called Pryor "the Frankenstein nominee—a stitching together of the worst parts of the worst nominees the president has sent us."[7]

All the other Judiciary Committee members had declared positions on Pryor, leaving me to decide whether he advanced to the Senate floor for a vote. With my 2004 Senate race roiling, both Toomey and Hoeffel hammered away. "Pryor is eminently qualified, and Sen. Specter refuses to support him thus far," Toomey told the press. "It is bad enough that Democrats have abused advise and consent, but it is appalling that he would be a contributor." From the left, Hoeffel chimed in: "My reaction is that he is selling out in order to keep the political support of the President."[8]

I had not planned to attend Pryor's hearing on June 11, 2003, as I had too much else brewing. At 1 p.m., I was rushing to the Senate dining room in the Capitol, already fifteen minutes late for lunch with the chairman and chief lobbyist of the American-Israel Public Affairs Committee (AIPAC). I had to walk past the Judiciary hearing room in the Dirksen Building, and decided to pop in. I figured I'd find a lot of other senators questioning Pryor and walk out, as senators often did at hearings.

I entered G-50 Dirksen, its two-story walls sheathed in enough rich wood paneling to build a ship. The only senators there were Jeff Sessions, who was Pryor's patron and former boss at the Alabama attorney general's office, Judiciary chairman Orrin Hatch, and ranking Democrat Patrick Leahy. Hatch had the floor. He asked Pryor whether there were some statements he might like to take back. Pryor declined the olive branch, or lifeline.

"Now, just for the record," Hatch asked, "what is your religious affiliation?" Hatch often spoke of his own Mormon faith.

"I'm a Roman Catholic," Pryor replied.

"Are you active in your church?" Hatch asked.

"I am," Pryor said.

"You believe in your religion."

"I do," Pryor affirmed.

With this exchange playing out, the AIPAC leaders would have to wait.

Hatch brought up Pryor's advocacy for the Alabama Religious Freedom Amendment to the Alabama Constitution, which made it more difficult for government to impose restrictions on the exercise of religion.

"And you were advocating for that?" Hatch asked.

"Yes," Pryor said.

"As a committed Catholic."

"Yes," Pryor said.

"For everybody, regardless of religious belief," Hatch said.

"Absolutely."

Guided by Hatch, Pryor maintained, "Even though I strongly disagree with *Roe v. Wade*, I have acted in accordance with it as Attorney General and would continue to do so as a Court of Appeals Judge."[9]

When Hatch finally finished his questioning, Leahy asked to make a "couple of quick points." I objected, noting it was not Leahy's turn. Hatch overruled me and let Leahy talk. As it turned out, I was glad he did.

"You were asked about your religion," Leahy told Pryor.

In 29 years in the Senate and thousands of nominations hearings in all the different committees I sit on, I have never asked a nominee what his or her religion was because I think that is irrelevant to our consideration. . . . Just as we are supposed to be colorblind, we should be religious-blind, as far as that is somebody's personal choice, and has nothing to do with their qualifications.

When Leahy finished, Hatch said:

. . . I do not usually ask that question, either, but lately we have been finding situations where some of the questions that come up clearly go to that issue. And I just wanted to make it very clear that he is a very strong Catholic who believes in what he is doing, but yet has abided by the law, and that is a very important point because some of the criticisms have been hitting below the belt, frankly.

Hatch turned to me. "Senator Specter?"

"Thank you, Mr. Chairman," I said. I looked at Hatch. "I withdraw my objection to Senator Leahy's latest intervention because I want to associate myself with his remarks. I do not believe that religion ought to be a question, either. If you have been attacked for being a Catholic, that is one thing." I asked Pryor if he had been attacked for being a Catholic. Before Pryor could finish answering, Hatch interrupted. I said, "If I may proceed, Mr. Chairman?"

"Sure," Hatch said.

I soon gave Pryor another chance to ease off some of his statements. I asked whether he had been accurately quoted as saying the 1992 Supreme Court decision in *Planned Parenthood v. Casey* "preserved the worst abomination of constitutional law in our history."

"Yes," Pryor said.

I asked him whether that comment fell in the category that Hatch had covered, of remarks Pryor might wish he had not made.

"No, I stand by that comment." Pryor was making it awfully hard for a senator in my position, whose constituents look to him to protect them from guys like that.

"Why do you consider it an abomination, Attorney General Pryor?" I asked.

"Well, I believe that not only is the case unsupported by the text and structure of the Constitution, but it had led to a morally wrong result," he said. "It has led to the slaughter of millions of innocent unborn children. That's my personal belief."[10]

He was just exacerbating the matter.

Hatch and Leahy sparred for another couple of rounds, with Leahy insisting that the committee should not ask nominees about their religious beliefs, which would "be a terrible, terrible precedent to start."

"Then let's get the outside groups to stop doing that," Hatch shot back. "We will recess until 3 o'clock."[11]

Although Hatch wasn't trying to criticize Pryor for being a Catholic, he was trying to excuse Pryor's statements on the basis of religious conviction, which would invite abuse. And the argument that a public servant's religious views color his judgment in exercising his official duties is akin to accusations thrown at John F. Kennedy, Al Smith, and other leaders who were Catholic. Smith, whose hand my father shook at the 1928 Wichita whistle stop, generated fears of the pope moving into the White House. After losing the election, Smith said that he sent the pope a one-word telegram: "Unpack!" Religion should have no place in politics, as JFK famously said, citing Article VI of the Constitution.

Later in the day, Hatch stopped me on the Senate floor, upset over my criticism of his remarks at the hearing. "You really shouldn't have done that," he said. "That really was embarrassing."

I said, "Listen, Orrin, it was mild compared to what I really thought about it. I thought that was really just outlandish. You opened the door to religion, and watch out—there'll be concerns next for the Mormons and the Jews."

My points seemed to hold little sway with Hatch. A month later, he was quoted in the *New York Times* as saying, "The left is trying to enforce an anti-religious litmus test [whereby] nominees who openly adhere to Catholic and Baptist doctrines, as a matter of personal faith, are unqualified for the federal bench in the eyes of the liberal Washington interest groups."[12]

Democrats, in response, accused Republicans of "religious McCarthyism." Leahy said at a Judiciary Committee meeting:

> A Republican-backed group was on one of the talk shows one Sunday morning and they attacked me as being anti-Catholic. Now, I didn't see the show because my wife and I were at mass at the time. The following Sunday, I prayed for their enlightenment, of course, as I am sure everybody else did in both parties.[13]

In late July 2003, Democrats tried to seize the offensive by seeking unanimous consent for a rules change to ban questions about a nominee's religion during confirmation proceedings. Hatch objected. The ongoing spat over nominees' religion, the *Washington Post* wrote, "plunged the already bitterly divided Senate into new depths of rancor."[14]

I mulled Pryor's nomination. One Judiciary Committee session was adjourned to allow me time to deliberate. It was hard for me to understand why a smart guy like Pryor, who aspired to the federal bench, would want to create a controversy with his remarks about *Roe*. I thought that if he got confirmed as a judge, he would tilt far right. But on the circuit bench, he wasn't going to Borkize the Supreme Court. And I thought of all the imperatives of trying to make the process work and get judges confirmed, and move forward. In the end, I decided Pryor was acceptable, and not worth a battle royal.

In July 2003, I cast the deciding vote in the Judiciary Committee to send Pryor to the floor. I took my consistent approach that the full Senate, not the committee, should decide on nominees. I issued a statement saying I still had concerns about Pryor and would reserve my final decision until the full Senate vote:

It is not unusual in coming to this vote on Attorney General Pryor that the other 18 Senators on the Committee are divided evenly nine to nine on party lines and my vote will be determinative. . . . The party-polarized Senate has become a way of life, in my opinion to the detriment of the public interest. Regrettably, few senators will even consider the other party's arguments and fewer dare to vote with the other party. In the interim between now and the floor vote, I will continue to listen to my constituents on this heavily lobbied nomination.

The decision was a political high-wire act. I satisfied the right by voting Pryor out of committee, and satisfied the left by not committing to vote for him on the floor.

A month later, in August 2003, Pryor became the point man for enforcing a federal court order against Alabama chief justice Charles Moore, who refused to remove a 5,300-pound monument to the Ten Commandments from his courthouse. Pryor maintained that while he personally found the monument legal and constitutional, he would enforce the federal order.

The Ten Commandments fight made front-page headlines across the country, and was likened to Alabama governor George Wallace's 1963 standoff against Attorney General Robert F. Kennedy over integrating the University of Alabama. I had seen the 1963 standoff from RFK's office as we discussed the Philadelphia Teamsters case, and now I also had a good vantage point on this twenty-first-century redux.

In November 2003, propelled by ethics charges Pryor filed against Moore, the chief justice was removed from office. Pryor's action infuriated some of his core supporters but proved his ability to divorce his own views from his law-enforcement duties.

In February 2004, President Bush gave Pryor a recess appointment, a month after installing Charles Pickering, another filibustered nominee, on the Fifth Circuit. Like Pickering, Pryor would serve only for the duration of the 108th Congress, until 2005, not for life. I had objected to recess appointments in years past, saying they poisoned the waters. But I did not object to Pickering's and Pryor's appointments, because the waters could not be poisoned any more than they already were by early 2004.

A month later, in late March 2004, Minority Leader Tom Daschle and the Democrats vowed no further action on judicial nominees unless Bush promised no further recess appointments. The president refused.

To break the gridlock, Majority Leader Frist and other Republicans conceived a parliamentary maneuver to change the Senate rules to require a simple majority vote on judicial nominees, essentially stripping the minority of its veto power through the filibuster. Under the plan, Vice President Cheney, presiding over the Senate, would rule that 51 votes—not the normal 60—could invoke cloture, cutting off debate. That ruling would then be appealed. Under Senate procedure, a majority of 51 votes, which Republican leaders figured they could muster, would sustain the chair's ruling. Proponents called their plan the "constitutional option" because it was based on an interpretation that the Constitution required only a majority for Senate confirmation. Opponents dubbed the plan "the nuclear option" because they said it would blow up the Senate.

If Republicans engaged the option, Democrats threatened to halt Senate action on all non-defense-related matters. On the Senate floor, Harry Reid called President Bush a liar over the option. Four years later, Reid would boast about his accusation in a book:

> "This nuclear option is very bad for the country, Mr. President," I said. "You shouldn't do this."
>
> Bush protested his innocence. "I'm not involved in it at all," he said. "Not my deal."
>
> It may not have been the president's deal, but it was Karl Rove's deal.
>
> A couple of days later, Dick Cheney spoke for the White House when he announced that the nuclear option was the way to go, and that he'd be honored to break a tie vote in the Senate when it was time to change the rules. The president had misled me and the Senate.
>
> And that was the second time I called George Bush a liar.

The first time was over the nuclear waste repository located at Yucca Mountain, in my home state of Nevada. . . . When one lies, one is a liar. I called him a liar then, and with his obvious duplicity on the nuclear option revealed by the Vice-President's pronouncement, I called the President a liar again.[15]

Reid's charge was absurd. And calling the president a liar demeaned the presidency and diminished Reid's stature as a leader. It's one thing to blurt such an accusation in the heat of passion, but another to repeat it at length years later in a book.

In 2004, I proposed a remedy to break the impasse and return the confirmation standard to professional competence and away from ideology. My resolution called for a ninety-day timetable: Within thirty days after the president submitted a judicial nomination, the Judiciary Committee would hold a hearing. Within thirty days of that hearing, the committee would vote on the nomination, and within another thirty days, the full Senate would vote. My protocol would also advance to the Senate floor any nominee whom the committee rejected on a party-line vote. Further, any Supreme Court nominee would be reported to the full Senate regardless of the Judiciary Committee vote, following Senate practice formalized in a 1991 letter signed by Hatch and Leahy. To retain ample discretion by the committee and the majority leader, the timetables could always be extended for cause, such as a need for more investigation or more hearings.

Bob Dole, for one, liked my idea. "My view is, Arlen's right, there ought to be a certain amount of time you have a hearing," he said. "I don't care what their party is, or their philosophy is, they're entitled to a hearing, they're entitled to a vote."

With that backdrop, conservative critics pounced in late 2004 on my post-election remarks. As a matter of fairness, a senator in my position was entitled to become Judiciary chairman as a function of seniority, absent some extraordinary disqualifier. Hatch was stepping down, under Republican conference rules that limited chairmen to six years.

Grassley was next on Judiciary, but he had opted to chair the Finance Committee, and a senator was not allowed to chair two major committees at the same time. That left me next in line to chair Judiciary in the 109th Congress, which would open in January 2005. I had served on the panel since joining the Senate in 1981. Republican conference rules technically required a majority vote of approval by committee Republicans followed by the full caucus's ratification. But those steps were considered formalities, and had never been used to block an incoming chairman.

And there was precedent. After the 1986 elections, Jesse Helms had challenged incumbent Richard Lugar for the top Republican spot on the Foreign Relations Committee. They had both served on the committee since 1979, but Helms had served in the Senate four years longer. Helms wanted to move from chairing Agriculture. Lowell Weicker, the hulking and fractious Connecticut maverick, detested Helms, a hard-charging, hard-line conservative. But Weicker made a strong case for Helms on the ground that chairmanships should go strictly by seniority. Otherwise, somebody as far to the left as Weicker could never get elected to anything by the right-dominated Republican caucus. On January 20, 1987, Senate Republicans elected Helms over Lugar 24–17.

For more than a year, since my ascension to Judiciary chairman had become a real prospect, some on the Republican right had grumbled. There had never been a challenge to my objectivity, but some suggested I would rely on my own views rather than on party dogma and that I might oppose some Bush nominees and block some conservative legislation. Bork made the argument in campaigning for Toomey. One of my Republican Judiciary colleagues had told the *Washington Times*—anonymously—that it would be "just awful" if I became chairman. "Arlen will go off with [the Democratic agenda] more often than he'll go with ours. Many of President Bush's nominees won't go through."[16] Now those voices grew louder.

A person in my position, recognized as a major contributor during twenty-four years on the Judiciary Committee, should not be disqualified because his views might not accord with those of one wing of the party. Nor was there any solid reason to think I would oppose any of Bush's nominees.

Calls swamped my press office. Every day, as many as twenty-eight news outlets requested—or demanded—interviews about my views and my prospects for the Judiciary chairmanship. My communications director told a Fox News producer who was phoning him every forty-five minutes, "You're a nice person, I always like to talk to you. But why are you fixated on this?" After all, he noted, Palestinian leader Yasir Arafat was dying, House Majority Leader Tom DeLay was mired in ethical troubles back in Texas, and war was raging in Sudan. Without hesitation, the producer replied gleefully, "You're the only scandal in town."

Some pundits, including Rush Limbaugh, recognized that the story had taken on a life of its own, with words put in my mouth. Brian Wilson of Fox News said, "My impression is that Senator Specter was the victim of some spin on the part of some reporters who took some comments and were looking for a kind of a good headline out of it."[17]

Some critics seemed less concerned about the facts. James Dobson was crusading to his 7 million radio listeners to keep the Judiciary gavel out of my hand. On ABC's *This Week*, he said:

> Senator Specter is a big-time problem for us, and we're very concerned about him. I campaigned against him . . . Senator Specter is a problem not only because of the Judiciary but because he has been the champion of stem cell—embryonic stem-cell research and so many other things. He's remembered most for having sabotaged Robert Bork. He is a problem, and he must be derailed.[18]

That weekend, I assuaged party activists at a Miami Republican Senatorial Campaign Committee event, where I was the hot topic. And I fired back at Dobson on CBS's *Face the Nation*. Those trying to derail my chairmanship, I said,

> are the same people who came to Pennsylvania from all over the country to try to defeat me in the primary election and they were unsuccessful. They do not like my independence, and I am, I believe, the only pro-choice Republican on the Judiciary Committee.

But that doesn't mean I have a litmus test or that I don't give appropriate deference to whom the president nominates.

I shifted back into campaign mode, this time for the Judiciary chairmanship, with Republican senators as the electorate. I filled eleven days with media interviews, meetings, and other efforts to set the record straight.

Calls, mostly from conservatives, swamped Capitol Hill phones and faxes. The Family Research Council urged its legions to phone Senate Republican leaders and Judiciary Committee members to oppose me, saying "a Specter chairmanship would be disastrous." John Cornyn's office reported getting several calls a minute about me.[19] Lindsey Graham changed his office phone message to say, "If you are calling Sen. Graham to leave a comment about the Judiciary Committee chairmanship, please press 1. If you would like to be connected to a staff member, please press 2. Senator Graham appreciates you taking the time to call, and have a great day."[20] Graham's deluge stemmed partly from his support for me. He told the press, "Based on his past performance during the time I've been on the committee, he seems to have given the president's nominees more than a fair shake."[21]

Among fellow Republican senators, I got my strongest endorsement from Larry Craig, who said he thought I would make a "hell of a chairman." Dole returned a call I had placed to his wife, Elizabeth, then a senator from North Carolina, not knowing which Senator Dole I was after. My old friend from Russell offered to make a statement on my behalf. McCain, Cornyn, Judd Gregg, Pat Roberts, Wayne Allard, Bob Bennett, Craig Thomas, Mel Martinez, Christopher Bond, and Hatch all expressed or pledged support. Most did not go public, though: maybe, following Elizabeth Dole's approach, which presumed I would probably not lose the chairmanship, they didn't want to inject themselves into the controversy.[22]

David Vitter, an apparent family-values conservative just elected to the Senate, told the press, "I have concerns about him being chairman."[23] The White House gave me a good character reference, but tepid support. Rove said on *Meet the Press* the Sunday following my remarks, "Senator Specter is a man of his word, and we'll take him at his word." As to whether Bush was comfortable with my becoming chairman, Rove said, "That's up to the United States Senate to decide, not the president of the United States."[24] Rove's comment was understandable. The president doesn't want to wade into an internal Senate fight.

Four days later, at a White House Veterans Day reception, Bush gave me a warm greeting, noting that I had been taking a lot of heat. I told him I stood by my commitments to prompt hearings and reporting his nominees from the committee to the full Senate. He smiled and, in effect, said that was good enough for him.[25]

David Brog, then my chief of staff, arranged an evening meeting in my Hart Building office with several evangelical and conservative leaders, including Gary Bauer, former head of the Family Research Council; Paul Weyrich of the Free Congress Foundation; Richard Land, a leader of the Southern Baptist Convention and radio host; and Ted Haggard, then head of the National Association of Evangelicals, who would resign in 2006 amid a scandal over paying for gay sex and crystal meth.

As Brog later recalled, the meeting was civil, though Weyrich, wheelchair-bound from a recent illness, could barely contain his disdain for me.[26] I maintained that I was a reliable shepherd of presidential nominees. I had supported all of Bush's nominees to that point, and had advanced Clinton's nominees for votes, which gave me even more credibility.

I reached out to other evangelical leaders, including Pat Robertson, whose media empire arguably surpassed even Dobson's; and Jay Sekulow, head of the American Center for Law and Justice, and a radio personality. After several meetings, we had essentially convinced them all to tone down the rhetoric and stop the push to bar me from the chairmanship—all except Dobson, who remained fiery and implacable. On November 10, Robertson said on *The 700 Club*, "I think what is being said about Senator Specter . . . just is a reflection of a media spin which was relatively inaccurate, and he has certainly clarified over and over again his position."[27] He pledged publicly not to oppose me. David Keene, the American Conservative Union chairman, wrote in *The Hill* that he, Limbaugh, and Robertson, among too few others, had taken the time to examine my comments. "What we found, of course, is that those so ready to believe the worst read things into the interview that weren't there. Specter neither threatened the president nor said he wouldn't support his nominees."[28]

A sense grew in the Senate, especially among some old bulls, that the seniority rules should be respected. The caucus was reluctant to upset the seniority system partly because members all wanted to be chairmen one day. Sessions gave me what the *Philadelphia Inquirer* described as a "ringing vote of confidence," touting my "great potential to lead the committee."[29]

My prospects still seemed uncertain when Majority Leader Frist went on *Fox News Sunday* to call my comments "disheartening" and to say I hadn't yet made a persuasive case to chair the committee.[30] The fringe was threatening to turn on Frist if he backed me. When I spoke with Frist the next evening, he was so supportive that it was hard to believe I was talking to the same guy who had appeared on Fox the day before.

I continued making my case to colleagues, and seemed to be building support. A feeling grew that senators wanted to put the matter to rest. But some opponents kept clamoring. Outside the Dirksen Senate Building, some twenty antiabortion activists held a "pray-in." One carried a "Bork Specter" sign.[31]

More meetings with Republican senators followed, and we decided I would craft a written statement. I preferred to put any commitment in writing, so nobody could later try to hold me to an oral promise I'd never made. My four-paragraph statement contained no views I hadn't been voicing for weeks, or years. The key line, drafted by Shanin, was: "I have no reason to believe that I'll be unable to support any individual President Bush finds worthy of nomination."

Hatch made a statement supporting me, prompting a *Roll Call* headline: "Hatch's Backing Boosts Specter." The outgoing Judiciary chairman had remained a good friend, even through some rocky exchanges. At 3:15 p.m. on November 18, Hatch convened Republican Judiciary Committee members for a news conference at the Senate Radio-TV Gallery. He opened by saying, "I'm pleased to announce that . . . there is unanimity among all current members of the committee, all of whom I believe will be on the committee after the first of the year, that Arlen Specter will be our next chairman of the Senate Judiciary Committee." The full GOP caucus would have to ratify the vote, but Hatch said, "It's a done deal." Answering a reporter's question, he said, "Our caucus is a broad, diverse caucus. And frankly, we love everybody in the Republican caucus."[32]

A reporter asked me after the news conference whether winning my Republican colleagues' support was one of the toughest efforts of my career. I replied, "Not one of the toughest—the toughest."

Some hard-right groups issued statements expressing disappointment with the committee's decision and putting me on notice. Tony Perkins, president of the Family Research Council, said, "This is an issue that will not subside, and the integrity of Senator Specter's word will be tested through his leadership on the Judiciary Committee."[33]

I had prevailed. But many in the Republican caucus had made it clear that they felt uncomfortable with me as chairman, which stirred my feelings of discomfort at being a Republican. It was a combustible mix.

The battle over judicial nominees was still raging in January 2005, when I took the committee gavel. I made three floor speeches urging senators to shuck party straitjackets and vote independently. I said many Democratic colleagues had told me they did not personally believe it was a good idea to filibuster Bush's nominees, that their unprecedented use of the filibuster damaged the Senate and infringed on the president's prerogatives. "Yet despite their concerns, they gave in to party loyalty and voted repeatedly to filibuster federal judges." Likewise, I said, many Republican senators questioned the wisdom of the constitutional or nuclear option, recognizing that such a move would deal a serious blow to the rights of the minority that had always distinguished the Senate from the House. "Knowing that the Senate is a body that depends upon collegiality and compromise to pass even the smallest resolution, they worry that the rule change will impair the ability of this institution to function. If we fail, then I fear this Senate will descend the staircase of political gamesmanship and division," I warned. "But if we succeed, our Senate will regain its place as the world's preeminent deliberative body."

Sen. Specter took the Judiciary Committee gavel in January 2005, after a long battle to overcome conservative opposition. Asked by a reporter whether winning his Republican colleagues' support was one of the toughest efforts of his career, Specter replied, "Not one of the toughest—the toughest." (CORBIS/REUTERS)

A shifting bipartisan coalition of fifteen to twenty senators began meeting to discuss a way out of the impasse. The talks were like a floating crap game. They moved around and the participants changed, and each new entrant brought modifications and made news. Twice, in mid-May 2005, I joined the meetings. Senate leaders Reid and Frist attended one of those sessions, giving the inchoate group their implicit blessings for what was essentially a coup d'etat, while officially hewing to their partisan stances. The far right was pressing Frist to ram the rule change down the Democrats' throats, while the far left was pressing Reid to filibuster forever.[34]

Eventually, the so-called Gang of 14 coalesced with seven Democrats and seven Republicans. I told McCain, the gang's de facto leader, "I'm prepared to join [the group] if you need me." I said that, as Judiciary chairman, I would prefer not to join. McCain told me they had enough members without enlisting me.

As Republicans bulled toward a vote on the nuclear or constitutional option, speculation swirled around a one-vote margin, with the uncertain vote being mine. Various media outlets reported my position both ways, forcing me to issue repeated denials. Fox News would report:

> Senior Republican sources tell Fox Senate Majority Leader Bill Frist and the Bush White House were worried enough about possibly losing the vote to end judicial filibusters that they dispatched two conservatives . . . to cut the best possible deal. The principal source of anxiety, Judiciary Committee Chairman Arlen Specter. Top GOP sources say it was unclear until the last minute how Specter would vote on abolishing Democratic judicial filibusters. . . . Without Specter, Frist and the Republicans would have been one vote short.[35]

On May 23, with a vote scheduled on invoking the rules change, I carefully prepared a floor statement on my position. Then I went to bed at 7:30 p.m., exhausted by chemotherapy treatments for Hodgkin's. I silenced my bedside phone, but slept fitfully, over both the statement and the cancer. Throughout the night, I later learned, colleagues and aides strained to phone me.

I woke at 5:30 the next morning. Those days, I felt lousy all the time, and it took a while to compose myself. In my bedroom, I turned on NPR. I wasn't exactly groggy, but close. I was anxious to read a piece in the *New York Times* by Sheryl Gay Stolberg on Arlen Specter, man in the middle of the nuclear/constitutional option battle. I knew Stolberg had written the story; she'd been pumping me hard as to what I was going to do.

At 6 a.m., NPR's news came on. I heard a breathless report of a last-minute deal brokered by the Gang of 14. The gang had agreed to a compromise to confirm three judges, including Pryor, and to reject two.

I said to myself, "Whew, what a close call."

With the Gang's seven Democrats and seven Republicans breaking party lines, the party caucuses lacked the votes to either maintain the filibusters or invoke the option. The Gang of 14 adopted a policy to condone filibusters only under "extraordinary circumstances," a term left deliberately vague. The key factor in this grand compromise was the uncertainty over how a vote on the constitutional/nuclear option would come out.

And then I thought, I'm glad I kept my judgment to myself, and I'm glad I kept it under lock and key, because no matter what I did, I was going to make a lot of people mad. I was enormously relieved to dodge that bullet, and for the Senate to dodge a potential nuclear bomb.

The option vote, now moot, was canceled. We never determined whether Republicans had enough votes to invoke the rules change. I never had to declare my position. Stolberg apparently rewrote her page 1 piece to focus on the compromise. She didn't give me a copy of her original. Maybe I could have traded it for my statement.

I continued guarding my position on the option. "I can do a lot better with divergent interests if I maintain as close to a centrist position as possible," I told the press. "And that means keeping quiet."[36]

At a Capitol Hill news conference days after the impasse broke, the *Philadelphia Inquirer* reported,

> he refused to say how he would have voted—"the statement is under seal in an envelope in a file cabinet which is locked in a location that is secret"—explaining that this would help preserve his mediation role on a contentious panel that may soon be weighing the direction of the Supreme Court.
>
> "I have to be the arbitrator among very, very divergent factions in the Judiciary Committee," a hoarse Specter said during a morning news conference. "Our committee has the most liberal Democrats and, some might say, the most conservative Republicans. And I have to pull that group together."[37]

Here now, unsealed, is my position on the nuclear option: I would have opposed it because it would have subverted the 60-vote filibuster, which had been a saving grace for slowing down precipitous action.

Since the nation's founding, Senate rules had saved vital institutions by restraining the temper and passions of the times. In 1805, the Senate saved the federal Judiciary's independence by acquitting impeached Supreme

Court Justice Samuel Chase. Chase, a former member of the Continental Congress, had signed the Declaration of Independence. He was also a Federalist, and advocated a strong central government and due process. President Thomas Jefferson, leader of the Republicans, disliked the idea of lifetime appointments for judges, fearing the Judiciary might grow too powerful. When Chase voiced Federalist views from the bench, Jefferson encouraged the House of Representatives to impeach him.

Chase's test case would determine whether judges could be ousted merely for their opinions. If Jefferson could get rid of Chase, other Federalist judges, notably Chief Justice John Marshall, would probably follow. The Senate acquitted Chase, with unlikely help from Jefferson's own vice president, Aaron Burr, who ran a fair trial.[38]

In 1868, the Senate saved the presidency's independence by acquitting impeached president Andrew Johnson. Johnson was charged with violating the Tenure of Office Act, passed the previous year. He had removed Secretary of War Edwin Stanton and even appointed a successor, but Stanton had refused to resign, barricading himself in his office. Opponents of the president charged that the Senate would have to relieve Stanton, just as they had to confirm him. The Senate acquitted Johnson by a single vote, cast by a courageous freshman from Kansas, Edmund Ross, whose valor would earn him a chapter in Senator John F. Kennedy's *Profiles in Courage*.

After the Gang of 14 ensured an up-or-down vote on Pryor, the Senate in June 2005 confirmed him 53–45. But the break in the partisan logjam would prove fleeting.

SIX

MANIFEST INJUSTICE

The Senate was out of session on September 1, 2007, when I heard on the news that night that Larry Craig had announced his resignation over a disorderly conduct conviction for an episode in an airport men's room. I read a transcript of the arresting officer's tape recording. It seemed insufficient evidence to constitute a crime.

Craig, an Idaho Republican, had been arrested on June 11, 2007, on charges of lewd conduct in a men's room at the Minneapolis–St. Paul airport. An undercover police officer who took the neighboring stall claimed that Craig had peered into the cop's stall, tapped his foot, touched the cop's foot with his own, and made hand motions understood to signal interest in sexual contact. Craig denied any attempt to solicit sex, and insisted he was not gay. As to touching the cop's foot, Craig famously explained that he took "a wide stance."

On August 8, Craig mailed in a guilty plea to a lesser charge of disorderly conduct, which carried a fine but no jail time. Clearly, he hoped the matter would never draw notice. *Roll Call* broke the story on August 27.

Republican leadership wanted Craig out, and quickly. He was a distraction and a spectacle and marred the party's family-values image. Top Republicans stripped Craig of his leadership posts on three panels, referred his case to the Senate Ethics Committee, and maneuvered for his ouster. Craig held a news conference a few days later to announce his intention to resign from the Senate within thirty days. It was evening coverage of that announcement that I saw on television.

Craig's situation, whatever his sexual orientation, recalled entrapment in Philadelphia that I had investigated during the 1964–65 magistrates probe. Magistrate Harry Schwartz had enlisted a bondsman and a constable in a racket to exploit gay men. In the early 1960s, homosexual acts were illegal in Philadelphia. Most gay men lived in dread of exposure. Once outed, they would pay anything to avoid prosecution and further notoriety. Schwartz traded on their despair.

Gay men gravitated to the Family Theatre, in the shadow of Philadelphia's city hall, for chance encounters with each other at all-night movies. Undercover cops from the morals squad went to the theater to mingle and make arrests. In a typical case, Schwartz and his cronies preyed on George Hubert, a quiet little German refugee who worked as a busboy at Horn and Hardart. They charged him $1,000 to fix the case. Every other week, Hubert had been depositing a few dollars scrimped from his paycheck. Later, when I looked at Hubert's savings book, noted the meticulous small deposits, and then saw the $1,000 withdrawal, I was livid.

With that in mind, I phoned Craig. He told me he'd already made a commitment to leave the Senate. "Well, you can change your mind," I said. "This was not with the advice of counsel, and there's no reason to resign on this."

The day after Craig announced plans to resign, I went on *Fox News Sunday*. "I'd like to see Larry Craig go back to court, seek to withdraw his guilty plea, and fight the case," I told host Chris Wallace. "I've had some experience in these kinds of matters since my days as Philadelphia district attorney, and on the evidence, Senator Craig wouldn't be convicted of anything." As for Craig's resignation, I said, "He hasn't resigned. . . . He said he intends to resign. Once you resign, you're out. But when you have a statement of intent to resign, that intent can change."

Leahy, who joined me on the Fox show, chimed in. "You've just heard from one of the best lawyers I've ever served with in the United States

Senate," the Judiciary chairman said. "Senator Specter has laid out as strong a legal case as I've heard."[1]

A week later, I pushed my point on CNN's *Late Edition with Wolf Blitzer*. On the air, Blitzer played a voice mail that Craig had left for an associate: "Arlen Specter is now willing to come out in my defense, arguing that it appears by all that he knows I've been railroaded and all of that. Having all of that, we've reshaped my statement a little bit to say it is my intent to resign on September 30."

I told Blitzer that Minnesota law allowed withdrawal of a guilty plea if there was manifest injustice, defined as a plea that was not intelligently made. "And what Senator Craig did was by no means intelligent."

Blitzer echoed popular sentiment that Craig was a U.S. senator who'd had two months to think between his arrest and his pleading guilty. I replied, "He's entitled to his day in court. . . . It was foolish of him to enter the plea. It was equally foolish of him not to consult with an attorney."

"So let me get this clear, Senator," an exercised Blitzer said. "You think he should still stay in the Senate and fight this?"

"I do," I said. "I think that Senator Craig is entitled to the same rights as any other person, no more or no less. . . . You have twenty-seven years in the Congress, you have his reputation, you have his whole life on the line. I think he's entitled to his day in court."

Senate Minority Leader McConnell, who had called Craig's conduct "unforgivable,"[2] grew furious, and so did David Vitter, the family-values conservative who had confessed publicly to "a very serious sin" two months earlier after his phone number appeared on a Washington prostitution ring's client list.[3]

Another of the Senate's moral paragons, Nevada Republican John Ensign, raised the prospect of public ethics hearings if Craig stayed in office. As head of the Republican Senate Campaign Committee, Ensign joined in a Senate leadership decision to strip Craig of his committee leadership posts.[4] A few years later, Ensign would admit to an affair with an aide's wife. He would cite "consequences to sin" and ongoing investigations and resign from the Senate in May 2011.[5]

Republican presidential candidate Mitt Romney fired Craig as a co-chair of his campaign and called Craig's reported actions "disgusting." That prompted Craig to say, "He not only threw me under his campaign bus, he backed up and ran over me again."[6]

Craig lawyered up and tried to withdraw his guilty plea. And he returned to the Senate. I patted him on the back on the Senate floor. Nobody else did.

Ultimately, the Minnesota courts let Craig's guilty plea stand. Craig did not run for re-election, but served out his term, retiring at the end of 2008.

I stood up for colleagues of all stripes when they got in trouble, like Craig, when I could lend some skill or expertise to help, especially in an era of intense media scrutiny and politics of personal destruction. Prominent people like senators get into difficulties in part because they're targets. As Witkin used to say, "The higher the monkey climbs the flagpole, the more his ass shows."

Behind all the uproar were a lot of guys doing a lot of foolish things. Some didn't know what their rights were, and I did. They were friends of mine, and I was in a position to help them, so I did. And I did it generally without asking them, and certainly without asking leadership, which was often eager to get rid of them. I've always had a soft spot for people in trouble. Maybe it's the flip side of my hounding public trustees for their official misdeeds.

I also defended Ted Stevens, a friend and Senate icon, when he was engulfed in a 2008 corruption scandal. Stevens was a self-styled curmudgeon known in Washington as "the Hulk," despite his welterweight stature, for the way he ran the Appropriations Committee. Alaskans called him "Uncle Ted" for his service ever since helping the territory win statehood in 1959.

Stevens was a target because of his extensive use of earmarks, the now-limited congressional practice of allocating funds for particular projects, generally in a member's home state or district. Earmarks could deliver vital projects for small or rural states that otherwise lacked clout to attract federal funding. I defended earmarks on the grounds that members knew better than Washington bureaucrats what was best for their states. If members abused earmarks, they should meet the same fate as former Congressman Randy "Duke" Cunningham, still serving an eight-year sentence for corruption.

Stevens was indicted in July 2008 for allegedly failing to report gifts including improvements to his Alaska home. The Department of Justice's elite public integrity section ran a prosecution so flawed that U.S. District Judge Emmet Sullivan lectured in open court: "In nearly twenty-five years on the bench, I've never seen anything approaching the mishandling and misconduct that I've seen in this case. Again and again, both during and after the trial in this case, the government was caught making false representations and not meeting its discovery obligations."

Daniel Inouye, Stevens's Democratic counterpart on the Appropriations Committee and a fellow World War II vet, testified to his character as the leadoff defense witness. "I can assure you, his word is good," Inouye told the court. "It's good enough to take to the bank." In October 2008, only weeks before the election in which Stevens was running for an eighth term, a jury convicted him on all seven counts.

I stayed abreast of the case and saw that Stevens had been mistreated. His lawyer sent me copies of voluminous materials he had filed. The prosecutors had failed to release exculpatory evidence to the defense, as required by law, according to an FBI agent's affidavit. The allegations looked serious on prosecutorial misconduct. But the worst hadn't yet come out.

The evening before Stevens's 2008 election, Anchorage radio station KENI phoned my press office to ask for an interview. Stevens had already been convicted, and supporting him publicly was politically risky. I defended the Hulk on the air, going as far out on a limb as I could while maintaining credibility.

"The federal trial judge has found that the prosecutors did engage in prosecutorial misconduct," I told host Mike Procaro. "They presented matters to the jury which they knew to be false. That is a very strong ground for a new trial." As for a motion to expel Stevens from the Senate, I said, "I believe that Senator Stevens, like any other citizen, is entitled to pursue all of his rights . . . and that is especially applicable here, where the trial judge, as I say, has already made a declaration of some misconduct by the prosecutors."

During Eric Holder's confirmation hearing for attorney general in early 2009, I met with Holder in my office, expressed my concerns about the Stevens prosecution, and asked him to personally review it. He immediately and readily agreed. The Department of Justice's Office of Professional Responsibility investigated.

The new prosecutors assigned to Stevens's case found some disturbing material. The key evidence had involved Bill Allen, an oil services company owner who cut a deal and became the prosecution's chief witness. Stevens's defense team had built its case around a letter from Stevens to Allen about renovations to Stevens's Alaska home:

> . . . Thanks for all the work on the chalet. You owe me a bill—remember Torricelli, my friend. Friendship is one thing—compliance with these ethics rules entirely different. I asked [Stevens's friend Bob Persons] to talk to you about this, so don't get P.O.'d at him—it just has to be done right.

Robert Torricelli, known as "the Torch," was a volatile New Jersey senator who had been forced to resign for accepting constituents' gifts.

Allen testified that he had not sent Stevens a bill or an invoice after getting the letter because Persons told him, "Oh, Bill, don't worry about getting a bill. . . . Ted is just covering his ass."

"The testimony turned Stevens's best evidence against him," Jeffrey Toobin would write in the *New Yorker*. "It seemed to show that the Torricelli note was actually part of Stevens's cover-up rather than proof of his innocence."[7] Then, in early 2009, the new prosecutors found earlier prosecutors' notes from an April 2008 interview with Allen, a bombshell that had not been shared with the defense. "In the interview, Allen said that he remembered receiving the Torricelli note but did not recall speaking to Persons about it."[8]

In April 2009, Holder asked Judge Sullivan to set aside the verdict against Stevens. The judge did. At lunch with Holder in October 2010, I thanked him. He said he appreciated my insights and my calling the matter to his attention.

The reversal came too late for Stevens. Days after the conviction, he had lost a close election, ending a career as the nation's longest-serving Republican senator. I communicated with him frequently, including exchanges of letters. I had lot of respect for his tenacity and his determination to help his state. Stevens greatly improved the quality of life for people on the tundra. He was tougher than nails. Nails were putty compared to Stevens.

In 2010, one of my squash partners, Larry Burton, who had worked for Stevens and become a long-time friend, asked me to craft a Sense of the Senate resolution essentially saying that Stevens was a man of good character, to clear his name. I prepared the document after consulting with Reid, McConnell, and Stevens's Senate successor, Mark Begich. But before I had a chance to introduce the measure, Stevens's lawyer asked me to defer, saying action was imminent on the prosecutors. Then, in August 2010, the plane Stevens was riding in en route to a fishing lodge crashed in the Alaska wilderness. When rescuers finally arrived, Stevens was dead. He was a few months shy of his eighty-seventh birthday, and had held up magnificently. The Senate wound up passing a resolution expressing "profound sorrow and deep regret" over his passing, and recognizing his service.

Separate investigations into prosecutorial misconduct, by the Justice Department and Judge Sullivan, continued. In September 2010, Nicholas Marsh, a thirty-seven-year-old prosecutor on the trial team, committed suicide. "Marsh and his colleagues took an important but fairly routine political corruption investigation in Alaska and tried to leverage it into a prosecution of one of the leading political figures in the country," Toobin concluded in a generally sympathetic portrait of Marsh. "In doing so, they failed themselves and the Justice Department."[9] And, as Stevens said in a statement after his conviction was overturned, "Their conduct had consequences for me that they will never realize and can never be reversed."

. . .

S enator John Tower, all of five feet five, was a dynamo and a bully. He once bullied Senator Jim Exon, a gruff but kindly Nebraska Democrat, to tears. Tower always dressed meticulously and immaculately in a pin-striped suit. The *New York Times* wrote of the former Armed Services Committee chairman, "Mr. Tower was once a Washington figure of a certain sort, wielding power and inspiring fear."[10]

I had a number of run-ins with Tower, including one over the so-called Black Box, which reportedly contained information on nuclear strikes. Tower wouldn't tell me what was in the Black Box but expected me to vote to fund it. I wouldn't. He summoned me to the cloakroom to tell me that first-termers didn't ask what was in the Black Box. I told him I wasn't voting for the appropriation unless I knew what was in the Black Box. Ultimately, I found out what was in it. It wasn't any great shakes. I voted for the appropriation.

The first President Bush, at the beginning of his administration in 1989, nominated Tower for secretary of defense, a job Tower had long dreamed of. The Senate, controlled by the Democrats, rejected him. The main rap against Tower was his drinking, including a scene in which he had danced atop a piano.

I defended Tower on the Senate floor, arguing that the matter should have been remanded to the Armed Services Committee for a factual determination as to what had happened. Tower drank a lot during the slew of all-night sessions when Baker was majority leader, I said, but he was never out of control. At all. About all you could say was that his tie was loose.

Dennis DeConcini went on about reports of Tower's drinking, and what the Arizona Democrat considered supporters' attempts to make a meaningless distinction between "inebriated" and "under the influence." He asked, "Isn't there any decency left in the Senate?"

I jumped in. DeConcini and I went back and forth until finally he said, "This senator has seen Senator Tower under the influence of alcohol, as he has seen other members. I have not seen him inebriated to the extent he could not perform his duties."

Tower, still seething two years later at those he had considered friends but who had voted against him, said, "They're pretty straightforward what they do in Beirut. They hurl a grenade at someone or shoot a machine gun. Up here, it's a little more subtle, but just as ruthless, just as brutal. They kill you in a different way."[11]

In a general atmosphere of intolerance and political correctness, Majority Leader Trent Lott was flayed in December 2002 for remarks at Strom Thurmond's one-hundredth-birthday party. The Mississippian said, "When Strom Thurmond ran for president, we voted for him. We're proud of it. And if the rest of the country had followed our lead, we wouldn't have had all these problems over the years, either."

Thurmond had run for president in 1948 on the segregationist Dixiecrat ticket. Lott was pilloried for endorsing racism. He was hardly the first senator who should have chosen his words more carefully. On the substance, his comment was certainly no worse than former Ku Klux Klan member Byrd's using the term "white nigger" on national television or Hollings's calling Hispanics "wetbacks." In April 2004, in a gaffe that would recall Lott's remark, Chris Dodd would gush that Byrd "would have been a great senator at any moment in American history." Lott would pay the higher price, though, because Democrats generally got leniency on civil rights, as they belonged to a party seen as more racially sensitive and sympathetic.[12]

I defended Lott, loudly and publicly. "I know Trent Lott very well from working with him for the last fourteen years and can vouch for the fact that he is no supporter of Senator Thurmond's 1948 platform," I said in a statement. "His comment was an inadvertent slip and his apology should end the discussion."

The *Philadelphia Inquirer* reported, "Specter has defended Lott since the controversy erupted, a position that has upset some of his supporters. But he denounced the drumbeat for Lott's punishment."[13]

"I know I'm losing political skin on this," I told the *Inquirer*. "I'm very much offended by what's happened to a very decent guy. . . . You had a very foolish statement [by Lott]. And I don't agree with many of Lott's votes, but this matter doesn't deserve the death penalty." Essentially, I said, Lott was praising a man on his one hundredth birthday. It wasn't a political speech or an endorsement. Lighten up.

Instead, the Senate booted Lott out of leadership. He stayed in the Senate, stripped of his stripes. Two years later, during my primary against Toomey, Lott gave me substantial support, partly in gratitude for my defending him in 2002. Lott, on the outs with the Republican fund-raising establishment, refused to contribute to the Republican Senate Committee in 2004, and gave only Congressman George Nethercutt of Washington, then running for Senate, and me the full $10,000 allowed from his PAC.

Lott would prove a real fighter. He came back several years later to challenge for assistant minority leader, the Republicans' number-two spot. He ran against Lamar Alexander, a former secretary of education. I wound up the decisive vote. I thought it over carefully, and didn't formulate a judgment until the morning of the election, because too often these issues go away. Why declare for somebody when it could prove moot? But not this time.

I voted for Lott. I told Alexander, "I think Trent will be stronger in helping those of us who are up in 2010, because of his experience. And, ideologically, Lamar, I'm much more disposed to you."

Lott won 25–24.

Bob Packwood, a fellow Republican moderate, consulted me in 1995 when he was mired in a sexual-harassment scandal and an issue arose over his diaries. Packwood had talked to a lawyer and was noodling a tricky question, the legality of destroying records when a known investigation was under way, but before they'd been subpoenaed. If the records had been subpoenaed, destroying them would have been obstruction of justice. It probably was anyway. Before I reached a conclusion, investigators issued a subpoena.

Packwood and I were squash partners. Packwood also often played with John Chafee, and they would rush back from the Capitol Hill Squash Club, racing onto the floor with their hair slicked back, to cast votes just as time expired. Arriving in the final moments was risky. Larry Pressler, a South Dakota Republican, burst into the well of the Senate in the final seconds of a tally and asked, "What's the farm vote?" The vote was on Planned Parenthood. Mark Hatfield, who was in the well managing the bill, told Pressler, "It depends on whether you have rubber trees in South Dakota." Pressler had an off-putting way, making him appear out of it, and making some wonder how he had acquired a Rhodes Scholarship and a Harvard Law degree. But he was very smart.

Laggards also had to fear the ire of Robert Byrd, the president pro tempore, éminence grise, and self-appointed guardian of Senate decorum. Bennett Johnston, a Louisiana Democrat who chaired the Energy Committee, would play tennis on the Dirksen Building's roof court and then dash to the Senate in his gym clothes. Johnston would steal to the door by the hallway entrance and stick his head in to vote, hiding his ill-clad body outside. If Byrd had seen Johnston's attire, he would have raised holy hell.

On the squash court, Packwood was rambunctious. If you had a good shot, he would throw himself in front of it to prevent you from making it. He wouldn't care if the ball hit him. He didn't want to lose the point. When I could stop my swing, I wouldn't hit the ball. I wasn't going to call him, so he got away with it. Things weren't so simple off the court.

On one occasion, Packwood swatted me across the face with his racket, carving a neat, straight gash. Fortunately, I was wearing goggles, as players always should. A plastic surgeon in Bethesda sewed six stitches and told me, "You have to stay off the squash court for six to seven weeks." About that time, a Washington hockey player suffered an eye injury and had a helmet fitted with a plastic mask that extended below his lip. I went out and bought a guard like the hockey player's and went back on the squash court the next day.

Packwood was oblivious to life and limb when he played squash. That was also apparently the way he treated women. Before the 1992 election, the *Portland Oregonian* was investigating sexual-harassment allegations against Packwood. He went before the newspaper's editorial board and assured them that everything was all right, not telling the truth.

By 1995, the Senate Ethics Committee was investigating accusations of sexual misconduct against Packwood by seventeen women who had worked for him or for the Senate, or who had wanted to work for him, going back to 1975. Packwood had forced himself on some women by grabbing them and sticking his tongue in their mouths, earning him the nickname "the Tongue." The committee was also investigating charges that Packwood had destroyed evidence. He had dictated detailed diaries that featured his sexual exploits. He explained the exercise as therapy. He described seducing one withdrawn staffer, saying, "I was feeling sorry for you and thinking I was doing my Christian duty by making love to you." He had a trusted aide transcribe the tapes. Packwood was accused of altering the tapes and transcripts by recording over and editing incriminating sections.

One day when we were in session, Packwood's secretary phoned one of my senior aides, distraught that her boss was about to commit suicide. My aide flagged me, and I rushed over to Packwood's office to talk to him. When I arrived, he was laughing. His staff had apparently misread him, and they offered a simple explanation for the suicide alarm. Packwood thought the alarm was funny.

The humor didn't last. In a 179-page decision bolstered by more than 10,000 pages of evidence, the Senate Ethics Committee unanimously recommended Packwood's expulsion for ethical misconduct. The Senate ultimately decided against open hearings, over my vote and despite public pressure. Packwood announced his resignation on September 7, 1995.

I made a statement on the floor, standing up for Packwood when few others would, and scoring the Senate for failing to hold public hearings.

We are losing an outstanding senator at a time when the Senate and the country need his expertise very badly. I believe that America was entitled to full disclosure. I believe the people who came forward with complaints were entitled to be heard, and I think Senator Packwood was entitled to have a defense. . . . I have had one other very painful experience with Senator Packwood when I got six stitches under my left eye a decade ago. But I consider this day much more painful.

As I was defending Packwood, Senator Barbara Mikulski, a Maryland Democrat and Ethics Committee member, asked me to yield, essentially asking me to stop and let her speak. I wouldn't yield to her. I was making a point for Packwood, and she was after his scalp. She got sore about that.

That day, I was with Dole and thought he should make a statement as leader. He went to the floor and gave a strong speech. Praising Packwood's ability to distill and convey complex financial concepts, Dole said, "I believe my colleagues on either side of the aisle will acknowledge that Bob Packwood has no peer." Praising Packwood's bipartisanship, Dole said:

> I can think of many, many times when he was able to bring us together . . . because of his explanations and illustration of forceful arguments. . . . I would just say he has been an outstanding legislator, an outstanding U.S. Senator, and someone whose legacy will be around for a long, long time, and a friend of mine.[14]

On a visit to my Senate office late in my last term, a former colleague, David Durenberger of Minnesota, stopped by to commiserate on the 2010 election results, and we reminisced about an incident in February 1994. Durenberger recalled the following version: The evening before his arraignment on corruption charges, I buttonholed him at the Capitol after the Senate adjourned and said, "I'd like you to come out with me." We walked downstairs and I spotted Al D'Amato and recruited him, and the three of us climbed into my car.

"Where the hell are we going?" Durenberger asked as I steered toward Constitution Avenue.

"We're going to my house," I said.

When we arrived at my Georgetown condo, D'Amato and I took chairs and Durenberger sat cross-legged on my living room rug. "I just remember being more comfortable than the rest of you guys, or so I *thought*," Durenberger recalled. "My mind was someplace else. I was thinking, Hey, this is not a bad way to start the life."[15]

By that night, Durenberger had been battling legal and ethical troubles for five years. The Senate Ethics Committee and the Department of Justice had both investigated him on charges that he submitted false expense claims to the Senate for his stays at a Minneapolis condo that he secretly owned, and that he had sidestepped the $2,000 speaking-fee limit by funneling payments through Piranha Press, the publisher of a book he wrote.

On July 25, 1990, the Senate had voted unanimously to denounce Durenberger for "bringing dishonor and disrepute to the Senate." That day, I had made a floor statement criticizing the way the investigations had been handled and mingled, raising concerns about confidentiality and about separating the prosecutor's and judge's functions.

Later, as the Justice Department investigation continued, Durenberger and I convened in Minority Whip Alan Simpson's office and discussed the background. I said, "Let's get [Janet] Reno on the phone." Three minutes later, Clinton's attorney general was on the line. Simpson did most of the talking, but I got on for part of the time.

Durenberger recalled later, "I don't hear her voice, but I can hear you explaining the background, telling her that you didn't think—it wasn't a matter of whether I deserved it or not—you didn't think on the facts that it merited taking it any farther."[16]

I was just making an inquiry, and making representations as a lawyer would. I wasn't retained and I wasn't formally on the case, but I had standing to speak. Reno didn't have to listen. I didn't threaten her or throw my weight around. I was talking about a man I knew. Durenberger had been a solid senator, and we had collaborated on important legislation. In 1990, when he was managing the Clean Air Act, I wanted a provision added, and he and I had a colloquy on the floor and worked it out.

Reno grew offended and indignant that we would inquire about a pending investigation. I didn't give a damn that she didn't like it.

The Justice Department moved ahead. In April 1993, Durenberger was indicted on felony fraud charges for taking $3,825 in reimbursements for his 1987 condo stays. In December 1993, a federal judge dismissed those charges on the ground that prosecutors had improperly developed the case with material gathered by a Senate committee, touching on my point on the Senate floor.

But Durenberger wasn't clear yet. In February 1994, a federal grand jury re-indicted him on charges that he had conspired to abuse his Senate expense account. If convicted, he faced up to ten years in prison and a $500,000 fine. It was before his arraignment on this second indictment that he recalled my bringing him to my Georgetown apartment.

I served martinis. "After about three of them, we're all hungry enough to say, 'Where's the food?'" Durenberger recalled. "Then I discovered you didn't have a great larder. I think it was canned tuna, canned sardines, you know, a bunch of stuff like that." He laughed at the memory. "That was our dinner that night. I suppose we talked about everything except me, and—everything under the sun."[17]

After midnight, Durenberger began to leave, to go home. "Dave, please, you've got to stay," he recalled my telling him. He slept in my spare bedroom.

"But I remember that night well," Durenberger told me sixteen years later. "That was very good. Very nice. All the rest of it—I mean, the next day was unpleasant. But you knew it would be. It was unpleasant having to plead not guilty, and getting fingerprinted. Being shown where the jail is—the Washington, D.C., jail—but not being put in it. Being told, because you're a senator, we're not going to put you in the jail. We're not going to reduce you, that sort of thing."

Durenberger maintained his innocence. He detailed to me how the charges grew from misunderstandings, colleagues' poor advice and false assurances, and payback from a powerful senator he had crossed.

Durenberger did not run for re-election in 1994, retiring at the end of his term. In August 1995, he made a deal to plead guilty to five counts involving cheating on his Senate expense accounts to convert $425 in public money to his personal use, all misdemeanors. In November 1995, he was sentenced to a year's probation, which he served in Washington doing good works on Medicaid and other projects, and fined $1,000. When he came to visit me in September 2010, he had kept his strong, patrician looks into his late seventies, accentuated now by a full head of silver hair, and his easy smile.

Apart from any criminal issues over paying for lodging in one's home state, some senators were offended by the idea of a senator calling Washington, D.C., home. In March 1982, Ted Stevens railed on the Senate floor against a proposal to eliminate members' $75-a-day tax deductions for expenses involved in living in Washington, D.C., winding up in a fiery debate with Bill Proxmire of Wisconsin, who had listed Washington as his hometown.

"God forbid someone should tell me that the city of Washington is my home," Stevens hollered. "I detest it!" He continued at full volume: "I can't think of a worse city in the world to have a capital. . . . And I don't care who knows it." Washington "has the worst crime and the worst schools," Stevens howled, and its foul air "will shorten our life spans."[18]

Stevens said he never lost his temper, that he always knew where it was. But that night, he showed a temperament that, I believe, would cost him. When Howard Baker left the Senate after the 1984 election, five candidates ran to succeed him as leader: Stevens, Dole, Lugar, Pete Domenici, and Jim McClure. Paul Weyrich, the conservative activist who helped found the Heritage Foundation and the Free Congress Foundation, made me an offer: if I supported McClure, the far right would back me for re-election in 1986. I responded with a resounding no.

After the first round of voting, the low man dropped out—McClure. After two more rounds, Stevens and Dole remained as the finalists. I had an easy choice because of my relationship with Dole, going back to our days in Russell. On the final ballots, Dole won 28–25.

Stevens's anti-Washington tirade probably cost him the victory by raising concerns about his temperament. Other factors, including some backroom deals, may also have shaded the voting. Dole was chairman of the Finance Committee, and Packwood was anxious to take that gavel if Dole became leader. Packwood was chairman of the Commerce Committee, and John Danforth was eager to take that spot if Packwood succeeded Dole on Finance.

I also crossed party lines to defend friends. In November 2006, the *Washington Post* ran a Ruth Marcus column headlined "Unfit for Majority Leader," decrying Pennsylvania congressman John Murtha's bid for the House Democrats' number-two spot, and citing his involvement in the 1980 ABSCAM scandal. Murtha had been videotaped meeting with the undercover operatives, offering to provide names of businesses and banks in his district where funds could be legally invested and then saying, "I'm not interested . . . at this point. [If] we do business for a while, maybe I'll be interested, maybe I won't." The U.S. attorney's office inferred that Murtha was trying to get investment in his district. In a letter I wrote, which the *Post* published, I opened by calling Murtha "a friend of mine for three decades." The letter continued:

> I begin with the proposition that everyone is entitled to the presumption of innocence as a fundamental principle of American law. . . .
> Mr. Murtha may have had a complete defense of entrapment. . . .
> What we do know is that Mr. Murtha was not indicted. If the government had a case that it thought would have produced a conviction, it is a virtual certainty that he would have been prosecuted . . .
> I have had many dealings with Mr. Murtha during the past 26 years in connection with his duties representing Pennsylvania, and I have always found him to be law-abiding and ethical.
>
> I would not be able to say the same for all colleagues.

SEVEN

STIMULUS

Vice President Cheney stepped into the walnut-paneled Mansfield Room, off the Senate floor, where the Republican caucus had gathered. The Senate had rushed to convene that day, October 1, 2008, to vote on TARP, President George W. Bush's $700 billion financial rescue.

Cheney had earned a reputation as a dry, factual, unemotional speaker, low-key and direct, here it is, take it or leave it. In the Mansfield Room, the vice president was impassioned. "If you don't pass this," he told us, "you're going to make George W. Bush into the Herbert Hoover of the twenty-first century."

The economy was in free fall. More than half a million workers were losing jobs each month, and unemployment had climbed by nearly 4 million. Driven by soured subprime loans, the housing sector was in crisis, with foreclosures burgeoning.

In response, President Bush had crafted the Troubled Asset Relief Program, or TARP. Congress had formalized the plan as the Emergency Economic Stabilization Act of 2008, better known as the financial bailout bill. Through TARP, the federal government would buy mortgages and other "troubled" assets from banks and other institutions, to strengthen and restore confidence in the buckling financial sector. Many of the toxic assets had been combined into securities and were difficult to price, driving fears that the taxpayer would get stuck with a massive tab.

Resistance to the proposal was high. On September 24, the day Bush had announced the plan, more than a hundred university economists sent an open letter to Congress warning of three "fatal pitfalls": unfairness, subsidizing investors at taxpayers' expense; ambiguity of the new agency and its mission; and long-term effects, including potential weakening of the markets.

The same day, the two major parties' presidential nominees, Senators Obama and McCain, issued a joint statement warning that "the effort to protect the American economy must not fail."

The next day, September 25, protests against TARP raged in more than a hundred U.S. cities. Opponents bridled at what they considered a Wall Street bailout funded at the expense of desperate regular Americans. Free marketers decried the massive government intervention. Jim Bunning, the fiery Kentucky Republican, lectured Treasury Secretary Henry Paulson at a Senate Banking Committee hearing: "This massive bailout is not a solution. It is financial socialism and it's un-American."[1]

On September 29, the House rejected the legislation by a vote of 228–205, with most Democrats in favor and most Republicans opposed. The Dow Jones average plunged 778 points, the largest single-day point drop in history. Nothing could be done immediately, since many in Congress, including me, were in synagogues across the country observing Rosh Hashanah that evening and the next day. The Senate was called into session on October 1.

When I was deciding how to vote on TARP, I sent a series of letters to Paulson, Fed Chairman Bernanke, and Senate leaders Reid and McConnell, raising a range of concerns. In a September 23, 2008, missive to Paulson and Bernanke, I noted the byzantine mortgage and foreclosure process and wrote: "Keeping people in their homes should be a, if not the, fundamental object of congressional action." Beyond that, I wrote, I was very skeptical of spending $700 billion without proof that such aid was essential to stabilizing the economy, without standards on who would get the funds, and without proper regulation and oversight.

I had not heard back from Paulson or Bernanke by October 1, when Cheney made his plea. The bill needed 60 votes for passage. The Senate version now contained $150 billion more than the defeated House bill, much of it pork and sweeteners that senators had larded on, with no time for the body to examine and eliminate them.

Dick Cheney was not exactly a wide-eyed liberal spender. But, by the Mansfield Room's white Vermont marble mantel, surrounded by American black walnut paneling, he implored us, saying that fast action was essential to stop the market slide and to prevent an economic crash and a worldwide domino effect.

Thirty-four Republican senators responded with aye votes, joining forty Democrats to pass the bill 74–25. I voted for the bailout to avoid the potential damage to the U.S. economy and its ominous global threat. Only Ted Kennedy, battling advanced brain cancer, did not vote.

On October 3, the House passed the Senate version, and within hours Bush signed the bill. It wasn't a pretty legislative process. The plan had begun as 3 pages and mushroomed into a gigantic 451-page bill, without appropriate hearings, analysis, debate, or deliberation. We had acted in haste, without following regular order.

TARP and its series of bailouts sparked widespread public resentment that would flare, among other forms, into the Tea Party limited-government movement.

Under TARP's broad charter, the Bush administration set—and changed several times—its spending rationale. Eleven days after the president signed the bill, Paulson announced that Treasury would infuse TARP funds directly, to loosen lending, by buying senior preferred stock and warrants in the nine largest U.S. banks. On November 12, Paulson indicated that in the second round of TARP spending, Treasury would bolster the consumer credit market. On December 19, Bush cited his executive authority to announce that TARP funds could be spent on any program he deemed necessary to stave off financial crisis. Bush then used

that authority to spend TARP money to bail out the flagging auto industry, mainly General Motors and Chrysler.

On November 14, 2008, I had written to Reid and McConnell about
financial aid to automakers. "There are many complex questions which
need to be answered before the Senate can even begin to make a prelimi-
nary assessment on aid to the auto manufacturers," I wrote.

What assurance would we have that these funds for the auto industry would be spent wisely, and as intended by Congress? Isn't it
wiser to let the market make those decisions? Insufficient consideration by the Treasury Department and the Federal Reserve followed by the rush to judgment by Congress on the $700 billion has
left my constituents perplexed about the competency of the federal
government to respond rationally to the current problems.

I never heard back from Paulson or Bernanke on any of my letters. On
January 15, 2009, Congress released the second $350 billion of TARP
funds, over my no vote. I was unhappy with Paulson's various directions
on the first installment. He didn't seem to grasp what he was doing, and
was going too fast.

The economy continued to wane. President-elect Obama went to
work on a stimulus bill. Just a week after taking the oath of office,
on January 27, 2009, the new president addressed the Republican Senate
caucus at our weekly Tuesday luncheon in the LBJ Room, the same
chamber that newly elected President Clinton had worked in 1993. Standing before mid-nineteenth-century fresco lunettes by Italian artist Con-
stantino Brumidi, known as the "Michelangelo of the United States Capitol";
hand-colored engravings of Washington from the 1830s; a carved, gilded
mirror; and late-nineteenth-century window valances, Obama was less
personable, more professional, but every bit as political as President Clinton. He brought none of the smartest-guy-in-the-room swagger he would
wield at later confrontations. He discoursed about the problems facing the

U.S. and world economies, including the ongoing hemorrhaging of jobs. He painted a frightening picture. The president said it was imperative that Congress pass the stimulus bill by Friday, February 13, before we recessed for a week for Presidents' Day, so that he could sign and promptly implement it.

When Obama took questions, I was the first to seek and get recognition. I asked, Why the urgency? It was an enormously complicated bill, I said. We should separate what belonged in the stimulus from what should go through the regular appropriations process. After TARP, I hesitated to support Obama's plea for legislation without taking time for study, hearings, and adequate floor debate.

Obama replied that the economy was so precarious, we couldn't wait. He said the country was heading toward catastrophe and needed the stimulus legislation by February 13 to avert a 1930s-type depression, and perhaps a world economic collapse.

A 1930s-type depression. My thoughts went back to 1935, when I was five, and the long, bumpy ride in the back of my father's pickup from Wichita to Philadelphia, and moving in with my aunt because my father couldn't earn a living. The president's warning resonated with me, channeling Cheney's earlier plea about George W. Bush becoming a latter-day Herbert Hoover if we didn't approve TARP.

But most Republicans gave Obama's appeal a cold reception. Jim De-Mint, a scorched-earth partisan, captured caucus sentiment by saying the president's agenda would be his "Waterloo," referring to the 1815 battle in which British and allied forces effectively ended Napoleon's reign, and that we would "break" Obama. DeMint's official Senate Web site boasted that "he was recently ranked as the Senate's most conservative member by *National Journal.*" The ink wasn't dry on the president's oath of office and opponents were laying plans to defeat him in 2012.

Months later, South Carolina Republican congressman Joe Wilson would again capture the vitriol by shouting "You lie!" during the president's health-care address. Those remarks carried an ugly undercurrent that bubbled below the surface of the Republican caucus and flowed more freely in other quarters.

Pat Gillespie, head of the Greater Philadelphia Building Trades Council, told me how he and John "Johnny Doc" Dougherty, business manager of the city electricians' union, had placed Obama signs during the 2008 campaign in white sections of northeast Philadelphia, where the city's black mayor, John Street, would never post signs. Gillespie said it took guts to put up a black man's sign in a white Philadelphia neighborhood. Obama did not do well in southwestern Pennsylvania. I used to figure my being Jewish cost me 3 percent in a statewide election. Obama's African ancestry may have cost him twice that.

Republicans had no viable alternative to Obama's stimulus plan. And a party has to do more than simply say no. McCain proposed $450 billion in tax cuts, which I supported. But that doesn't put people to work immediately.

Following the policy lunch with the new president, I gave an interview in the Senate TV Gallery about Attorney General–designate Eric Holder. That week would be a marathon of stimulus talks intermingled with confirmation proceedings on the president's cabinet.

That same day, January 27, at an Appropriations Committee hearing, I circulated an amendment to the stimulus bill to increase funding for the National Institutes of Health by $6.5 billion, for a total of $10 billion. The NIH is the crown jewel of the federal government, maybe the only jewel. The NIH has advanced medical research to the threshold of conquering dreaded ailments including cancer, heart disease, Alzheimer's, and Parkinson's disease.

I had strained to nearly triple NIH funding, and now the institutes were being starved. The budget crunch had killed cost-of-living adjustments and brought across-the-board cuts that sliced $5.2 billion in NIH funding over the previous seven years. Grant applications had piled up. Breaking that logjam would put an estimated seventy thousand people to work in research and reduce America's medical bills. What better way is there to cut health-care costs than to prevent illness and cure deadly diseases? I had found an offset, from the State Fiscal Stabilization Fund, which seemed neither a priority nor an economic stimulator.

Majority Whip Dick Durbin approached me in the Appropriations

Committee chamber and pulled Tom Harkin and me into a back room used by committee staff, away from the cameras and the crush. Durbin was in a bind because Democrats had promised the Appropriations chairman, Dan Inouye, that no amendments would be offered or accepted. Durbin told me, "Don't offer it now because I don't want to have to vote against it." He promised that he and other Democrats would support my amendment if I introduced it on the Senate floor.

"Okay," I said.

As the *New York Times* would report a couple of weeks later:

Mr. Durbin said later that he almost had occasion to regret that promise. When the majority leader, Senator Harry Reid of Nevada, asked him whether he had extracted an agreement from Mr. Specter to vote for the bill, Mr. Durbin had to admit he did not know.

"I flunked Politics 101; I never asked him that," Mr. Durbin said. . . . "I gave away $10 billion but never got his commitment."[2]

After my exchange with Durbin, Reid told me on the Senate floor, "We'll give you the $10 billion, but we expect a vote for the bill in return."

"I'm not trading any votes," I told Reid. "I never have, and I never will."

I had a rough history with Reid. In July 2008, we had a terrible fight over the way he ran the Senate. Reid, a former amateur boxer, exploited protocol to block Republicans from introducing amendments. Those minority proposals, combined with virtually unlimited debate, made the Senate the world's greatest deliberative body, where ideas could be expressed, the public could hear and understand them, and momentous matters of public policy were decided. The process hung on any senator's being able to offer any amendment on any subject at any time. On the Senate floor, I accused Reid of "tyranny."

In blocking Republican amendments, Reid was trying to protect his members from politically perilous votes. But he should have stood up in the Democratic caucus and said, "Hey, ladies and gentlemen, we're here to vote, and we're going to have some tough votes, but if we want to have Republicans on our bills, we're going to have to take some chances." Instead,

Reid blocked any Republican ideas. And the Republican minority, with no alternative, resorted to their only pressure point, the filibuster. Why should they let a bill go forward if they had no input, if only one side could offer amendments?

Several years earlier, when Reid had helped lead Democratic filibusters against George W. Bush's judicial nominees, he lacked Republicans' later justification. Reid had filibustered confirmations, which were simple up-or-down votes, while Republicans filibustered because they wanted to offer legislative amendments.

If Reid had been willing to discuss legislation with Republicans, bills could have changed and maybe improved. By 2009, the air was so poisoned that Republicans showed no interest in discussing the stimulus.

The following day, Wednesday, January 28, I met at 7:30 a.m. with Ed Rendell and a lobbyist for UPMC, a Pittsburgh-based global medical enterprise. They wanted $600 million in stimulus funds to create a vaccine manufacturing and development facility. At 6:30 that evening, I attended a fund-raiser for DeMint. I tried to stop by any caucus member's event, if I was invited.

On Sunday, February 1, Joan and I took the 1:12 p.m. Amtrak from Philadelphia to Washington to attend the White House Super Bowl party. Obama was hosting members of Congress from Pennsylvania and Arizona, among some seventy-five guests, to watch the Pittsburgh Steelers play the Arizona Cardinals in Super Bowl XLIII. McCain, the Arizona senator whom Obama had defeated for the presidency three months before, did not attend.

The game marked Obama's debut as White House host. In a white checked shirt, sleeves rolled up, the president moved among his guests in the White House movie theater, a deep red, wood-trimmed auditorium that seated about fifty on wide, deeply padded chairs. The game aired on a giant screen. The president looked, acted, and talked like the new kid on the block. Clearly, he was enjoying the White House. He was charming with women, putting his arm around Joan for smiling photographs.

A boy asked the president, "Where's the bathroom?"

"I've only been here ten days," Obama replied. "Ask someone in the hall."

The president abandoned any pretense of neutrality and rooted for the Steelers. He told me he had become a fan growing up in Hawaii, which had no pro football team, during the Steelers' 1970s heyday. As a Chicagoan, he was for the Bears, but liked the Steelers. I told the president that I rooted for three teams: The Philadelphia Eagles, the Pittsburgh Steelers, and whoever was playing Dallas.

The president razzed me for putting on a tie. I was wearing a navy blazer and a patterned blue tie over a white shirt with blue windowpane checks, a version of my usual sporting-event attire. The president's shirt was like mine but with tighter blue checks.

The food was simple—hot dogs, sandwiches, salad, and soda, with hard liquor available but having few takers. I had a chicken sandwich and an Iron City beer, made in Pennsylvania, and some fruit. The president circulated with a platter of freshly baked oatmeal raisin cookies.

Amid cheers for Steelers touchdowns and groans over Cardinal advances and scores, the president lobbied not so subtly for the stimulus package. Obama said he was going to ask me to come in to discuss some of my ideas one-on-one.

Durbin told me he would support my amendment to increase NIH funding. "I'm keeping my word."[3] That's a vow we had in the Senate, your word, and Durbin was an honorable man.

The game turned out to be a 27–23 nail-biter, perhaps the most exciting Super Bowl in history, with the commander in chief hooting like the rest of us at acrobatic interceptions and 100-yard runbacks. The battle ended well, with the Steelers capturing a record sixth Super Bowl victory.

It was a heady experience to join the glamorous new president, first lady Michelle, and the others for the big sporting event. Obama picked up a lot of goodwill, but the votes on the stimulus package and his larger agenda would ride on hard facts and practical considerations.

The next day, I told Andrea Mitchell of MSNBC that I would support the stimulus only if it would put people back to work immediately. "There are a lot of good programs, but we ought to be taking them up in the regular budget process where we establish priorities." I wanted to see more on bridges, highways, mass transit, high-speed rail.

Mitchell and I had grown up together; she had covered me in Philadelphia as a cub reporter at KYW Radio when I was district attorney. When I announced for the Senate in 1976, she got into a fight with a rival reporter in the den of my East Falls home. After I had finished speaking, Norm Fastow of WCAU Radio asked if he could use my phone. Sure, I said. He had asked first. Mitchell grabbed the handset. She and Fastow had a simmering enmity. She wouldn't let go.

I backed up Fastow. I said I had told him he could have the first call. Mitchell was unmoved. Fastow pressed one of the phone's plungers, disconnecting her call. The spat ended with Mitchell irate that she had been cut off in the middle of a live broadcast.

From Philadelphia, Mitchell went on to a dazzling career in national media, and she continued to invite me on her shows. At dinner with her and her husband, Alan Greenspan, he said that no matter how exhausted Mitchell was after coming back from a globetrotting assignment, if you put a mic in front of her, she would brighten, electrically.

Mitchell closed our February 2, 2009, interview as she had opened it, congratulating me on the Steelers' Super Bowl victory. "It's better to win than lose."[4]

In another interview, I told Pittsburgh's KDKA Radio that we had to stimulate the economy, and that we needed to work on a bipartisan basis, but that "the current bill as it stands now is not good, not right. . . . I think people, understandably, are a little put off with the $700 billion we passed last year where we had so many problems with the financial system, so we've got to narrow in on it and get the job done with a rifle shot, not a shotgun blast."

During the week, heavy meetings on the stimulus drew ten to fifteen Democratic senators and five Republicans: Susan Collins, Mel Martinez, Lisa Murkowski, George Voinovich, and me. We centrists were nicknamed "the Gang of 18." Reid pressed hard for my vote and Collins's. Olympia

Snowe did not attend any of the sessions, and we figured she had already committed to Obama and Reid to support the bill.

At 11:45 a.m. on February 3, I had an appointment with the president on the stimulus bill. Obama wanted support, and especially Republican support, to make the bill bipartisan after the House's 246–183 party-line vote, and to lock up a filibuster-proof 60 votes. On the button, I was escorted into the Oval Office.

The president was in shirtsleeves. I had been in the Oval Office many times over the years, going back to my first meeting with President Nixon in 1971. I had sat in a chair beside Nixon's desk. At most of the later meetings, with Reagan and Bush, I sat in a large padded armchair. At a meeting with Clinton, the president's chocolate Labrador, Buddy, joined us. Despite my father's dream of my becoming "presidential timber," and my own 1996-cycle run, I never fantasized about occupying the Oval Office. I had no illusions about winning the presidency.

Obama and I sat on large chairs. I told the president what I had said publicly and on the Senate floor, that we needed a stimulus, but that we also needed to follow established procedures, including hearings, mark-ups, and detailed analysis, which we had not done with TARP. Hearings would give us a chance to digest it all, and to get public input, I said.

I told the president the bill didn't contain enough tax cuts, which could magnify the stimulus effect; didn't contain enough infrastructure spending; and carried a $79 billion provision for the states' Fiscal Stabilization Fund, which was essentially discretionary spending for governors, which I didn't consider stimulus. I also said a lot of programs in the legislation were good, but were not designed to stimulate the economy, and should go through the regular appropriations process later rather than boosting the deficit now.

The president maintained that the bill was an emergency. But he said the Senate had an opportunity to make changes. I inferred that if the legislation stayed within the president's overall figure and direction, he would allow the Senate's modifications as a matter of congressional judgment.

He asked me to give bipartisan support to his stimulus package. He didn't ask me for a commitment on the spot. I told him I thought we needed a stimulus, but I had the concerns I'd expressed. He said, Let's see what the amendments bring and see if the concerns you have are allayed.

We then discussed a couple of other matters. We talked about trying to seat judges who would be acceptable to all sides. The president did not make a commitment to run judges by me or other Senate Republicans. But he was looking for bipartisan support for his nominees. He wasn't looking to ram through his judges. On the NIH, I mentioned my amendment to increase funding by $10 billion.

Around noon, the president made some body motion that signaled the meeting was ending. I don't think he looked at his watch. We talked two or three more minutes, and I left.

B ack in the Senate, I tried to help tighten and shape the stimulus bill. The $920 billion price tag dwarfed even the TARP package. As to the number of jobs created, I said on *The News Hour with Jim Lehrer* that I was willing to accept the president's estimates, but that the exercise reminded me of Philadelphia police commissioner Frank Rizzo estimating crowd size. "It's pretty speculative."[5] Rizzo would sometimes concoct wildly inflated numbers.

When the *NewsHour* reporter asked whether senators had "a big existential objection to this kind of thing," I said, "We don't have existential objections. We have very concrete specific objections. We object to spending more than we have to for a purpose which is not really crystallized and defined."[6]

Meanwhile, the president was ratcheting up the rhetoric. On the evening of February 5, as I was dismissing existential qualms on PBS, Obama told a Democratic group in Virginia:

Then you get the argument, well, this is not a stimulus bill, this is a spending bill. What do you think a stimulus is? That's the whole point! We are not going to get relief by turning back to the very

same policies that, for the last eight years, doubled the national debt
and threw our economy into a tailspin.[7]

That kind of red-meat campaign rhetoric made good television, but
hurt efforts to solve the problem. As I told Michael Smerconish on Philadelphia radio WPHT:

> He asked me to come see him and I sat down and we talked ratio-
> nally about what was going to go on. . . . Then he goes to Virginia
> and makes a red-meat speech to the Democrats, and frankly, I was
> embarrassed by it. I'm trying to work it out with the president and
> he's down there talking raw politics and then my colleagues say,
> "Look at what he's doing." Then I say that I'm not going to make
> any excuses for him but I'm not going to let that guide me, either.[8]

Reid was also sharpening his words. The majority leader publicly warned
our Gang of 18, "Don't overreach. . . . You cannot hold the president of
the United States hostage on this."

On Fox News the next morning, anchor Megyn Kelly asked me what
I thought of Reid's warning. I said,

> I think Senator Reid ought to read the Constitution, on the clause
> which calls for separation of power and the other clause which says
> that the appropriations process, that is, the spending of money, is
> the primary responsibility of the Congress of the United States. . . .
> So we're not holding anybody hostage and we're not going to be
> held hostage. We're doing our job.

Because of our well-known friendship, Joe Biden was assigned one-
on-one coverage of Arlen Specter on the stimulus. Biden played it like
man-to-man coverage in a basketball game. A newspaper reporter told
me, "Biden claims he talked to you fourteen times. Is that true?"

I didn't know whether Biden had talked to me fourteen times. He might have; he was heavily invested in delivering my vote to the White House. It sounded like something Biden would say, to emphasize how hard he was working on it. My date book for one day that week, February 4, showed four calls from the vice president. I said, "I didn't count, but it sounds like it could be."

The content of the conversations with Biden, however many there were, was always the same: how important the stimulus was to the country, how important it was to the president. In one call, Biden told me that if I voted for the stimulus, I would "not have a race." I didn't ask what he meant because I didn't want to get into any discussions about selling my vote for an uncontested election. I took it to mean that I wouldn't have any Democratic opposition in the 2010 general election. Biden certainly couldn't control what would happen to me in a Republican primary. I didn't think he could control what Senate Democrats would do if I were a Republican nominee. Biden was sometimes exuberant, and he wanted my vote very badly. I was going to make my decision on the merits. His no-race remark was loose talk, and couldn't have any role in our discussions.

I consulted the family. On a cold morning in late January, I phoned Shanin on the New Jersey shore, where he had a weekend house.

"I knew when I was having the conversation that I would never forget it," my elder son recalled. There seemed a consensus of rational thought that a stimulus was a good idea, Shanin said later, coupled with a drumbeat that the country was sliding off a cliff and that beginning the Obama presidency with an enormous failure would harm the nation. Shanin had also just finished reading a biography of Franklin Roosevelt that explored what my son called "the most potent use of the stimulus in American history."

"But I thought politically it was somewhere between bad and disastrous to vote for it," Shanin said later, given my long-standing vulnerabilities in Republican primaries and Toomey's potential Senate candidacy.

He said to me, "I think if you vote for it, it's going to be a problem in a primary. But I think that it's important to do it. There are some things that are more important than getting re-elected."

I said, "I feel the same way. I've been thinking to myself, I wonder how

I'd feel if I were fifty-eight instead of seventy-eight. But I just think it's too important to do this."

Shanin had an absolute standard—Do what you think is right—and never deviated from it. Not ever. "Do what you think is right, Dad." Joan thought it was the right vote too. She didn't express a political opinion on the consequences.

In the end, I acted on my own judgment. My father had often told me, "Use your own judgment, Arlen." Something would come up about work in the junkyard, and my dad would say, "Use your own judgment." When I had to choose which college to attend, "Use your own judgment." My father said that to me so often that he instilled some confidence in using my own judgment. That has led me to make some risky moves, including voting "Not Proven" on Clinton's impeachment and taking the lead in questioning Anita Hill. My aunt Rose had phoned me the night before Hill was scheduled to testify and urged, "Don't do it, Buzzy Boy." But I used my own judgment.

It had been a long journey from the junkyard, oil fields, and wheat fields of Russell, Kansas, to being a five-term senator. It was a lot to put at risk on the stimulus vote. When I decided to vote aye, I called Biden to let him take the credit.

In round-the-clock talks, the Gang of 18 emphasized shovel-ready projects on highways, bridges, and mass transit, and strengthening the safety net. We were trying to cut what we Republican centrists had identified as $100 billion not directed to stimulating the economy, even though it covered some good programs, some of which I had supported for decades. I wanted the final price tag under $800 billion.

The revolving bipartisan meetings did not accomplish much. Martinez didn't have a great deal to say and soon dropped out under considerable caucus pressure. I had always found Martinez sensible, moderate, willing to talk, and even willing to listen, a relative rarity. I had come to know him when he was secretary of Housing and Urban Development. Pennsylvania had heavy contact on housing and redevelopment projects, and Martinez was always helpful and cooperative. We had a cordial relationship and I liked him. A few months later, Martinez would abruptly resign from the Senate, saying he didn't want to finish the remaining year and a half of his term. He would leave Florida governor Charlie Crist to appoint a Republican replacement, Crist's former chief of staff George LeMieux, so the Senate numbers stayed the same.

Murkowski followed Martinez's exit, with speculation that she was worried about a challenge in her 2010 re-election bid from Sarah Palin, whose persona was growing. A Murkowski-Palin feud had raged since at least 2002, when Lisa's father, Frank Murkowski, left the Senate to become Alaska governor. In preparing to name his Senate successor, Frank interviewed then–Wasilla mayor Palin, among others. Frank ultimately appointed Lisa, then the Alaska House's new majority leader. Palin, in her book *Going Rogue*, denounced Frank's giving "the most coveted job in the state" to his daughter. When Frank came up for re-election for governor in 2006, Palin unseated him in the Republican primary.

I first heard about Palin during the 2008 presidential campaign. McCain had scheduled his running-mate announcement for a time when I would be on a flight. I knew I'd be asked about the Republican veep nominee as soon as I got off the plane, so when we touched down I made a cell phone call to get intel.

I said, "Who?" I'd never heard of Palin. On the ground, the best I could do was say, "I have confidence in Senator McCain. It's traditionally the province of the candidate to pick his running mate."

Months later, I introduced McCain and Palin at a big outdoor rally in Delaware County, Pennsylvania. I rode to the rally grounds with the Republican candidates in McCain's bus, sitting on a bench in the rear, opposite Palin. I told McCain that it would be very popular in the suburban counties for him to come out for embryonic stem cell research, which I had championed. While I was giving this advice, Palin sat silent. This archconservative, who had a name for decrying efforts like stem cells, said nothing.

Still, she was a total charmer, very friendly. The few things she said were intelligent. We were sitting virtually knee to knee in the cramped bus, and she radiated sensuality. Her skirt rode above her knees—not exactly short, but close. I also met one of her daughters and her husband, Todd,

Sen. Specter introduces the Republican nominees for President and Vice President, Sen. John McCain and Gov. Sarah Palin, at a September 2008 rally in Delaware County, Pennsylvannia. (GETTY)

the First Dude. He seemed like a rugged, good-looking guy. Later, at the rally onstage, we talked about the rigors of being a rising star's spouse.

Murkowski told me later that at the outset of the stimulus talks, she thought there was genuine interest to figure out if we could come to satisfactory terms on both sides. But she said she saw a host of junior senators at the first meeting, with Democrats outnumbering Republicans two to one, and wondered whether we'd be able to pull anything together. She said she spent some hours on the effort and spoke to Voinovich, and both felt it wasn't coming together.

"There just really wasn't a willingness on the part of Republicans to even talk about it," she recalled. She said she needed to do "assessments on analysis," but that such work was beyond the scope of her personal staff's expertise. "Tough, tough stuff."[9]

Amid the stimulus talks, Rendell phoned to tell me how urgent passage of the bill was for Pennsylvania. "We've just gotta have it." Without the stimulus funds, the governor warned, our state would have to make

Sens. Specter and Susan Collins confer at the elevator near Sen. Reid's conference room just after leaving a meeting with Democratic senators. (GETTY)

massive, crippling layoffs. I knew Rendell didn't overstate and didn't ask for things he didn't need. I also knew that the former DNC chairman appreciated the political difficulty of the vote. Rendell's comments were influential.

The negotiations ended up in Reid's office on Friday, February 6, with several meetings that day among Democrats Reid, Lieberman, and Ben Nelson; Republicans Collins, Voinovich, and me; and White House Chief of Staff Rahm Emanuel.

Voinovich was one of the Senate's smartest and most practical members, experienced at national, state, and local government. He had been an outstanding Cleveland mayor and Ohio governor. Then-governor Voinovich had attracted a lot of attention in 1995, when he ordered his plane to take off from a Columbus airport during an airspace restriction still in effect even though then-president Clinton had landed more than an hour earlier at the main Columbus airport several miles away. Voinovich reportedly grabbed a mic and told the tower it could shoot down his plane.

Voinovich wound up paying a $1,500 federal fine and $3,500 in legal fees. He wrote to the Federal Aviation Administration, "I should have exercised more restraint, not lost my temper and remained at the airport until this confusing situation was cleared up."[10]

In one of our first meetings after his Senate election in 1998, I told him I admired his spunk. He insisted he had been wrong and wouldn't be placated. Voinovich joined me in December 2000 for part of a trip to Europe and the Middle East, meeting with, among others, Egyptian president Hosni Mubarak, Israeli prime minister Ehud Barak, and newly elected Yugoslav president Vojislav Koštunica. While America struggled with partisan gridlock, Yugoslavia faced structural gridlock, paying for ten years of corruption and mismanagement under Slobodan Milošević. In Belgrade, rolling blackouts highlighted the lack of basic public services and health care. In Bosnia, Voinovich and I went on a patrol through the towns of Flipovici and Katonovici with soldiers of the Third Infantry Division.

At the February 6 stimulus meeting, Voinovich did not have much to say. He appeared uneasy. I stepped out for a few minutes to meet a constituent group at the Capitol Visitors Center. In retrospect, it was foolish to leave that vital meeting, but senators always stretch to cover all bases. When I got back, Voinovich had left, never to return.

My first thought was that the pressure had grown too heavy for Voinovich and he simply didn't want to participate further. And the pressure was great. It's tough to be one of four who walk away from thirty-seven other Republicans bent on scuttling the president's agenda. However, Voinovich, like Martinez, had already announced his intention not to seek re-election, so he didn't face the potential wrath of angry voters.

Later, I talked to Voinovich about it, and he used the word "betrayed." He thought that Collins and I had made our own deal. I raised my voice a little, saying that was not true. He didn't like the package. I didn't like the package either. We cut back a lot of items, and I thought a lot more should have been handled through the appropriations process.

But I had grown convinced that the stimulus was indispensable to avert a depression. I was disgusted by the Republican caucus's refusal to engage the issue. Everyday citizens don't plumb the ins and outs of complex legislation, but they draw confidence when the two parties come together in a bipartisan manner.

On the GOP side, it was now down to Collins and me, with Snowe inactive but presumably aboard. "Olympia was in a separate orbit," working directly with Reid, Durbin later told me. "You and Susan, it's true, were more directly and personally involved."[11] McCain was quoted as saying that three Republicans didn't make it bipartisan. But that's the best we could do, given the caucus's attitude.

Collins and I were trying to reduce the House's $920 billion figure, largely for cosmetics. Obama's figure had begun at $600 billion and ballooned to more than $1 trillion. Collins and I thought the public would balk at such a massive stimulus, given mounting debts and deficits, so we insisted on holding the figure under $800 billion.

Lieberman, who was heavily involved in the effort, told me later that without downward pressure on the price tag from us Republicans, "it could have gone up, up and away." He likened the negotiating process to slogging through mud in combat, just trying to keep moving forward.[12]

Collins and I didn't have time or the staff analysis from the committees that dealt with the fine points of substance and the financing of programs under consideration, which we would have needed to negotiate content in any meaningful way. On education, we wound up striking a nearly $20 billion school construction program but increasing a general state fund, some of which could be used to rebuild schools. We also added tens of billions in spending through Pell grants and other programs.

One issue, Medicaid reimbursement, did get a detailed look. Nebraska and Pennsylvania had different rates. The bill included $90 billion in Medicaid funding, provided to the states through a combination of two formulas. First, each state got an automatic 6.2 percent increase in federal contributions to its Medicaid program. Second, each state got additional increases based on its unemployment rate. The House and Senate came up with different weights for the unemployment-based increases. The final negotiated rate was to be the mean of the two chambers' rates. But Nelson of Nebraska pushed to increase the weight of the automatic portion of the increase, favoring states—like Nebraska, but unlike Pennsylvania—with low unemployment.

Amy Klobuchar had lobbied me to hang tough because Minnesota's interests matched Pennsylvania's. Emanuel, who had been with Nelson, made short shrift of the controversy, immediately agreeing with us because my vote—as a Republican—was more important than Nelson's, which they already had.

In midafternoon on February 6, Collins and I reached an impasse with Reid and the other Democrats. Collins and I insisted on delivering a final bill under $800 billion. They wanted a higher figure. Reid was adamant. The negotiations broke down. I suggested to Collins that we retire to my hideaway, a two-minute walk to the floor below, and reconnoiter.

Visitors to my Capitol office generally focused on two framed items: a poster of former Palestinian chairman Yasir Arafat and an original edition of the articles of impeachment against President Clinton, each of its two pages covered with the signatures of all one hundred senators. I had picked up the campaign-style poster in December 1998 when I accompanied Clinton to Israel. The poster, in photomontage, showed Clinton giving a thumbs-up and Arafat raising his hand in a peace symbol. In March 1999, Arafat visited me in the hideaway and was delighted to find the poster framed and hanging just inside the door. He insisted on having his picture taken in front of his picture. That photo now hung beside the poster.

On the articles of impeachment, I had collected the signatures of all the House managers, the White House defense team, and even the chief justice. I needed one more autograph. One day in 1999, I set out to get it. I had a meeting with President Clinton at the Old Executive Office Building. I had a Shanin family reunion that day, and brought my aunts for photos with the president. In preparation, Rose went back to the hotel to change clothes, into a dress that happened to be low-cut. She was eighty-eight. When Annie came back from the meeting, her son Jay later told me, she reported that the president was charming and handsome, adding, "I don't blame Monica a bit."

I told a presidential aide that I needed the president to sign a memento, and the staffer volunteered to arrange it. "No," I said, "I want to do it personally." When the time came, I presented the photos with Rose, Anne, and Joyce, and the impeachment articles, in sequence. By the time Clinton got to the document, he was in a signing mood. He glanced at the page and said, "You got Chuck Ruff to sign," referring to White House Counsel Charles Ruff. Whether Clinton knew what he was signing, I don't know. But he didn't hesitate a bit in emblazoning his left-handed signature. But as Collins and I walked into my hideaway in February 2009, she wasn't distracted, and I wasn't giving my customary travelogue.

We agreed that the consequences of inaction could be catastrophic. The thought of a 1930s depression was never far from my mind. I didn't want to be responsible for a repeat. The president's mandate also weighed on me. The American people had spoken. They were expecting the new president to take the lead. I recalled how FDR had brought Keynesian economics to take the lead.

Collins was equally concerned and perplexed. We had to find a compromise. We discussed a number of items we didn't like, but agreed that we didn't have enough data or time to negotiate them. We simply weren't equipped to go through the entire bill and adjust areas that affected and crossed multiple committee jurisdictions. If the various committee chairmen had come in and said, This is what we need on schools, highways, environmental protection, and so on, we could have crafted a precise, strategic bill. If the Republican leadership had participated, staff assistance could have helped direct funds to stimulate the economy immediately and create jobs. When the TARP package came up, we had gone to the leaders. But the Republican leadership refused to participate in the stimulus; the GOP had its eyes on Waterloo.

So Collins and I did the best we could. We crafted our last best proposal, with a figure of $780 billion. Our negotiations had reduced the spending by $110 billion and increased the tax cut to 36 percent of the total cost. The House version had reduced tax cuts to 22 percent of the total.[13] We went back upstairs to Reid's office.

Reid pressed for $7 billion more to accommodate a Mikulski tax provision, and the historic $787 billion was set.

"You drove a hard bargain," Durbin told me later. "I was in the room when you did. . . . I wish there had been more on the Republican side who had joined you. But each one who did—Snowe, Collins, and yourself—had a definite impact on the outcome of that debate, and what the stimulus bill looked like."[14] The president phoned, and the call was routed to my hideaway. Obama thanked me for standing up against pressure from my party, for advancing the bill, and for my patriotism. I kept a thought to myself: this wasn't patriotism, just rationality. The president also phoned Snowe and Collins.[15]

That evening, Friday, February 6, Scott Hoeflich and my campaign manager, Chris Nicholas, were at the Republican State Committee's meeting in Harrisburg, where I was planning to speak the next morning. Hoeflich later recalled, "Everything was fine, because Toomey had announced he was going to run for governor. We had a clear shot, everyone loved us, and the biggest problem we had was how we were going to vote on Employee Free Choice." The Employee Free Choice Act would make it easier to unionize through "card check," which provided for union certification if 51 percent of the members signed a card requesting it.

Former senator Santorum phoned my chief of staff at 5:45 p.m. Hoeflich walked outside and asked, "Senator, how can I help you?"

"I'm not calling for help; I'm calling to help *you*," Santorum told him. "Rumors are, Arlen's going to vote for the stimulus package. If you do that, you're going to pull a primary challenge, and you're going to lose."

Hoeflich trotted upstairs and phoned me. "Senator, I got a call from Santorum. You can't vote for the stimulus package. Everything is fine right now; we've got a clear shot to re-election. Don't do this."

"Scott, tell everyone I'm down in D.C. doing official Senate business. This is the right thing to do. I'll see you tomorrow morning."

"Next thing you know, BlackBerrys start going off," Hoeflich recalled. "It's out; the boss is going to vote for the stimulus package. Game over."[16]

Just after 8 p.m., we announced our agreement to an army of reporters near the Ohio clock outside the Senate chamber and prepared to speak on the Senate floor. It was a fitting site. The eleven-foot clock had weathered various storms during its two hundred years, and had stood in its current post since 1859. Rumors circulated that senators used to hide whiskey in its case, and reporters from the 1940s confessed to doing so. A blast from a bomb planted in 1983 outside the Senate chamber, purportedly in retaliation for U.S. military action in Granada and Lebanon, had broken the clock's glass face cover. But still it ticked. The clock had been made in Philadelphia, as the face stated, and its Ohio designation remained a mystery.[17]

I began by congratulating Nelson, Collins, and Lieberman for their leadership and for taking on an unpopular but necessary job. "If we do not act and act decisively and boldly, the psychological impact would be felt beyond Wall Street to Main Street, but really on the face of the globe."

Lieberman was gracious, saying essentially that it was easy for Democrats to vote for the bill, but tough for Republicans.

> I'd say that Sen. Collins and Sen. Specter really deserve the Medal of Honor for what they've done here tonight. They put national interest ahead of party interest. It's not easy; it's often lonely, but the American people will benefit from what they have helped us accomplish here in the Senate tonight.[18]

Collins said, "Tonight is a victory for the American people. We demonstrated that we can come together to tackle the most important problem facing our nation."

A reporter asked me, "Senator Specter, you're the only Republican that's up in 2010. I'm sure you're seeing the right wing of your party as really going after you in a [big] way. What do you say to those critics?"

I was the only dissident up in the 2010 election cycle, while Snowe had a cushion until 2012 and Collins until 2014. Two or four years are a lifetime in politics, with lots of time for redemption, forgiveness, or forgetfulness.

What could I say? A story about Abraham Lincoln came to mind. A boy reportedly asked Lincoln whether he always voted his conscience. Honest Abe replied that he voted his conscience 90 percent of the time. The boy pressed, asking about the other 10 percent. "That's so I can vote my conscience 90 percent of the time." There was an obvious temptation to vote no on the stimulus and justify it to myself on the Lincoln 10 percent doctrine. A no vote would almost guarantee my political survival. But the national and global consequences could be catastrophic.

"Well, there are material risks in the position I'm taking, which may well impact in a primary," I told the reporters. "Those thoughts have not escaped my attention. And I believe that my duty is to follow my conscience and vote what I think is in the best interests of the country. And the political risks will have to abide."

Minutes later, Hoeflich and Santorum exchanged BlackBerry e-mails:

Hoeflich—8:21:35 PM
I tried and failed. He will be 61 [the sixty-first aye vote for the stimulus].
Santorum—8:40:07 PM
It's his butt.
Hoeflich—8:40:26 PM
And mine!

We went to the Senate floor to announce our positions. I had visions of Congresswoman Marjorie Margolies Mezvinsky, who had represented the Philadelphia suburbs, then cast the decisive vote for President Clinton's 1993 tax increases and became a House one-termer. I had known 3M, as she was called, since she was an anchorwoman for a Philadelphia TV affiliate around the time I was first elected to the Senate. She would hit the news again in July 2010, when her son Marc married Clinton's daughter, Chelsea.

In October 2010, I would run into Mezvinsky at the wedding of one of my senior Philadelphia aides, and she would tell me how she had negotiated with Clinton for her 1993 vote. "I need your vote," the president had told her. She couldn't, she said; it would cost her her seat. "I have to have it," Clinton insisted. "I'll give you anything." She told the president he might not want to meet her price. Anything, Clinton repeated. She told him, "The price I'm exacting is your firstborn."

By the next morning at the state committee confab in Harrisburg, Nicholas recalled later, "we [were] getting lots of cold stares from people." Toomey had scheduled an initial meeting for the following Monday about running for governor. "And as the state committee meeting broke up Saturday afternoon," Nicholas said, "a lot of hard-core conservatives were saying, 'We're going to that meeting and telling Pat he's got to run for Senate. Specter's betrayed us by helping get the stimulus package through.'"

On the Senate floor, I asked Lugar to join on the stimulus. The Indiana Republican had tremendous ability and carried great respect. He listened politely and said he would consider it. When Lugar had to be on the floor, he would sit in the back of his row, always working and reading, and never hang around. He was the fastest guy in and out of the Senate. He strode in on votes and strode out. We marveled that he didn't run. Lugar would wind up voting no.

Voting against the party's wishes was one thing, but advocating such a position was something else. You are forgiven a lot more easily for a wayward vote than for taking a leadership role in urging others to do the same. On the stimulus, though, the difference may have shrunk; there was no place to hide. In for a dime, in for a dollar. In for a vote, in for a trillion.

After making my statement on the stimulus, I walked off the Senate floor into the Republican cloakroom. Bob Bennett of Utah walked over. "Arlen, I'm proud of you," he said.

"Thanks very much, Bob. Are you going to vote with me?"

He promptly replied, "No, I couldn't do that, it would cost me a primary." The people on one end of the political spectrum don't like the government spending, Bennett said. As it turned out, Bennett could have voted aye. In the May 2010 state Republican nominating convention, activists would derail the three-term senator, setting up a runoff between two political neophytes. Bennett's vote for TARP, along with his co-sponsorship of the Wyden-Bennett health reform bill, would cost him his seat, despite a 93 percent favorable rating from the American Conservative Union and solid conservative bona fides. Purity tests would reign among Tea Party activists and the Club for Growth, who dominated Utah's unique system. At the convention, activists would mock Bennett as "Bailout Bob" and jeer, "TARP, TARP, TARP!"[19]

Bennett was among the many, perhaps the majority of, Senate Republicans who would have been happy to see the stimulus bill pass, but without their fingerprints on it. The rest were hard-core conservative opponents. The U.S. and world economies had sunk closer to depression than when thirty-four GOP senators had voted for TARP. But the pressure to vote the party line was tremendous, the strongest I had seen in my twenty-nine-year tenure. The risk of retribution was enormous.

The next day, Saturday, the Pennsylvania Republican State Committee threatened to censure me. Conservative members of the Lehigh County Republican Party's executive committee soon submitted an actual letter of censure.[20]

Reid called Rendell over the weekend to ask the governor if I would stick with the Democrats, saying that if Arlen Specter went south, the women—the Maine senators—would never stand up. Rendell assured Reid that I was solid once I had given my word.

On Sunday, twenty picketers descended on my Allentown office. One brought a gun. The anger also registered in comments on the street wherever I went. Opposition to the bill mounted on both ends of the political spectrum: from those who said there was too much spending, and from those who said there wasn't enough. Irate callers from around the nation jammed my office phone lines in Washington and in Pennsylvania with threats of political reprisals. Kate Schramm, deputy director of my Philadelphia office at the time, said one Pennsylvania man told her it had taken him days to get through to talk to her about a pending visa.[21]

The tide might turn, I thought, because the Chamber of Commerce, a prime voice for corporate and conservative America, had issued a letter supporting the stimulus, citing the economy's continuing slide.

Conservative talk radio hosts blasted me. The day of the cloture vote, Monday, February 9, 2009, Laura Ingraham asked me early in a live interview, "How can you, in good conscience, move forward and support this, Senator?" A few minutes later, she asked, "Is it nice to be wined and dined at the White House? You're treated pretty well, when you're a Republican bucking other Republicans, right, Senator?"

That one made my pulse pound. "Oh, now, let's get off it, Laura," I said. "I'm not drinking any wine at the White House and I don't dine at the White House. If the president wants to talk to me, I talk to him, and I make my own independent judgment."

Later that day, I spoke to Sean Hannity on a cell phone while riding Amtrak from Philadelphia to Washington. I missed his opening and we got disconnected a couple of times, but we got through the interview.

Hannity inveighed, "All of this crap is in here, and if you were to stand up and say, 'I won't support it,' this bill wouldn't pass in its current form. You are the defining vote here, Senator—you can literally stand on conservative fiscal principles and stop this reckless spending." Hannity urged Reagan-style tax cuts, which I had supported.

"We have very substantial tax cuts in the bill," I said. "I would have been delighted to have rewritten the whole thing, but that wasn't realistic."

"You can make that happen," Hannity pleaded. "Without you, Republicans are united, Republicans stop this bill. It dies in the Senate with your vote, Senator. You can stop this; you have that power."

"When I gave my word last week, that's it," I said. "I'm looking at a monstrosity of an economy which is going to hell worse day by day with thousands of people losing their jobs and mortgage foreclosures. And I'm not prepared to sit on the sidelines. If anybody else had come in, I would have gladly given them my spot at the table."

Shortly before 5:30 p.m. that Monday, Harry Reid took the Senate floor and told America, "Help is on the way."

Mark Udall of Colorado, the Senate's presiding officer—the job generally went to majority party freshmen—called for the ayes and nays on the motion to invoke cloture on the stimulus debate. This was the key vote. If supporters could muster 60 ayes to cut off debate, the underlying bill would certainly draw 51 votes for actual passage.

Before heading to the floor, I had a few matters to wrap up in the office.

I made it a practice not to leave for votes or other appointments any sooner than I had to, out of a drive never to waste a minute, from a morbid sense of how finite life is.

Ted Kennedy braced on a cane as he stepped into the chamber, his first official Washington appearance since collapsing at a postinauguration luncheon. Kennedy had been battling brain cancer, resting in Florida. He chatted with some colleagues, voted aye, and soon left.[22]

With just over five minutes left in the fifteen-minute vote, the Senate clerk called the roll, enunciating each senator's name in a strong alto. Two-thirds of the senators had gathered, and the final tally would clearly be close. I was on the underground tram from the Hart Building to the Capitol. With 1:53 left on the clock, I strode into the chamber. I headed straight for the well, where the clerk was tallying votes. None of my colleagues tried to intercept or engage me. They knew what I was going to do. I got the clerk's attention by gesturing as though I were calling a strike on a batter, more animated than my usual hand signal.

She promptly looked over. "Mr. Specter," she said, her mic booming her voice on national television.

"Aye," I said.

"Mr. Specter, aye."

I felt, to paraphrase Ross Perot, a giant sucking sound—my political career going south.

The two Maine senators also voted aye.

When time ran out, the clerk intoned, "On this vote, the yeas are 61, the nays are 36. Three-fifths of the senators duly chosen and sworn, having voted in the affirmative, the motion is agreed to." The filibuster was broken.

The stimulus was one of ten thousand votes I had cast. From the beginning, I had been successful doing it my way, using my own judgment, through independent actions like opposing Bork and funding stem cell and other medical research, education, and foreign aid. I figured I might be successful again with the stimulus, but the odds were long against me. Terry Madonna, the Pennsylvania political oracle, would write: "Specter throughout his political career almost has seemed a force of nature. He always found a way to win and survived whatever challenge was thrown against him."[23] Still, I knew my vote was probably politically fatal, especially in the context of my tenuous relationship with the GOP.

The morning of the vote on final passage, February 10, I interrupted the first game of my morning squash match to call R. J. Harris of WHP Radio in Harrisburg live.

"Well, I have to tell you, Senator, I have never seen anything like it," Harris began.

> Number one, I have never had more e-mails on any one topic. Never had more phone calls. . . . People cannot understand, including me, how you, Arlen Specter . . . could be voting for this spending bill. . . . They are calling you a turncoat, they are saying that a yes vote is a career-ending vote for you. . . . One called you a political transvestite, another "Republican in Democratic clothes."

Toward the end of our talk, Harris said he appreciated my defending my views. "I do appreciate that, but boy oh boy, you are going to get—there will be some hell to pay for you."

Dana Bash of CNN asked me later that day, "You've been through so many elections and primary challenges, how concerned are you that this could be the thing that costs you your seat?"

"I'm very concerned about it," I said.[24]

I had issued a statement saying that if the stimulus bill remained "virtually intact" from the version the Senate had passed, I would support final passage. It did, and I did.

Vengeance was swift. As John Roberts told me the next morning when I appeared on CNN's *American Morning,* "You had a tough primary in 2004. It looks like this one is going to be even tougher. You've got the powerful National Republican Trust threatening to pour millions of dollars into a challenger, whatever it takes to defeat you."[25]

A *Pittsburgh Post-Gazette* reporter told me, "We had some national Republican groups vow that you were a 'marked man' because of your vote on the stimulus package."[26]

On February 11, Biden phoned for me five times. The final stimulus votes were looming, on the conference report to reconcile the House and Senate versions of the bill, officially H.R. 1, the American Recovery and Reinvestment Act of 2009. The vice president reached me the first two times, and bragged to the president that we had spoken, according to Hoeflich's e-mails with the vice president's office. Later that day, Biden couldn't get through to me. So he phoned my chief of staff. According to Hoeflich's notes that day, "Same message (need to reach Arlen, Stim is very important, if he votes for it he won't have a race in 2010)."[27]

That evening, Hoeflich couldn't reach me to convey Biden's latest message. Undeterred, the vice president phoned Joan, who told him that I had probably gone to sleep and that I often took the phone off the hook when I did. Biden phoned Hoeflich again. "Scott, have Arlen call me first thing in the morning—first thing, this is very important."[28]

The next day, February 12, was my seventy-ninth birthday. Bill O'Reilly, Fox's volatile conservative, was cordial and complimentary when he interviewed me.

> I can't possibly predict whether this is going to work and I don't believe any human being can. . . . Whenever you have Bush and Obama, who are diametrically opposed politically, saying the same thing, smart people are going to pay attention. . . . Look, Senator, I've known you a long time. . . . You're no bomb thrower, you're no Nancy Pelosi, you're a deliberative man and I respect your decision. I mean I don't know what I would have done if I were in your shoes.

O'Reilly closed the interview by saying, "It was a very worthy conversation, and we really appreciate it."[29]

Ted Kennedy's wife, Vicki, phoned about the vote on the conference report, which reconciled the House and Senate versions of the bill. "Would

you mind if Ted didn't come in?" she asked. "He's not well." Without
Kennedy, I would be the decisive sixtieth vote. Whether Vicki called
Snowe and Collins, I don't know. I told Vicki of course he didn't have to
come in.

I held a seventy-five-minute telephone conference call with several
hundred members of the Pennsylvania Republican State Committee. "I
know that you're taking a lot of heat," I told them, "because I'm taking a
lot of heat."

Bucks County chairman Harry Fawkes spoke first when I opened for
questions. "I was worried more about you and what could happen to you
for voting that way," he said. "I don't want to see you lose; you've always
been my friend."

A committeewoman told me:

I'm under the firing pin in Elk County like you have never in your
life seen. The people up here are not happy with this bill and they
wish that you would have stayed the course and not had been the
one that was one of the sixty-one. . . . I pray for my country because
right now I think that the United States of America—because it's
going down the tube because of the direction Mr. Obama—I call
him that because I don't consider him my president—because the
direction Mr. Obama is taking us.

A committeewoman from York County groused, "Spending this money
and making my kids and grandkids pay the interest on this is just abomi-
nable."

There were pockets of support. One committeeman said:

I'm a conservative Republican and I don't think that there are
many conservative Republicans that are happy with this bill but
I'm very proud of you because I believe that the bill was absolutely
essential. . . . Although people are beating on me night and day
about it and my shoulders aren't as broad as yours, but we all have
to hang together and try to explain to people that it was a very cou-

rageous thing that you did on behalf of your nation and we've got to rally around.

His vocal support was the exception that proved the rule.

The next day, February 13, hours before the conference report vote, Hoeflich attended a monthly meeting of conservative Republicans in Harrisburg run by my good friend and supporter Charlie Gerow, CEO of the public affairs firm Quantum Communications. "I was the most hated person in the room and they were all yelling at me," Hoeflich recalled. "I then left and went to another conservative meeting the same day in D.C. One guy stood up and said, 'I will offer my media services for free to any person or group who opposes Arlen Specter.'"[30]

Just before 5:30 p.m. on February 13, the day between my birthday and Valentine's Day, we voted on final passage of the conference report. The tally was 60–38, with Kennedy absent and the Minnesota seat vacant, pending a recount between Republican Norm Coleman and Democrat Al Franken.

If Republicans were calling my stimulus vote a career ender, Democrats were equally eager for my political hide. Senator Bob Menendez of New Jersey, head of the Democratic Senatorial Campaign Committee, said, "We're going to do everything we can to beat Arlen Specter."

A *Philadelphia Inquirer* reporter asked me, "How does it feel to get it . . . from the Democrats and Republicans?" She ended the interview by saying, "I wish you luck. I hope you have good protection when you go back."

On February 16, *Washington Post* reporter Ruth Marcus began an interview by saying, "Congratulations, you had a big achievement there."

"Did you say commiserations?" I asked.

"No," Marcus said. "I say, 'Congratulations.'"

"Yeah, I heard you, Ruth."

The increased NIH funding added some solace. As the *New York Times* reported:

For years, Senator Arlen Specter of Pennsylvania has been the National Institutes of Health's most ardent champion on Capitol Hill. . . . He has long insisted that research that results in medical cures is the best service that government can provide.

But even lobbyists are stunned by the coup Mr. Specter pulled off this week. In return for providing one of only three Republican votes in the Senate for the Obama administration's $787 billion economic stimulus package, he was able to secure a 34 percent increase in the health agency's budget—to $39 billion from $29 billion.

After money intended for highways, schools and states, it is the largest chunk of financing in the budget and is almost three times the $3.5 billion first approved by the House.

. . . And once [Specter] voted for the [stimulus] bill, Mr. Durbin said that he made sure that the additional $10 billion for the N.I.H. was protected in conference negotiations with the House.[31]

No quid pro quo was involved; there was no deal of my vote for the NIH funding.

A year and a half later, at an Appropriations subcommittee hearing on September 16, 2010, I would take the opportunity to ask NIH director Dr. Francis Collins about the $10 billion, and what use the institutes were making of it.

Collins effused. The funds, he said, had given "an enormous infusion of energy, capability, and excitement" to a community that had been struggling, reviving many innovative ideas that had lagged for lack of support. That work, he said, had produced some of the most exciting science grants, in turn producing breakthroughs in fighting cancer, heart disease, diabetes, and other diseases. "I want to thank you for your remarkable leadership in making that possible."

Experts would later confirm the stimulus's vital role in our economic rescue. The *New York Times* would run a piece in July 2010 headlined "In Study, 2 Economists Say Intervention Helped Avert a 2nd Depression," reporting:

Like a mantra, officials from both the Bush and Obama administrations have trumpeted how the government's sweeping interventions to prop up the economy since 2008 helped avert a second Depression.

Now, two leading economists wielding complex quantitative models say that assertion can be empirically proved.

In a new paper, the economists argue that without the Wall Street bailout, the bank stress tests, the emergency lending and asset purchases by the Federal Reserve, and the Obama administration's fiscal stimulus program, the nation's gross domestic product would be about 6.5 percent lower this year.

In addition, there would be about 8.5 million fewer jobs, on top of the more than 8 million already lost; and the economy would be experiencing deflation, instead of low inflation.[32]

In September 2010, experts would declare the recession officially over as of June 2009, and Treasury would report that TARP would cost taxpayers $29 billion, a fraction of the original $350 billion estimate. The automobile industry had rebounded, and banks had repaid many of the TARP loans, some with interest. Still, economic indicators would continue to show a slow recovery, adding proof that the stimulus package had been necessary. And while the contents of the stimulus were popular, the public found the stimulus itself toxic, studies showed.[33]

But the economists' findings would come too late for my political prospects.

Soon after the stimulus votes, Pat Toomey abandoned his gubernatorial campaign to challenge me again for the Senate.

Jim DeMint approached me in the Marble Room, the senators' private chamber off the floor where senators respect one another's privacy and seldom interrupt. "I'm going to support Toomey," DeMint said. The two had served together in the House. DeMint had once proclaimed that he'd rather have "thirty Republicans in the Senate who believe in principles of freedom than sixty who don't believe in anything."

Saying, "This conversation is over," I rose and walked away.

I had \$7 million in the bank, and I wasn't going to be run out of Washington by the right wing and Toomey. But my approval rating among Republicans had plummeted 30 points. A comfortable lead in a fall 2008 poll of a prospective Specter-Toomey Republican Senate primary had turned into a sizable deficit. Also, more than 200,000 moderate Pennsylvania Republicans had re-registered as Democrats to vote in the 2008 Obama–Hillary Clinton primary and because they were, polls showed, "turned off by the Republican Party's rightward drift."[34]

Many Republican critics weren't interested in hearing my side. A longtime close friend, Fred Anton, chairman of the Pennsylvania Manufacturers Association, wouldn't invite me to speak to the conservative Republican group he led, and which I had addressed in 2006 and 2007. Anton told me that two-thirds of the members would boycott the event. I had made him chairman of the Pennsylvania federal judicial nominating panels. But he wouldn't invite me to defend myself before his group. I understood his dilemma and didn't blame him for the position he had to take.

Gerow did gather his group of conservative Republicans in Harrisburg for me. The meeting drew a cordial, overflow crowd to his office. When you have a chance to talk to people, to lay out your reasons, you can often gain their understanding and even their respect, if not their approval. Operating on that hope, I had met every year with pro-life groups who descended on Washington on the anniversary of the *Roe v. Wade* decision.

I asked Republican state chairman Rob Gleason whether my opposition to "card check," the bill providing for union certification if 51 percent of members signed a card requesting it, could make a difference in bringing back conservative Republicans. Madonna the political scientist had told the national press the week of the stimulus votes: "Card check is shaping up to be a pivotal vote for Specter—in some respects more important than the stimulus." The Saturday before the votes, the state Republican committee had urged Pennsylvania's congressional delegation to oppose the Employee Free Choice Act.[35]

Gleason said, "You've got to be against card check."

I said I was. I had opposed the measure because of my strongly held view that the secret ballot was indispensable. Election cards offered too many opportunities for coercion. I asked, "Do you think that would balance out the stimulus?"

He said yes, he thought it could, that it was possible. But Gleason was generally unsupportive. His uncle Andy Gleason, 104 at this writing, whom I had visited often on my many trips to Johnstown, was a powerhouse going back to the days of Billy Meehan's father. Rob, a scion, was picked for state chairman, an impossible job. I didn't completely fault him, because supporting me would have meant making a lot of enemies in the Republican Party. But a strong chairman would have defended and backed a long-standing senator. It might have made a difference, if I'd had the state chairman standing up for me and rallying the troops, urging me to continue the fight. Gleason could have said, "We have a five-term senator, let's not throw that away over one vote."

Some Pennsylvania Republican congressmen were even less helpful. Todd Platts, a moderate whose Web site boasted of his efforts to reach across the aisle, and who had spoken forcefully for me in 2004, wouldn't return my phone call. Bill Shuster wouldn't endorse me for re-election. His father, then-representative Bud Shuster, had once praised me at an Altoona campaign event by saying that a senator's single most important vote was the first one, on organization to select the majority leader and other officers. That was all the elder Shuster had to say on my behalf.

I began a statewide tour, talking to Republicans to see if my candidacy could be salvaged. I went to the Lehigh Valley, Pittsburgh, and a dozen places between. Everywhere, it was the same. I came to see the issue, borrowing language from domestic-relations law, as irreconcilable differences with Republicans.

The crescendo came from Charlie Roberts, a Northampton County party worker who had been one of my most avid supporters since my 1978 gubernatorial primary run. When I phoned Roberts to discuss the stimulus vote, he wouldn't take my call. So I phoned him the next day. On the second call, he told me, "Call me back in an hour."

I phoned him again an hour later. The interlude gave him some time to cool down, but not by much. He still didn't want to talk to me. A friend for thirty-plus years. He was indignant about the vote. But he was even more embarrassed, for speaking up for me all those years to so many people who were now angry at him.

Roberts had been proud of our close friendship, which had given him some added status and prestige with his friends and fellow party workers. When I voted for the stimulus, many turned on him. Roberts was passing his and their anger to me.

When Charlie Roberts wouldn't take my call, I knew it was futile.

EIGHT

TOO CANDID

Visiting the Republican leader's grand suite had always felt like entering a sanctum–until my trip on April 27, 2009. I'd been to the Capitol rooms thousands of times, beginning thirty years earlier, when Howard Baker occupied them. I'd sat with the Republican leader, sometimes alone, sometimes with others, and engaged in congenial conversation on what course to take. I'd hashed out countless issues over the decades in that suite with Baker and then with Dole, Lott, Frist, and now McConnell.

The room's architecture and history added to the warmth. The leader's office, in the oldest part of the Capitol, offered a majestic view of the Washington Monument and the Mall. Above intricate marble mantels and amid frescoes, a frieze of thirty-two medallions featured lawmakers from ancient Rome and Greece. Early nineteenth-century presidents, with no designated space of their own in the Capitol, had shared the rooms with their veeps. Supreme Court justices, including Oliver Wendell Holmes, Louis Brandeis, and Chief Justice William Howard Taft, had used the spaces as a "Robing Room" from 1860 until the Court moved into its own building in 1935. In 1981, the suite had become the permanent Republican leader's room when minority leader Baker was elected majority leader, but decided to keep the spaces rather than moving around the corner. Three years later, Congress passed legislation designating S-230 the Howard H. Baker Jr. Room.

That spring evening in 2009, facing Mitch McConnell in that chamber, felt different, and tense. I told the minority leader that I planned to change parties, to become a Democrat.

I had known McConnell since 1984, when he came to testify before the Judiciary Committee on juvenile justice. He was then judge-executive of Jefferson County, Kentucky, which included Louisville. He was also running for the Senate against an incumbent Democrat, and waging a solid campaign that featured a powerful ad. I was giving him a little publicity.

McConnell and I had never been close. But we had always been congenial, even through a little tension over some of my policy disagreements with his wife, Elaine Chao, when she served as George W. Bush's secretary of labor. Chao was very attractive and petite. Strom Thurmond's assessment was "He married that Chinese woman."

I always respected McConnell's political astuteness. He made no pretenses about subordinating policy to politics, and luxuriated in Senate process. McConnell rates near the top of the Senate on political savvy and near the bottom on public policy.

When I told him I was going to change parties, he was visibly displeased, but not ruffled. Mostly, he was taciturn. He asked about my thinking. I told him Pennsylvania Republicans were unforgiving about my stimulus vote, that it had been an uncomfortable relationship for decades, and that the camel's back was broken—and not by a straw, but by a log.

McConnell and I had a serious discussion. He was very nice and very professional.

"Don't do it," he said. "It'd be a big mistake. Serve out your time as a Republican and retire gracefully."

I said, "I'll sleep on it." I thought that the Republican leader was entitled to have me consider his views, and that his views were worth considering, on the merits.

. . .

I had decided to switch parties several days earlier, after getting the results of a poll we had commissioned from the major Republican firm
Public Opinion Strategies. The family gathered in Shanin and Tracey's
kitchen over the weekend to discuss my political options, all of them un-
appealing.

I called Shanin's house in the Philadelphia suburb of Gladwyne my
center of gravity, where my four granddaughters dashed and darted. We
sat around the island in the earth-tone kitchen, an idyllic spring day just
outside the windows.

Shanin later recalled:

My mantra was, "Look, here are your options—you can stay a Republican, run, and lose badly; you can retire; you can run as an independent and you'll finish third; or you can switch parties."

And I thought if he switched parties, that he would probably
win the primary, although it was not clear that he would, and I
thought he would probably beat Toomey in the fall—but, again, it
was not clear. Being at 30 percent popularity among Republicans is
high enough if you're a Democrat–it's just not high enough if you're
a Republican.

Joan recalled later, "I thought he could do it, and was very supportive.
Then I said I wanted to come to Washington to be part of it."

Tracey didn't say much. A political natural, she knew the party switch
would make her situation as chair of the Republican Committee of Lower
Merion and Narberth very difficult, and perhaps untenable. She had
worked her way up through the party ranks over twenty years, and had
led the committee the last seven. But she was intensely loyal to my interests and willing to put up with whatever problem a party change would
give her. Tracey later described herself as "the one dissenter" at the family
meeting. She said she thought that, practically, a party switch would be

better, but on principle, I shouldn't do it. "That was my opinion. . . . But I could see the other side. And I agreed to it." She also recalled:

> Arlen—he so cared about my situation. . . . He really was interested
> in how I would feel, and how [a party switch] would affect me. I
> wasn't telling him all the negativity, but he knew. He felt really bad,
> and he was always apologizing . . . which I really appreciated, and
> really helped, I have to say.

My eldest granddaughter, fifteen-year-old Silvi, encouraged me to run as a Democrat.

My private poll tracked with a public Rasmussen Reports poll the previous week that had me 21 points behind Toomey among Pennsylvania Republicans. After the stimulus vote, my approval rating among the state's Republicans had sunk to 30 percent. The numbers might have been even worse if not for ads I was running about Toomey's actions as a Wall Street trader that had contributed to the ensuing financial mess, an endorsement letter from National Republican Senatorial Committee head John Cornyn, and other efforts. The new poll confirmed what I had heard during my travels across the state and my calls to Charlie Roberts and others. I could not win a Republican primary.

Meanwhile, my standing with Democrats had risen. A March Quinnipiac poll gave me a 71 percent approval rating among Pennsylvania Democrats.[1] Democrats who had long urged me to return to my roots had intensified their efforts. Rendell's voice was second only to Biden's. Some weeks earlier, Biden had convened the White House's Middle Class Task Force for a hearing at the University of Pennsylvania's Irvine Auditorium, and in front of cabinet secretaries, the governor, and a host of mayors and other officials, he urged me to return to my Democratic roots.

"I was a little surprised the vice president said it," fellow Pennsylvania senator Bob Casey later recalled, saying this was the first time he had heard the long-simmering speculation aired publicly.[2]

Rendell, whom the press called "the most prolific fundraiser in the state's political history,"[3] said he'd raise money for me. I said that if I became a Democrat, I wouldn't need him to help me raise money. But I would take it. I wasn't quite foolish enough to stand by that.

For decades, I had been offering principled resistance to the Democrats' party-changing pressures. I had told *The Hill* as recently as March 17, "I am staying a Republican because I think I have an important role, a more important role, to play there. The United States very desperately needs a two-party system. That's the basis of politics in America. I'm afraid we are becoming a one-party system."

A frustrated Rendell had told the press around that time, "We've tried—myself, Sen. Casey, Vice President Biden. We've tried to talk him into it, but he's bound and determined to stay a Republican. He doesn't want to see Republican moderates vanish from the earth."[4]

I was seventy-nine, but still full of vim, vigor, and vitality, and eager to continue advancing medical research, holding the federal judiciary accountable, and pressing other fights. I had raised $7 million for a re-election effort,

Vice President Biden and Sen. Specter discuss the use of stimulus funds while traveling to Philadelphia for the first meeting of the vice president's Middle Class Task Force. While serving together in the Senate, the two commuted together by train between Washington and Philadelphia and Wilmington for nearly thirty years. (WHITE HOUSE)

and I was not going to be driven out of the Senate by Pat Toomey and the Club for Growth. As I had told the *Washington Post* during my first re-election campaign: "I had a rocky road getting here and I'm going to do my damnedest to stay here. This is a fascinating job, challenging, demanding, a great opportunity to serve. Every problem in the world comes to the U.S. government and every problem in the government comes to the U.S. Senate."

I had considered running as an independent. I even made a public statement to that effect, telling *The Hill*, when pressed, that as a last resort I would leave open the possibility of running as an independent, if I could caucus with the Republicans. My attempt to distance myself from the prospect produced a front-page article headlined "Specter Won't Rule Out Run as an Independent." An *Allentown Morning Call* reporter followed up, and I told him, "It is an abstract possibility, but I am not making any plans on it. It is a possibility in the sense that almost anything is a possibility." That drew another page 1 story the next day, which declared, "He's not ruling out the chance that he'll run as an independent."[5]

Shanin got annoyed with me. He counseled me to say, "I'm a Republican and going to stay a Republican." I soon dismissed the idea of running as an independent anyway. There's no party behind you; I just didn't think I could get enough votes. Nobody had ever been elected statewide in Pennsylvania running as an independent. Yes, Lieberman famously won election to his Senate seat running as an independent after losing a Democratic primary, but Connecticut had a weak Republican Party, really no Republican Party. And even that option wasn't open to me. Pennsylvania law, unlike Connecticut law, barred a candidate who lost a primary from running an independent general-election campaign.

We put out a statement April 16: "I am a Republican, I am going to be running on the Republican ticket in the Republican primary." That would come back to haunt me.

I weighed my options, and then analyzed them again. In the end, I relied on my own judgment. I decided to become a Democrat. It was a wrenching decision, just as becoming a Republican had been a wrenching decision in 1965. The difference, though, was that there was never any real philosophical drive behind my becoming a Republican. It made sense to run as a Republican for district attorney, hewing to La Guardia's dictum that there's no Democratic or Republican way to clean the streets. It wasn't a matter of embracing Republican dogma of limited government and lower taxes. That first run for DA seemed a suicide mission. It wasn't the Republican Party that elected me. It was an individual effort, with help from Meehan and Witkin, and with heavy support from Americans for Democratic Action and Democrats for Specter. For years after my DA days, Republican leaders repeatedly supported my primary opponents, until I finally beat one of their anointed candidates in 1980. But even then, I was not elected to the Senate on Ronald Reagan's coattails; we had different constituencies.

And in the Senate, I'd always been issue-oriented. I wouldn't even call it pragmatism. It was a matter of using my own judgment and doing what I thought was right, on a case-by-case basis, on whatever issue came up. That approach had led to a host of Republican apostasies. As Appropriations subcommittee chairman, I took the lead in increasing education funding by 153 percent; tripling NIH funding; advancing stem cell research; and enhancing worker safety through OSHA and the NLRB. I voted to increase Social Security payments and to boost funding for veterans, and Jim Jeffords, Linc Chafee, and I had cast the key votes to knock $250 billion out of George W. Bush's $1.6 trillion tax cut. But I did believe in a constitutional amendment for a balanced budget and a line-item veto.

I had never really felt comfortable in the Republican caucus. I made many friends, but I didn't speak up much at weekly policy lunches and other gatherings, because I knew that what I had to say would not be well received. So I didn't go out of my way to start an argument.

Some may have sensed my discomfort. I went to the White House in April 1996 for a ceremony on the lawn as President Clinton signed the Antiterrorism and Effective Death Penalty Act, which included my provisions on habeas corpus reform. After the photos, I bumped into the president as he was coming downstairs from the first floor. He said, "Arlen, after the election, I want to make it worth your while to become a Democrat."

"There's no way you can make it worth my while to become a Democrat," I said. "It's a nonnegotiable issue." I told Clinton I had once been a Democrat.

He said, "Yeah, I know."

I said, "You only have one sex change."

Still, while I guarded my independence, I remained a loyal Republican, even as the party's centrist bloc shrank. In 2001, I labored to convince Jeffords to stay a Republican, even writing that he should have worked within the party. I proposed a rule, never adopted, to bar senators from making party switches that would shift the balance of Senate power. I followed that approach for another eight years—until it became impossible.

Since the stimulus vote, pundits from across Pennsylvania had been urging me to leave the GOP, to become either a Democrat or an independent. Dick Polman, the *Philadelphia Inquirer*'s national political columnist, wrote a March 2009 piece headlined "Time for Specter to Join a New Party; He'd Be More at Home Ideologically and Safer Politically as a Democrat." Polman began: "I'm talking to you, Arlen Specter. You might want to do yourself a favor by switching teams and joining the Democrats."[6] Dan Simpson, a retired U.S. ambassador turned *Pittsburgh Post-Gazette* associate editor, wrote in a column headlined "Switch Sides, Sen. Specter": "Still, there would be no satisfaction in seeing a great senator, who has served Pennsylvania in a long career, defeated by a lightweight ideologue in the nasty, personal campaign that this one already has become."[7] *Post-Gazette* columnist Sally Kalson wrote in a piece headlined "Abandon Ship, Arlen; Why Does Specter Stay in a Party That's Listing So Far to the Right?":

> Does the senator really feel he still belongs in a group that has purged so many moderates from its ranks, that consider it apostasy to work with majority Democrats in addressing the worst economic train wreck since the Great Depression? . . . If Mr. Specter is holding on to his membership in hopes of bringing his party back to its senses, well, that ship has sailed. It's not too late to jump.[8]

On Sunday, April 26, as I was weighing an imminent party switch, I worked a fund-raiser for the Republican nomination. Mark Aronchick, a prominent Philadelphia lawyer, held a 4:30 p.m. event for me at his Narberth home. I watched my syntax very carefully. I'm always careful, but that evening I chose my words with extreme care, making sure that whatever I said wouldn't be inconsistent with being a Democrat. Listening to me, a guest at that event would never know I was going to change parties, but also wouldn't be surprised later to learn I had.

The next day, Monday, April 27, I went to the annual Teamsters meeting in Washington and had lunch with union president Jimmy Hoffa Jr., who had become a good friend. I exercised the same care. I knew that people at both the Sunday event and the Monday lunch would later get the sense that I had kept something from them. But I thought that, upon reflection, they would understand. I wasn't going to make any casual disclosures on such a weighty subject.

In fact, both Aronchick and Hoffa would later comment about how closemouthed I had been. "The next day I turned on the television," Hoffa would tell me, "and you were a Democrat!" I would tell them I was being consistent with what I had been doing, and not inconsistent with what I was about to do. I was always meticulous about being candid and open, but also hewed to my father's dictum, "Know what you say, don't say what you know."

Their comments reminded me of a story about Siddhartha Gautama, the founder of Buddhism, that a professor told in a 1950 religion course at Penn. Siddhartha Gautama went off to the woods to contemplate, and to go to people's houses to beg for food. In the course of his wanderings as a mendicant, he knocked on his own mother's door. She fed him, and he didn't acknowledge that he was her son. Later, when the townspeople told her that her visitor was her own child, she thought, Oh, what a wonderful man. He could be at our household and maintain his composure and contemplation, not being distracted by earthly things, including his mother. At a more modest level, that's how I felt.

Monday afternoon, Joan and Shanin came to Washington, and we huddled in my office. Joan generally came to D.C. on Wednesdays for a weekly

Reporters pursue Sen. Specter and his wife, Joan, for comments on his reregistration as a Democrat. (GETTY)

dinner and evening together; a Monday visit was unusual. Shanin may have come to my Capitol Hill office five times in thirty years. "When I walked in there," Shanin later recalled, "I knew everybody was looking at me, with the thought in their mind, Oh my goodness, what's going on?" At least one of my aides worried that I had a new health problem.

We broke for a 5:30 p.m. vote. Joan and Shanin watched from the Senate balcony as I sat silently at my desk on the floor, waiting for Reid to vote.

"I knew that was going to be an historic moment," Shanin said later. "I wanted to see it for myself."

After Reid finally voted, I walked over and said, "Harry, I need a minute of your time."

"Okay."

"I'd like to talk in your office."

"Okay."

We went back to his leadership office in the Capitol. Reid had a beautiful chamber with vaulted ceilings, huge windows that overlooked the Mall and the Capitol dome, a nineteenth-century chandelier, and a fireplace mantel carved in green marble. Reid had painted the walls beige, which highlighted the wood trim, and covered the floor with a rich blue-and-red oriental rug. A large oil portrait of Mark Twain sitting with legs crossed in a white vested suit hung above Reid's desk, glaring down at us.

Reid and I had a history, apart from his various overtures over the years to become a Democrat. There was our July 2008 fight on the floor about the "tyrannical" way he ran the Senate. He had written in his book *The Good Fight*, "Arlen Specter of Pennsylvania is always with us when we don't need him."[9] He was saying that he wanted me with him all the time. Sometimes I could be, and sometimes I couldn't be. It was true that I hadn't supported him many times when he came and asked for support. And it was also true that I had voted with him when I felt such a vote was the right thing to do, when he didn't need me. But I wasn't going to structure my votes according to when Reid thought I was needed. I was certainly with him on the stimulus, when he craved my vote. Reid had a flip tongue—smart-alecky, really. He should have appreciated when I was with him instead of griping when I didn't suit his wishes, as though I should have been in his pocket.

I said, "Harry, I've decided to become a Democrat. And I want to know how I'll be received."

"We'll welcome you with open arms."

"Well, to be more specific, Harry, I want the seniority as if I had been elected as a Democrat in 1980."

"Arlen, you got it."

"And what I have in mind, Harry, to specify, is that, if, as and when Leahy becomes chairman of Appropriations—he's behind Inouye, who's in his mid-eighties—I don't know if Inouye were to leave; I can't control that—but if he does, Leahy would take Appropriations, I'd be right behind Leahy in seniority, ahead of everybody else. And I'd be chairman of Judiciary." I wasn't looking to become a party's junior member without any significant committee assignments.

"Arlen, you got it."

That was the same commitment Reid had made to Jeffords in 2001, when Jeffords became an independent and caucused with the Democrats. Jeffords wrote shortly after his party switch: "I had been assured that my seniority would be honored. . . . Harry Reid also had very generously told me that he would be willing to step down as chairman of the Environment and Public Works Committee so that I would retain a chairmanship."[10]

I didn't ask for any concessions from Reid, and he didn't offer any. We didn't discuss any issues. I had nothing in writing. I considered it sufficient to take the majority leader's word. After watching Jeffords vacillate and hold numerous meetings with Democrats who were urging him to go and Republicans who were urging him to stay, I decided I would not take that course or anything remotely like it. I would make a decision, announce it, and not subject the matter to negotiation or vacillation. It was a big decision, and the worst way to handle it would be to appear uncertain or as if I were trying to extract concessions one way or another.

I went around the corner and had my serious discussion with McConnell, resolving that I would sleep on the Republican leader's advice. I then returned to Reid's office. The Democratic leader seemed perturbed. He'd had this fish in his hand, and now the fish might be escaping. Reid had negotiated Jeffords's party switch eight years earlier and had written that at one point, "Daschle and I were worried that his decision would not hold."[11]

I returned to my Hart Building office, where Joan and Shanin had gathered, and called Hoeflich to join us. I told them, "I have three options: I can stay a Republican and lose in the primary to Toomey. I can switch to Democrat and run as a Democrat. Or I can retire." I had already caucused with Joan and Shanin, so I asked my chief of staff, "What do you think I should do?"

Hoeflich asked about my health and fitness, which I assured him were fine. He said, "Whatever you decide, I'm on board." Then he said we had a lot of issues to discuss, primarily seniority.

I said, "I've been assured by Majority Leader Reid that I will retain my seniority as if I were elected as a Democrat in 1980." I closed by telling Hoeflich, "Keep this to yourself. I haven't made any decisions yet; I'm going to go home and think about this. But be ready."

The next morning, Tuesday, April 28, I arrived at the Hart Building shortly after nine and summoned Hoeflich to my private office. "I've thought about it, and we're going to do this," I said. I had already drafted a statement. I asked my chief of staff for a list of phone calls he thought I should make.

"The whole day was a blur," Hoeflich remembered later. "I actually created a separate folder in my Gmail account for 'Two Weeks of Craziness,' I called it. You didn't know what the hell was going on, you couldn't keep track of it." Office phone lines would soon jam.

I began making calls, trying first to reach President George W. Bush, Obama, Rendell, and Biden. Then I headed to the Capitol to tell Reid and McConnell, in turn.

Meanwhile, in the Oval Office, the president was getting his daily economic briefing at 10:25 a.m. when an aide handed him a note that read, "Specter is announcing he is changing parties."[12] Obama's spokesman, Robert Gibbs, would tell the media, "The President is quite pleased. And that is the understatement of the day."[13] At 10:32 a.m., while Hoeflich and I were on the basement tram nearing the Dirksen Building on the way back from the Capitol, my executive assistant, Patricia Haag, got a phone call from the president. She promptly routed the call to Hoeflich's cell.

I dashed off the tram onto the catwalk at the Dirksen Building and talked to Obama. The call dropped off a couple of times, but the message came through. The president told me, "You have my full support. . . . We are thrilled to have you."

In practical terms, once I had made an overture to become a Democrat, it would have been impossible to go back on it. And I wouldn't, in any case, once I had given my word. I thought that I was on solid ground in relying on the majority leader's word, that he spoke for his caucus.

I had scheduled a staff meeting for 11 a.m. to tell the crew. I wanted to spell out the situation and reassure them. The news would be especially tough for my twenty-person Judiciary Committee Republican staff, whose jobs would be in jeopardy. But first I needed to make a few more key calls. I tried Bush again; Senators Casey, Santorum, and Harkin; Karl Rove; Chamber of Commerce president Tom Donohue; and others.

As I worked the phones, Hoeflich checked periodically on the staff, who had packed the big conference room adjacent to my office. "Thanks for your patience," he told them. "I need you to keep being patient."

When I reached Bush, I said, "Mr. President, I want to tell you, so you don't read about it in the newspaper or hear about it on the radio, that I've decided to change parties. There's no future in the Republican Party for me with what has happened."

"Well, listen, I understand, Arlen." Bush was cordial. Essentially, he said he understood my point of view, without indicating that he approved.

I had written him a letter in November 2008, as his term was ending:

Congratulations on your distinguished service as President of the United States.

In my judgment, historians will rank your tenure as an outstanding President. No one can deny that the security of the country since September 11, 2001, under your stewardship has been successful. The seeds of democracy which you have sown in Iraq and Afghanistan may change that entire region and have the potential to spread to other parts of the world.

During the course of the past eight years from our extensive personal contacts, I have come to know, admire and respect you. As I have so often said in describing your presidency, your private persona up close is so much different from your public persona as portrayed by the news media.

In the historical context, I think of how President Truman was criticized and ridiculed. Now, he is regarded as one of America's great Presidents. Similarly, President Ford was chastised for the pardon of President Nixon. Now, that pardon is viewed as one of the great acts of presidential statesmanship.

At sixty-one, it is my speculation that you will yet be called upon for more important public and worldwide community service.

Joan joins me in wishing you, Laura, and your family the very best in the days ahead.

In our conversations, I found Bush to be very much engaged. His popularity and approval have begun to rebound, but for years angry claques demeaned his abilities. When I'd give speeches, I'd frequently be asked about Bush. And I would always defend him. I would feel it relevant to say, "I know in defending President Bush my credibility may be questioned, but that's how I see it. I see some eyebrows raised when I tell you I think he was engaged and competent."

While I believe Bush was a good president, I did not agree with him about Iraq. In October 2002, I had taken the Senate floor to register my very strong concerns with the resolution authorizing the use of force, which I equated with a declaration of war. Despite CIA director George Tenet's now-infamous assurance that Iraq's having weapons of mass destruction was a "slam-dunk," we did not have specifics or proof. And we lacked plans for handling Iraq after we defeated Saddam Hussein. Further, unilateral U.S. action could set a precedent for some other nation to take unilateral action, such as China on Taiwan, or India or Pakistan on each other.

"This is a matter which requires discussion and analysis," I said on the floor. "I do not believe it helps the president of the United States to have the Senate rush to judgment."

I pressed my concerns in statements and exchanges. Lieberman, a leading proponent of the bill, replied, "This resolution is intended to send a message to Saddam: Disarm, as you promised to do eleven years ago at the end of the Gulf War, or we will use force to disarm you with our allies and the international community." In other words, we might get Saddam to back down, if he knew President Bush had the authority to use force against Iraq whenever he chose. I considered that point a strong argument in favor of authorizing force. Ultimately, notwithstanding my serious reservations about the resolution as crafted and the Senate's rushed procedure, I supported the authorization of force against Iraq.

Congress should have been informed about the specifics, rather than having to rely on vague assurances. Several months later, in February 2003, Secretary of State Colin Powell laid out the administration's case to the United Nations, vouching for CIA intelligence in accusing Iraq of harboring weapons of mass destruction. As it turned out, Powell should have been a lot more insistent on finding out the specifics of whatever factual basis the administration had for concluding that Saddam had WMD. Powell would later call his UN presentation a "blot on my record."

Members of Congress are not privy to the nuances of the intelligence available to the president, the secretary of state, or the CIA director. Even when I served as chairman of the Intelligence Committee in the 104th Congress, I could not get to the bottom of many of the representations by the administration on intelligence matters. Had Congress known Saddam Hussein did not have the weapons of mass destruction to justify the invasion, we never would have voted for the resolution. By going to war without adequate evidence, Bush, Powell, and Tenet failed to exercise the requisite due diligence.

News of my party switch had hit cyberspace. In the big conference room, Scott Boos, my legislative assistant for financial issues, got an e-mail from a woman he knew in England, the executive producer of BBC's *Newsnight*, asking for confirmation.

Hoeflich placed a stack of papers on the conference room table, the statement I had prepared. Each staffer grabbed one. The room was silent as they read.

By the time I entered the conference room with Joan and Shanin, closer to 11:30 a.m., the news was out, running on CNN and Fox News and buzzing on BlackBerrys. I outlined my rationale, fully and frankly.

One aide asked, "Why can't you run as an independent?"

"In Pennsylvania, people pull a whole-party lever," I said. "If you're an independent, you're lost."

The Judiciary Committee staffers were understandably distraught, and there were some tears. Nearly all of the twenty would soon get picked up, especially as Senate offices staffed up for Sonia Sotomayor's coming Supreme Court confirmation. I would be able to reclaim one staffer, whom I brought to my personal office as a legal adviser.

At 11:52 a.m., as the staff meeting was breaking, Hoeflich got an e-mail from a reporter flagging him that Republicans had called a noon emergency meeting at McConnell's office over my switch. Across the Capitol, House leaders also scrambled into impromptu meetings to discuss how my switch would affect their priorities.[14] Representative Charlie Pingree, a Maine Democrat, Tweeted, "Everyone distracted by Specter switch today."[15]

When my aides returned to their desks, Boos, then thirty, phoned his mother. "There are moments when you call your mother," he recalled. "When you get into a car accident, when you get married, when you break your leg, when Arlen Specter becomes a Democrat. April 28, 2009, will forever be engraved in my mind as 'Arlen Specter Switch to Be a Democrat Day.'" The day was also Boos's brother's thirty-fifth birthday. But in the bustle, Boos forgot to phone his brother. "I don't think my mother even reminded me."[16]

Bob Casey was a guest at a Senate Commerce Committee hearing on formaldehyde when his BlackBerry began to vibrate incessantly. He had messages saying Rendell and others had phoned his office. Casey stepped out of the hearing. "It was electric," he recalled.

There was electricity in the air—however you want to define that. The reporters were all buzzing about it. There was an excitement, and a sense of momentum we didn't have before. Because now we had a senior member of the United States Senate from the other party joining our caucus. . . . It had that dramatic and crucial feature, which was that it would allow us to get legislation passed—like health care, or other substantial pieces of legislation we couldn't pass otherwise.[17]

My new caucus mates sent out a flurry of news releases welcoming me. As *Roll Call* reported:

> Democrats might be thrilled to have Sen. Arlen Specter join their ranks, but there are a few things they don't know about the Pennsylvanian—like how to spell the guy's name. At least two Democratic Senators and one interest group misspelled Specter's name (they opted for "Spector" . . .) in press releases reacting to word of Specter's party switch.[18]

Word quickly spread through Capitol Hill and beyond. I was besieged by a throng of questioning reporters when I rode the subway and took the escalator on my way to the Senate chamber. Reporters customarily congregate around the chamber, but the crowd that followed me to the weekly Republican caucus luncheon was larger than anything I had ever seen.

I spoke at the Republican lunch at 12:30 p.m. in the LBJ Room. That ten-minute session would be my last meeting with the Republican caucus, after twenty-nine years. By this point, as *The Hill* put it, "the story had exploded on TV and the Internet,"[19] so I wasn't surprising anyone. Hoeflich waited outside the closed door. Reporters gathered "like a pack of angry wolves waiting to tear flesh to the bone," he recalled.

Inside, Thad Cochran, the Appropriations chairman from Mississippi, broke the ice. "Well, at least I won't have to go to Erie anymore." Cochran had campaigned for me in Erie, an industrial city on Lake Erie, which could get severe weather. When I next went to Erie and repeated his remark, they would get upset.

It was a hard speech to make. A lot of articles had said I was not loved, but was respected and admired. The room that day included many good friends. The brew of emotions roiled at that lunch, though everybody was outwardly pleasant.

McConnell asked me in front of the others if I was going to criticize him or the Republican caucus for my decision. He was worried that I might blame him.

Absolutely not, I said.

The session ended with warm handshakes. While I knew many were disappointed, I took the cordiality to mean that they respected my sincerity, what I had done in the Senate, and what I intended to keep doing. Several approached me afterward and told me how they'd been challenged by the Club for Growth.

Outside the room, as I headed toward the elevator, the press swarmed. Packs of cameras had been following me everywhere I walked. Hoeflich and I said only that we were holding a news conference at 2:15 p.m. Reporters persisted, even shouting questions as elevator doors closed between us. "I'll give you an answer at 2:15," I said.

Meanwhile, the tone was different at the Democrats' Tuesday lunch.

"That lunch meeting was pretty intense," Casey later recalled. "'Celebratory' does not adequately describe it. There was a sense of real optimism— we were on our way to getting support for a bill like health care, or several other pieces of legislation. So it was a dramatic moment."[20]

When they heard I had become a Democrat, Lieberman later told me, there was "cheering, throwing food in the air."

Then the subject of my retaining my seniority came up, Lieberman said, "and everyone went, 'What!?'" A senator told Reid that he had heard the majority leader had promised to let me keep my seniority, Lieberman recalled. "Harry said, 'Yes.' Then, it all blew up."[21]

An hour later, the news conference at the Senate Radio-TV Gallery was jammed, cameras lining the riser in the rear, Bigfoot reporters filling the chairs. The networks all covered.

When Shanin, Joan, and I had discussed what I should say about my reasons for the party change, Shanin had advised me to be candid and say I couldn't win as a Republican. I modified that, albeit slightly, by saying I "found that the prospects for winning a Republican primary are bleak."

"Switching parties raises questions in people's minds—why did you do it? I thought and continue to think that the only way to handle it is to tell the whole truth," Shanin recalled later.

Sen. Specter holds a packed news conference in the Capitol on April 29, 2009, to an-
nounce his switch to the Democratic Party. Opponents would seize on elements of his
candid account of his reasoning and views. (AP)

He could have said simply that he was no longer in step with the
Republican Party, more in step with the Democratic Party, and that
would have been true. But that would have left others to say, "You
knew you couldn't win as a Republican, and that's why you switched."
And a denial of that would sound kind of hollow. So I thought it
better not to get involved in that issue.

I told the media, "Since my election in 1980, as part of the Reagan Big
Tent, the Republican Party has moved far to the right. . . . I now find my
political philosophy more in line with Democrats than Republicans." I
noted that the year before, more than 200,000 Pennsylvania Republicans
had reregistered as Democrats.

It has become clear to me that the stimulus vote caused a schism
which makes our differences irreconcilable. On this state of the record, I am unwilling to have my twenty-nine-year Senate record

judged by the Pennsylvania Republican primary electorate. I have not represented the Republican Party. I have represented the people of Pennsylvania.

. . . I deeply regret that I will be disappointing many friends and supporters. I can understand their disappointment. I am also disappointed that so many in the party I have worked for for more than four decades do not want me to be their candidate. It is very painful on both sides.

I made a point to say, "I thank especially Senators McConnell and Cornyn for their forbearance." I said I was running for re-election because I had a significant contribution to make on many key issues, especially medical research. "And my seniority is very important to continue to bring important projects vital to Pennsylvania's economy.

"Upon request," I volunteered, "I will return campaign contributions contributed during this cycle.

"My change in party affiliation does not mean that I will be a party-line voter any more for the Democrats than I have been for the Republicans," I stressed. "Unlike Senator Jeffords's switch, which changed party control, I will not be an automatic sixtieth vote for cloture." The next day, in fact, I would vote against the president's budget. I didn't like a reconciliation provision that would have allowed the health-care plan to sail through with only a majority vote. And in the next big vote, I would help kill a Democratic measure to let bankruptcy judges modify homeowners' mortgage terms.

I concluded, "Whatever my party affiliation, I will continue to be guided by President Kennedy's statement that sometimes party asks too much. When it does, I will continue my independent voting and follow my conscience on what I think is best for Pennsylvania and America."

When reporters asked me how the Republican Party had sunk to its current state, I said, "Because most of the people do not participate in the political process. . . . If the electorate as a whole participated in the political process and in the primary process, Joe Lieberman would win the primary in Connecticut hands down. And I'd do the same thing in Pennsylvania."

I didn't pass up a chance to credit the Club for Growth for the centrist scalps they had collected over the years.

> Remember Linc Chafee? They made him spend all his money in the primary and he lost the general. And had Linc Chafee been elected in 2006, the Republicans would have controlled the Senate in 2007 and '08 and I would have been chairman of the [Judiciary] Committee. . . . And for the people who are Republicans that just sit by and allow them to continue to dominate the party after they beat Chafee, cost us the Republican control of the Senate, and cost us thirty-four federal judges, there ought to be a rebellion. There ought to be an uprising. So thanks for asking the question about what are the Republicans like here.

I stressed my agreement with Reid. "In discussing that issue with Senator Reid, the fair approach, which we both agreed to, was to be where I would be had I been a Democrat coming into the Senate with my election in 1980."

It's hard to figure out what's best to say at the moment, but I came to believe we would have been in a better position had I stated a principled position that I could no longer agree with Republican obstructionism against President Obama. I could have said I was becoming a Democrat to support the administration's position on key issues such as the stimulus and to provide the sixtieth vote to cut off Republican filibusters and pass comprehensive health-care reform.

Shanin was probably right that it was more candid to say that I had changed parties because my re-election prospects as a Republican were bleak. Without that admission, my critics would have been limited to a good argument. With it, they would construct a powerful, perhaps decisive TV ad against me, using my own words.

I was too candid. You can't be too honest, but you can be too candid. I had ignored my father's dictum to know what you say, not say what you know.

Right after the news conference, around 3 p.m., we were in the hide-away when Hoeflich got a call on his cell from a blocked number. It was his day-to-day liaison at the White House. The president and vice president wanted me to come over to the White House for a news conference the next morning.

"I'll be there," I said.

The day I made the party change, for some reason I talked to Ron Perelman, the investor and philanthropist whose properties had included Revlon and Marvel Comics. Perelman was in a car in Los Angeles coming from the airport. He said, "You smart son of a bitch." The unspoken words were *You couldn't win a Republican primary; you figured out a way to survive.*

Within hours, Republican leadership instructed my GOP committee aides that I was no longer in their caucus, and that they could no longer work for me, since they could not expend Republican funds to do work for a Democrat. Over the course of the next two weeks, the only Judiciary work my team could process would be prior prepared materials I had requested. The afternoon of my announcement, one aide was scheduled to lead a meeting with some IT people. "No, I'm not staffing it," she told Hoeflich. "He's no longer a Republican."

Some Republican leaders took a broader view. Elsie Hillman, Pennsylvania's former Republican National Committeewoman, issued a statement:

> . . . Today's announcement is disappointing to some, but should come as a surprise to none. . . . I have seen our party move further to the right, leaving little room for those of us in the middle. . . . While I am saddened that Arlen has left the Republican Party, he does so as 200,000 other Pennsylvania Republicans did last year. I believe that he is the brightest member of the United States Senate and I will continue to support him and will vote for him in next year's general election.

Susan Collins said, "I do think our party needs to make clear that centrists are welcome." Olympia Snowe called my switch a "wakeup call" to the GOP.[22]

Shortly after my announcement, Orrin Hatch said: "Arlen's very torn up about it. He's my friend and he had to face reality. I think he has a better chance of winning in Pennsylvania as a Democrat than as a Republican . . . but I was surprised." Asked whether he respected my decision, Hatch said: "I always respect his decisions. I feel really badly about it. But we're close. I intend to remain close."[23]

Even some conservatives read the tea leaves—in various senses. "My initial reaction on hearing the news was that after generating a bunch of Democratic House seats, the Club for Growth has now produced its first Democratic senator," wrote Ramesh Ponnuru of *National Review Online*.[24]

Ambassador David Girard-diCarlo, who co-chaired President Bush's 2004 campaign in Pennsylvania, told *USA Today* that he shared my frustrations. "The Republican Party should take a hard look at itself. If we can't be a national party, then we have some serious introspection that I think must occur."[25]

Steve Schmidt, who managed John McCain's 2008 presidential campaign, said that my switching "because his party no longer welcomes him is a pitiful commentary on the state of the party, based on the fact that we continue to shrink when we should focus on trying to grow."[26]

Other Republican lights burned less warmly.

Cornyn, the National Republican Senatorial Committee head, issued a statement ninety minutes after I had thanked him and McConnell for their "forbearance": ". . . Senator Specter's decision today represents the height of political self-preservation." Cornyn was a friend, and he might have toned down his remarks. Even so, the NRSC promptly flooded Pennsylvania with phone calls reminding Democratic voters of my support in 2004 from Bush and Cheney.[27]

Shortly after I changed parties, I wanted five minutes on the Senate floor, and John McCain indignantly told me to get it from the leader, meaning Reid.

The *New York Times* captured the Republicans' passions:

"Party switching has all the emotional edges and baggage of divorce," said Mark McKinnon, a longtime Democratic media maestro who fell hard for George W. Bush in 1997 and remained one of his closest aides and confidants into his White House years. "Rejection, betrayal, humiliation, jealousy and anger for the aggrieved party. Jubilation, titillation, pride and power for the successful seducer. Everything but the broken glass." That pretty much summed up the vibe on Capital Hill after Mr. Specter announced his switch on Tuesday.[28]

Jilted Republicans also acted out of self-interest. My departure kept their party in the wilderness, and kept them from regaining their committee chairmanships.

J ust before 3 p.m., Reid held a media availability in the Radio-TV Gallery about my party switch. A reporter asked the majority leader, "[Specter] said he would be coming in as if he were elected, in 1980, a Democrat."

"That's right," Reid said.

"What will you do on the subcommittee that Sen. Harkin now chairs?" a reporter asked, referring to the Appropriations Subcommittee on Labor, Health and Human Services and Education.

"Senator Specter knows that no one will be dumped off of a full committee or a subcommittee, unless it's done on some voluntary basis," Reid replied. "Of course in a year and a half, as we start every Congress, it's a new game. And Senator Specter has seniority, over a number of people, in the committees that he wants to serve on."[29]

Late that afternoon, I phoned Joe Torsella, who had launched a candidacy for the Democratic Senate nomination in February and quickly raised $600,000. I knew Torsella, a Rhodes Scholar who had served as a deputy mayor under Rendell and later as president and CEO of the National Constitution Center in Philadelphia. He called back on Hoeflich's cell. I took the call in a Hart Building hallway in front of Sherrod Brown's office, which little more than a year earlier had been Senator Obama's.

"Joe," I said, "I wanted to let you know that I've decided to switch parties, and I'll be seeking the nomination in the Democratic primary."

Torsella was cordial. But he vowed to stay in the race. "Nothing about today's news regarding Sen. Specter changes that," he told the *Allentown Morning Call*.[30] Rendell had shifted his support to me, and Torsella would drop his bid a couple of weeks later. He would provide significant help, endorsing me publicly, contributing, and giving us insights on Sestak.

I phoned a dozen friends and colleagues the day of the party switch. I'd begin, "I just want to let you know—I don't want you to read about it in the newspaper—that I'm switching parties. I had no choice, the way the Republicans are going." They'd say, "Appreciate the call." And they'd immediately tell their friends.

In retrospect, I should have phoned Sestak. For months, the congressman had been making noises about running for Senate, and he had banked $3.3 million. He made a trip around the state to sound people out, musing to local media that he was in, and then backing off.

A phone call might have had some impact, by offering Sestak a little courtesy. I would have said, "Joe, I understand you may be considering running for the Senate. I just want you to know from me directly that I've become a Democrat and I've changed my party affiliation, hope to be the Democratic nominee, hope to be re-elected. Just want to give you the courtesy of letting you know from me directly."

After an utterly exhausting day, as Joan and I turned out the lights a little after 10 p.m., the phone rang. It was our younger son, Steve, suddenly interested in politics. On a personal level, Steve's reaction was the most unusual. After college at Penn in Philadelphia, he had continued his education and career in faraway places and was in residency in psychiatry at UCLA. He wanted to know all about my switch, at great length in a long conversation. His interest was supplemented by many pointed and sophisticated questions, with his repeated use of the word, "Huge, huge, huge!" From all the reactions, his impressed me the most.

Still, I was astounded, really shocked, by the newspaper coverage the next day. The *New York Times, Washington Post, Los Angeles Times,* and *Wall Street Journal* carried headlines on multiple columns on the top right

Hundreds of newspapers throughout the nation prominently reported Sen. Specter's party switch, running headlines ranging from "Specter Shockwave" (The Hill) to "Specter of Doom for GOP" (New York Post). USA Today *began its front-page piece,* "Pennsylvania Senator Arlen Specter shook the capital's political order . . ."

of their front pages. The Newseum provided my press secretary, Kate Kelly, with copies of front pages of 134 newspapers that carried items on my switch, ranging from Anchorage, Alaska, to Bangor, Maine, to Miami to Honolulu. Overseas accounts included those in the *Australian* and China's Xinhua General News Service, and four columns across page 1 of the *London Financial Times*.

The media played my party switch as a "seismic" "game changer" that would give Democrats a filibuster-proof 60-vote majority, once Franken was seated after the Minnesota courts certified his recount victory over Coleman. Headlines blared "Specter Shockwave" (*The Hill*), "Defection Reshapes Senate" (*The Hill*), "Specter Defection Roils Senate; Move Is Ultimate Transfer of Power" (*Roll Call*), and "Specter's Survival Switch: Death Knell for Moderate Wing of GOP" (*Philadelphia Daily News*). The *New York Post* ran a piece headlined "Specter of Doom for GOP" that began: "Sen. Arlen Specter threw Congress into chaos yesterday with the blockbuster announcement of his defection from the Republican Party, potentially giving Democrats the ability to quash any effort to block their agenda in the upper house."[31] *USA Today* began its front-page piece, "Pennsylvania Senator Arlen Specter shook the capital's political order . . ."[32]

At the White House event on April 29, which also marked Obama's first hundred days in office, Joe Biden introduced me:

> Arlen Specter has been my friend and my confidant and my partner, and I his partner, in scores and scores of major, major pieces of legislation and issues for a long time. And beyond that, Mr. President, he's been there for me every time things have been tough for me, and I hope I have been there for him.

When my turn came, I turned to Obama and said, "I think I can be of assistance to you, Mr. President."

Obama said, "Let me start off by saying I'm thrilled to have Arlen in the Democratic caucus. I have told him that he will have my full support in the Democratic primary. Joe Biden has said the same thing."[33] He added, "We are confident that Arlen Specter is going to get a sixth term." The president then detoured into efforts to combat "the ongoing challenge posed by the H1N1 flu virus," better known as swine flu.

Soon afterward, at his daily briefing, White House spokesman Gibbs repeated the president's pledge of "full support." A reporter asked about the possibility of my facing a Democratic primary. "Full support means full support," Gibbs replied.[34]

My phone calls were piling up faster than I could take or return them. Many left a simple message: "Welcome!"

Joe and Valerie Plame Wilson, the ambassador and his exposed-spy wife, now international celebrities, each sent warm notes. "Like Valerie I would be honored to do what I can for your reelection, campaign, stay away, praise you or condemn you," Joe Wilson wrote. "Whatever helps."

The Wilsons had burst onto the international stage in 2003, when syndicated columnist Robert Novak revealed that Plame was a covert CIA officer, based on information apparently leaked in retribution for Joe Wilson's criticisms that the United States had manipulated intelligence to justify invading Iraq. Vice President Cheney's chief of staff, Lewis "Scooter" Libby, was ultimately convicted of obstructing justice and perjury, though not for actually revealing Plame's identity. Plame wrote a best-selling book, *Fair Game*, which was adapted into a 2010 film in which Naomi Watts played Valerie and Sean Penn played Joe.

I first met Joe Wilson in 1990, when he was chargé in Baghdad and I arrived to meet with then–Iraqi dictator Saddam Hussein. I later met the Wilsons at a cancer fund-raiser, and we struck up a conversation. Valerie had Pennsylvania roots, graduating from high school in Huntington Valley and then from Penn State. When the Wilsons e-mailed about my party change, Valerie had been asked to serve as grand marshal at Penn State's homecoming that October. "I will bring Joe and the children with me for the weekend," she wrote. "Is there any way that you and Mrs. Specter

At 7:30 a.m. on the day following Sen. Specter's reregistration, President Obama and Vice President Biden welcome him to the Democratic Party. (GETTY)

could join us?" I wanted to go for political reasons. Centre County, where Penn State was based, was tough. But foul weather would prevent the trip.

Others were less enthusiastic. Bob Dole e-mailed me: "Arlen, We are taking down your sign in Russell and putting up pictures of Pat Toomey and [perennial conservative candidate] Peg Luksik. Then I plan to move to Pennsylvania and run for the Senate as a Republican."

Eighteen months later, Dole I would talk for nearly an hour at Walter Reed Army Medical Center in Washington, about the party and a range of issues. At that meeting, Dole told me I had done the right thing, that I had done a terrific job as a senator, been involved in a lot of projects, been very active, and hadn't gotten credit for a lot of the stuff that I had done. He said that I faced a dead end with what was happening in the Republican Party.

I said, "Bob, I think it's very meaningful when you say that I did the right thing, in the party change."

He said, "Well," and then paused and thought for a few seconds. Then he said, "I probably would have done the same thing."[35]

In my meeting with David Durenberger around the same time, my former colleague made similar comments. "I'm still a Republican," Durenberger said. "I'm a Minnesota Republican, and I come out of a tradition that is a progressive tradition. Period . . . I don't know what would have happened to me had I stayed here as long as [you] did. But it's easier if you are a retired member and the party moves away from you to say, 'I'm still a Republican,' than if you're sitting here with ninety-nine other people.

"You've got to decide: How long can you take the crap that guys like Arlen and Jim Jeffords and these other people take?"

I asked, "So you think you might have become a Democrat?"

"It's— I don't know," Durenberger replied. "I've never had to really think seriously about it."[36]

After returning from the White House event, I met again with Reid in his leadership office. Our chiefs of staff, Gary Myrick and Scott Hoeflich, joined the twenty-minute session. We sat in four chairs in the room's four corners. Mark Twain again glowered at us from the wall. Twain had famously advised, "If you tell the truth, you don't have to remember anything" and "It ain't what you don't know that gets you into trouble. It's what you know for sure that just ain't so."

Reid opened by saying, "Arlen, I'm here to do everything I can possibly do for you."

We began with rumors about Sestak and other House members running for my Senate seat. Reid said he had spoken to the Democratic Senatorial Campaign Committee and his understanding was that the field was clear, and that they would help us keep it clear, because they had

welcomed me to the Democratic caucus. There was still the possibility of
Sestak's running, but no one knew.

We discussed the logistics of seniority, as to committee assignments
and funding. Reid said, "Arlen, you will retain your seniority as if you
were elected in 1980—with the exception of committees. We cannot go
back to reorganizing the committees with regards to chairmanships and
ranking members."

Members of each committee elect their chairmen and ranking members. Reid was saying he wouldn't hold another election midway through
the 111th Congress, and that I would not become a chairman or ranking
member until the 112th Congress, beginning in January 2011. Then I
would chair Judiciary, or whatever available committee seemed most appealing as senators shifted assignments. Meantime, would I sit beside the
chairmen, as a chairman-in-waiting? We hadn't nailed that down.

Reid suggested that there might be a subcommittee chairmanship
coming my way shortly.

We next asked about money. Republicans had rescinded my funds. It
was nearly May, and committee budgets had already been doled out. Chairmen customarily give committee members part of their budgets. Those funds
can allow a member to hire some of the biggest brains in public policy as
aides, as I had done on Judiciary before I became chairman, and as I had
helped Hatch do after succeeding him as chairman.

"Good point," Reid said. The meeting ended with an understanding
that Myrick would work with Chuck Schumer's staff to get some funds
released to us on the various committees. Schumer chaired the Rules Committee, which could tap an emergency pot of money reserved for the inevitable special event that required additional staff, such as a Supreme
Court confirmation.

Meanwhile, we were getting an early inkling of rumblings among
Senate Democrats over Reid's promise to treat my seniority as though I
had been elected as a Democrat in 1980. Kate Kelly got an e-mail from
The Hill reporter Alexander Bolton just after 12:30 on April 29, under the
subject "Dem pushback on Specter deal":

. . . Just want to let you know there's some resistance developing in the Democratic caucus to Specter's deal with Reid.

I've just spoken to a few senior Democratic Senators who are not happy at all that Sen. Reid has agreed to let Sen. Specter to [*sic*] import his seniority to the Democratic caucus . . . .

The Democratic lawmaker told me "That's his deal and not the caucus's," of Reid's agreement with Specter. Furthermore, the law-maker said Democrats did Specter a favor by giving him a chance to remain a U.S. Senator. He was a "cooked goose," said the lawmaker. "He was going to lose to Toomey and we were going to beat Toomey."

Does your office have any comment?

I gave Kelly a comment for Bolton: "I feel comfortable relying on the arrangements I made with Senator Reid. I've talked to many Democratic senators in the past couple of days and they have all greeted me with open arms."

A few hours later, I summoned my senior staff to my hideaway.

"He wanted to give us a pep talk," my finance issues aide Boos recalled. "Everything was going to be okay; he was going to keep his seniority."[37] Hoeflich called the meeting a "gut check." Both were right.

When we broke up, I headed to speak to Pennsylvania postmasters at the Phoenix Park Hotel, and Boos walked me out. I said, "I don't under-stand why all the long faces."

"Never in my right mind, would I work for a Democrat out of the blue," Boos told me. "You need to give people space and time to digest this. When people seem frustrated or have long faces, they're processing this."

That was the most direct my financial policy aide had ever been with me, and I heard him out. I told Boos I didn't understand how anyone could keep working with extremists who had taken over the Republican Party, and that I had no choice.

"He was under attack, and I saw him explain himself more than I'd ever seen him explain himself," Boos recalled. "Even to staff. Arlen Spec-ter explaining himself to staff."[38]

My aides stayed loyal. Only two left, and reluctantly, because they had strong Republican ties. One would send me a nice Christmas card.

Later that day, April 29, I gave a rush interview in a hallway to Deborah Solomon of the *New York Times* for a Sunday magazine profile. I was asked to pose for a photo that would show me standing against a blank background. I declined; I thought it was a phony deal. So they used another photo of me, an unflattering one. That was my first mistake.

Solomon asked, "Are you surprised by the titanic public reaction to your announcement? How does it feel to know that you've overshadowed swine flu?"

"I'm startled by being on the front page of every newspaper I've seen and several columns of the top right on the *New York Times*," I said. "It's a new experience. I doubt if I'll ever have it again." That prediction would soon prove wrong.

Solomon asked, "With your departure from the Republican Party, there are no more Jewish Republicans in the Senate. Do you care about that?"

"I sure do," I said. "There's still time for the Minnesota courts to do justice and declare Norm Coleman the winner." Franken and Coleman were still locked in a recount battle. Without realizing it, I intuitively said "Coleman"; he was my friend, and it just slipped out.

The next day Bolton's story came out in *The Hill*, headlined "Top Dems Rebel on Specter":

Senior Senate Democrats are objecting to the deal Majority Leader Harry Reid made with Sen. Arlen Specter, saying they will vote against letting the former Republican shoot to the top of powerful committees after he switches parties. Several Democrats are furious with Sen. Reid (D-Nev.) for agreeing to let Specter (Pa.) keep his seniority, accrued over more than 28 years as a GOP senator. That agreement would allow Specter to leap past senior Democrats on powerful panels—including the Appropriations and Judiciary committees. . . . Under his deal with Reid, Specter would jump ahead of all but a few Democrats when it comes time to dole out committee chairmanships and assignments. "That's his deal and not the caucus's," the senior lawmaker said of Reid's agreement with Specter. . . . Harkin buttonholed [Appropriations chairman] Inouye on the Senate floor Tuesday evening, giving Inouye an earful of his concerns, according to a senator who overheard the conversation.

Bolton closed his story with the quote I had sent him, saying I trusted Reid to keep his word, adding: "Specter, however, is confident that his deal will hold."[39]

At a May 1 media availability at Philadelphia's Thirtieth Street Station, I said, "My change in party will enable me to be re-elected and I have heard that again and again and again on the street: 'Senator, we're glad you'll be able to stay in the Senate and help the state and the nation.'"

And there was enthusiasm on the street—literally. We got reports that at the thirtieth annual Blue Cross Broad Street Run in Philadelphia on May 3, runners forfeited precious time to dash up to Rendell in the middle of the ten-mile race, shake the governor's hand, and thank him for getting Arlen Specter to switch parties.

I got admiring glances and an enormous number of compliments. Joan and I went to dinner in Philadelphia's Rittenhouse Square the weekend after I switched, on an idyllic spring night on which restaurants' sidewalk tables bustled. I wound up shaking so many hands amid a cheering throng that I lost my bearings and headed briefly to the wrong eatery. In Washington, I went to dinner at Charlie Palmer's on Capitol Hill, and it took me five minutes to reach the table where my guests were waiting, because a stream of diners left their tables to come over and shake my hand.

My party change did not please all my constituents. When I went to a big industrial plant in northeast Philadelphia, an older employee told me that I was elected as a Republican and should have stayed a Republican. In effect, he was saying that I had breached my trust or duty to the GOP.

I thought of other senators who had changed parties, with few if any major repercussions. Richard Shelby, elected as a Democrat in 1986, became a Republican in 1994, a day after the GOP took control of the

Senate, changing political philosophy without so much as a sound. Shelby told me he got very few complaints. Ben Nighthorse Campbell of Colorado, elected as a Democrat in 1992, became a Republican in 1995, again with few waves. The senator who arguably made the most ethical party switch was Phil Gramm of Texas, who as a Democratic House member resigned his seat in 1983 and won re-election as a Republican the next year. Gramm was one of four Democrats who became Republicans during Reagan's presidency. All kept their seniority and committee assignments.[40]

Solomon's *New York Times* profile came out, quoting my hopes for a Coleman victory. *Politico* wrote that I was "urging the Minnesota Supreme Court to overturn the results of the recount and lower-court ruling declaring Al Franken the victor."[41]

Reid found me on the Senate floor and asked, "Arlen, what's going on here?"

I said I had forgotten which team I was on. I corrected the record with the press, saying I had misspoken. "In the swirl of moving from one caucus to another, I have to get used to my new teammates."

The Coleman remark caused an uproar in the Democratic caucus. Reid told me holy hell was raised. I misspoke out of long-standing habit, not deliberately. It's hard to be a Republican for so long and not have a slip of the tongue. It really was no big deal, but it gave a toehold to Democrats *The Hill* had described as "furious" over my deal with Reid.

Over the coming months, I would make the Democrat-Republican gaffe a number of times. At an Allegheny County Democratic dinner, I would twice cite the Allegheny County Republican Committee, which didn't go over well. The same when the Penn State College Democrats endorsed me.

After twenty-nine years as a Republican, I was lucky I didn't do it more often. Joan wanted me to abbreviate my speeches, so I wouldn't screw up. She wanted me not to take any questions one evening; she thought I'd make the mistake again. When I concentrated, I didn't make the mistake.

Hoeflich also caught flack over the Coleman remark, first from Reid's chief of staff Myrick and then from Franken's top aide, Drew Littman.

"I was in my first Democrats chiefs-of-staff meeting," Hoeflich recalled, "and I'm introducing myself to everybody, and it's nerve-racking as
it is, to be welcomed into this group, and I said, 'Hey, Drew, I'm Scott
Hoeflich, Specter's chief, I just want to apologize for the comment. We're
all on the Democratic team.' He says, 'Yeah, it was a pretty big fuckup.'"[42]

Howard Baker wrote a book called *No Margin for Error*—well, that's
my profession.

Significant public opinion crystallized around a view that I was being
opportunistic in switching parties. David Broder, the syndicated
Washington Post columnist and dean of political pundits, wrote a piece
headlined "Specter the Defector." The *Wall Street Journal* editorialized
that I was "America's champion of political opportunism."[43]

Hoeflich asked a senior Washington correspondent for a frank assessment of the media's view on my switch. "I think it's split," the newsman
reported. "There's some who see it as purely an exercise in self-preservation,
those who see it as an indictment of the GOP's drift into regionalism, and
those who see it as both. I'd say most probably fall into the 'both' category." He added in a separate note, "You know you're doing something
right when bitter, out-of-touch David Broder shits in your hat."

Back in the 1980s, Richard Fenno had captured the crux of the "opportunism" charge:

> First as a prosecutor, later as a candidate, and finally as a senator, he
> had cultivated a reputation as someone who "calls 'em as he sees
> 'em," who makes up his own mind and charges ahead. Of course,
> one person's independence is another person's inconsistency. And
> one person's judgment call is another person's opportunism.[44]

Matt Bai, in a *New York Times* think piece about an anti-incumbent
tsunami roaring toward Washington, would postulate that my statement
went through the prism of "a sense that Washington acts from expedience
and little else." So, he explained,

while Mr. Specter may have thought he was being transparent by announcing to the world that he was switching parties in hopes of continuing to pursue his life's work, what a lot of voters probably heard is that his beliefs were fungible in the service of his own ambition—a vulnerability that Mr. Sestak exploited with one of the most eviscerating advertisements in recent history.[45]

Yes, I was candid about wanting to keep my job. "There are people who would give their right arm or spend their fortunes to be in the Senate," I told the *New York Times*. "I don't deny that there is an aspect of self-interest involved. But there's more to it than that."[46]

As I told Michael Smerconish the day after my switch, I had twenty-nine years on the line, and I didn't want to have it judged by that stacked jury, in the Republican primary. "Is it personal? Sure. But is it public-spirited public policy? You bet."

Some months later, a friend handed me a photocopy of a passage from *The Lords of Finance*, an acclaimed history of twentieth-century international bankers. The pages described the ire and distrust swirling around a party-switching official.

Within political circles, he was almost universally distrusted as a man who had changed parties not just once, but twice . . . one minister complaining that he could not understand "how anybody can put their faith in a man who changes sides, just when he thinks it is to his own personal advantage to do so."[47]

The party switcher went on to win even higher office. His name was Winston Churchill.

I reached out to Pennsylvania Democratic leaders. I called up the chairmen of the four suburban Philadelphia counties and invited them to dinner at the Capital Grille, near city hall, on a Saturday night. All of them came. They were cordial and supportive. They all had agendas, and they knew they had a senator with access to the White House and seniority to secure appointments and federal grants.

Montgomery County Democratic chairman Marcel Groen told me, "I've admired you for a long time." He noted that he was a law partner at a prominent Philadelphia firm with two good friends of mine. "They think the world of you, and, of course, I was always on the other side," he said. "I'm glad you're a Democrat, look forward to working with you, helping you to be re-elected. But you've got to realize that Democrats, including me, have been working for thirty years to beat your brains out. Personally, I'm delighted to be with you, but now I have to go back to the troops, do a U-turn, and urge them to work for the guy we've fought for decades."

A few weeks later, at a breakfast for Democratic leaders in Montgomery County, one diner asked me, "Why should we back you when any Democrat can win?" At that point, the political picture looked very bright for Obama and the Democrats.

I said that my candidacy would be the strongest, and that nothing is ever sure in any election. I noted my support for Democratic principles, especially the stimulus vote, and my adding a sixtieth Democratic vote to overcome Republican filibusters.

At the breakfast, Joe Hoeffel, whom I had beaten by 11 points in the 2004 general election, pitched for Sestak. Hoeffel, a liberal organization Democrat, spoke about Democratic principles. He incarnated Groen's point about my seeking support from people who'd been trying to beat in my brains for thirty years.

My party switch went no smoother physically. The secretary of the Senate notified us that they couldn't unbolt my desk and move it across the aisle until their office got certification from the Pennsylvania Board of Elections that I had registered as a Democrat.

Meanwhile, we rewrote our campaign plan.

"I did a triage plan, because we had an entire campaign organization up and running," Hoeflich recalled. "And it totally got wiped out, like a

tsunami would take out a house on stilts. We had to basically rebuild everything. And we were so far advanced, had a whole fund-raising operation
moving forward in 2007. And we were adding components as we went.
And now we needed to build a political and fund-raising operation immediately."

On Wednesday, May 5, I attended my first Democratic caucus lunch,
heading to the Mansfield Room instead of the LBJ Room. My new caucus mates gave me a warm welcome. Reid seated me at the leadership table, usually reserved for the majority leader, Durbin, Schumer, and Patty
Murray. I spoke about my party switch, and my approach of making independent judgments.

The Hill reported that three senators contradicted Reid's characteriza-
tion that I had received a standing ovation, insisting I had drawn only
"warm" or "strong" applause, and "a fourth senator, a senior member of
the conference, said that many of his colleagues continue to question
whether Specter's arrival is a good deal. The lawmaker argued that Specter's switch has done little to alter the structure of the Senate."[48]

That night, I hosted a dinner for several of my top aides at my Georgetown condo. Just after 9 p.m., as we lounged in the living room, preparing
to dive into platters of cold cuts, crab meat, salad, and smoked salmon,
Hoeflich got an e-mail from Kelly, my press secretary, with a *Roll Call*
story headlined "Specter will Be Junior Democrat on Committees."

Despite promises from Senate Majority Leader Harry Reid (D-Nev.)
that Sen. Arlen Specter would retain his seniority after switching
parties, Specter will be put at the end of the seniority line on all his
committees but one under a resolution expected to be passed on the
floor late Tuesday.

A Democratic aide acknowledged Tuesday that under the modified organizing resolution, Specter would not keep his committee
seniority on any of the five committees that he serves on and would
be the junior Democrat on all but one—the chamber's Special Committee on Aging. On that committee, he will be next to last in seniority.[49]

By the time the *Roll Call* story reached us, Reid had in fact already introduced the resolution during wrap-up, shortly before the Senate adjourned an hour earlier. Not even a customary "Hotline" e-mail had alerted Senate offices that the majority leader was going to introduce a resolution. But beyond neglecting the Hotline, Reid violated a fundamental Senate practice to give personal notice to a senator directly affected by the substance of a unanimous consent agreement. Had I had notice, I would have come to the floor and objected, which would have prevented its passage. Where a consent agreement calling for elimination of my twenty-eight years of seniority was involved, it was unfathomable not to be personally notified. Instead, Reid stood at his dais on the near-empty Senate floor and said, matter-of-factly, "I ask that the Senate move to consideration of Senate Resolution 130, which is at the desk."

Udall of Colorado, stuck with evening duty, ordered, "The clerk will report."

A clerk intoned, "S. Res. 130, to constitute the majority party's membership on certain committees for the 111th Congress, or until their successors are chosen."

Reid quickly said, "Mr. President, I ask unanimous consent that the Senate now proceed to consideration of S. Res. 131," which was a Republican companion, presumably listing revised Republican committee rosters with my name removed now that I had left the GOP caucus.

Udall promptly said, "Without objection, so ordered." Nobody was on the floor *to* object. "Without objection, the two resolutions are adopted en bloc."

And it was done. That was the first and only official Senate action on my party switch.

Reid had said nothing to me in our talks that afternoon. Nothing had been said to suggest his commitment on my seniority would not be honored. Reid had explicitly told me that I would retain my seniority "as if elected, in 1980, as a Democrat." That was amplified in our discussion, that I would retain my seniority on the Judiciary Committee so that I would take over as chairman if Leahy moved to Appropriations. I had explicitly asked for those terms and Reid had assured me on both counts.

Although Hoeflich told me about the *Roll Call* story in the midst of our noisy condo and Shanin and I had a brief telephone conversation, the impact did not fully register until I opened the *Washington Post* at 6:30 the next morning. I was in a car approaching the Russell Building, which houses the Senate gym. In the swirl of events following my party change, I tried to maintain my exercise routine to keep my head clear. Chemotherapy had caused problems on my balance, so I was alternating exercise in the Senate gym every other day with squash. As we drove past the security post, I read a version of the story, which began, "The Senate last night stripped Sen. Arlen Specter (Pa.) of his seniority on committees. . . ." In an understatement, the *Post* noted, "The loss of seniority could prove costly to Specter in his campaign to win reelection in 2010, denying him the ability to distinguish himself from a newcomer in his ability to claim key positions."[50]

I was stunned. In heavy competition, it was the worst moment of my life. I had taken some heavy blows in the past: losing the Philadelphia mayor's race in 1967 by 1 percent; losing my bid for a third term as district attorney in 1973, just ten days after the Saturday Night Massacre. But nothing like this.

I had worked twenty-eight and a half grueling years to build up the seniority that they had stolen in an after-hours ploy. They had broken a specific, unmistakable commitment from Reid, and taken away what most everyone recognized as my status. My immediate thought was to pack it in, to abandon my campaign for re-election and just serve out my term.

Joan was just as shocked when I called her to tell her what had happened, but she was fighting mad. A stirring lecture followed. "Don't you even consider that! You are bigger than all of that. You are Arlen Specter. You are Arlen Specter. You are a giant in the Senate. You have done so many things. You are bigger than all of them." She just kept repeating, "You are Arlen Specter. You are Arlen Specter. Don't forget that!" In retrospect, at that moment, I had.

"I just thought he shouldn't give up," Joan recalled later. "He loved the Senate—it was his life . . . and he should do everything possible to stay in the Senate."

Then I thought about an interview I had in October 1980 with Professor Dick Fenno, who taught political science at the University of Rochester. Fenno and I were riding along Interstate 80 in northwestern Pennsylvania shortly before Election Day. He pressed me as to how I had the perseverance to run for the United States Senate after suffering defeats in four of my last five elections. In addition to losing for mayor in 1967 and district attorney in 1973, I had lost the 1976 Senate primary to John Heinz and the 1978 governor's primary to Dick Thornburgh. My response was: "I don't discourage easily; in fact, I don't discourage at all." That conversation came forcefully to mind after Joan's lecture. I also thought about my determination in my fight against Hodgkin's and the advice I had given others in my book *Never Give In*.

I phoned Reid. The majority leader told me that his chief of staff, Gary Myrick, had alerted my chief of staff, Scott Hoeflich, about the seniority-stripping resolution, which wasn't true. Reid's spokesman would go even further, and in his falsification tell the Associated Press that I had not only known about the resolution, but had joined in a deal to draft it. The AP filed a report that day stating, "The resolution was passed after an agreement was reached between leadership in both parties and Specter, said Jim Manley, a spokesman for Senate Majority Leader Harry Reid."[51] I had never known about the resolution to break me to the Senate's most junior member, and had certainly not helped craft its terms.

Near 8:30 a.m., I phoned Hoeflich. "Tell me the story again—did you know about this?"

"Absolutely not," Hoeflich insisted. "I did not know any of this was happening. No way in hell."

I called Reid again. He ducked me.

Hoeflich soon phoned Myrick and said, "Let me just get something straight—you and I never discussed this resolution; I had no idea this was going through; I had no idea this was [in process] to do this. And you're telling your boss to tell my boss that I knew."

"No, you're right," Myrick told Hoeflich. "I didn't tell you. It's my fault."[52]

I put out a statement that day: "Senator Reid assured me that I would keep my committee assignments and that I would have the same seniority as if I had been elected as a Democrat in 1980. It was understood that the issue of subcommittee chairmanships would not be decided until after the 2010 election. . . . I am confident my seniority will be maintained under the arrangement I worked out with Senator Reid. . . ."

I was faced with awful alternatives. If I chose to fight for my seniority in the Democratic caucus, the chances of winning were slim. That would elevate the issue and make my loss more of a campaign problem. I could follow Reid's line, that I could regain my seniority after the midterm election; but even I didn't believe that. I decided to work quietly within the caucus, be a team player, provide the sixtieth vote to stop Republican filibusters, and rely on the goodwill and fairness of Democratic senators with whom I had worked in crossing the aisle for more than twenty-eight years.

Meanwhile, some of my former Republican colleagues seemed amused. The *White House Bulletin* posted a story headlined "GOP Gleeful with Specter's Demotion."

> "This is the talk on our side," said an adviser to GOP leadership. "He must be steamed with Reid. Nice," added the adviser. Other Republican aides said that demotion would rob Specter of senior staff on his committees. "This really jams his committee staff too," said a Republican consultant.[53]

That afternoon, Reid appeared on CNN's *Situation Room with Wolf Blitzer* to hawk his book *The Good Fight*, which was out in paperback with an addendum on the 2008 elections. Before getting to the book, Blitzer wanted to discuss my situation.

> **BLITZER:** . . . There's I guess some sort of misunderstanding between you and him over whether or not you promised him that he would be able to retain his seniority on these committees. . . .

REID: . . . He has his seniority. He's now seated on the Senate floor between Senators Leahy and Dodd, which is fairly significant. Senator Specter and his chief of staff always were told that we couldn't interrupt any of the subcommittee chairs or the chairs until the next Congress. And his seniority will be determined next Congress.

BLITZER: So going between now and the next election in 2010, and the new Congress in 2011, he's going to be the most junior member of the Senate Judiciary Committee? He'll ask the next Supreme Court nominees questions last in line?

REID: Well, I think that we kind of exaggerate where people sit. Arlen is a senior member of the Senate, and that's significant. I think, also, we can try to work something out with individual chairmen. And I'm certainly doing that. . . . The seniority in the— I'm sorry, in the Senate is determined every new year with the caucus. Now, we did pass a resolution. That I did so I could put him on the Environment Committee. . . . So he's on all the committees that he said he wanted to be on. . . . He is a person that's been in the Senate since 1980. I think he should be able to handle himself.

BLITZER: Because even as recently as today, he's told our people up here on the Hill that he thought he had an understanding with you that was different than what has now emerged . . . but this was basically your decision, Harry Reid. You're the majority leader. You could have done something else, but this is the way you wanted it as far as Arlen Specter is concerned?

REID: Yes, I think that's a fair statement.

BLITZER: Okay. So it's not just the whole caucus, all the Democrats getting together and thinking about it? It's you.[54]

Reid knew he was misstating the facts when he said he had told me I would lose my seniority. You can say, well, I should have known that it was a caucus decision, but I thought that Reid's representation could be relied upon. And I wasn't in a position to negotiate the arrangement in public.

I tried to enlist some friends. Inouye wouldn't get involved in any dispute over seniority. Neither would Leahy. I found you couldn't touch seniority. It's the Senate's third rail.

I threw my shoulders back, held my head high, and walked that gauntlet, because walking through the center aisle on the Senate floor was a gauntlet. Maintaining poise and dignity was the toughest thing I've ever done. Joan's words—"You are Arlen Specter. You are Arlen Specter"—kept me going. And Mort Witkin's dictum, Never let your face show how hard your ass has been kicked.

A five-term senator nearing eighty, I now found myself senior only to Al Franken, who had just been awarded the Minnesota seat. I entered an Appropriations Committee hearing while Secretary of State Hillary Clinton was testifying. I instinctively took a seat closest to the door, which happened to be at the end of the table, where the seniority line ended. I didn't really focus on the significance of the spot, which seems absurd in retrospect. But I read about it in newspapers the next day. I was particularly anxious to move up on Appropriations, on which I'd sat since joining the Senate in 1981, because if Republicans gained seats in the 2010 election I could be bumped off the committee.

On the Judiciary Committee, my seat was near the end, with only Franken a notch down. Franken had arrived with national renown as a comedian. He had written and starred on NBC's *Saturday Night Live*, creating the indelible self-affirming Stuart Smalley. He later wrote bestselling books of political commentary. I first met Franken when he interviewed me for Comedy Central at the 1996 Republican convention. He introduced me as "the first Jew to come closest to being elected President."[55] Franken was jovial by nature and a rabid kibitzer. A fair number of his expressions were Jewish.

When I sat next to Franken, he told me, "It really just isn't right, considering what you've done in the Senate, especially in Judiciary Committee, being chairman and questioning all the Supreme Court nominees—and now you're sitting next to me—a *pischer*." The Yiddish term *pischer*, which I recalled from years gone by, characterized a youngster who figuratively wet his pants.

It was ignominious, to say the least. Tough to sit in the last Democratic chair in the Judiciary Committee, which I had chaired just a few years before. Tough to sit in the last Democratic chair in the Appropriations Committee, where a few years before I had been next to chairman Thad Cochran, next in line for that position.

Then the Sotomayor Supreme Court confirmation hearings came up. I asked Herb Kohl to let me sit next to Leahy, just for the hearings. Kohl was a fine and intelligent guy and had always been a good friend. After he was elected in 1988, the first thing he told me was that he had contributed to my '86 campaign. I think Kohl was shocked. He said, "I'll think about it." Then he phoned me at home. He felt I was asking him to give up his seniority, which I really wasn't. It was just for that one event. But he said he wasn't going to give up any seniority.

It was hard to consider it anything but humiliating to sit near the end of the line for Sotomayor's hearing, especially after chairing the previous two Supreme Court hearings, on Roberts and Alito. I stayed away from the morning sessions. I went in the afternoon and sat at the end of the line, behind Ted Kaufman, who had recently been appointed to replace now–vice president Biden, and the *pischer*.

A newspaper reporter asked me, "Well, what's it like being in this Judiciary hearing when you used to be chairman, and then you were ranking, and now you're way down the line?"

I made the best I could of it spontaneously, saying it's not a matter of where you sit, it's a matter of what you say, and that I had been influential on Bork and Thomas when I was junior.

A brouhaha arose at the hearing about Sotomayor's boast that a "wise Latina woman" might have advantages on the bench over a white man. The statement had prompted charges of racism from Rush Limbaugh and Newt Gingrich and sparked a national furor. My committee colleagues were punching all over the place. When it came to me, I said,

The criticisms made of her on the "wise Latina woman," I thought, were not only ill-founded, but I appreciated the comment. When you consider that women were not given the right to vote until 1920, and when you consider . . . that there is still a tremendous glass ceiling . . . I could go on and on and on about the appropriateness of a woman standing up for women. . . . And when she refers to being a Latina, that's a little ethnic pride. . . . I didn't find fault with the "wise Latina woman." I thought it was commendable.

That wasn't exactly a stroke of brilliance. It was just a stroke of being awake.

Even apart from the seniority issue, I never felt comfortable in the Democratic caucus or at their Tuesday lunches. My Democratic colleagues were all cordial and many appeared to go out of their way to make me feel welcome. I had known most of them for years, some for decades, and had worked with them on important substantive matters, often on the same side. But I felt like a man without a country, or more precisely, without a party.

Entering the Senate chamber, the most direct route from the elevators was down the aisle on the Republican side. I had always felt most comfortable walking down the center aisle to the well where we cast votes. It wasn't quite like crossing the street to avoid somebody you don't want to say hello to, but it had some uncomfortable similarities.

For the most part, Republican senators were also congenial. DeMint aside, they never showed hostility or resentment over the party switch. Many mornings, I bumped into Cornyn at the gym as the Texan ground through a tough workout, and Alexander, who would put some time on an exercise bike and move on. John Thune, who looked like a movie star in or out of clothes, was constantly stretching. His lanky body seemed to have some kinks to iron out. Sessions always spent a lot of time on the treadmill, and at a brisk pace. They were all peaches and cream on a personal level. The gym had always been a haven and a bonding place, where

Ted Kennedy slid into the whirlpool with me, where Bumpers told his bawdy jokes, where Randolph sprawled across three massage tables.

I think my former caucus mates all understood what I was going through, understood my interest in being re-elected, and had no recriminations. Their attitude seemed to be, You did a tough thing, and we respect it and really admire it. Their looks and words reminded me of the reaction when I was battling cancer, about how tough and tenacious I was going through chemotherapy. Those guys saw me walk into that chamber every day for months without any hair, and then saw it grow back and then leave again. Brownback, also a cancer survivor, told me I was a "tough old bird," and Coburn, a two-time cancer survivor, generously called me the toughest man he'd ever met.

Reid had told me four Republican senators would oppose me in a primary. None had openly signaled they would join DeMint. I could only speculate who the other three were.

At Ted Kennedy's funeral in August 2009, Joan and I arrived early, and I approached Vicki to express my condolences. She threw her arms around me, gave me a kiss, and thanked me for sparing her husband from the February vote on the stimulus conference report.

As we waited for the service to begin, I struck up a conversation with Arnold Schwarzenegger, who was married to Kennedy's niece Maria Shriver. He was now nearing the end of his tenure as governor of California. Even though at this point I was a Democrat, I asked him to appear at a fund-raiser for me. He agreed, but the event would never come off.

After Kennedy's death, Tom Harkin succeeded him as chairman of Health, Education, Labor, and Pensions, known as HELP, the authorizing committee that handled all of the issues subject to appropriations by our subcommittee. Harkin and I had alternated as chairman of the Appropriations subcommittee since 1996.

Reid had promised to work with members of both the Appropriations and Judiciary Committees to try to advance my seniority. Early on, Dick Durbin had given me his chairmanship of the Judiciary Subcommittee on

Crime and Drugs. He was busy with duties as assistant majority leader and didn't have much time for that subcommittee. But even so, it was a generous move, considering how zealously senators guarded every perk.

Durbin and Schumer also let me climb ahead of them on the Judiciary seniority ladder. Schumer, like Durbin, was busy with his number-three leadership post, his key Banking Committee assignments, and chairing the Rules Committee. But, also like Durbin, he acted with generosity. The newer members of the committee, Sheldon Whitehouse, Ben Cardin, Klobuchar, and Kaufman, all agreed to my moving ahead. They shared the general feeling that I should be accorded some extra seniority.

As a senior Republican on Judiciary, I had gone out of my way to sponsor Whitehouse's legislation. Similarly, I had worked closely with Cardin on Chesapeake Bay issues and other matters concerning our bordering states. Kaufman had been a good friend for years when he served as then–senator Biden's top aide. Klobuchar and I had common backgrounds from our prosecutor days, and I had won a key point of mutual interest, the Medicare reimbursement rates, on the stimulus bill.

Kohl, Dianne Feinstein, and Russell Feingold refused to budge on seniority. Maybe they were motivated by the thought that they were getting closer to chairing the Judiciary Committee and guarded that possibility.

Overall, my sense was that Reid didn't extend himself much to advance my seniority on either committee. Meanwhile, Joe Sestak was making an issue of my being ninety-seventh in Senate seniority. He pounded away at it in our televised debate and elsewhere. The one significant advantage I had thought I would have in a primary against him was my seniority. It had been a big factor in my argument for re-election. People believed me over Reid. But my vaunted seniority was gone.

I went to Durbin and Schumer and asked for their help in regaining the chairmanship of the Appropriations Subcommittee on Labor, Health, Human Services, and Education, at least until after the election. Schumer told me that he, Reid, Inouye, and Durbin would try to persuade Harkin. Weeks passed and I heard nothing, so one day in the gym I asked Schumer what was happening. He later told me Harkin had agreed to come to me with a proposal.

Then one day in April 2010, during a vote, Harkin sat down in Dodd's seat next to me. He asked me if I had any special requests for funding on the subcommittee's appropriation bill. I said that the one request I had was for him to let me have the chairmanship, at least through the election, that it was vital, really indispensable, for my re-election.

He said, "I couldn't do that."

"Why not?" I asked. As chairman of the authorizing committee on Health, Education, Labor, and Pensions, he had full jurisdiction to hold hearings or to take any other action open to him as Appropriations subcommittee chair.

Harkin said that he sometimes had had problems with Mike Enzi, the HELP Committee's top Republican. That was a lame excuse. Harkin had the votes and could do what he chose on the full committee.

He said I wouldn't do it for him if the roles were reversed.

It was the only heated argument I ever had with a Senate colleague during my thirty-year tenure. I reminded him that when I had chaired the subcommittee and he had served as ranking Democrat, he had made many requests, and I had agreed to every one of them. Harkin's conduct ranked very close to Reid's duplicity.

Around 4 p.m. on May 17, the day before my primary, I was in my charter plane in the Wilkes-Barre airport about to take off for Allentown, making a final statewide swing, when I got a call from Harkin. He said he thought my re-election looked good. I replied with the bleak facts. He obviously felt very guilty.

NINE

"GOD'S GOING TO STAND BEFORE YOU"

Driving toward my August 2009 town meeting in Lebanon, Pennsylvania, I was shocked to see half a dozen network TV trucks lining the quaint streets around the community college satellite campus. CNN, MSNBC, and Fox would all broadcast at least part of the meeting live. I had held hundreds of town meetings during my years in the Senate and never drawn a network television camera, much less three going live. My Lebanon town meetings usually drew 85 to 100 local residents. An estimated 1,200 had descended on the school for this forum, some by bus, some before dawn. Hundreds more came to demonstrate. The Lebanon police chief told Hoeflich that he had hadn't seen so many people lined up since *American Idol*.

The cameras, and a troupe of print journalists, had come to capture the opening salvo in the Tea Party revolution, or certainly the nascent movement's most muscular public display to that point. Little more than a week earlier, as I prepared for the nation's first town hall on President Obama's health-care plan, nobody had forecast the coming storm.

. . .

On Sunday, August 2, 2009, Secretary of Health and Human Services Kathleen Sebelius and I found ourselves the luncheon speakers at a Philadelphia gathering of the Inner Circle of Advocates, a group of nationally prominent trial lawyers. Shanin's law partner, Tom Kline, was president of the Inner Circle and was hosting the conference, and had suggested that my meeting the membership could help raise campaign funds. Kline had enlisted Sebelius, a former executive director of the Kansas Trial Lawyers Association, to address the group.

While Sebelius was in Philadelphia, the administration apparently decided that she should hold a town meeting on the president's health-care plan. The health-care overhaul, the most sweeping social legislation in a generation, was becoming Obama's defining legislative initiative.[1] The goal was to provide health insurance to every American, and the administration promised to reduce the cost of a bloated and burgeoning system in the process. Critics of "ObamaCare" blasted it as an arrogant government takeover of one-sixth of the U.S. economy, burying Americans and their grandchildren in debt. As Durbin framed it, "This is a real debate over whether or not health care is going to be a right or a privilege in America."[2] The president had been pressing to get the health package passed in time for him to sign it into law on Labor Day. But squabbling and haggling over financing had delayed the effort.

Sebelius's Philadelphia forum was scheduled for August 2, minutes after the lawyers' meeting, at the National Constitution Center on Independence Mall. I was asked to join her. With my recent party switch, I was the expected sixtieth Senate vote that would override a filibuster and deliver the health-care legislation. As such, *USA Today* wrote, I "was a particular target for those in opposition." Months later, the newspaper would run a front-page retrospective on the health-care bill, which it called a saga worthy of Shakespeare. The Constitution Center meeting would rank as the second of "eight key moments" in the drama.[3]

The health-care overhaul capped an ambitious, expensive agenda the

Democratic president and Congress were pressing, including the $787 billion stimulus package, which had supplemented the Bush administration's $700 billion TARP program. The House had passed cap-and-trade legislation to combat climate change, derided as a $3 trillion tax.

Congress adjourned for the August 2009 recess the week before our Philadelphia event. In July, after action by three House committees, comprehensive health-care reform legislation expected to cost more than $1 trillion had been introduced in the House. The Senate did not yet have a bill. The HELP Committee had passed its portion of the bill at the end of July, but the Finance Committee had not yet acted on its portion. Legislation moves much quicker through the House than through the Senate. The upper chamber runs a more deliberative committee process and demands considerable preparation to organize 60 votes against a filibuster. But even by Senate standards, the health-care bill was crawling, and leadership was guarding details.

We had the broad parameters but didn't know what the Senate bill would ultimately look like. But the House bill was out, and activists had been blasting warnings across the country that the legislation would let the government invade your bank account and your medical records, publicly fund abortions, and promote assisted suicide, among other fabrications. Palin charged on Facebook that the legislation would bring an America "in which my parents or my baby with Down Syndrome will have to stand in front of Obama's 'death panel.'" Obama kept insisting he would not "pull the plug on Grandma."[4]

With the annual deficit projected at $1.7 trillion and the national debt at $12 trillion, concern mounted about the public response to the health-care bill's additional cost. Polls consistently showed tepid public support for the plan. Vitriol was brewing on all sides, characterized by DeMint's "Waterloo" remark.

The Tea Party formed in this miasma. In suburban Philadelphia, Diana Reimer, sixty-seven, wife of a Navy retiree, feared that the health-care bill would bring higher taxes and more government control, which she did not consider "America the free." So Reimer, who had never attended a protest, joined the Tea Party Patriots in 2009 and organized some fifty others who shared her fears to deploy to our Constitution Center meeting.[5]

As we prepared for the Philadelphia forum, my chief health-care aide, John Myers, said, "You know things aren't going to be nice. There are going to be challenging questions." But none of us forecast the coming storm.

The National Constitution Center was usually friendly ground. In 1988, I had spearheaded legislation that led to building the limestone-and-glass museum two blocks from Independence Hall and the Liberty Bell. The center billed itself as "America's most interactive history museum," which would prove true that day on several counts.

After meeting with the lawyers, Sebelius and I went upstairs to a rounded auditorium whose towering glass walls showcased Independence Mall. Above us, a colorful array of flags ringed the stone walls. Sebelius and I stood on a short platform before the glass wall. Uniformed police were posted at the stage's edge.

The size of the crowd—more than four hundred, including standees—surprised us. And while many had come to ask legitimate questions, an angry faction railed against abortion and assisted suicide, which were not covered in the plan, demanded that government hew to the founders' ideals, and drowned any discourse in jeers and heckles.

Sebelius and I stood our ground. "Excuse me," she said when hecklers interrupted her opening statement. "We can stand here and shout at one another and we can leave the stage, or we can have a conversation. It's really up to you." She seemed light on her feet, with a runner's lean build. She had run a state, and had grown up in politics, the daughter of an Ohio governor.

I made a brief opening statement, mostly suggesting that the crowd keep quiet between questions and answers, with no applause and no response. When we opened the floor to questions, dozens stood to get in line, escalating the chaos.

One man charged that the health bill would ration care and force us into a European-style system. Another said Congress couldn't be trusted. One posed a two-part question: The government should not be in charge

of health records because it couldn't be trusted; and why did the bill require coverage of abortions, which would shut down hospitals as a result?

One woman told me, "I look at this health-care plan and I see nothing
that is about health or about care. What I see is a bureaucratic nightmare,
Senator. Medicaid is broke, Medicare is broke, Social Security is broke,
and you want us to believe that a government that can't even run a cash-
for-clunkers program is going to run one-seventh of our U.S. economy?
No sir, no."

I replied, but was drowned out by boos, heckling, and shouts of "That's
a lie!"

A Philadelphia woman said she had emigrated from Brazil in 1986.
"My question to you is why we are turning this country, the land I've
learned to love so much during the past twenty-two years, into a land of
entitlement?"

I told her the entitlements she was talking about were Medicaid,
Medicare, and Social Security, which were sensible but needed to be
brought under control.

In its retrospective, *USA Today* would write of the Philadelphia forum:
"The raucous scene . . . , aired on newscasts and posted on YouTube, would
shake Democrats, embolden Republicans and force the White House to
accelerate its strategy. It nearly succeeded in upending Obama's initiative."[6]

But the anger targeted more than the health-care plan. The Constitution
Center event showcased what was, to that point, the largest formal display
of Tea Party rage.

The week of the Philadelphia forum, a Tea Party affiliate's strategy
memo for disrupting upcoming congressional town hall meetings on health
care flew around the Web. The memo outlined best practices that "could
be useful to activists in just about any district where their Congressperson
has supported the socialist agenda of the Democrat leadership in Washington."

The memo offered a detailed "playbook" that included preparing and
distributing "embarrassing and damning" questions and "packing the hall."
It advised,

You need to rock the boat early in the Rep's presentation. Watch for an opportunity to yell out and challenge the Rep's statements early. . . . The goal is to rattle him, get him off his prepared script and agenda. . . . Look for these opportunities before he even takes questions. . . . When called on, ask a specific prepared question that puts the onus on him to answer. It can be a long question including lots of statistics/facts. . . . The balance of the group should applaud when the question is asked, further putting the Rep on the defensive.[7]

The day after the Philadelphia forum, *Talking Points Memo* reported, "If these tactics catch on, and August recess health care events are characterized by organized agitprop, it could have a dramatic impact on the tenor of the health care debate, and the media coverage of the events this month. Buckle your seatbelts."[8]

I had scheduled my regular town meetings across Pennsylvania for the following week, in Lebanon, Bloomsburg, State College, and Kittanning. Since my election in 1980, I had visited nearly all sixty-seven Pennsylvania counties every year, and town meetings were a staple. The sessions let me test public sentiment and stay in close contact with my constituents. I went on a basic proposition: If you can't defend to all these people what you've done, you've done something wrong.

The essence of my treatment of people was to listen to them. And I was genuinely sympathetic. I gave them straight, direct, sensible answers, and they generally appreciated it. I didn't feel like I was descending from Olympus when I entered a VFW hall or a community college auditorium. I felt like I was from Russell. I couldn't perform miracles for them. So you listen to them, hear them out, and do what you can. It's like a story Marv Katz told about a boy playing in the street who got run over by a steamroller. The driver knocked on the mother's door and said, "I'm sorry to tell you this, but your child just got run over by the paving machine." The mother said, "Slip him under the door." You do what you can.

After the Philadelphia forum, John Myers told Hoeflich that we would need police protection for the coming meetings. Hoeflich asked the Capitol

Hill police for security, and they turned him down, citing lack of a credible threat. He worked with Rendell's chief of staff, and we were assigned three Pennsylvania state troopers, two in uniform and one undercover, for each meeting.

Anticipating donnybrooks, Hoeflich convened the senior staff to plan logistics. At each meeting, they would hand out thirty cards, on a first-come, first-served basis, to those who wanted to ask me questions. They would ban signs inside. And no standees.

On Saturday, August 8, my Lehigh Valley director, Adrienne Baker, phoned Hoeflich. She had received a call from a friend, and was alarmed. The night before, Baker's friend had overheard groups of men talking at a diner about their plans to bring guns to my town hall meeting Monday in Lebanon, to demonstrate their constitutional right to bear arms. Hoeflich called me and recommended that we cancel the meeting.

Instead, I phoned Baker's friend to hear his account firsthand. Then Hoeflich and I worked the phones that weekend, talking to the state police commandant, the Senate sergeant at arms and deputy sergeant at arms, and the police chiefs in the four towns where we had scheduled meetings. At 9 p.m. Monday, Hoeflich got a call from Frank Leitera, head of Durbin's Capitol Hill police detail. The assistant majority leader had headed to Illinois for the recess, freeing the officers. "Scott," Leitera said, "we've been assigned to the senator. What are the details?"[9] Game on.

Leitera, beefy and compact with a shorn rim of gray hair, and his team of Capitol Hill police officers would prove models of professionalism and precision, a boon to us and a credit to the federal government.

Hoeflich asked me about ejecting unruly guests from the meetings. I told him I didn't want anybody ejected unless it got to the point where I told the person, "You need to leave." My chief of staff considered that approach a security nightmare, but complied.

My round of town hall meetings began Monday, August 11, in Lebanon, seat of a south-central Pennsylvania county of rolling hills, parks, farms, and eighteenth-century buildings. The city's Web page boasted, "Lebanon has been recognized as the second least stressful city in the United States." For that first meeting, we had only three state troopers and two Capitol Hill police officers; the departments hadn't had time to mobilize full security teams. And we couldn't get portable metal detectors because no law-enforcement agency would provide operators.

Before heading to the 9:30 a.m. town meeting at Harrisburg Area Community College's Lebanon campus, I met with some local Democrats at their nearby headquarters. A classic red convertible was cruising downtown Lebanon bearing signs, "RETIRE SENATOR SPECTER 2010."

At breakfast meetings like the session with the Lebanon Democrats, I sometimes told gags about my friend and former colleague Bob Dole. I said that every year I phoned Dole on July 22, his birthday. The last time, I said, "Congratulations. How do you feel?" He said, "Arlen, I feel like a teenager. But the problem is, I can't find one."

Depending on the crowd, I might continue the routine. Dole said, "I just came down for breakfast and I saw Elizabeth and I said, 'Elizabeth, I just shaved, and I feel ten years younger.' Elizabeth scowled at me and said, 'Bob, why didn't you shave last night?'"

Dole then told me that Elizabeth had been very irritated with him lately because he had been complaining about the cost of Viagra. He said, "Arlen, do you know that Viagra costs $10 a pill?" I said, "Bob, how would I know about the cost of Viagra?" Then he said, "Elizabeth really is mad at me because she thinks I can afford $40 a year." That humor, although a little off-color, relaxed the crowd and maybe even improved my too-serious image.

Several of my Washington-based aides arrived at the college around 8:30 a.m. I always wanted my D.C. staff to see what was going on in the state. A line already stretched fifty yards from the front door on State Route 422, called Cumberland Street on that downtown stretch, and would eventually ring the block. Many had learned of the meeting from conservative and antitax groups' e-mail alerts, including the Berks County Tea Party.[10]

"Some staffers were wary of parking where anybody would see us," James Warner, my environmental aide, recalled. They worried about their cars and themselves being targeted.

Some among the masses wore tea bags affixed to T-shirts and hats. Health-care advocates, urged to attend by unions and liberal groups, generally arrived too late to get numbered question cards. As the *New York Times* reported, "It was the angriest people who got in line first."[11]

Inside the auditorium, my aides helped set 250 green folding chairs on the light gray carpet and coordinated with local and Capitol Hill police. The cops discussed escape routes, Warner recalled. "If we have to get him out the back door, this is how we're going to do it," one officer told another.

The crowd was polite as they filed in. Only 250 could sit, and we had determined not to allow standees. When aides shut the doors, some groused that they'd driven far and waited long, but stepped back.

When I arrived and spotted the TV trucks, I told my aides that I was a little concerned—not for myself, but for television viewers across the country who wouldn't be able to do much surfing for different programs.

Protesters massed around the college, many waving signs reading "Obama Healthcare—Down Right Evil" and "Benedict Arlen—Don't Reelect a Traitor!" The *Times* photographed a white-haired woman in metal-rimmed glasses and a floral print dress holding a handwritten sign, "I Love You ARLEN," as a younger woman jabbed a finger at her. The caption read, "Nancy Gusti, 73, of Lebanon, stood her ground as a passerby berated her outside the meeting."

Joe Sciarra, my driver, was anxious. Sciarra had joined my staff four years earlier, after thirty years as a Philadelphia police officer.

I had always made it a point to talk to protesters. When a Sestak crowd picketed one of my Montgomery County campaign events, I walked over, chatted, and offered my hand. Most shook it.

Michael Smerconish recounted an incident during my first Senate re-election campaign:

Senator Specter invited me to be the campaign manager for Philadelphia in his 1986 race against Bob Edgar. . . . I remember a particular day, he was in Center City and was due at headquarters at some point. We had protesters arrive on our sidewalk. What they were protesting, I don't remember, but I felt obliged to call and warn him so he could delay his return to avoid the protesters. In what I learned to be typical Specter, all that made him do was have the driver floor it to get back to the campaign headquarters, where the action was.[12]

In Lebanon, we took a rear entrance and wound through the building, past what looked like a stage area, to a small room where we had arranged a brief meeting with several area residents suffering from health problems exacerbated by the health-care bureaucracy. I wanted these people in the hall, for ready testimony about the need for health-care reform, though there would be no opportunity for them to speak.

After that five-minute meeting, I stepped into the auditorium. In a navy suit, white shirt, and muted blue tie, I stood on a parquet island toward the front of the gray-carpeted room. I faced the crowd, most in short-sleeved knits and shorts against the August heat, and a massive green steam locomotive roaring down the tracks on a mural that covered most of the rear wall. Mountain and town scenes cast a placid aura from the adjacent walls. Evading our sign ban, several people carried small placards with slogans such as "Kill the Bill." One man raised sheets of colored copy paper, laser-printed with slogans including "You are no longer trusted" and "Keep your hand out of my pocket. The well is dry!" He wore pink paper cutouts over his ears, maybe to symbolize that he was listening carefully, or not at all.

Outside, Joe Sciarra stayed with the car, a maroon 2005 Lincoln, in the rear parking lot off Spring Street. Sciarra could cast a chilling patrolman's glare, and stowed a revolver at the base of the driver's seat. But he grew uneasy as the protesters massed. He found a Lebanon police officer, asked for his supervisor, and then told the sergeant that we needed more support.

I made a six-and-a-half-minute introduction, which I said was as long as anybody should speak, laying out the problems of the current health-care system, including taxpayers' covering steep emergency room fees, and the ground rules for the meeting: ninety minutes, and questions only from those thirty holding cards.

My staff had arranged for Hoeflich's assistant, Robert Jones, to hold a

Unruffled, Sen. Specter confronts a hostile constituent town meeting in Lebanon, Penn-sylvannia, in August 2009. (GETTY)

portable mic for questioners. Jones stood six feet four, and weighed a solid 225 pounds, and dissuaded dissent. But he would also bark, "Get to your question, get to your question." I soon took the mic and circulated through the room, standing in front of each questioner—not crowding him or her, but eyeball to eyeball. I had developed the technique long ago, to make it harder for protesters to holler at me.

When I asked whoever had card number 1 to come forward, a middle-aged blonde in a turquoise top and white pants demanded that her senators and representatives also carry whatever health plan we approved for her. "I understand at this point you're not," she said, chopping the air. The crowd gave a burst of applause.

I responded, as I had before, that all Americans should have the same plan, including members of Congress.

Questioner 2, in a blue blouse and off-white Capri pants, shouted that she didn't like her elected officials running around calling her un-American, a rabble-rouser, a mobster, and a Nazi. "I'm sick of the lies," she said, jabbing

The New York Times *front page captures a furious constituent, Craig Anthony Miller, at Sen. Specter's Lebanon, Pennsylvannia, town meeting in August 2009. Their televised exchange, rebroadcast for months, made Miller a media star.* (THE NEW YORK TIMES)

a finger at me, her voice strong but tense. "I don't like being lied to; I don't like being lied about." She ended by declaring, "I want you as my senator to go back to Washington, D.C. . . . Shut up and get out of the way."

More applause.

Before I could call on the next questioner, a heavyset man with trimmed gray hair and beard, later identified as Craig Anthony Miller, fifty-nine, charged down the aisle toward me. Face flushed, Miller waved a sheaf of papers, a water bottle wedged under one arm, a pen in the pocket of his gray T-shirt. He hollered that he wanted to speak, had been assured that he could speak, but then didn't get one of the thirty cards: a victim of more government lies.

I strode toward Miller, closing the gap.

From the side of the room, Leitera, the Capitol Hill police team leader, hissed into his cufflink mic, "Jesus Christ, he's going in!"

Leitera lunged forward, and his partner rushed in from the rear. Before they could reach the action, a burly neighbor in a white ball cap grabbed Miller and steered and then shoved him toward a row of seats.

Now, half a dozen cops and security guards were racing toward us. I shouted, "Wait a minute!"—twelve times.

I stood firm and told the closest officer not to remove or even touch Miller. I didn't want the headline to read "Citizen Evicted." I wanted "Senator Keeps His Cool."

The cops stood down.

Miller, quivering, finger poking at me, shouted that he wanted to leave. I told him that was his right. He said, "I'm going to speak my mind before I leave." Inches away, he shouted at me, "I don't care how crooked you are. I'm not a lobbyist with all kinds of money to stuff in your pocket so that you can cheat the citizens of this country. . . . One day God's going to stand before you, and he's going to judge you and the rest of your damn cronies up on the Hill. . . ."

He gave senators credit for a bit too much power.

Shouting, "I'm leaving!" Miller stormed out of the hall, a beefy security officer clearing the way.

I held up my hand in a stop gesture. "Okay," I said, "we've just had a demonstration of democracy." As for Miller's charge that his constitutional rights were being trampled, I said, "I'm encouraging constitutional rights by coming to Lebanon to talk to my constituents."

The next day, the *New York Times* would run a front-page, above-the-fold photo of Miller gesturing menacingly at me, as I listened with arms folded. Network television would replay the scene constantly for days and periodically air it even months later to show Tea Party rage. The performance would land Miller guest spots on Fox and MSNBC talk shows. Nearly a year later, *Roll Call* would write:

> The video of a white-bearded, bespectacled man in a T-shirt yelling and thrusting his finger in Sen. Arlen Specter's face during a town hall meeting last August has become an iconic personification of voter rage.

The outrage that the Pennsylvania Republican-turned-Democrat faced boiled across the country during the debate over health care reform and still simmers heading into the midterm elections.[13]

Questioner 4, a middle-aged woman, told me, "I do not want to pay on a health-care plan that includes the right for a woman to kill her unborn baby."

I responded that although we didn't yet have a Senate bill, I anticipated subscribers would have the option to have a plan that excluded abortion coverage while others could have the coverage if they so elected.

Questioner 6, a portly, balding, gray-haired man, hit the heart of the government-intrusion rebellion in a soft, reasoned, almost beseeching tone. He said the health-care plan was obviously written with the "assumption that government has the right to control our lives from prebirth to death." He noted "a few problems: The illegals; they shouldn't even be here." He ended by imploring, "Would you leave us alone?"

Questioner 7, Katy Abram from North Cornwall Township, stood to make a speech that would launch the self-described stay-at-home mother to national celebrity. Abram and her husband, Sam, had brought a video camera and taped each other as they questioned me. Katy Abram trembled when she took the mic, her dark curly hair framing a fair complexion over an aqua T-shirt, olive shorts, and white sneakers. Gesturing with her left arm as she spoke, her voice occasionally breaking and rising, Abram said:

Thank you. I am a Republican, but I'm first and foremost, I'm a conservative. I don't believe this is just about health care. It's not about TARP, it's not about left and right. This is about the systematic dismantling of this country. I'm only thirty-five years old. I have never been interested in politics. You have awakened a sleeping giant. We are tired of this. This is why everybody in this room is so ticked off. I don't want this country turning into Russia, turning into a socialized country. My question for you is, what are you going to do to restore this country back to what our founders created, according to the Constitution?

The room erupted. One man, joining his neighbors in a standing ovation, raised his hands over his head and brought them together in thunderous claps.

I said, "Well, there are a few people who didn't stand up and applaud, but not too many."

Abram would soon guest on CNN's *American Morning*, Fox News's *Hannity*, and MSNBC's *Hardball*, and headline Tea Party rallies as far away as Florida. A year after the Lebanon meeting, in August 2010, at a ceremony in Washington, D.C., Abram would receive the first Liberty Heart Award from the 9-12 Project, founded by conservative idol and Fox News host Glenn Beck.

"Basically, the reason they nominated me was of course because of the town hall meeting," Abram would tell the *Lebanon Daily News*. "There are different principles and values the group believes in, and they were saying that my comments had emboldened them."

McCain had launched Palin into the conservative stratosphere; my payload was Katy Abram.

Questioner 9, a clean-cut, russet-haired man in a blue oxford shirt, complained: "The government hasn't done anything right. . . . You're taking our kids' future and driving it right into the toilet."

More applause.

Questioner 14, a strawberry blonde in a maize blouse, introduced herself as a nurse from Lebanon and thanked me profusely for coming. Then she extolled the health plan.

"Thank you for your positive comment," I said when she had finished. "I knew that if I looked hard enough, far enough in this large group, I'd find someone who likes the health-care plan. Thank you."

By this time, after some trouble with the sound system, I had been handing my mic in turn to each questioner.

Questioner 17, a heavyset, soft-spoken older man with a vigorous white beard below thinning white hair, identified himself as a former Republican committeeman who had supported me. "But now you defected." He then said the Koran calls for slaying nonbelievers, offered to cite verses, and asked me whether I had read the Muslim holy book.

I eventually took off my suit coat and circulated in shirtsleeves.

As the meeting neared its end, Questioner 28, a burly, bearded young man in a T-shirt printed with the word "DAD," told me, "There are many people here that would like to have a word with you and may I remind you that you work for us. We are your employer and if the employer is willing to sit around and have a chat with his employee, I think the employee should oblige them."

I told the man I was due in Lewisburg. "You are my employers, but you have to realize I have 12 million."

The final participant, Questioner 30, stood, a woman in a blue T-shirt that proclaimed in white uppercase: "PROUD MEMBER OF THE MOB." Middle-aged in short brown hair and glasses, she seemed an unlikely rebel.

Immediately following the meeting, I held a media availability, cramming into a classroom near the building's rear exit with thirty reporters and eight TV cameras. From a security standpoint, we chose the wrong space. The classroom had a wall of windows that offered a full view to the seven hundred protesters and others who had been unable to get into the meeting and had gathered outside.[14] They saw me, Sciarra, and the maroon Lincoln. Soon a hundred people, many waving signs, surrounded the car.

The Lebanon police brought in eight marked cruisers and created a barricade to protect the Lincoln, the Capitol Hill police Suburban, and our exit route.

As soon I came out, shouts flew. Close to me, a dark-haired man in his late thirties, screamed, "You're nothing but a fucking traitor!" Another man yelled, "Hey, Arlen, enjoy your next sixteen months, because it's the last sixteen months—because you're done." Nearby, a third man chanted, as though running for office, "No to socialist health care! No to socialism!"

We hopped into our vehicles and caravanned off toward Interstate 81 and our next stop.

The next meetings drew even larger crowds and longer lines. Later that day in Lewisburg, a farming area sixty miles north of Harrisburg, a woman in the audience told me:

> My main concern is our freedoms. I am very, very, very scared. I believe we are going down, I think this health-care reform act is a vehicle not for health care—this is a vehicle to take us down a path of socialism and totalitarianism. . . . So I ask you, what are you going to do to uphold our freedoms?

I began, "Well, I'm glad to say only about a third of the crowd stood up."

The following day, some 1,500 people gathered for my meeting in State College, home to Penn State University. Our planned route would have taken me entirely through public areas. My security team found a tunnel that could take me through the complex, so that no one could even see me, and redrew our route. But I didn't know anything about those plans at the time.

"Funny thing was," Hoeflich later recalled, "before and afterward, he decided he wanted to use the bathroom. So we had done all this work to prevent him from being anywhere near the public, and it turned out [with him] standing at a urinal next to a guy."

By the State College meeting, the crowd seemed to have developed a grudging respect.

"Hello Senator," Questioner 4 began:

> I want to thank you for taking, having the courage to come here and do a meeting today. . . . What is to become of freedom in America? People in Washington have been on what looks to me like a socialism juggernaut. . . . The health-care bill is simply the battlefield where we meet now. But the war in my mind is really American freedom.

The next questioner told me:

> I do have to congratulate you for having the courage that a lot of your other buddies don't have to come and have a town hall meet-

ing; I consider them cowards, quite honestly. . . . But you're going to tell me how I should have my health care. I don't like that. I think that's arrogant. . . . I know you value re-election, more than life itself it seems sometimes.

Questioner 18 told me, "I feel you do not have the right, the authority under the Constitution, to get involved in health care. . . . And if you do not understand this, you may want to review it in the Constitution." She offered a booklet. "Here is a copy of the Constitution."

I said, "Well, I have a copy of the Constitution, but I'm always glad to get another copy." In fact, I always carried a copy, and so did most of my staff. "Okay, okay, I'll read it again."

When I told Questioner 20 that the proposed health-care plan would not operate at a deficit, he replied, "I'm sorry, sir, I just don't believe you."

Questioner 23 told me:

Senator, first of all I want to thank you very much for coming here today and showing the courage to do that, unlike some other senators who are weaseling out of these things. And of course unlike our president you didn't, as far as I can see, you didn't stack the deck before the people came in.

"If I stacked the deck," I replied, "I did a hell of a poor job."

One questioner made a proposition: "Senator Specter, would you agree that if you vote yes and the facts and figures presented to the public are wrong, you should be held criminally liable?"

"No!" I said.

By the week's final town hall meeting, in Kittanning, a borough in a former industrial area forty-five miles northeast of Pittsburgh, everybody knew our routine. At my first meetings, our thirty numbered question cards had shocked the activists, spoiling their playbook to bombard me with questions. By the fourth meeting, they had learned that they could game our process simply by yelling louder.

Some 2,200 people descended on our Kittanning meeting, wedging us in bumper-to-bumper traffic approaching a bottleneck intersection. Protesters waved the usual signs, and debuted "Don't Tread on Me" flags. I recognized several people from the previous day's Lewisburg forum.

The hall at the Belmont Complex, a recreational facility, was smaller than at the other meetings, pressing bodies together. The tight quarters also meant cameras were within kissing distance to my face. Hoeflich told the crew from Pittsburgh's KDKA-TV, which was shooting live for CNN, three times to stand back. Finally, he grabbed the cameraman by the belt and yanked him back.

Toward the end, a woman in the fifth row stood to ask a question, showing her numbered card, and a man lost control. We had filled the room front to back, which meant the first thirty people—those with question cards—should all have been in the front couple of rows. The man smelled fraud. And, worse, the card-holding woman in the fifth row was wearing a sports jersey, as were many of the troops that unions had sent.

"You planted this question, she's with the union—she said she is—and how does she get a goddamn fucking question?" the man screamed. "All the questions are in the front, and she's in the back!"

In fact, the woman had gotten the card on the way in from one of her friends, who had decided to let her ask a question instead. While my staff denied any ploys, the woman with the ticket screamed back at her accuser. The man stormed out.

The session produced mostly variations on what had become a familiar theme. Questioner 25 told me, "I come here today as a man under authority. I'm a born-again Christian under the authority of almighty God. I'm a United States citizen under the authority of the Constitution." The man said he did not care for the proposed health-care plan. "Therefore, I find it outrageous that a citizen of the United States would be forced to go against their biblical religious beliefs. This is unconstitutional. . . . It is 100 percent socialism and should not be tolerated."

The crowd cheered.

After the thirty questions, we left the hall, to find a man hollering at me, "I hope you die!"

More than a year later, Hoeflich recalled, "If I saw his face today, I'd still remember the guy: mustache, blond, around forty years old, kind of balding. Screaming, 'I hope you die, I hope you die!' Screaming."

State police nudged throngs out of the way with their cruisers to clear our route to the cars. We finally got into the Lincoln, buffered by the Capitol Hill police Suburban and two state police cruisers, and pulled out. People chased us down the street on foot as other state police cars tried to set up a perimeter.

The Kittanning forum moved Salon.com, which covered some of my meetings, to headline one of its pieces with a comment addressed to me: "You're a Socialist, Fascist Pig!" The journal reported:

> . . . You try being yelled at by a woman dressed elaborately as Betsy Ross who keeps asking why you never read the House—not Senate— bill on healthcare reform; or being called a "Socialist, Fascist pig" by a furious guy who storms out of the room. . . . Getting hassled by a bunch of Tea Party loons, day in and day out, adds such a layer of absurdity to the business of governing that even a longtime survivor like Specter must wish he could escape it all.
>
> Arlen being Arlen, though, he mostly shrugged all the hostility off. . . . He kept calm, defending the healthcare bill no matter who was yelling about it, and answering friendly questions in the same "I've seen it all" tone that the angry ones generated.[14]

The encounters recalled a town meeting shortly after I was elected to the Senate, when a man in an upturned clerical collar stood up, berated me at some length for my centrist views, and concluded by ordering me, "Resign and repent!"

"Wouldn't one or the other be sufficient?" I asked.

My August 2009 meetings, and others like them that Cardin and Grassley and other lawmakers faced, nearly killed town meetings. The *New York Times* reported that only a handful of the 255 Democrats in the House held town meetings during recess a year later.

If the time-honored tradition of the political town hall is not quite dead, it seems to be teetering closer to extinction. . . . With images of overheated, finger-waving crowds still seared into their minds from the discontent of last August, many Democrats heeded the advice of party leaders and tried to avoid unscripted question-and-answer sessions.[15]

Sestak held only one town meeting, in a friendly black church in Center City, Philadelphia. Murtha eschewed live forums in favor of a series of telephone town halls, and caught hell. Murtha's opponent charged, "At some point, [Murtha] has decided that he no longer has to listen to his constituents."[16]

Political pundit Peggy Noonan called the 2009 "town hall rebellion" a turning point in both parties' fortunes. "That is when the first resistance to Washington's plans on health care became manifest, and it's when a more generalized resistance rose and spread."[17]

On ABC's *This Week* the Sunday following my August 2009 meetings, host Jake Tapper played some video highlights of the sessions. "That's a lot of anger," Tapper told me. "Where does it come from, Senator Specter?"

"A variety of factors, Jake," I said. "I think people are very nervous because so many have lost their jobs, and I think that the uncertainty of the health-care bill . . . I think we have to bear in mind that, although these people need to be heard and have a right to be heard, that they're not really representative of America, in my opinion."

I was wrong. The Tea Party protesters were not Astroturf, a movement manufactured and orchestrated by professional activists, but grassroots.

At 7 a.m. on Christmas Eve 2009, the Senate voted on the health-care bill. The tally was 60–39, along strict party lines, with no margin. I cast the key sixtieth vote. The House passed its bill 219–212 on March 21, 2010, with only Democratic support. Not a single Republican in either chamber voted for final passage. That's the disintegration of the center.

On March 23, the president signed the bill into law, and the House and Senate followed two days later by passing a package of final fixes.

The legislation requires most Americans to buy health insurance and subsidizes those who cannot afford it, covering an estimated 94 percent. It adds 16 million to Medicaid's rolls. Small businesses and the uninsured can shop for coverage in insurance exchanges, to be created in 2014. Employers have to offer coverage to employees or pay penalties. The law bars insurance companies from imposing lifetime caps or denying coverage to patients because of preexisting conditions. It raises payroll taxes on individuals making more than $200,000 and couples making more than $250,000, taxes their investment income, and taxes high-cost employer-sponsored health plans.

Obama said at a late-night ceremony after House passage, "In the end, what this day represents is another stone firmly laid in the foundation of the American dream. Tonight, we answered the call of history."[18]

The fight did not end with the president's signature on the bill; to some, it was only escalating. As the *New York Times* reported, "Around the country, reaction to the bill's passage was emotional, and in some cases violent." Arizona representative Gabrielle Giffords found a glass door of her Tucson office shattered after she voted for the bill. In January 2011, Giffords would suffer a far more severe outburst of irrational rage.

A day before the president inked the bill, Republicans launched a campaign to repeal the legislation, in whole through Congress or in pieces through local lawsuits challenging particular provisions. They vowed to wield the new law against Democrats in the midterm elections and beyond.[19]

But the health-care debate, weighty as the issue was, had always been about more than health care. Two months after my Lebanon town meeting, Katy Abram, who had risen to fame confronting me with America-as-Russia charges, crashed my October 17 Lebanon County Democratic Committee Dinner. I rarely attended county political banquets, but I drove hundreds of miles throughout Pennsylvania that night to hit two of them, in Lebanon and Lancaster, to build ties with local Democrats.

The "infamous town hall woman," as the *Lebanon Daily News* called her, raised her hand and asked me another question. "With the health-care reform that's going on," Abram began, "I feel like everybody is missing the big picture. The Constitution says we're supposed to promote the general welfare, not provide it. . . . Why is this a federal-government thing?"

Before I could reply, Abram would recount, a woman in the audience yelled, "She's not one of us; don't worry about her." Turning to Abram, the woman yelled, "We don't need you here!"

But I answered Abram's question. "The lady puts her finger on the spot," I began. "We have a federal system, a central government of limited power. . . . But the Supreme Court of the United States has said that the general welfare clause is important, and we have come to believe that in terms of morality and in terms of humanitarian principles, that people are entitled to Social Security. They pay for it; they worked hard."[20]

People are also entitled to affordable health care. And to Medicaid and Medicare. And to a Department of Education and an Environmental Protection Agency. Some argue that the federal government's role should be limited to establishing post roads and an army and a navy; the Constitution says nothing about an air force. But inherent in the Constitution is the notion that a civilized society must provide a social safety net.

The Tea Party continues to wobble the Republican Party, toppling viable centrist candidates, and to damage the country. The movement's antitax, pro-entitlement crusade may have found its embodiment in the irate man who demanded at a town hall meeting, "I don't want the government messing with my Medicare!" The Tea Party invokes a warning attributed to the nineteenth-century French political thinker Alexis de Tocqueville: "A democracy cannot exist as a permanent form of government. It can only exist until the voters discover they can vote themselves largesse out of the public treasury."

TEN

RED MEAT

Some five hundred jeering union activists staged a rally in June 2009 to pressure me to support the legislation known as card check. They commandeered a plaza across from Pittsburgh's Westin Convention Center Hotel, where Pennsylvania Democrats were holding their annual meeting with their "newest darling," as one newspaper described me, as featured attraction.[1] The Democratic leaders were doing their best to formally welcome me to the party. Their reception, replete with one of the few speaking slots, was enthusiastic. I didn't sense the ambivalence and opposition that probably festered behind some smiles. At the rally, the friction was all in the open.

I could understand Tea Party activists hurling catcalls and insults at me when Obama's health-care plan was hot. But I hadn't thought the steelworkers—the loudest among the AFL-CIO crowd that Saturday morning—would be so hostile, considering what I had done for them over the years. For decades, organized labor had been supporting me for a variety of reasons, from my health-care push to my stand against striker replacements to my support for prevailing wages in federal contracts under Davis-Bacon. As chairman of the Appropriations Subcommittee on Labor,

I had added critical funding for workers' safety and training to replace jobs lost to dumped imports.

But card check, officially the Employee Free Choice Act, provoked visceral reactions. "I cannot remember an issue this emotional in all my years in the Senate," I told the *New York Times* that summer. The paper reported, "Labor had called the bill its No. 1 objective, and both labor and business deployed their largest, most expensive lobbying campaigns ever in the battle over it."[2]

As the rally raged, I stepped onto a platform and into the summer sun to face the union activists. Some booed. Others chanted, "Free choice! Pass the vote!"

The bill would require an employer to recognize a union when a majority of workers signed cards showing support, replacing elections by secret ballot, and would require an employer and a union to submit to binding arbitration. Decades-old law, with only narrow exceptions, required recognition only upon a union's showing majority support in an election conducted by the National Labor Relations Board. Labor was counting on the act to reverse a steep decline in union membership. Just 7.6 percent of private-sector workers belonged to unions in mid-2009, down 80 percent from a half century earlier.[3]

Seven weeks earlier, I had announced my opposition to card check. Until then, some had considered me a supporter because I favored labor reform. But I had never been willing to give up the secret ballot, a cornerstone of democracy that protects voters from coercion. I had been trying to work out a compromise to expedite union certification, as part of a group of six Democratic senators.

Standing in the plaza below, Mike Oscar, my southeastern Pennsylvania executive director, began to sweat, and not only from the June heat. "The perspiration on my brow was intense," Oscar recalled later. He had been working with union leaders, and this was the first time I was addressing labor as a whole since announcing my card check decision. "We didn't know how the event was going to play out."

Bill George, the Pennsylvania AFL-CIO president, had warmed up—or spun up—the crowd, pacing the platform like a lion and roaring about fairness and clout. Their appetites whetted, the workers were ravenous for more red meat, and George introduced me. Since my party change five weeks earlier, union leadership had been inciting the rank and file to pressure me at every point.

Rich Trumka, the AFL-CIO's national secretary-treasurer and next president, and George had both said publicly that the AFL-CIO was not inclined to support me for re-election in 2010 if I did not back the Employee Free Choice Act. The AFL-CIO, 900,000 strong in Pennsylvania, was the most powerful voting bloc in the state. And nearly all its members were Democrats. Trumka, raised in Pennsylvania, had been a good friend. Jimmy Hoffa Jr., the Teamsters general president and another strong supporter, had said that if I didn't come around on card check, he would support Sestak. I called Hoffa promptly to tell him about my efforts to reach a compromise, and that calmed him down.

At the rally, Eileen Connelly, executive director of the Pennsylvania State Council of the Service Employees International Union (SEIU), stood among George and other union leaders on the platform when I spoke. She recalled, "We won the [2008] election with Obama. We thought that we could get it all, without any compromises and any real fights." Democrats controlled the White House and both chambers of Congress, with near-filibuster-proof numbers in the Senate. "I think labor said way too early, right after the election, this is our line in the sand—we have to have card check, and that's it."[4]

Connelly had been a close ally for years. She brought strength and clout. The SEIU was widely considered the most powerful union in Pennsylvania, with nearly 100,000 members in the state. The SEIU was the nation's largest health-care union, the largest property services union, and the second-largest public employees union, behind the American Federation of State, County and Municipal Employees (AFSCME).

Connelly had an indelible image of me from an early encounter, when she had testified at a 2003 Philadelphia field hearing that I chaired on labor law reform. After I heard testimony from a worker disciplined for trying to organize a union, Connelly recalled, I pointed my finger at a right-to-work witness and asked whether she really thought the worker should have gotten in trouble for organizing a union. "And that's the vision I have of you, pointing your finger," she told me privately. "The room just started clapping. . . . That was pretty cool. And that was the first time, Senator, that I thought you really, really enjoyed working people. Liked being around them and talking to them." Connelly also said I reminded her of her father, who was generally quiet but could be cutting when he spoke.[5]

A perception pervaded labor, at least in Pennsylvania, that I had killed card check. Feinstein came out against card check, and other Democratic senators whose votes labor was courting or counting on, including Blanche Lincoln and Mark Pryor, also ultimately demurred. But, as Connelly told me, "in Pennsylvania, it was all Senator Specter. Workers didn't really understand what had happened to the Employee Free Choice Act. So they were caught up, especially western Pennsylvania, in all of that stuff about 'Specter killed card check.'" Connelly was an idealist, but she was also direct and tenacious, like a pit bull, and strained to educate my critics. "But when you have the head of the Pennsylvania AFL-CIO and people like [national president] Leo Girard from the Steelworkers . . . not saying the same thing," she said, "it's kind of hard to get union members from Pennsylvania to believe you."[6]

To Connelly's point, three days before the Pittsburgh rally, George's statements about me appeared in the press: "He did give us the vote two years ago, and our rank and file don't know why he can't give us the vote now, when it's exactly the same bill. And I can't explain it to our members."[7] The fact was, I hadn't voted that way. I had voted for cloture to cut off debate to take up the bill, but that did not mean I supported circumventing the secret ballot. But that nuance escaped the crowd.

Some Democratic leaders also defended me on card check but couldn't cut through the noise. Pennsylvania chairman T. J. Rooney told the press: "I know firsthand from Sen. Specter that he has been working daily over the past few weeks to come to compromise language to be able to get 60 votes to survive a filibuster. I can't think of anybody better to bring about a resolution, especially among other Senators who have concerns."[8]

I wouldn't avoid speaking at the rally. And I didn't want to. I had a long record of standing up to tough crowds. As I took the mic and planted myself on the platform, workers waved signs demanding "Free Choice— Now!" Behind me, a red, white, and blue banner beside a giant Pennsylvania AFL-CIO seal screamed, "Employee Free Choice Act—It's About Workers Rights."

I slid my hand behind my tie. "Ed Rendell gave me this tie last night," I said, holding out the blue strip of silk emblazoned with white donkeys. "It's the symbol of the Democratic Party. . . . And I'm proud to wear this tie and carry the Democratic banner." I told them, "I'm working on legislation which will be a little different from what's in the Employee Free Choice Act, but will pass the Senate." The crowd rumbled. "I'm committed to find an answer which will satisfy you."

"What's wrong with card check?" a woman shouted.

I said, "I agree with Bill George," who was still standing nearby, "when he says if you want to be elected in this state, you have to come to labor." That was especially true in a Democratic primary.

"I voted for you in the past," a man shouted from below and to my right. "You want my vote, I want yours!"

Others clapped and took up the chant. "You want my vote, I want yours!"

"I understand your jobs are on the line," I said. "And I understand my job is on the line."

They hooted. A big man to my right heckled.

"I think you will be satisfied with my vote on this issue," I told them. Just as they had been satisfied with my other votes for labor: to raise the minimum wage, extend unemployment compensation, reform the NLRB, and deliver the stimulus.

More jeers.

Stan Caldwell, my Pittsburgh director, also at the plaza, grew concerned. "Billy George was trying to turn the tide, and the response from the crowd wasn't turning," he recalled. "It was basically, we don't believe you're with us. Rank and file had been pummeled for eighteen months, with their leadership saying, 'Specter turned on us, he's not with us, with card check.' We could see the momentum was so strong, and labor leaders couldn't turn it around."

It was almost as though a lightbulb went on in George's mind. He had been applying maximum pressure and working the rank and file to apply pressure. George seemed to realize that he and the other leaders were going to have to change their tune. But he also saw, at that moment, that it was already too late.

My coronation across the plaza at the Democratic convention also wasn't swaying the rank and file. They may also have been demonstrating their independence, that labor wasn't always bound to the Democratic Party.

"Free choice!"

"Pass the vote!"

"Free choice!"

"Pass the vote!"

In November 2003, Ted Kennedy had introduced the Employee Free Choice Act. I co-sponsored the bill in 2004, largely at Connelly's request. The bill hadn't been aired and hadn't had any hearings. I wanted to advance it and give it some bipartisan support.

In 2005, I co-sponsored it again, in the same framework. Ben Campbell was willing to co-sponsor it with me. In 2007, when Kennedy submitted the bill again, Campbell didn't run for re-election, and I couldn't find a co-sponsor. Labor wanted me to co-sponsor, and I refused, not wanting to be party to a naked reverse, out alone without any blockers. I told AFL-CIO president John Sweeney that if he found me a co-sponsor, I would consider it. He couldn't. Even so, alone among Republicans, I voted for cloture in June 2007, stressing that my vote was procedural and that I was expressing no conclusion on the underlying merits. I said I was withholding co-sponsorship to let both sides give me their views and to give me more time to deliberate.

That cloture vote got me into a lot of trouble with conservative Republicans, at a time when I was watching my right flank over the prospect of another bruising primary. Card check was such a hot issue for Republicans that I got an earful nearly everywhere I went. At a Chicago fund-raiser, the head of a big retail chain sat next to me at lunch and wailed about how terrible card check was. An Altoona manufacturer told me he had supported me in the past, but would not support me again unless I promised to vote against the bill. Technically, that was a bribe offer, and I wouldn't go near it. Then state GOP chairman Gleason urged me to make a statement against the bill, saying that might neutralize Republican ire over my stimulus vote. Republicans were raising money on card check, and added me to their warnings after my party switch.

"Everywhere we turned around, it was card check, card check, card check, card check," Hoeflich recalled. He even got pelted at the Pennsylvania Society's 2009 weekend in Manhattan, an endless stream of cocktail parties and sumptuous meals, where players from politics, government, and industry gathered but avoided talking business.

During the Pennsylvania Society confab, Bob Asher, a good friend with whom I'd collaborated on a number of efforts, took me aside at a bar area at the Waldorf. Asher, a candy manufacturer, told me how devastating card check would be to his business. He chose his words carefully, but the music was that he couldn't support anyone who was for card check.

Asher and I had a long history that began when he supported Thornburgh's primary candidate, Haabestad, against me in the 1980 Senate primary. Asher liked what I did in my first term and was solidly on board until Thornburgh threatened to primary me after I opposed William Bradford Reynolds. Asher's support moved to Thornburgh.

In December 1986, Asher, then the Pennsylvania Republican chairman, and R. Budd Dwyer, the state treasurer, were convicted on eleven federal charges for rigging a $4.6 million state contract award to a California data-processing firm in exchange for a $300,000 bribe. One of the conspirators testified that when Asher found out about the bribe to Dwyer, he ordered it diverted to the Republican State Committee.[9] Asher was sentenced to a year and a day in jail and a $205,000 fine. The day before Dwyer was scheduled for sentencing, the treasurer held a packed news conference at his Harrisburg office. With television broadcasting live, Dwyer protested his innocence, pulled a .357 Magnum revolver from a manila envelope, put the barrel in his mouth, and pulled the trigger. That suicide lingers among journalists and others present as a moment of un-paralleled horror.

While Asher was in jail, Steve Dunkle, then executive director of my Harrisburg office, persuaded me that Asher had been mistreated. Dunkle wanted my help to get Asher into a halfway house. No one was helping him. I put aside the past and helped get him into a halfway house. He has since totally rehabilitated himself, becoming Pennsylvania's Republican national commiteeman in 1998, but media commentary about his case persists. Card check was just too big for him to swallow.

Asher and other business leaders warned about added costs that would drive more companies out of business or overseas. The Chamber of Commerce produced, among other materials, a bumper sticker that showed eyes peering through a hole in a stone wall beside text that asked: "Mind If the Unions Watch *You* Vote? Say NO to CARD CHECK!" Local chambers throughout Pennsylvania, which generally activated only on local issues, held card check meetings, prompted and organized by the national chamber. I spoke at many.

I felt strongly about the sanctity of the secret ballot. Card check reminded me of the battle forty years earlier, when I was running for mayor of Philadelphia, to give state aid to Pennsylvania's parochial schools. I stuck to my principled opposition and it cost me heavily. In 2009, with card check again before the Senate, the prospects for the next cloture vote were virtually the same. Franken's Minnesota victory remained uncertain at the time, so it appeared the fifty-nine Democrats would vote to proceed, with the forty Republicans opposed. The decisive vote would be mine.

I would announce my decision on the Senate floor on March 24, 2009. I would not support the Employee Free Choice Act. The day of my announcement, I invited Trumka to my Capitol Hill office to tell him personally in the late morning about my decision before my planned afternoon floor statement. I can't remember a more difficult conversation.

Trumka had helped me as far back as my 1992 campaign, when he was president of the United Mine Workers of America. We had bonded in the early 1990s when I took up the fight for mine worker retirement benefits. Trumka also had an ego. He was robust and hale, powerful and fit well into middle age. We had played squash once, Trumka's debut at the game, and he got incensed when he didn't win. It didn't matter that I had been playing daily for decades, or that we played on one of my home courts, at the Capitol Hill Squash Club. After the game, he was disconsolate. I've joshed him about it for years.

The Trumka game reminded me of my one squash match with John Heinz, my former Pennsylvania Senate colleague, on the same court. Heinz, a natural athlete and solid tennis player, was also unhappy at losing. I had loaned Heinz a racket, which he broke. The scion of the Heinz food fortune bought me a replacement, worn and secondhand.

When I told Trumka my card check decision, he grew furious. He thought the issue boiled down to loyalty. I believe in loyalty and act on it. But loyalty has its limits when dealing with a public issue that has so much impact, and when the sanctity of the secret ballot is involved.

Trumka argued with me about how important the bill was, and how employers had taken advantage of unions. I told him I agreed. "But the answer is speedy elections, not drowned out by long publicity campaigns, which they're better at than you are." I told him, as I had always stressed, that both sides used excessive tactics and that card check allowed too much opportunity to coerce major union-management decisions like certification. I wanted to level the playing field, but not to the point where intimidation could govern. I was not going to replace employer intimidation with union intimidation. The compromise I was working on would get him arbitration, I said.

None of that was sufficient. Trumka thought card check was the golden key to reviving the union movement in America. When he got back to his office near the White House, he phoned me. I listened and responded. The second conversation went about the same as the first, on the substance. Our close relationship survived that difference, and Trumka wound up doing all that could be expected in promoting my candidacy.

I also invited Hoffa to come to see me that day, and broke the news to him face-to-face. That wasn't easy either. Hoffa inevitably evokes images of his more famous father, whose goons I prosecuted as an assistant Philadelphia DA. But the son projected a more pensive and mellow air, though he could thunder in a baritone, and was physically bigger and heavier than his father. Notwithstanding our differences on card check, Hoffa would be fully supportive in the primary.

That morning at AFL-CIO state headquarters in Pennsylvania, my campaign manager, Chris Nicholas, was outside Bill George's office preparing for an 11 a.m. meeting about how the union could help us in a Republican primary—I had not yet switched parties. Both sides knew that the union couldn't do much for us in a GOP primary, Nicholas said, but every little bit helps. Nicholas had been trying to schedule the appointment for more than a month.

Fifteen minutes before the meeting, Nicholas got an e-mail from Hoeflich saying that I was going to take the Senate floor to announce that I would not support the Employee Free Choice Act. My campaign manager knew that George would soon be alerted. As Nicholas recalled:

> So now I'm . . . waiting for Bill George to show up, knowing that Specter was not going to be with him. So he shows up a little bit late, kind of walks past me, goes into this office, slams the door, does a few things in there, and then opens the door and, "Chris, get in here."
>
> So we get in the meeting, and I forget which one of us said it, but one of us said, "I guess we don't have that much to talk about now."
>
> And to Bill's credit, he was a perfect gentleman toward me. He was upset, he was pissed, he was disappointed, but he didn't rant and rave against me. . . . So we had about a twenty-minute meeting, and just had some nice chitchat, and said, "Okay."
>
> And I was thinking to myself, only in the Specter-palooza could I pick the exact moment in time the boss announces his position on this huge issue to have a meeting with the people who want him on the other side of the issue.[10]

On the Senate floor, I said I could not support card check and eliminate the secret ballot. As to arbitration, I said that it was worth considering on "last best offer," in which an arbitrator selects between the two sides' final offers, which generally forces the sides toward more moderate, reasonable positions. On the merits, I said, the Employee Free Choice Act was a close call. Labor had a valid point that it had suffered from outsourced jobs and losses in pension and health benefits. But the better way to expand labor's clout in collective bargaining was through amendments to the National Labor Relations Act.

Although my card check position had remained consistent, it was complex to explain, and many thought I had flip-flopped. With my announcement, the media pronounced card check dead, and cited me as the cause. Rank-and-file labor largely wrote me off. "I had gone to some labor meetings after that," Caldwell later recalled, "and it went from 'We're pressuring you to do the right thing' to 'We're done with you.'"[11]

When I switched parties a month later, on April 28, 2009, I noted in my floor statement that I would not change my decision on card check—no matter how much support it would bring me from labor. I was changing my party, not my principles, and I wasn't going to abandon a belief just because I had first expressed it while registered as a Republican.

Even so, labor thought that facing a Democratic primary, I would yield and support card check. Labor declared victory, on card check and other parts of its agenda. "This is a new day for the Employee Free Choice Act and labor law reform," AFL-CIO legislative director Bill Samuel gushed to the press.[12] Hoffa issued a statement saying he had been talking with me about my position on the Employee Free Choice Act since my March decision to oppose the bill, and that my party change showed there was still a chance to pass the legislation.

The Hill reported, "Hoffa joins other figures in the organized labor community in celebrating Specter's decision and professing optimism that Specter would switch back on EFCA, despite pledging not to in his statement today."[13] What part of "no" did they not understand?

My ongoing refusal triggered labor's renewed coercion campaign. In addition to the Pittsburgh rally, they held smaller card check rallies outside my state offices. They stuffed Democratic voters' mailboxes across Pennsylvania with postcards and ran field operations knocking on voters' doors, all urging them to press me to vote for the Employee Free Choice Act.[14] Those voters, along with activists and automated calls, barraged my phones. Former representative David Bonior, head of American Rights at Work, issued a statement saying he hoped I heeded the more than 100,000 calls they had ginned up to pressure me on card check.

Labor was also battling other Senate Democrats on card check. Unions backed a primary challenge against Lincoln. Pryor, also from Arkansas, was skittish about card check. When I mentioned the Employee Free Choice Act to Mark Warner of Virginia, a co-founder of the cell phone company Nextel and a champion of small business, he reacted negatively. During a lull at a moderate senators meeting on health care, I said, "Let me discuss what we're doing on card check." Michael Bennet, a Colorado Democrat, got up and walked out of the room.

Meanwhile, Reid had picked six of us Democratic senators to try to work it out: Harkin, senior Democrat on the HELP Committee, as chairman, Pryor, Sherrod Brown, Tom Carper, Schumer, and me. Ultimately, our effort would get us as close as we have come to a major overhaul of the National Labor Relations Act since the Taft-Hartley Act, which labor called the "slave-labor bill," was enacted over President Truman's veto in 1947.

We met in Schumer's conference room, off his reception area. Each senator brought one or two staffers. I usually arrived first. We saved the chairman's spot at the end of the table for Harkin, who generally arrived five to ten minutes late. Harkin was basically standing in for ailing Ted Kennedy, the HELP Committee chairman, apparently at Kennedy's request. Harkin wasn't focused or well prepared. But he had expert aides from the HELP Committee along with one staffer from his personal office. He relied mostly on one-page staff memos and added little to the discussions, which were carried largely by Schumer, Carper, Pryor, and me.

The meetings ran at least an hour. We shared the table with some union leaders and senior staff, including AFL-CIO president Sweeney, who said almost nothing, and legislative director Samuel; Larry Cohen, president of the Communications Workers of America; SEIU president Andy Stern, who was a strong voice throughout the process; and SEIU general counsel Judy Scott. Trumka came to one of the later meetings.

Pryor was thoughtful. Carper was helpful in negotiations and the closest in that group to a conservative. Brown, an outspoken liberal, was open to compromise. Schumer, always the pragmatist, offered the best ideas to maneuver for a compromise. He saw all the foibles and was able to work his way through. Schumer was really the de facto chairman. We met half a dozen times. We hammered out broad outlines and turned them over to staff to work out details.

Card check was off the table. We were not going to kill the secret ballot. That wasn't only my view. Pryor and Carper were also on board, and so, presumably, were other centrist Democrats not at the table. But those others said nothing, content to stay on the sidelines and let the group work out the process.

To expedite union elections, we were looking at requiring votes within ten or fifteen days after 30 percent of workers signed cards for unionization. At the time, most unionization campaigns were running two months, some much longer.

The elephant in the room was the provision mandating arbitration. "Binding arbitration is an absolute non-starter for us," an umbrella business group announced. "We see it as a hostile act to have arbitrators telling business what they have to do."[15]

I studied bill texts and proposed a series of a half dozen counteroffers, some variations on others, that I hoped the business community wound find palatable, to try to reach middle ground. At one point, I asked to share a copy with McConnell. Harkin "reacted hostilely," as one participant recalled, in an understatement.

I was searching for a way to justify compelling arbitration over business's objection. A management failure to operate in good faith, I thought, should trigger compulsory arbitration. I called the NLRB's general counsel and one of its regional directors, among other experts, to research specific cases of a finding on bad faith. I finally concluded that it was impossible to define it with sufficient precision, and not realistic to expect to persuade labor to go along.

Meanwhile, Senate staffers were meeting regularly in Harkin's conference room, joined by union officials. Harkin's aides would crank out drafts.

My general counsel, Matthew Wiener, a former labor lawyer, did an outstanding job representing me. He gave me an update during the crush of negotiations and mentioned an upcoming staff meeting. I asked Wiener when the meeting was scheduled, and he told me, but didn't say where. It wasn't too hard to figure out. When the time came, I knocked on the door.

"There were a lot of surprised faces," Wiener recalled. "I'd never seen a senator at a staff meeting."

I attended staff meetings from time to time. I found it an effective way to get progress on stuff I wanted done. Invariably, I was the only senator there. Senators don't attend staff meetings. I would come in to emphasize my view of the importance of the issue and help to find a compromise.

I grew uncomfortable with the process because we were hearing only one side, labor's. And I said so, more than once. One day, the union crew brought cookies to an Employee Free Choice Act staff meeting. The half dozen Senate staffers placed change or small bills on the table to pay for any cookies they ate, to avoid an appearance of a quid pro quo. Wiener, along with aides to Carper and Pryor, voiced concern to HELP Committee staffers about the unions being in the room while Senate staff was crafting legislation. The HELP staffers agreed, and decreed that union reps would not attend future sessions while staff was drafting legislation.

Shortly afterward, as the August 2009 recess approached, it became clear we didn't have 60 votes for cloture. Two supporters, Kennedy and Byrd, were in failing health. Harkin grew concerned. He didn't want our proposal out there for the business community to take shots at. The group suspended negotiations until we could get a reasonable assurance of 60 votes. Then, they figured, we could reconvene and need only two to three weeks to finish.

I alone wanted to move ahead. "I want an agreement reached," I told the others. I talked off-line a lot to Pryor, who was interested in reaching a solution. He was sympathetic to my efforts, but cautious, and never quite committed himself. I thought he would have been a solid ally if I could bring somebody else along.

At the AFL-CIO's convention in Pittsburgh on September 15, 2009, Trumka, the union's incoming national president, stood on the stage right behind me to my right. I laid out the card check compromise in detail before some five hundred labor zealots, and said Rich Trumka has agreed with this. I said it because he had. I turned and looked at Trumka, made eye contact, and gestured at him.

Trumka smiled. He said nothing, tacitly agreeing.

When I finished speaking, I walked back and shook Trumka's hand, and he embraced me. It was a typical embrace between friends and colleagues—but one that we both knew was being observed by many, and was made for effect.

But it was too late. The workers were sorer than hell. Our card check compromise efforts carried little sway.

The SEIU's Connelly said, "It was tough to sell a compromise on the bill to the membership. I think the biggest part was, there was nothing to sell. . . . What was happening behind closed doors in terms of the compromise being reached—[was] not public."

I talked about the details. So did Connelly. And so did other supportive labor leaders. Connelly told *The Hill*, "In my view, card-check left the Employee Free Choice Act a long time ago. . . . Sen. Specter was key in working out a compromise on the bill with a small group of senators that I believe most if not all of labor could support."[16] Stern shared details of the compromise with his executive board, in writing, according to Connelly. "I don't know that any other union did that. It was so frustrating."[17]

Our statements, even though credible, were not enough. To overcome the rank and file's skepticism and win them over, we needed repetition and publicity, a drumbeat.

Union leaders' disappointment with me was mutual. Some ringleaders should have been for me, loud and up front. I was invited to the Steelworkers' annual convention in Atlantic City, where I had attended several times before. Then I was disinvited. The ringleader who disinvited me, Phil Hughes, was an officer at a Delaware County local, and tight with his neighbor Sestak. United Steelworkers president Girard didn't intervene. Girard wasn't going to say anything that would buy problems with his troops, even though he was constantly pressing me to appear before the International Trade Commission about stopping unfair imports, which I did more than once, on principle.

To endorse me, labor leaders would have to surmount rank-and-file resistance. Making a Democratic primary endorsement itself was tough. Labor generally hadn't jumped into primaries, saving its fire for general elections. Labor leaders didn't seem comfortable going against a pro-labor Democrat such as Joe Sestak. They were better at going after bad guys rather than at supporting a better guy over a good guy. One union leader told the press that endorsing in a Democratic primary was "mindless." "It does not take a pundit to recognize that November is going to be ugly for Democrats and eating our own in primaries makes no sense."[18]

To the extent that labor jumped into the 2010 primary cycle, the Supreme Court's January 2010 *Citizens United* ruling, which freed union as well as corporate campaign spending, gave much of the push. When labor did choose sides in a Democratic primary, it was often to punish what it considered a wayward candidate, such as Senator Lincoln, who had opposed card check.

As *Roll Call* wrote, "For years, Pennsylvania Sen. Arlen Specter was organized Labor's best friend in the Republican Conference. But now that the state's senior senator is a Democrat, local union leaders said his record might not pass muster in a 2010 primary."[19]

Connelly said, "Initially, there was big pushback on me and on SEIU to not support Senator Specter in that election. It really was about a Democrat; it was about Sestak." Sestak was a hard-line liberal. In mid-2009, the AFL-CIO had rated my lifetime voting record at 61 percent but had given Sestak a 96 percent rating.

Connelly said she felt strongly about supporting me because of my consistent efforts over the years for labor. "It was very basic. . . . You just don't turn your back on somebody who's done that. . . . It was extremely, extremely emotional for me. I shed lots of tears over that one fighting with my board." An eight-member SEIU board made endorsement decisions for 2010.

Despite their discomfort about primaries and my card check stance, the AFL-CIO eventually endorsed me, by a vote of more than 75 percent of its executive board of some sixty-four labor leaders. The SEIU also came through. I ultimately got a slew of labor endorsements, from the United Auto Workers, the United Transportation Union, the Building and Construction Trades, the International Brotherhood of Electrical Work, AFSCME, and firefighters and teachers locals, among others.

The Teamsters endorsed me at a big ceremony at the Hotel Hershey, a landmark 1930s complex on a hilltop overlooking Hershey, Pennsylvania. Hoffa wanted to introduce me, so we had to change the time and wait for the general president to arrive. The Teamsters gave me a unanimous endorsement. The entire room stood and hollered, "Arlen! Arlen!"

Now Bill George, the Pennsylvania AFL-CIO chief, also stood up for me publicly. *The Hill* reported: "George said Specter has been with the Obama administration on healthcare reform, trade and other key issues for labor. 'OK, he was not right on this one issue,' the union leader said about EFCA."[20]

I think Trumka and labor leadership always knew they'd be for me over Sestak, just as they had endorsed me in 2004 when I was a Republican, because my heart was in the right place and I'd proved it with what I'd done on funding for the NLRB and the Mining Safety and Health Administration, raising the minimum wage, and extending unemployment compensation, which are my core beliefs. But until then, they would squeeze me as much as they could on card check. I was the guy they needed to win the general election. In the end, only one union came out strong for Sestak, the United Food and Commercial Workers International. But the message didn't filter down to the rank and file.

My card check stance nearly cost me support from the Philadelphia Black Clergy, a key element of my coalition. African American laborers, many of them devout churchgoers, strongly supported the Employee

Free Choice Act. Mike Oscar sensed that the Black Clergy's support was waning and arranged to meet with their elders. He asked to go alone to the church, and I told him, "It's in your hands."

Oscar recounted my record in detail, telling the elders they needed to get past the Employee Free Choice Act and support a senator who had been with them for decades, delivering a host of vital efforts including workforce development grants and Department of Justice mentoring programs.

The elders asked Oscar to leave the room. They took a vote and called him back. They told him they would support me.[21] And they did, including signing an endorsement letter for me that we mailed and used to blanket church parking lots.

We unveiled the letter at an event at Philadelphia's Comcast Center, where Senators Cardin and Roland Burris came in for me. Burris, appointed by disgraced Illinois governor Rod Blagojevich, gave a rousing "we-need-this-man" speech, putting my fights for civil rights in the continuum with Martin Luther King Jr., essentially calling me a historical figure. One Friday night, I went to a big event at an African American church, and Bishop Ernest Morris recognized me with equal enthusiasm.

ELEVEN

FATALLY FLAWED

The 2010 Pennsylvania Democratic Senate primary was a referendum on me. Sestak was an irrelevancy. In a poll a few days before the primary, 52 percent of voters said they didn't know enough about the congressman to form an opinion. Headlines on the race called him "Specter Foe." Even Sestak defined himself as my foe.

"Sestak defines himself to voters in terms of his opponent," CBS News's *Political Hotsheet* reported the day before the primary.

> "Hey, I'm Joe Sestak, the guy who's running against Arlen Specter," he says as he hands out campaign fliers at a check cashing store. He doesn't say: "I'm Joe Sestak and I'm running for the Senate" or "I'm Joe Sestak and I could use your vote Tuesday." As simply as possible, he's saying that he's the guy who's NOT the guy who's been in Washington for 30 years.[1]

The entire Democratic political establishment came out for me, from the president and vice president to the governor and Congressman Bob Brady, a ward leader who ran the Philadelphia Democratic Committee. Brady arranged for me to speak to his organization and came to a number of rallies. One thing he didn't do was endorse me early, before the city committee endorsed. But I could understand that. He was always cordial, really solicitous, even insisting on carrying my suitcase when we met on the train between Philadelphia and Washington.

At the national level, Bob Menendez, head of the Democratic Senatorial Campaign Committee, came to Philadelphia to headline a rally for me at the landmark Tierra Colombiana Restaurant in the heart of the Latino community. I had heavy support among Hispanics, largely from my push for comprehensive immigration reform, and Menendez was one of their heroes. Oscar likened Menendez's arrival that day to the Second Coming.

Menendez and I arrived in separate cars. He reached the restaurant first, and we got bogged down in traffic. Sciarra nearly had a fit trying various routes, all clogged. Finally, northbound on Fifth Street, as we neared the restaurant thirty minutes late, we saw a swarm on the street. At least a hundred people, many wearing Specter T-shirts, were waving Mexican and American flags, hoisting banners and signs, hollering into bullhorns. Kids and even seniors hung out of windows, watching and hollering. Music blared, and crowds devoured quesadillas and tortillas, and drank margaritas. By a Rite Aid drugstore across the street from the restaurant, police cruisers and patrol officers managed the crowds. It was our own event that had jammed the traffic.

When we pulled up, cries rang out, "It's Specter!" And then chants, "Ar-len!"

Menendez spoke for ten minutes, delivering a line in Spanish and then making his own English translation. He hailed me as "someone in the U.S. Senate, that on the critical issues of the day, is willing to vote his conscience, willing to stand with the president, willing to do what is necessary to move this country forward. . . . Senator Arlen Specter was there fighting for us each and every time and now it's our turn to fight for him." Menendez was fighting a feverish illness but wanted to come out for me. He stayed more than an hour, working a post-rally fund-raiser in the restaurant's wine cellar.

Menendez also let me use $1.1 million that I had raised when Obama headlined a Philadelphia event for me. Technically, the money belonged to the party, but the party could spend the proceeds for me if I needed them.

That generosity was largely offset when I had to return $800,000 in donations, through a ploy by the Club for Growth. The Club seized on my statement, when I switched parties, that I would return donations upon request. They asked the FEC for permission to contact my donors to urge them to seek refunds. No third party had ever taken such a step. A strict FEC rule barred anyone from using somebody else's list as a database to target donors for fund-raising, advocacy, or any other purpose. The FEC invited my campaign and the Club to express our views.

My team decided not to engage in the FEC process, but to post notice that donors had a deadline of October 15, 2009, to request refunds. With no response from our campaign, the FEC allowed the Club for Growth to send its letters. Sure enough, the day we posted the deadline notice, the Club's packages began hitting my donors' mailboxes. They even included envelopes addressed to my campaign, with instructions on how to request refunds. In retrospect, we should have set a time limit on refund requests when I first made the offer in May 2009.

Beyond the Club-staged refunds, I promptly cut checks for all my Republican colleagues who had made PAC contributions—except for Richard Shelby, who told the press April 29 that he would not ask for his money back. He said he hadn't refunded money when he switched parties from Democrat to Republican.[2]

A reporter asked at my May 1 Philadelphia news conference about gifts I had made through my Big Tent PAC, and whether I had asked for refunds from those senators whose donations I had refunded. "No, I gave them Big Tent money because I wanted a big tent," I said. "They fit in my tent. I just don't fit in theirs."

I snatched an hour when I could to make fund-raising calls. I meticulously avoided phoning from federal property, which had gotten Al Gore into so much trouble as vice president when he made forty-five fund-raising calls from his White House office in late 1995 and early 1996.

With a Boston trip planned, I decided to call Robert Kraft, owner of the New England Patriots. I had heard what a great guy Bob Kraft was. He was an unlikely target, though. In 2008, I had called for an independent investigation into the Patriots' stealing opponents' signals, known as "Spygate," dismissing the NFL commissioner's investigation as a whitewash. The Patriots had been caught in September 2007 filming the Jets coaches' defensive signals. I grew concerned that they might also have stolen the Eagles' signals in February 2005 in beating my home team in Super Bowl XXXIX, which I had flown to Jacksonville to watch.

I moved against the signal stealing under my thesis that the NFL owns America, and thinks it can do whatever it pleases and get away with it. We're addicted to pro football in a way that we've never been addicted to baseball. Or to heroin. The NFL exists through the grace of federal legislation, the Sports Broadcasting Act of 1961, which allows the teams to share equally in TV revenue. I had long found the teams' approach offensive. They would extract large sums for stadium construction on a threat of moving to another city, as the Colts did in the middle of the night in 1984 from Baltimore to Indianapolis. I was the only Republican senator with a team in the league, except for Mathias of Maryland, who was indifferent on the issue.

I'd been after the NFL since 1983, when it threatened to move the Eagles from Philadelphia to Phoenix. I had filed legislation that conditioned the league's antitrust exemption on not blackmailing teams to change locales. I got then–Judiciary chairman Thurmond to hold a hearing that pitted NFL commissioner Pete Rozelle against Raiders owner Al Davis, in a titanic struggle. Davis was fighting to move his team to Los Angeles from Oakland, and the league was blocking him. Davis ate Rozelle's lunch. Davis eventually won a jury verdict that the NFL had violated antitrust laws, and received $50 million.

In 1986, I pressed legislation to make it tougher for owners to move teams without approval from the league or the local communities. I warned at a 1989 hearing that losing antitrust exemptions was "a distinct possibility" if organized sports cut programming on conventional television in favor of pay TV.

On the signal stealing, a mutual friend told me that if I laid off the Patriots, there'd be a lot of money in Palm Beach. I replied, "I couldn't care less."

I met with NFL commissioner Roger Goodell, did my own research, and blasted Goodell on the Senate floor for his whitewashing, replete with destroying tapes, notes, and other evidence, saying, "On the totality of the available evidence and the potential unknown evidence, the commissioner's investigation has been fatally flawed." I carried it as far as I could. Those who had videotapes had nothing more than the tapes. Ultimately, I said I wouldn't pursue hearings on the Patriots, given more pressing matters before Congress.

In 2009, I heard from Ken Langone, the venture capitalist and Home Depot co-founder, how upset Kraft was with the entire Spygate situation. Kraft was an upright guy who felt the Patriots had been unfairly treated. He had never disputed the facts I had amassed, but felt the publicity unfairly cast a pall on his reputation, and Kraft was known for good works in the community and charitable events.

As long as I was going to be in the Boston area, I figured I'd try for a meeting with Kraft. In the back of my mind— far back—I considered the possibility of fund-raising. But I realized the prospect of bearding that lion in his den was remote. I phoned Kraft. In fund-raising, I'd call people even if I thought it was a long shot. People I knew, people I didn't know, people I'd like to know. All they could do was say no. My fundraising relied on chutzpah, bravado, and self-confidence.

We arranged to meet on Monday, March 16, between a fund-raising breakfast and lunch. My staff reserved the biggest suite I'd ever seen, and I'd seen a few suites, in a historic Boston hotel. Kraft walked in wearing a shirt with a white collar and cuffs and a striped body, the kind I kid people about: "Your shirtmaker ran out of material."

Kraft began by saying his entire staff had urged him not to take my call. Then he said, "Let me get off my chest some things you did to the Patriots which were very unfair. Just very unfair."

I decided not to argue with him.

Kraft said he had a lot of admiration for what I'd done on the NIH and cancer, and told me that he and some of his relatives had had cancer. He said he also admired my efforts for Israel. We began talking about our careers and our activities and wound up having a cordial conversation, two not-so-young Jewish guys who some would think had at least partially succeeded in the world. I did not pursue it beyond that point. I didn't ask for his support.

I t was a lot easier for me to operate in the Democratic caucus than in the Republican one. The issues made it comfortable to vote with the Democrats. It became easier to support labor. But I didn't hesitate to disagree with the administration, from opposing the budget the day after I switched parties to later opposing thirty thousand additional troops for Afghanistan, criticizing the administration's giving Miranda warnings to terror suspects, and challenging the administration's policy in failing to act against Chinese currency manipulation and its policy toward Israel in failing to understand the difference between Jerusalem and the West Bank.

My stump speech stressed that on the big issues, I had always voted more often with the Democrats: supporting a woman's right to choose on abortion; extending unemployment compensation; raising the minimum wage; increasing funding for education and health care, including more than doubling NIH funding; backing the nuclear test ban treaty and federal funding for embryonic stem cell research; opposing warrantless wiretaps; and blocking Bork.

Obama spoke to the Democratic caucus in a televised meeting, and it was arranged that those of us with tough races would get to ask the president a question. I got the first question. I asked about trade with China. Ben Nelson said sotto voce, but loudly enough to be heard: "So much for softballs."

T he support from Obama, Brady, and others was heartening, but 2010 proved a bad year to be an establishment Democrat. Less than a week before the primary, the *New York Times* wrote:

On the face of it, Mr. Specter should be the dominant candidate in this race. He has the support of Mr. Obama, and this is the only Democratic primary where the Democratic Senatorial Campaign Committee is pouring in money on behalf of an incumbent. He has the support of most of the state's political leadership, including Gov. Edward G. Rendell, and labor unions, critical to any get-out-the-vote effort here.

But Mr. Specter has been firmly identified as a Washington politician at a time when such an identification has proved toxic to other incumbents in competitive primaries. And he is viewed with suspicion by Democrats, given his political history. It is difficult enough to be an incumbent these days, but it is particularly tough to be an incumbent without a loyal party base.[3]

In the campaign's final week, Sestak ran a TV ad considered among the political cycle's most devastating. I knew he would show photos of me with Bush, McCain, and Palin, which would be tough for liberal Democrats to swallow. The party's left wing controlled the Democratic primary, just as the Republicans' right wing chose the GOP nominee. Society Hill liberals in Philadelphia wanted money for education and drug control, and despised George W. Bush.

Democrats, especially liberal Democrats, found it more palatable to support me as a maverick Republican who backed them on key issues, lending a bipartisan quality. They expected uniform, total support from Democrats. Labor also liked me better as a renegade Republican than as a Democrat who wouldn't blithely follow the party line.

On the issues, I could have done more as a Republican, supporting Obama. My voice would have been louder. I made that point to an *Allentown Morning Call* reporter, but the line got butchered. Instead, I faced the grave difficulty that any fresh party switcher would find in a primary.

In his ad, Sestak extracted out of context the statement from my media availability that I changed parties so that I could be re-elected, omitting the rest of the thought: that I would use my job to save others' jobs. His

spot showed me hairless from chemotherapy between replays of my trun-
cated statement and endorsements from Bush. He also used footage from
my Delaware County campaign event with McCain and Palin. The ad
wrapped with the narrator crowing, "Arlen Specter switched parties to
save one job: his. Not yours."

Rendell called Sestak's ad the worst kind of politics: a below-the-belt
shot. "That ad is a bunch of BS," the governor told the press. "It's done by
the media consultants who've run all my campaigns, they're terrific, but
it's a bunch of BS."[4]

At first, we didn't know where Sestak had found the "re-elected" footage. It was only after the commercial had aired for several days that a reporter from WNET-TV in Wilkes-Barre found my fuller statement—that
I had changed parties to keep my job after hearing so many constituents
say I should do that to help them keep their jobs. Until then, it wasn't like
looking for a needle in a haystack. We didn't even know where the haystack was.

Even with the fuller statement, our media pro recommended cutting a
radio spot to correct the record, since we couldn't explain it in thirty seconds on TV. That probably was a mistake, though by the campaign's final
days we lacked time and funds for an extensive TV reply. And the damage
was done. The *New York Times* reported:

He has clearly been staggered this week by an advertisement released by Mr. Sestak showing former President George W. Bush
praising Mr. Specter as a "firm ally." That is precisely the kind of
advertisement Democrats are planning to use against Republicans
this fall. Democrats and some of Mr. Specter's supporters said the
advertisement, which also shows the senator appearing alongside
Sarah Palin and a clip of Mr. Specter arching an eyebrow as he
declared, "My change in party will enable me to be re-elected," was
crystallizing concerns about him among both Democratic partisans
and voters weary with Washington. "It's been a rugged time, candidly," Mr. Specter said.[5]

My campaign comptroller, Ellen Tighe, saw Sestak's ad at the office, and then again while she was staying with her parents in Carlyle, Pennsylvania. "I never, ever wanted to see it again," she recalled months after the election. "It's awful to watch, even now."

My argument for leaving an increasingly extremist GOP should have gained sway as Florida's centrist Republican governor, Charlie Crist, plunged toward his fate. Crist had announced for the Senate seat Mel Martinez was vacating, opening his campaign as the all-but-anointed Republican nominee. Then the Tea Party, the Club for Growth, and other staunch conservatives backed a primary challenge by Marco Rubio, a former Speaker of the Florida House of Representatives. Crist slipped behind Rubio by double digits among a hard-right GOP primary jury after Crist hugged Obama at an economic stimulus rally in early 2009. The governor bolted the Republican Party to run as an independent, in an ultimately failed bid.

Even after winning the union endorsements, we couldn't get much of the rank and file to help us with the actual work. "After the endorsement, all of the union leadership had indicated to the senator and to the political and executive staff, 'Hey, we're with you now, we'll get our guys on the ground and everything will fall into place,'" Caldwell recalled later. "But when we went to get bodies to do activities, phone calls or door-to-door, we couldn't get them out."[6] In the campaign's final month, my team set up command posts around the state on at least two Saturdays. We set up phone banks just for labor, including one at AFSCME's spaces in downtown Pittsburgh. We got little or no turnout in Pittsburgh, Harrisburg, and Scranton. After a cathartic card check meeting with Philadelphia heads of the AFL-CIO and the Building Trades Council, Philadelphia did turn some out some bodies.

Sestak essentially had to show only that he was a viable alternative. And he was, at least on paper. He was a perfect candidate to run as a qualified outsider against a long-term incumbent, despite his career on public payrolls. A Naval Academy salutatorian with a Harvard Ph.D., he had reached vice admiral during a thirty-one-year Navy career. He had served on President Clinton's National Security Council as director for defense policy. He was serving his second term in the House, representing suburban Philadelphia. And he entered the race with more than $4 million in his campaign account.

Once Sestak aired his bio spot on April 20, I lost a couple of points every day in our internal polls. That sixty-second spot featured a photo of Sestak in Navy whites in the Oval Office with Clinton. That image elevated Sestak to a legitimate contender and made the difference, my longtime media consultant Chris Mottola later said. Sestak's slashing thirty-second "re-elected" ad, surprisingly, caused little further erosion, at least according to the tracking polls. It was the bio spot—and not the "re-elected" ad—that proved decisive.

"The fundamental problem for Specter was that more than two-thirds of Democratic primary voters had already voted against him in an election," Mottola later said. "In order for Specter to win, Democratic primary voters had to vote for a guy they had voted against, instead of a guy they had voted for."

By the end, Sestak had pulled into a tie with us, after opening down more than 20 points. I saw those polls starting to mount up for him, and felt like I was in the middle of an avalanche, or maybe a volcanic eruption.

Four months before the primary, an unneeded distraction set off what the *Allentown Morning Call* called a weeklong "nationwide uproar."[7] Dom Giordano, a personality on Philadelphia's WPHT Radio, came to Washington to broadcast his show on January 20, the one-year anniversary of Obama's inauguration. I was the leadoff interview. Around 6 p.m., while I was on, Tea Party favorite Michele Bachmann, a feisty Minnesota congresswoman, walked in, and Giordano invited her to join us. I didn't object. I enjoy a challenge, even though I saw I was being set up.

Bachmann, a telegenic and media-savvy ultraconservative, had a burgeoning national following. In June 2011, she would announce her candidacy for president.

On Giordano's show, as the *Los Angeles Times* reported, "Bachmann was going on and on about killing 'Obamacare' and cutting taxes and common-sense conservatism. Hey, you talk till the ref blows the whistle."[8]

Eventually, I tried to jump in to correct the record. As the *Minneapolis Star-Tribune* reported:

Specter had asked Bachmann what she has proposed or supported this year and was in the middle of criticizing her answer when she interjected.

"Now wait a minute. I'll stop and you can talk," Specter said. "I'll treat you like a lady. So act like one."

"I am a lady," Bachmann replied.

Specter later went after Bachmann for saying she voted for "prosperity."

"She said 'I voted for prosperity,'" Specter said. "Well, prosperity wasn't a bill."

"Well why don't we make it a bill?" Bachmann responded.

"Now wait a minute, don't interrupt me," he said. "I didn't interrupt you. Act like a lady."

When Bachmann said, "I think I am a lady," Specter toned down the rhetoric a bit. "I think you are too, that's why I'm treating you like one."[9]

The media convulsed. *New York Times* columnist Gail Collins penned a piece headlined "The Lady and the Arlen."

I told the *Philadelphia Inquirer* that I looked forward to more frank, but less testy, discussions on issues. "While Representative Bachmann and national Republican leaders talk about what they're against, I am focusing on creating jobs, reducing the deficit, and moving our country out of this deep recession."

That hardly quelled the furor. As Paul Carpenter of the *Morning Call* pointed out, "the word 'lady' in modern conversations is demeaning to women, as is any suggestion that women should refrain from displaying what old fuddy-duddies once considered bad manners."[10] And my tough questioning of Anita Hill had continued to shade perceptions of my demeanor toward women. Still, Carpenter also noted, "The fuss is not over Bachmann's loutish behavior; it is over Specter's request."

Bachmann wasted no time capitalizing. She told Fox's Hannity that she was "stunned at the arrogance" of my comments and felt as though I had treated her like a little girl.

The story metastasized. The conflict sparked generational and gender angst and reignited the debate over my questioning of Hill. I could see how "Act like a lady" could be seen as a put-down, like an elder scolding a woman for misbehaving. In the modern world, where people leap to scream "sexism," I could see the charge. And I had put myself in the crosshairs by not handling the interview better. People in my position wear big bull's-eyes on their backs.

I don't apologize unless I've done something really wrong. I just don't do it. But I decided to make an exception here because it was the politic thing to do. So I phoned Bachmann. I left a message on her answering machine. "I called to apologize. Maybe it was generational, but I didn't think that calling somebody a 'lady' was problemsome."

She called back. She was very cordial, really peaches and cream, nothing like the on-air firebrand I had faced. "Oh, it was so nice of you to call. Well, don't give it another thought."

And that snuffed it out, like a candle in a vacuum.

The *Morning Call*'s Carpenter, for one, was disappointed that I had yielded. "Over the years, I've been a harsh critic of Specter at times," he wrote, "but this time the only fault I found in him was for apologizing to Bachmann when it should have been Bachmann who apologized to him."[11]

Even so, my comments lived on. On February 19, Bachmann drew a wild ovation when she burst onstage at the Conservative Political Action Conference, the annual right-wing confab, as Tom Jones's "She's a Lady" bellowed throughout the Marriott Wardman Park ballroom.

On February 18, 2010, in an event that would prove significant during the campaign and spark a national donnybrook afterward, Sestak told a local Philadelphia television host that he had rebuffed a White House offer of an appointment in exchange for dropping his primary challenge against me. Larry Kane prompted Sestak's claim on Comcast's *The Voice of Reason:*

KANE: I don't know how accurate this is, but a lot of reports are that the party has tried very hard to get you out of this race.

SESTAK: Haha, yes.

KANE: Were you ever offered a federal job to get out of this race?

SESTAK: Yes.

KANE: Was it the Navy Secretary?

SESTAK: No comment. I—let me—

KANE: Was it high-ranking?

SESTAK: Let me just say that both here in Pennsylvania and down there, I was called quite a few times and all I've said is, look, I felt when a deal was made that it was hurting the democratic process, I got into this because I think that deal started getting us off the track of where the Democratic party should go. I would never get out for a deal. I'm in this for the Democratic principles and working families.

KANE: Okay, but, was there a job offered to you by the White House? . . .

SESTAK: Yes. Someone offered—yeah.

KANE: It was big, right?

SESTAK: It was—never—let me not comment on it. . . .[12]

Sestak got a lot of mileage out of a vague charge, repeatedly talking about the alleged offer, constantly reminding people that he was the man against the machine. When pressed, Sestak refused to say anything. He also refused my demands to release his records, when I noted the circumstances of his resignation from the Navy. A *Navy Times* report at the time said Sestak had created "a poor command climate."

Sestak accused us of swift-boating him, likening our points to attacks during the 2004 presidential campaign against John Kerry's Navy record. I asked Kerry to make a statement that our points were nothing like swift-boating. A prompt, forceful statement at the outset could have been helpful. Instead, Kerry vacillated, under a pretense of considering, and came out after a long delay with a long, meandering—and near-useless—statement.

Around this time, I asked Kerry's wife, Teresa, whom I had known since she was John Heinz's wife, to host a fund-raiser for me. Word came back that she was upset over an old remark I had made about her current husband, that Kerry had been a senator for twenty years and didn't have one bill to his credit.

Meanwhile, Sestak continued to milk the job-offer controversy. A March 10 exchange with Bret Baier, host of Fox News's *Special Report,* was typical:

BAIER: Did the White House offer you a job to not get in the primary?

SESTAK: And I answered that yes, and I answered it honestly. But to go beyond that, Bret, doesn't serve any purpose.

BAIER: Was it Navy secretary?

SESTAK: As I said, there's nothing to be gained by focusing on this politics stuff.

I immediately said that Sestak should identify the offerer and specify what the offer was, when and where it was made, and under what circumstances. I pressed Sestak hard. If he disclosed those details, you could run an investigation. The Department of Justice should have investigated, but how can you investigate when the guy won't say anything? You can't give him immunity or compel his testimony by putting him in thumbscrews.

The White House, which was taking heat for allegedly arranging the offer, asked me to keep quiet about what would become known as Jobgate and Offergate. I wouldn't. I checked the criminal statute, and the conduct fit squarely. And I said so when the subject came up.

The issue erupted again on March 12, when Gary Sutton and Jim Horn, two savvy and aggressive morning radio hosts on WSBA in York, Pennsylvania, pressed me and then Sestak in separate interviews. "He has made the charge to get a lot of political mileage out of it," I said. "Trying to play the role of the underdog without being specific at all with names, dates, and places."

Sutton persisted, asking me twice whether I thought Sestak was lying about the offer. I said, "There's no credibility. When you have something that happened, the first thing you do is make a prompt complaint. A prompt complaint is an indication of credibility. He says it happened last summer, and he mentioned it a couple of weeks ago."

Sutton asked, "Wouldn't Representative Sestak have an obligation to have reported this alleged job offer to the Ethics Committee?"

"I think he would have," I said. "Some people have commented it's a violation of federal law. . . . There is a crime called misprision of a felony, Gary and Jim; misprision of a felony is when you don't report a crime."

When Sestak's turn came, he doggedly refused to disclose any specifics about the offer, telling WSBA that people didn't care about such "nonsense." Sutton pressed, telling him:

People *do* want to know if someone tried to buy you off. . . . How do you live with that, going out every day saying, 'Well, I'm a Democrat, I'm going to Washington, and I'm going to work with the very same people that tried to buy me off if I get elected to this job.' . . . People care about this. And again, you're talking about your honesty? Your integrity?

The York radio interview apparently gave the White House political crew agita. They railed at Hoeflich, "We told you guys not to raise it." Hoeflich told them, Blame Gary Sutton.

I wasn't a party to Sestak's job offer. But I sure wasn't opposed to it. And while I had never asked anybody to clear the field, I had been glad to hear Reid and other top Democrats say that they considered me their choice for 2010 and wanted a smooth ride to my nomination, for the good of the party. When the Jobgate chatter was simmering, Joan would ask me, "Did they offer him a job?" And I would say, "I don't know, I wouldn't be surprised if they did."

Fingers began pointing at former president Clinton as the intermediary. That turned out to be the case. Sestak had worked for Clinton and was reportedly at Clinton's Georgetown home to discuss running for my Senate seat the evening he found out I was going to switch parties.[13]

The offer, the White House would claim in a formal statement ten days after the primary, was for an unpaid spot on a defense-related presidential advisory commission. The White House would insist it had broken no laws because it had offered nothing of monetary value. An advisory board position seemed small inducement to drop a viable U.S. Senate bid. And it would turn out that Sestak, as a sitting member of Congress, was ineligible to serve on the board anyway. The explanation made no sense.

Early in the campaign, I asked for Clinton's endorsement. The former president phoned me when I was in California to tell me he couldn't, because Sestak had worked for him and they had grown close. But Clinton assured me he would stay neutral in the race, out of gratitude for my vote in his 1999 impeachment trial. I had voted "Not proven, therefore not guilty," which hadn't changed the Senate's verdict—two-thirds were required to convict—but had given Clinton a moral victory of 50 percent support.

A week before the primary, the White House provided another unneeded distraction, when the president nominated Elena Kagan for the Supreme Court to replace retiring justice John Paul Stevens. I had voted against Kagan the year before for solicitor general. I told the press I was keeping an open mind. "I voted against her for solicitor general because she wouldn't answer basic questions about her standards for handling that job. It is a distinctly different position than that of a Supreme Court justice."

The Kagan flap wasn't earthshaking in itself, just another slash in a death by a thousand cuts. Other cuts—many self-inflicted—included opposing Obama's budget; helping to kill the Democratic measure to let bankruptcy judges modify homeowners' mortgage terms; and opposing Obama's nomination of Dawn Johnsen, a hard lefty who equated pro-life views with slavery, to head the Department of Justice's Office of Legal Counsel.

Shortly before the primary, Montgomery County Democratic chairman Marcel Groen held a rally for me in King of Prussia. Attendees that evening were lukewarm, really bordering on indifferent. This was a county that I had carried by big numbers in the 2004 general election.

The Saturday before the election, Pennsylvania labor leaders staged a rally that drew more than two hundred rugged longshoremen and members of related unions to the Philadelphia riverfront by the Walt Whitman Bridge, where I had led efforts for nearly three decades to deepen the channel to forty-five feet from forty. This time, the workers' signs were for me. Boise Butler, head of the local longshoremen's union, a giant who must have weighed 350 pounds, blared that despite my missteps, they wouldn't have been where they were without me. Combined with the activities of "Johnny Doc" Dougherty of the IBEW and Pat Gillespie of the Building Trades, they proved a significant factor. Unfortunately, other union locals did not make similar efforts.

The next day, the Sunday before the primary, I covered Pittsburgh, so we could begin a statewide swing Monday in Erie. As I reached a building walkway, with TV cameras everywhere, a Democratic party worker from the Pittsburgh suburbs stepped up and challenged me. She told me, essentially, "You ought to apologize for the way you treated Anita Hill."

I knew that this festering decades-old problem, which had fed my brouhaha with Bachmann months earlier, was now going to be televised within thirty-six hours of the polls opening. I told the woman that I had treated Hill professionally, and when accusations are made, it's the job of the committee to find out if they're disqualifiers, and that they weren't in that case.

A t the end, White House support sputtered. My advisers insisted that the president should come in and campaign. With daily slippage in the polls, we obviously needed heavier Philadelphia turnout. That meant African American voters. I had a strong record with the African American community and all the endorsements, from the Black Clergy to Mayor Michael Nutter. But motivating that bloc on Election Day would be tough. Maybe even the president couldn't do it. But if anybody could, it was Obama.

A black minister in Pittsburgh told me my election was about Obama, not about me, and that the president's detractors would use my candidacy as a channel to attack the president. That was the message we needed to convey. That was also close to the message I had conveyed at the end of the 2004 Republican primary, when I drafted the ad framing the contest as Toomey versus President Bush. That's what it would have taken to get the full black vote in May 2010. Arlen Specter is not a candidate in this election; it's Barack Obama.

Hoeflich pressed me to call Jim Messina, Obama's deputy chief of staff, to make a personal request for the president's appearance, and I did. I didn't press him, and I wasn't enthusiastic about the president's coming in. I doubted my plea, however strenuous, would change Obama's mind. I also doubted the plea, however urgent, would do any good. And I also thought it was a little demeaning, with my long record, to have to plead for help.

Rendell told *Politico* that he thought an Obama visit would do more good than harm, but that it carried risk. "You know, among conservative Democrats the president may be a double-edged sword."[14]

The White House turned me down, although nobody there knew my personal reservations about making the request. I realized that the president and his advisers were gun-shy about supporting my candidacy after being stung by Obama's failed rescue attempts for New Jersey governor

Jon Corzine and Massachusetts attorney general Martha Coakley. They were reluctant to become victims of a trifecta.

The media said the White House threw me under the bus. The *New York Times* reported: "Democrats . . . said the White House is not eager to be embarrassed by having the president make a last-minute visit on behalf of a candidate who goes on to lose, as happened in the Massachusetts Senate and New Jersey governor's races."[15] *Politico* ran a long election-eve piece headlined "Obama Steers Clear of Shaky Specter."

It looked especially bad when the president, on the Thursday before the election, flew over Philadelphia en route to New York City, and then on Primary Day flew over Pittsburgh to visit a factory in Youngstown, Ohio, twenty-two miles from the Pennsylvania border, for a stimulus event. Footage of the president and me descending from the Philadelphia skies in Air Force One, followed by a joint rally, might have made a difference.

A last-minute appearance by the vice president was a different matter. I had turned down Biden's offer to come in the last Friday before the election because of cost. We had paid $18,000 to bring his retinue to Scranton two weeks before. I told our people to have him do a round of statewide radio interviews instead, which he did.

But the night before the election, I held a final rally before the Phillies game at Citizens Bank Park, at the end of a statewide fly-around. Biden was only a few blocks away at Penn at a prearranged appearance. In the scramble of my statewide swing, I didn't connect personally with Biden to urge his appearance. A staff-to-staff request failed. While not decisive and maybe not even weighty, it was disappointing not to have my old friend travel a few blocks to help rally the troops.

This issue of reciprocity again brings to mind the admonition of a sage Philadelphia lawyer, Harry Shapiro, who said, "Never explain, never complain," and Truman's famous advice, "If you want a friend in Washington, get a dog."

TWELVE

COLD RAIN

Shortly after 8:30 p.m. on primary night, Joan and I reached the Sheraton's inner room, which my team had dubbed the "war room," taking a private entrance to avoid the throngs in the adjacent ball-room. The results were coming in.

In the long, windowless chamber, Shanin, Chris Nicholas, Scott Hoeflich, and the rest of my brain trust had circled a small round table, watching numbers appear and change on laptop computer screens and taking notes. Organizing for America had created a Google spreadsheet that updated constantly, showing the score we needed in each county for a win, and then the numbers that were actually arriving. Across Pennsylvania and in a smattering of offices in Washington, some fifteen to twenty people with subscription rights to this document pored over the numbers. In the inner room, eight laptops lay open, all feeding off wireless modems to show the automatic updates.

Some of my aides sat at a large conference table that dominated the room, covered in a tablecloth and set with unused glasses. A few guests, including some of my close friends, sat in two club chairs and where they could find seats, or stood. Ed Rosen, whom I had known since the 1950s from a Jewish fraternal organization, walked in. He apparently hadn't been invited, but should have been. He asked to bring in a couple of other close friends. I said, "Of course, bring them in." A lot of people who should have been in the inner room were out in the ballroom. I didn't have anything to do with the invitations for the inner room. Gradually, some of them trickled in.

Joan was struck by the lack of bustle in the war room. "It was very quiet," she later recalled. "Normally, I would hear the numbers coming in. So I would have a sense of what was happening. In this case, I didn't. In this case, they sort of kept to themselves, taking the numbers themselves, and they weren't very open, announcing the numbers in any way."

For a while, the numbers moved slowly. Whenever doctors examined me or viewed X-rays or other test results in front of me, I always tried to read their faces, to gauge their thoughts. I did the same now with my aides. At first, I saw mostly clamped jaws beneath narrowed eyes that stared at the screens. They were bracing.

Jeff Pollack, our pollster, sat next to me at one point. Shanin got up from the small table and moved to the conference table, still watching a computer screen. Hoeflich worked his computer, bouncing among CNN, MSNBC, and Philly.com, and searching for Associated Press reports. A Pennsylvania Web site with key data kept going down. The continually flashing screens made little sense to me.

"It was hard even for me to figure out what was happening," Hoeflich later recalled. He was also working his BlackBerry, updating the vice president's office constantly; *We're up. We're down. We're starting to move.*

Outside in the Independence Ballroom, some danced to Lou Rawls's "You'll Never Find Another Love Like Mine." A *Bye-Bye Birdie* classic urged, "Gray skies are gonna clear up, put on a happy face." Guests devoured scallops, salad, shrimp, and beef, watched the newscasts, and reveled for more than half an hour in the early returns, which showed me leading. Union leaders, though far fewer than at my 2004 reception, mingled with friends and aides. Some former staffers who had lost their jobs when I switched parties also showed up. They asked others not to mention their attendance. They didn't want their new Republican bosses to know they'd joined a Democrat's election-night gala.

Camera crews and some forty reporters kept pushing out the ropes from their area, encroaching on the floor. "The space between the stage and the media was getting smaller and smaller," Maria Plakoudas, my scheduler who had arranged the Sheraton event, recalled. My staff had set up a separate room for print reporters, and had already moved one bar to give the media more space. Crews had spent much of the day building additional risers for the TV cameras and lining up more power and outlets for the media's equipment. Plakoudas had told the media they could set up in the ballroom at 2 p.m. At 10:30 a.m., she got an anxious call from the Sheraton concierge, saying camera crews were marking off their spots, standing where they wanted to be that night, some on dining room chairs. The hotel was worried about liability.

Whenever one of the ballroom televisions showed a tally, cheers erupted, led by my staff. They knew those early returns were from Philadelphia, and would need to offset other areas, especially some rural regions and other pockets of Sestak strength. But they couldn't see the numbers flashing on the war room computers, and so kept their grins, even as the bustle quieted.

Alex Halper, my aide for homeland security and infrastructure issues, visited the bar repeatedly for Arlentinis, four or five over the course of the night. Each hit hard, with two ounces of Beefeater and a splash of dry vermouth, along with extra olives. Halper generally preferred a dirty martini with olive juice, not straight up like mine, but he was also going for mood. "I thought it was a nice way to pay tribute to our boss."

The drinks flew off the bar, including the "Sparkling Specter," a champagne, gin, lemon juice, and simple syrup concoction; the "Keystone Cocktail," a brew of vodka, sour mix, and curaçao; and the "Spectini," a vodka, triple sec, cranberry juice, and lime juice cocktail. Guests asked Plakoudas for the recipes. Like most of my staff, Halper and Plakoudas had volunteered to take vacation time that day to phone voters from a call center and post signs at polling places. Halper's wife, pregnant with their first child, watched from home.

As the evening wore on, the ballroom cheering died. Ken Altman, my legislative aide for appropriations, found the shifting momentum especially disappointing after phoning some two hundred registered Democrats from a call center in Montgomery County that day. He had told them, "Remember to get out and vote—the polls are still open," and nearly all had assured him that they'd already voted for me, or would. But that's how it is in elections.

In the ballroom, Pat Haag told Joe Sciarra, "I don't think it looks good." In the war room, the OFA spreadsheet showed we were underperforming in a lot of counties, but not overperforming anywhere.

My special adviser John Gillespie made his way from the ballroom into the war room. He wasn't sure he could gain entry, but nobody stopped him. He sidled next to Susan Segal, one of my top Philadelphia aides. "How are things going?" he asked.

"Look around," Susan told him.

The war room smiles had already faded.

Nicholas stared at the changing results from the sixty-seven counties with a poker face, but even that facade began to show signs of despair.

I asked my campaign comptroller, Ellen Tighe, sitting nearby, "How does it look?"

"Sir," she replied, "I think Pete and the folks who watch the numbers regularly are better equipped to answer that question." Pete Jones was our research director. Tighe was thinking it didn't look good, but that she didn't want to be the one to deliver that assessment to me. Her reply gave me the answer, though.

My nine-year-old granddaughter Hatti walked up to me, threw her arms around me, barely reaching my waist, and said, "I'm scared."

I told Hatti I was, too.

Around 9:20 p.m., Shanin, in shirtsleeves, pulled me to the side. He said the Associated Press was going to call the race soon. The scattered returns showing on television still had us with a lead.

"Call the race?" I said. "For us?" I should have known better.

"No," Shanin said. "For Sestak."

"It was clear to me that we were about to fall behind," Shanin recalled later, "and I knew that we could never catch up, because we were running behind in every market in the state by a few points, and there's just no place to make it up."

I didn't say anything.

A couple of minutes later, the AP did call the race.

Shanin said, "I think you ought to call Sestak. Let's get this done."

I agreed, and said I wanted to go up to my room on the twenty-fourth floor.

"I didn't want him to go to back up to the room," Shanin later recalled, "because I didn't want him to have to walk out to an elevator, to pass a lot of people, go up in an elevator, go to his room, make a phone call, come back down. Why take all the time, and why expose yourself to all those people, if you don't have to?" Shanin walked outside to see if the hallway by the war room was empty, and it was. He suggested we call from there.

I said okay. We got Sestak on the line at his party in Wayne, Pennsylvania, on the Main Line in Delaware County. I made it short and sweet: Congratulations and I will support you in the fall.

Meanwhile, Plakoudas had just stepped into the war room. "Everybody was in tears, holding each other's hands," she recalled later. "Everybody started crying. Then we said to each other, *Stay strong, don't cry.* Then I saw the grandchildren, and I lost it."

I walked back into the inner room. I made a short statement, trying to pick up their spirits, which really wasn't possible.

As Hoeflich remembered it, "The boss walks in, says, 'I just called the congressman, I conceded.' And he's holding back, you can just see—he's holding something back emotionally. But he's strong. He's strong. The granddaughters are crying. Maria is bawling. Jennifer Bloom—the body person when he does fund-raising travel—bawling."

Tracey told Perri, who may have been crying hardest of all, "It'll be okay." My four granddaughters were born when I was in my third and fourth Senate terms. They called me "Arlen," but had wrapped my job into their identity.

David Urban, my former chief of staff, changed the channel on a television set to a basketball game. Nobody objected. Urban had played nose tackle for West Point before commanding artillery forces in the first Gulf War, and probably would not have drawn arguments under any circumstances.

"It was just so fast, and then it was over," Joan recalled later. The moment left her numb. "I think that was for me the most shocking part of it—not losing, but the fact that it was so fast, there was no time to reflect; *Here are the numbers—well, we're not doing so well here, but it's doing a little bit better there.* There was none of that. It was just, we just lost."

I looked over at my wife. "Joan, let's go on out."

In the ballroom, a hushed melancholy pervaded amid the jaunty streamers. "Nobody really said anything," recalled Altman, who looked around and found glassy eyes. "I saw people hugging each other."

Smerconish mused to John Gillespie about what might have been. Tighe scanned the crowd for fellow staffers. "Everybody looked shell-shocked," she recalled.

Joan, Shanin, and I strode into the ballroom. As we left the war room, a friend told Joan, "Oh, I'm coming in."

Joan said, "Ruth, we just lost."

"She was shocked, " Joan recalled. "She couldn't believe it. She just was shocked. She may have said something like, 'We just got here.'"

Nearby, CNN's Candy Crowley reported: "I tell you, this room, you could have heard a pin drop. . . . He walked in and an aide came running over and asked them to dump the music. And it was almost immediately quiet. This was such a subdued room."[1]

Sciarra later described my expression as "his typical look" before the cameras. Shanin and Joan were smiling.

Mike Oscar began an "Arlen!" cheer and the several hundred remaining guests applauded and joined, chanting, "Arlen, Arlen!"

"For just a moment," Altman recalled, "I thought Specter was going to say, 'I'm not ready to concede.' . . . I thought just for a second, *There has to be more.* . . . I think it was hope; I was grasping for things. It had been drilled into us for so long—we have battles where Specter always survives. . . . Even when things didn't look good, there had to be a way we survived. . . . It was always, we survived." Like my granddaughters, much of my staff had known me only as a senator. Altman was born in Pennsylvania early in my first term.

The welcome was warm but carried the pain of defeat. If we'd won, the greeting would have been tumultuous. "It wasn't like the clapping of victory," as Hoeflich described it. "It was the clapping of respect."

Joan and I stepped onto the stage, and I settled behind the podium. Shanin quickly joined us to the left, followed by Tracey, Silvi, Perri, Lilli, and Hatti. All the girls were in tears. So were many in the crowd, which had thinned to leave the ballroom half full.

The media throng was still at full strength.

I thought carefully through my concession speech. I was going to make it brief. And I wasn't going to say anything that could remotely be construed as an excuse. I wasn't going to talk about the problem of incumbency. I wasn't going to mention Sestak's "re-elected" ad that took my words out of context and showed me bald from chemotherapy. I wasn't going to cite Sestak's slur at a rally two days before the election about my potential victory: "We can't have a dead man walking." I wasn't going to talk about the difficulties of changing parties.

That was what I thought. I wouldn't allow myself to feel anything more. I focused on advice from Mort Witkin half a century earlier: *Never let your face show how hard your ass is being kicked*. My overarching consideration was not only to keep a stiff upper lip, but to keep both stiff.

"He gives a speech," Hoeflich recalled. "And it's like time stood still the entire speech. There was nothing I could do anymore."

As I spoke, Chris Mottola recalled, he thought of Atticus Finch arguing Tom Robinson's uphill case in *To Kill a Mockingbird*, and then taking defeat with grace. Still emotional about the race a year later, Mottola said:

> There's a generation of people passing by that were better than us. He's part of that Greatest Generation. That's what I thought when I saw him giving his concession, because he was the last of the Depression-baby senators who actually deliver for a state and make people well and make people good and deliver jobs. A generation had passed . . . a legacy of a postwar culture—that we should sacrifice for the next generation, that we should negotiate, that we should talk to each other. . . . I think he was the last of the guys.

And the fact that that kind of guy cannot exist anymore in our political culture and our social culture—it's very sad.

My speech was short. "Good evening to my supporters—and most of the media in the Western Hemisphere," I began. "I have just called Congressman Sestak to congratulate him and tell him that I think it is vital that we keep this seat with the Democratic Party and that I will support him in the election." I then thanked my family and key Senate and campaign aides. When I mentioned Hoeflich, a nice round of applause burst out. "I don't know why he got more applause than I did," I quipped, "but he deserves it." Joan smiled at my side, unflappable, radiant.

"It's been a great privilege to serve the people of Pennsylvania, and it's been a great privilege to be in the United States Senate," I said. "I'll be working very, very hard for the people of the commonwealth in the coming months. Thank you all."

I lived up to Witkin's dictum, and so did Joan. She looked like a movie star in a photo in the *New York Times'* late edition. Calm and poised. No tears, no regrets.

Tom Fitzgerald of the *Philadelphia Inquirer* would report that my eyes were moist. That was probably true, since they tear much of the time as an ongoing side effect of chemotherapy.

As I was closing my speech, Shanin made eye contact with Sciarra and gave a helicopter takeoff sign, his index finger up and rotating in a tight circle. Sciarra made for the door and the car. I followed moments later.

As Hoeflich recalled:

And then the speech ends, and suddenly Shanin and I are playing linebacker, and we're blocking—the press. Because he doesn't want to talk to the press; he just wants to leave. And the press won't leave him alone. They're hounding him everywhere.

I just remember, pushing through and clearing the way, so he and Joan and Shanin could get out of the room, and after the room they got on the escalator, and the escalator's packed, and people are running down the up escalator to get the photo, and they're running everywhere, they're trying to get in his face, and he just wants to be left alone.

And we get downstairs, and there's fifty, sixty media people, just chasing after him, and there's just so many people down in the lobby. He's walking to the car. He's not really sure where he's going at this point, there's so many people obscuring the view of the lobby and the doors.

I yell, "Senator!"

And Shanin pulls his arm and points to me, and we walk out this other door. There Joe is with the car.[2]

Sciarra saw us come out, followed by a horde of reporters wielding boom mics, cameras, and handhelds. The former Philadelphia patrolman saw Joan nearly trampled and took her arm. "Come on, ma'am," Sciarra said. "I don't want to see you get hurt." She climbed in on one side of the car.

Hoeflich, on the other side of the Lincoln with me, was ordering, "Give him some room!" I climbed into the car.

"I close the door, and I'm holding back the media," Hoeflich recalled. "There's guys sitting in front of the car, they won't get out of the way, the car can't pull out, we've got to push them out of the way, and the car pulls a foot or two and stops and the window comes down."

It had begun to rain again. "What about our coats?" I asked Hoeflich. "We need our coats."

"We're getting them, we'll get them to Joe," he assured me. "They'll be at the house shortly."

A TV reporter seized the opportunity to jab a boom mic through my open window.

"I'm leaving," Sciarra recalled thinking. "I don't care if that boom mic gets caught inside the car." He pressed the accelerator.

We pulled out of the Sheraton. Sciarra steered up Sixteenth Street, heavy on the gas, racing toward Vine Street and the Schuylkill Expressway. He checked the mirrors repeatedly to make sure nobody was following us. But the reporters had been on foot.

I was not surprised by the result, which would eventually be certified as 54–46. I had plenty of advance notice that losing was not only a distinct possibility, but a likelihood. With the polls even, you would pretty well conclude that the majority of the 16 percent undecided would go to the challenger. Still, the vaunted Democratic National Committee polling algorithms, played out on so many computer screens and handhelds, had given hope. But they had been off by 50 percent. The DNC had predicted a turnout of 1.5 million voters, beyond expectations, the kind of showing we needed. Just over a million voters had actually cast ballots.

As we crossed Sixteenth and Vine, I said, "There's no need to rush, Joe." For the first time in decades, I wasn't in a hurry.

I had lost elections before, but those losses had been more than thirty years earlier, and never from the pinnacle as a five-term senator. Still, I had been in active or intense competition since I was fifteen, and many defeats along the way had prepared me for primary election night 2010. In the car, I recalled some of the bitter losses of high-school debate tournaments, in some ways the most intense competitions I ever joined, and my three tries in college at winning the West Point national title.

After about six minutes in the car, when we were cruising along the Schuylkill Expressway, Sciarra's cell phone rang. "This is Joe," he said into the device.

"Joe, this is Joe Biden." After a pause, the voice said, "Joe, is the senator with you?"

Sciarra said, "Yes, sir." He handed the phone back to me and said, "It's the vice president."

Before the conversation was very old, I asked Biden, "How's your boy?" His forty-one-year-old son Beau, Delaware's attorney general, had suffered a stroke a week earlier, shortly after returning from a year in Iraq with the Army National Guard.

Biden said, "Oh, there you are, Arlen, terrible night for you, and you're thinking about somebody else."

Biden phoned me again later that night, at home. He obviously felt bad, and felt responsible. A lot of people felt bad about what had happened, and I think that was genuine.

By Rendell's account, the cold early-morning rain dealt the final blow. "The rain killed Arlen," he told the press. Rendell also gave a eulogy for the city's political clubhouse. "You can't really say there's a Philadelphia machine anymore, because if there was one, Arlen would still be standing," he told the *New York Times*. "We backed him, and the turnout in Philadelphia was less than 17 percent."[3]

Within hours of my primary, some seers began pronouncing the collapse of the political center. "Specter is now gone," G. Terry Madonna, Franklin and Marshall's political sage, eulogized in a day-after column. "The moderate politics he epitomized seems not far behind."[4]

THIRTEEN

THE AFTERMATH

Around 10:30 the morning after my primary, a private phone line rang in my Washington office. The Hart Building suite was nearly deserted, with my press secretary the ranking officer on deck. Kate Kelly, a trim ash blonde in her late twenties, had a toughness at variance with her size and age. She picked up the phone to find herself on the line with Reid's aides who tracked votes. She later recalled the exchange:

"Where is the senator?" No pleasantries, like How are you doing, sorry about your loss—nothing, just "Where's the senator?"

I said, "I don't know."

There's a pause, and then you could just hear the incredulousness in their voice, saying, "What do you *mean,* you don't know?"

I said, "I don't know where he is."

"Well, there's a vote this afternoon. Is he coming in?"

I said, "I don't know."

They said, "Well, we need to find out, because it's a really big vote. I'm sure you understand that this is a big situation for us."

This was the cloture vote for . . . financial reg reform.

I said, "I'm sure that *you* know that last night was a really big night for us." And I said, "Frankly, I don't know what to tell you. I don't know where the senator is, and I don't know if he's going to come in to vote."

So then they hung up and called back, thinking that somebody else might answer it, they had to get their line, and I said, "It's still just me. I don't know where the senator is."[1]

As Kelly was talking to Reid's men, I was in Philadelphia wrapping up a 9:30 a.m. squash match with Pop Shenian.

"It was like a death in the family," Shenian recalled. "You don't know what's the appropriate thing to say. He's not one who needs happy talk. He doesn't need consoling. He's a stand-up guy.

"He was at the bench getting changed. I just gave him a hug and a pat on the shoulder and said I loved him, let's go play squash. I could tell he was anxious as hell to get on the squash court. When he's on the court, all his troubles go away."

I wound up booking a seat on the next day's 11 a.m. Amtrak to Washington. Reid had postponed the vote, on cloture for a Wall Street reform bill, until the following afternoon. He needed to lock in more support.

That evening, the family gathered for dinner at Shanin's house. Losing a high-visibility political campaign can traumatize experienced adults, so the impact on a nine-year-old like my granddaughter Hatti or even a twelve-year-old like her sister Lilli could be devastating.

"My sense was my kids were extremely upset," Tracey later recalled.

And I think that that was still settling in at that point, that Arlen didn't win. . . . It's kind of hard to picture your grandfather, who's always been a senator for Pennsylvania—always been front and center, and they've traveled with him, they did the fly-around with him . . . just heard about it all the time . . . To them, he was their grandfather, but also a senator.

I'd been through tough election losses, and I'd had warnings from the polls, providing some insulation, but defeats are still extremely difficult, no matter how much your skin resembles rhinoceros hide. I'd never become a good loser. I subscribed to Knute Rockne's dictum, "Show me a good and gracious loser and I'll show you a failure."

Shanin later offered a variation on that theme, beginning with an observation that most people in my position would not have made the 2010 run.

> Most people seventy-nine years old, thirty years in Senate, all that he'd accomplished, all that legacy stuff—would say, Okay, I'm going to ride out of here on a white horse and retire. A lot of them have done that. And sort of ignore the fact that you're retiring because you can't get re-elected. But he has never been afraid to lose. Most people are afraid to lose . . . In my view, that's why he's a winner. When you're able to accept defeat, then you've really licked the core ingredient of success, which is the willingness to try.

At the dinner table, I tried to soften the blow of the election loss by explaining some of the circumstances to my granddaughters. As Shanin had said repeatedly, we won all the battles. We got the president, the vice president, the governor. We got the AFL-CIO endorsement. We got the Democratic State Committee's endorsement. We got most of the counties' endorsements. And that superstructure all turned into sawdust under Milton Shapp's campaign doctrine of "Man against Machine."

Maybe I should have focused more on that lesson, from my own experience in 1980 beating Bud Haabestad in the Republican Senate primary. He had the governor, both senators, and the state party chairman in his corner.

My party change was clearly a big factor, with a number of dimensions. Democrats doubted that I was a real Democrat. Some looked at my support for Clarence Thomas and my leadership in conducting hearings on Roberts and Alito as persuasive evidence that I was not one of them. Another big factor was the lack of enthusiastic labor support I had enjoyed in previous campaigns, and had been counting on. Card check had poisoned the well with the rank and file.

The Club for Growth and its former president, Pat Toomey, also contributed. "If you want to know how Sen. Arlen Specter was driven from office, look beyond the Democratic primary he lost Tuesday," the *Washington Post* wrote. "Instead, consider the role played by a small conservative group called the Club for Growth."[2]

G. Terry Madonna wrote in his day-after column, headlined "Arlen Specter's Perfect Storm":

> Everything went wrong for him: he was running for re-election against a tide of virulent anti-incumbency; he was the quintessential moderate in an era given over to the politics of polarization; he drew a younger, vigorous primary opponent not experienced enough to know he couldn't win; his age and many medical problems appeared to enfeeble him; and his five terms in office weighed him down with too many votes that had angered too many people.[3]

Sestak's "re-elected" ad, in the end, probably drove little movement. Mottola had tested attacks in focus groups similar to all those Sestak would eventually launch, and the "re-elected" point proved weak. *Of course he wants to be re-elected; he's a politician.* And while Sestak had distorted my statement, I'd been saying all over Pennsylvania that I had changed parties to help my electoral prospects. Mottola said later, "I always thought it was funny—the Sestak spot ended with 'Specter voted to save one job—his own.' I thought the spot should have ended, 'His vote cost only one job—his own.'"

Perri said she didn't want to talk about it. Lilli was quiet but nonplussed, and Hatti flitted in and out of the conversation. Silvi listened closely and seemed to be impressed with my point that it was important to compete and to take your chances on winning or losing. I would have liked to give them the background on the loss to perhaps make it easier to take. Maybe it was a combination of various factors, Madonna's perfect storm. Certainly, the decisive blow was a viable alternative. But we didn't dwell on the campaign, trying to put it behind us.

The next day, Thursday, I arrived in Washington near 1 p.m. and had a working lunch with Hoeflich that felt like a hospice meeting, discussing the office shutdown, the staff, and a host of other issues involved in closing a thirty-year Senate career. I had arranged with Reid's office to vote at 2:30 p.m., then get the 3 p.m. train back to Philadelphia and drive with Joan to the New Jersey shore, where we had a house.

At 3 p.m., as the train was pulling out of Union Station, Reid's people called my office to say they were planning more votes and needed me to stay. Hoeflich told them, "I'm very sorry," but that I had left as arranged. As Joan and I were on the road to New Jersey, Reid got me on the phone. "We need you for another vote," he said. "Where are you?" I was already too far away to reach Washington in time. The majority leader proposed sending a plane for me, but he was eventually able to convince Susan Collins to vote his way. The day seemed a replay of the episode weeks earlier when I needed to fly to Pittsburgh for the Allegheny County dinner, and Reid's votes were off, then on, then off.

On the media front, I tried to correct the record. Shanin drafted an e-mail to Katharine Q. Seelye of the *New York Times*, whose post-election story disappointed us, saying that I was not afraid of losing, as was proven by my 1980 Senate run following a string of losses. He crafted the missive under unusual circumstances. He did not want to talk to Seelye and was willing to communicate with her only by e-mail. As he told me, he wouldn't send the note unless I was willing to speak to her. Meanwhile, Seelye pressed. She offered a front-page Sunday story if I agreed to an interview. I agreed, but only to be interviewed by telephone. She said a phone interview wouldn't warrant a front-page piece. I found the bribe offer of a page 1 story more than surprising; it was shocking. Shanin and I agreed that we didn't want to get involved in negotiations on story placement. We ended the discussion.

Seelye's piece ran that Sunday, on page 14, with a line "Mr. Specter declined to be interviewed for this article." Tom Harkin, who the day before the election had phoned to tell me I was going to win, told Seelye, "The lesson is to be true to yourself. . . . Maybe there comes a time when people think, 'Should I run anymore—is there a time to bow out grace-fully?' But that's not Arlen's style. He's a fighter. And he was going to go down fighting."4

A rlen Specter Inc. had gone bankrupt, wiping out all its shareholders. The loss affected a lot of people. As Joan said, "You're the go-to guy." For nearly two generations, supporters had given blood, sweat, tears, and money. They were making emotional investments, but also more than that. They weren't getting anything tangible, but they were associated with the power structure, with those who were running things. They were a part of the action, a part of the greater glory. And now their investments had gone bust. During my 1976 Senate run, a top aide, Elliot Curson, had turned to me while we were filming some TV spots. Curson had written a Clio-winning ad during my 1969 DA campaign. "For you, this is just another election," he told me. "For me, it's important."

Shortly after the primary, I phoned Dr. Howard Weitz to talk about professional health care. I had known Weitz since he was fifteen, when he stuffed envelopes for my 1967 mayoral campaign. He had since gone on to become an eminent cardiologist. A year earlier, I had arranged his ap-pointment to a key commission.

Weitz asked, in a tone somewhere between a friend's and a physician's, "How are you feeling?"

"Fine," I said. "Occupational hazard. You have to learn how to take a punch in this line of work." I said I was sorry I wouldn't be able to con-tinue raising funds for the NIH.

Weitz said he hadn't gotten over the election. "I'm heartbroken about what happened, and all you've done."

I got a phone call from my Russell High School debate coach, Ada Mae Gressinger, now Haury, who had contributed the most to my development, outside of my family. She was also worried about me. Haury, then ninety-four, told me about a student she had coached in another Kansas town before going to Russell. That team had won the state championship in the B League, for small schools. This former student, now a prominent cardiologist, had sent her a caricature of me from a post-election issue of the *Economist*, a ghastly drawing showing me run over by a donkey-driven car, tire tracks through my severed limbs, as an elephant cheers.

The only way the debater-turned-doctor would have known about me was from Haury. I'm guessing that he was fed up hearing about what a great guy Arlen Specter was, Haury's most prominent student. So when he saw the *Economist* drawing, he sent it to Haury with relish. Haury was so angry at this student of hers—whom she had obviously been very fond of and proud of, to maintain contact so long—that she not only wouldn't answer him, but told me about what he'd done it.

Bettilou Taylor, a top aide for twenty-one years and a health-care and legislative whiz who had run my Appropriations subcommittee, wrote me shortly after the primary:

. . . You always had my back. . . . Your quick action meant so much to me.

Over the years, we had our disagreements. . . . When I think back on those occasions, it makes me smile. . . .

For me not having you in the Senate leaves a big hole. I will miss seeing you in the halls, in hearings and on the floor, your teasing about my wardrobe, your singing and your jokes . . .

When I think of your work in the Senate, I am reminded of a quote by Oliver Wendell Holmes Jr.: "It is required of a man that he should share the passion and action of the time, at peril of being judged not to have lived."

When I went into that office, I was just Arlen Specter, pile driving, raising hell, going through the line at 100 miles per hour, no matter how many tacklers came in front of me. And my bench seemed to appreciate that.

On June 1, Hoeflich sent me a message that the president was flying from Washington to Pittsburgh the next day, but that members were not invited. I had planned to travel to D.C. in any event to attend former transportation secretary Bill Coleman's ninetieth birthday party on June 2. When I was in the gym, Hoeflich asked if I'd be interested in going to Pittsburgh if there was a seat for me. Sure, I told him. He worked some magic, and I wound up on Air Force One.

As we were landing, I got an invitation to join the president in his cabin. Obama said he hadn't known I was on the plane, that he thought I would join him on the ride from Pittsburgh back to Washington.

Obama and I talked briefly about Kagan's pending nomination to the Supreme Court, to replace Stevens. Nominated by President Ford in 1975, Stevens was the only sitting justice whose confirmation I had not participated in. But I knew Stevens from bumping into him in the Senate barbershop and the attending physician's office. The Supreme Court is just across the street from the Hart Senate Building.

When I read in early 2010 that Stevens, then ninety, was planning to retire, I wrote him a letter urging him to stay on the bench, to avoid a filibuster on his replacement. His timing would work better a year later, I suggested. I also invited him to lunch.

Stevens didn't reply. Then, in April 2010, I read in the paper that he was retiring. He phoned and invited me to come over and see him. To me, Stevens had always seemed a jovial guy. Walking into his chambers, I said, "Justice Stevens, I have a question for you."

"Yeah?"

I said, "Do you think I'm too old to be your replacement?"

He smiled and said, "*Well,*" drawing out the word, "if they appointed someone younger, they could serve longer."

We had a wide-ranging discussion about cases, including the incendiary habeas corpus case on detainees at Guantánamo. He smiled, not revealing any Court topics. One day shortly afterward, I went to a dermatologist's office around 4 p.m. I'd found that I could often get seen if I showed up because another patient might be late for an appointment. After seeing the doctor, I came out to spot a patient waiting for another turn at his 4 p.m. appointment: Stevens.

On Kagan, I told the president that I had become persuaded by then-senator Obama's view that a nominee's professional qualification was not enough to merit a senator's support, but that a senator's vote ought to turn on agreement with the nominee's philosophy. I didn't say so, but that view jibed with my recent floor statements that the Supreme Court conference room had become an ideological battleground. The president smiled and said he thought that was a fair standard to apply on confirmation.

I then told Obama that I intended to ask Kagan what cases she would consider for Supreme Court decisions—though not how she would decide any specific case. To that end, I said, I had written to Kagan noting three issues: the terrorist surveillance program, which the high court had ducked by denying review based on lack of standing; a case brought by Holocaust victims against an Italian insurance company where the administration opposed review on the ground that the insurance claims should be handled through executive negotiations; and a lawsuit brought by survivors of 9/11 victims against Saudi officials.

The president said that those issues involved considerations of foreign policy, which would affect whether the Supreme Court wanted to become involved. I said, really in jest, that it sounded like President Obama had a slightly different view on those issues than Senator Obama. The president began to defend his position, and I interjected that I was really only kidding.

It was then time to deplane, ending our talk. The president gave a speech at Carnegie Mellon University, and I was a little surprised when he did not acknowledge my presence, especially when he started off thanking Pittsburgh mayor Luke Ravenstahl for meeting him at the airport, looking straight at Ravenstahl and me sitting together in the audience's front row. He acknowledged a number of people, but not me.

Obama commented about how important the stimulus was, saving the country, and it would have been a perfect opportunity to throw me a mention. He spoke about health care and cited the invective, without naming DeMint, about "Waterloo" and "break him." There, again, I had provided the sixtieth vote.

He surely had a lot on his mind. But we had just talked on the plane. He knew that I'd just lost an election, and as a professional politician, he knew the impact of that. I don't think he intended to overlook me. But the omission did reflect his state of mind—my situation wasn't of sufficient concern to have on his mind. If you're looking for appreciation, especially in my business, don't be surprised when it isn't there. Truman's famous statement is worth repeating often: "If you want a friend in Washington, get a dog." Notwithstanding all that, I'd be less than candid—and less than conscious—if I didn't say that it hurt.

Whatever the president's thinking, his omission affected my sense of personal satisfaction from my stimulus vote. Still, as proof mounts that the stimulus saved the country from a depression, that vote, which cost me so dearly, should count as the most important of my ten thousand Senate votes—hard to compare with trebling NIH funding, but in the same league.

That evening, I was watching *Hardball* and saw Chris Matthews make a big deal out of my accompanying the president, showing us descending Air Force One's steps. Matthews sarcastically asked why the president had taken me along, since I was a lame duck, instead of taking Sestak, the Democratic nominee.

Sestak had his own problems. A firestorm had erupted over Jobgate. On *Fox News Sunday*, Rendell called the job offer "hard-knuckle politics," but said the administration's dodging questions for months was "not smart."[5] A *Washington Post* editorial knocked Sestak for "less-than-full disclosure" and me for calling Sestak's alleged deal a crime, but blamed the matter mostly on the White House.[6]

Nearly 90 percent of all complaints to the Office of Congressional Ethics during the second quarter of 2010 concerned the Sestak offer.[7] Republicans demanded investigations and hearings. They thundered that laws were broken on interfering with a federal election by attempting to bribe a candidate to drop out. Critics grew even louder when a similar scenario erupted involving former Colorado House Speaker Andrew Romanoff, who had challenged appointed senator Michael Bennet, a fellow Democrat.

The controversy got a further boost on August 12, 2010, when Bill Clinton told the media during a Sestak rally in Scranton that he had not tried to convince Sestak to drop his primary challenge against me—

contrary to the White House's written statement. "I didn't try to get him out of the race," Clinton said. "I did not. In fact, I wasn't even accused of that."[8]

Clinton's on-camera denial prompted speculation that the former president was splitting hairs, as he had famously done when he told aides during the Monica Lewinsky scandal, "There's nothing going on between us," and later defended that statement before a grand jury by saying, "It depends on what the meaning of the word 'is' is."

Republican National Committee chairman Michael Steele wrote Attorney General Holder, "It has become clear that the only way to get to the bottom of this is for the Department of Justice to begin a formal investigation."[9] Hearings seemed overkill. It wasn't a defense to say such offers were made all the time, but pressing would-be challengers to drop bids was a legitimate party leadership tool, to try to save money on a primary.

By 1999, Republican Senate moderates could have met in a telephone booth. A decade later, by the end of 2010, the phone booth would have been empty. By the time the Tea Party emerged, helping to defeat Bob Bennett and Mike Castle and to nearly unseat Lisa Murkowski, there was no moderate GOP senator.

In my final Congress ending in January 2011, Democrats held fifty-nine seats, but not a single Republican would provide the sixtieth vote for many important legislative initiatives. The decisive vote came on the Disclose Act, to identify campaign contributors and stop secret contributions, in the wake of *Citizens United*, which had gutted the power of "one person, one vote" by letting corporations and unions pay for political advertising. The forty-one Republican naysayers included several who had vocally supported disclosure not long before. As Dick Polman, the *Philadelphia Inquirer* columnist, wrote:

> The public has the right to know who's laying out the big bucks for all those special interest ads; if well-heeled donors are free to spend whatever they want, then at least tell the public who they are.

And that's precisely what the Republicans have always argued in the past. That was candidate George W. Bush's position during the 2000 campaign.

That was Senator Mitch McConnell's position in 2000, when he said on *Meet the Press,* "Republicans are in favor of disclosure."

That was Senator Lamar Alexander's position in 1999 when he was running for president: "I support . . . free speech and full disclosure. In other words, any individual can give whatever they want as long as it is disclosed every day on the Internet."

That was Senator Jeff Sessions' position just three months ago: "I don't like it when a large source of money is out there funding ads and is unaccountable . . . I tend to favor disclosure."

That was Senator John Cornyn's philosophical position just three months ago: "I think the system needs more transparency, so people can reach their own conclusions."[10]

The *Washington Post* found that Republican candidates were reaping the vast majority of the hidden funds.[11] Four Republicans who opposed the Disclose Act had sponsored and voted for the sweeping McCain-Feingold campaign reform act in 2001: McCain himself and Cochran, Snowe, and Collins. When that 2001 vote ended, McCain had gathered up his forces, the two Maine women, to march up to take bows and primp in front of the cameras, a common practice after passing major legislation.

The Disclose vote was the most significant case of party over policy, but the same scenario played out on unemployment compensation and a host of other bills in late 2010. On election night 2010, after Republicans had gained half a dozen Senate seats, McConnell said, "The single most important thing we want to achieve is for President Obama to be a one-term President."[12]

But at least the racism seemed to recede. In South Carolina's Republican primary runoffs, Nikki Haley, an Indian American woman, won the gubernatorial nomination with 65 percent of the vote over a sitting congressman; and Tim Scott, an African American man, won a congressional nomination 68–32 over Strom Thurmond's son. Both nominees were Tea Party favorites. Both went on to general election wins.

I n the Senate, a season of farewells and valedictories began. But I wasn't ready to go yet. I gave a passionate hour-long floor speech on the courts, constitutional law, and the eroding balance of power as we prepared to vote on Kagan's nomination.

> The difficulty with the recent trend in the Supreme Court decisions, as I see it, is that there has been an abrogation of the fundamental doctrine of separation of powers. . . . The Court has further significantly affected the balance of power and the separation of power by deciding not to decide certain cases. In exercising their discretion not to take cases, they have let rulings stand which have given an enormous amount of what is legitimately, in my opinion, congressional authority to the executive branch of the government. . . .

"The Court has really become an ideological battleground," I said, citing the *Citizens United* decision, which upset a hundred years of precedent in allowing corporations and labor unions to pay for political advertising. I cited Chief Justice Roberts, who said on C-SPAN in early 2010: "I think the most important thing for the public to understand is that we are not a political branch of government. They didn't elect us. If they don't like what we're doing, it's more or less just too bad."[13]

"I am not prepared to accept that in a democracy," I said. "I am not prepared to accept that when we have the learning of Justice Brandeis and know from our own practical experience that sunlight is the best disinfectant. Publicity has a tremendous effect on the way government operates on all levels, including, I submit, the Supreme Court of the United States." I then pressed my long-standing effort to televise Supreme Court proceedings, so that Americans could see the justices tackle cutting-edge cases and could hold them accountable.

With his portrait in the background, Sen. Specter speaks at the November 2008 unveiling ceremony at the Constitution Center in Philadelphia. The painting, by Michael Shane Neal, was commissioned by Yale University, where Specter graduated from law school, now hangs in the law school's library. (AP)

Senator Feinstein gave me an effusive handwritten letter that concluded, "How lucky I am to be your colleague and learn from you." When the Judiciary Committee met the next day, she repeated her praise, and Leahy joined in, saying that he had packed a transcript of my speech to read that weekend. "With all due respect to everybody here, not everybody's speech goes to Vermont with me."

Scaife's *Pittsburgh Tribune-Review* ran an item on the Judiciary Committee comments, concluding: "Specter thanked Feinstein and Leahy for the praise, then made an offer. 'I wouldn't want to burden people with reading the dry text. I'd be very pleased to repeat it,' Specter said." The newspaper's headline read "Thanks but No Thanks."[14]

Republicans turned to obstructionism, a virtual scorched-earth policy to defeat Obama and his agenda. Filibusters were often frivolous and dilatory, evidenced by judges winning confirmation by overwhelming majorities, some 99–0, after cloture was invoked. Each time senators invoked cloture, they could not take up any other business for thirty hours, leaving little time to address other vital legislation.

Obviously, all Democrats do not routinely come to one conclusion and all Republicans to the opposite conclusion by expressing their individual objective judgments. Senators' sentiments expressed in the cloakroom frequently differ dramatically from their votes on the floor. Still, the emphasis on bipartisanship is misplaced. There is no special virtue in having some Republicans and some Democrats take similar positions. The real value and goal is independent thought and objective judgment.

Incivility and extremism pervaded, driven largely by the media, which in turn was trying to keep up with frantic Internet blather. CNN anchor Campbell Brown resigned, saying she couldn't or wouldn't deliver the incendiary barbs needed to compete with the likes of Bill O'Reilly. CNN talk show fixture Larry King quit a couple of months later, closing a show that the *Washington Post*'s Pulitzer-winning TV columnist Tom Shales called "an increasingly lonely outpost of humane civility in a mephitic menagerie of hotheads, saber rattlers, cretins and crackpots." Shales mused:

> Maybe Larry Kings cannot thrive or even survive in a world where the norms for discourse are rage, vehemence and character assassination. . . . And what happens on television invariably affects— and sometimes infects—American life, manners and mores.[15]

Politico captured the broad interest in heat over light in a piece headlined "The Age of Rage":

> What is different these days is the emergence of an industry—a political-media complex—for which ideological conflict is central to the business model. . . . If media executives hunger for ratings, politicians hunger for campaign cash and fame. . . . There is only a small market for moderation and reason.[16]

Michael Smerconish painted an even darker picture in a *Washington Post* op-ed:

The climate in Washington is being shaped by an artificial presentation of attitudes on cable TV and talk radio. To view and to listen is to become convinced that there are only two, diametrically opposed philosophical approaches to the issues. . . . Opinions from the middle are underrepresented, even shunned, in the modern debate. . . . Unfortunately, this approach is rewarded with ratings, because ratings are driven by passion, not universal appeal or general acceptance. . . . Sen. Arlen Specter's decisive loss in Pennsylvania and Sen. John McCain's fight for his political life in Arizona are signs of the vulnerability of non-ideologues running in primaries that cater to the passions at the ends of the spectrum. . . . All of which leaves more elected officials beholden to the fringe elements of their parties, which in turn means less gets done.[17]

The rhetoric boiled over on January 8, 2011, when a twenty-two-year-old, mentally ill nihilist and Internet babble devotee gunned down Representative Gabrielle Giffords and eighteen others while she was holding a Congress on Your Corner constituent service session outside a suburban Tucson supermarket. Fox News president Roger Ailes called for on-air disarmament. "I told all of our guys, shut up, tone it down, make your argument intellectually . . . You don't have to do it with bombast. I hope the other side does that."[18] Obama, speaking at a memorial service in Tucson, called for Americans to usher in more civility in public discourse, to "talk with each other in a way that heals, not a way that wounds."

In the November 2010 general election, boosted by the Tea Party and the Club for Growth, Toomey edged Sestak 51–49. Republicans also captured control of the House. The GOP gained five seats in the Senate, but fell short of a majority because extremist Tea Party candidates had knocked out mainstream Republicans in primaries. Most notably, Christine O'Donnell of Delaware, an unemployed perennial candidate, ousted Representative Michael Castle, a popular former governor, only to get trounced in November by Democrat Chris Coons. O'Donnell had made a series of bizarre statements over the years, ranging from claiming academic degrees she did not hold, including a bachelor's, to volunteering that she had dabbled in witchcraft. She opened an ad by gazing into the camera and declaring, "I am not a witch."

Lisa Murkowski scored the season's biggest triumph, beating Tea Party darling Joe Miller, who had ousted her in a Republican primary, to capture the first write-in Senate victory since Strom Thurmond's in 1954. After Murkowski launched her write-in campaign in September 2010, the Club for Growth ran the same playbook they had used against me in 2009, urging her Republican donors to request refunds. Unlike me, though, Murkowski had not volunteered to return donations. And she was running as an independent, not a Democrat.

More than one supporter told Murkowski, "I got that letter—it made me so mad, I wrote you a second check." Murkowski's chief of staff phoned any donor who requested a refund and explained what was going on. In the end, Murkowski said, she refunded "less than a handful" of donations.[19]

Shortly after launching her write-in bid, Murkowski resigned as vice chair of the Senate Republican Conference. She said she told Mitch McConnell it would be inappropriate to keep the post while running against a Republican nominee. But she kept her position as top Republican on the Energy and Natural Resources Committee. The committee had scheduled no further meetings or hearings for the balance of the 2010 session, and energy was a huge issue in Alaska.

Jim DeMint went to McConnell and said they couldn't have a person running against a Republican nominee as ranking Republican on a committee. "It was purely political," Murkowski said. "To rattle me . . . People recognized that it was a vengeful, spiteful act."[20]

The Republican caucus would vote by secret ballot on whether to strip Murkowski of her Energy post. "When I heard all this was going on, I thought, I need to get on a plane and get back," she recalled. A flight to D.C. would take ten hours.

I thought, They're going to delay this, they're going to think about it. But they acted literally within a twenty-four-hour period. And I thought, Okay, well, I should make some calls, lobby my colleagues, let them know they need to help me.

Then I thought, No. The party has not helped me throughout this whole write-in campaign. I have basically been written off by the senatorial committee. And I'm not going to go back begging and pleading. My relationships will either stand on their own or not. And I didn't make a phone call, or urge anyone to help me out.[21]

The caucus voted to let Murkowski keep her Energy post. She said De-Mint didn't endear himself to other Republican senators, who viewed him as petty and out of sync with the spirit in which the Senate operated.[22]

Even into December 2010, DeMint financed Miller's challenge of Murkowski's write-in win, insisting that any ballot that deviated from precise spelling of Murkowski's full name shouldn't be counted. A large color photo of Miller and a solicitation dominated DeMint's PAC's home page.

Murkowski told me that when she returned to Washington the week before the Thanksgiving recess, DeMint was the only senator who didn't offer good wishes. But she said he did send her an e-mail after she was declared the winner, just one line that said "Congratulations." "But then he continued to raise money for [Miller's recount effort]. . . . Sending me an e-mail congratulations and then continuing to provide money doesn't cut it."[23]

In late December, the *Washington Post* asked me to select a Washington Person of the Year for 2010, for publication in a Sunday package. I chose DeMint, by dint of his impact. That was a standard *Time* magazine had set, most famously by naming Adolf Hitler its Man of the Year for 1938. I wrote:

Sen. Jim DeMint warrants recognition as the emerging political power of the year here. By leveraging the Tea Party movement, he has in many ways dominated the Senate. Placing party purity above pragmatism and even electoral success, he has made some Republican senators worry that a single vote will end their careers, as evidenced by the experience of Utah Republican Sen. Robert Bennett.

Fear of being targeted in their next primary has caused some to change positions and refuse to provide the 60th vote for cloture to move legislation forward and avoid gridlock on many important bills. The Tea Party left three Senate seats—Delaware, Nevada and arguably Colorado—on the table by endorsing unacceptable candidates. Hopefully, DeMint's power will be undercut. But, unless centrists such as Sen. Lisa Murkowski (R-Alaska) can rouse voters to defeat Tea Party candidates, DeMint's power will only grow.

At least pockets of bipartisanship survived. Soon after the November elections, Bob Casey invited his incoming Republican colleague, Pat Toomey, to lunch. Casey said he was inspired by my having taken him to lunch on his first day as a senator in January 2007, and attending his swearing-in reception that day.

Casey's reception had been packed. His father, Robert Casey Sr., had served as a state senator, auditor general, and governor, and Bob had served as state auditor general and treasurer, but Washington was new turf for the Caseys. As Bob recalled, I made my way through the crowd to the stage, which was at least three feet high, where Bob and his wife, Terese, were standing. Just as Bob was beginning a speech, Terese tapped him on the shoulder and told him I was on the other side of the stage. Not realizing there was another stairway onto the stage, Bob said, he walked over to me. He recalled:

> He shook my hand and then before we knew it, I started to pull him up. He started to try to climb up. And I had this moment where I thought, *My goodness, I don't know if I can do this. And if he falls or I fall or both, this is going to be a bad start.* Somehow he grabbed on and pulled hard enough and I was pulling, we got him up on the stage. . . . He was climbing and I was pulling. . . . It was a manifestation of a team working together.[24]

I had a long relationship with the Caseys. I met Bob's parents at the May 1966 funeral service for Walter Alessandroni, the state attorney general who had sponsored my magistrates investigation, killed in a plane crash while running for lieutenant governor. Casey Sr. was strikingly handsome with salt-and-pepper hair, and Ellen was beautiful.

In 1969, when Casey Sr. was state auditor general, he published a report on welfare fraud in Philadelphia. A mob went after him, charging racism. I read the report and made half a dozen arrests based on it, because it was correct. Casey Sr. never forgot that.

Both Casey Sr. and I racked up a series of losses before winning high office. He lost primaries for governor in 1966 and 1970. In 1978, he and I both ran for governor and placed second in our respective primaries. We were considered losing candidates. Casey Sr. was called "the three-time loss from Holy Cross." My 1980 Senate win emboldened him to run again, I was told. After all, I had been a four-time loser. Casey Sr. won for governor in 1986, on his fourth try. But once you win one, people forget the losses.

Casey Sr. drew national attention in 1992, when Democrats refused to let him speak at their nominating convention because of his pro-life views. They figured that showcasing that kind of dissenting voice would weaken them politically and offend the pro-choice faithful. It was atrocious that they wouldn't let a sitting governor who deviated from the party platform express himself candidly and openly.

On the same day in June 1993, Casey Sr. got a double heart-and-liver transplant to combat a rare disease and I underwent surgery to remove a benign brain tumor. The *Philadelphia Daily News* ran the headline "AN-GUISH" above photos of the two of us, juxtaposed so that we were facing each other. The legislative and executive branches of state government closed for the day for the stated purpose of expressing respect. Some thought the Harrisburg crowd was figuring out who would replace each of us, and then who would replace those replacements, and so on.

We both recovered. When I visited the Casey home in Scranton where the governor was recuperating, Ellen could rattle off the birthdates of all thirty-five of their grandchildren.

For the 2007 lunch with Casey Jr., we took the underground tram to the Capitol, accompanied by Terese and one of Bob's top aides. Bob expected that just the two of us would have lunch, but I invited the others to join us. In the Senate Dining Room, we had crab cakes and chicken salad. I cautioned Casey's aide against the tomato pie. I told Bob, as he recalled, "It's important that people see us work together."

"At the time, it didn't mean much to me," Bob said. "Because we were going to work together anyway. Both of us were genuinely committed to doing that." It wasn't until much later, he said, especially with today's partisan rancor, that he realized how powerful even a little signal like that could be.[25]

Inspired by our lunch, Casey took Toomey to the Radisson Hotel buffet, in a grand neoclassical historic landmark that once served as Scranton's train station. Casey gave Toomey some history on Pennsylvania's first two senators, Robert Morris and William Maclay, who were the first U.S. senators ever seated, in June 1787, because Pennsylvania's legislature acted first. Until 1913, when the Seventeenth Amendment established direct election of U.S. senators, state legislatures appointed U.S. senators.

As Casey was giving his history lesson, a wealthy man of about eighty, who had known Casey's parents, walked by. "He saw me and he said, 'Hello, Bob,'" Casey recalled.

And he turned and he looked at Pat Toomey. Just as I was saying, "Here's Pat Toomey," he said, "This is great, that you're having lunch together. This is wonderful." And he walked away. As soon as he did that, I thought back to what Arlen said. People—they get a few messages we send—and they damned well better be positive. . . . If they get an impression about . . . two senators who are going to work together, that matters a lot. They'll say, Well, at least you're trying.[26]

THE WAY OUT

T he country and the world are confronting historic challenges. Tom Coburn said at Kagan's June 2010 confirmation hearings:

> I'm traveling all over this country today and I see something I've never seen in my 62 years of life: an absolute fear that we're losing it, that our institutions are failing us, that we're ignoring the basic document that combines us and puts us together, and that with the abandonment of that, we're liable to lose a whole lot more than just our short-term gains and income. . . . The fact is, is today our kids' future has been mortgaged, and the confidence that we can get out of that is waning, and that we need to build that back up.[1]

Judicial activism has reached unprecedented heights. Supreme Court nominees commit to fundamental principles, but once confirmed pursue their own ideological agendas. The extremes in both parties have dominated the political process. The result is a gridlocked Congress with members unwilling to offend their bases for fear of being ousted in their next primary. The silent moderate majority sits on its hands. If anything, Coburn underestimated the problem.

There is a way out because this country can still be governed by "We the People." If mainstream Republicans had been as active as Tea Party Republicans in the 2010 Utah, Alaska, and Delaware primaries, Bennett, Murkowski, and Castle would have won. That would have given heart to other Republican senators that their records would be judged by sufficiently large bases to give them fighting chances to survive.

Instead, Republican senators contributed to their colleagues' primary defeats. Eating or defeating your own is a form of sophisticated cannibalism. Similarly, on the other side of the aisle, Joe Lieberman, a great senator, could not win his 2006 Democratic primary and announced his retirement in January 2011 because he saw no path to re-election in 2012.

Still, Lisa Murkowski's spectacular write-in win and the defeat of other Tea Party candidates in the 2010 general elections show there is a way to counter right-wing extremists. Murkowski demonstrated that a moderate can win by informing and arousing the general electorate. Her victory proves that America still wants to be and can be governed by the center.

Politics is routinely described as the art of the possible or the art of compromise. The Senate itself was created by the so-called Great Compromise, in which the framers decreed that states would be represented equally in the Senate and proportionate to their populations in the House. As Senate historian Richard Baker noted, "Without that compromise, there would likely have been no Constitution, no Senate, and no United States as we know it today."

But in some quarters, "compromise" has become a dirty word. Ideological purity has become a precondition for support. Politics is no longer the art of the possible when senators are intransigent in their positions. Polarization of the political parties has followed. The Republican Party frequently abandons Reagan's "Big Tent." A single vote out of thousands cast can cost an incumbent his seat. The far right in Utah rejected Bennett because of his vote for TARP. It didn't matter that Vice President Cheney had pleaded with the Republican caucus to support TARP, warning that President Bush would become a modern Herbert Hoover. It didn't matter that twenty-four of the forty-nine other Republican senators had voted for TARP. Bennett's 93 percent conservative rating was insufficient. Repeatedly, senior Republican senators abandoned long-held positions out of fear of losing their seats over a single vote or because of party discipline, most notably on the Disclose Act to reveal donors to political campaigns.

Senator Margaret Chase Smith of Maine had it right when she said we need to distinguish between the compromise of principle and the principle of compromise. The two-party system is based on advocacy of differing approaches to governance, which ultimately seeks middle ground or compromise. That is virtually indispensible to reach a supermajority of 60. When one party insists on ideological purity, compromise is thwarted and the two-party system fails to function.

Notwithstanding the perils, senators can return to independence in voting and crossing party lines, as they did thirty years ago. John F. Kennedy's *Profiles in Courage* shows the way. Sometimes a party does ask too much. The model for an elected official's independence in a representative democracy has never been stated more accurately than in 1774 by Edmund Burke, in the British House of Commons, when he said that the elected representative's "unbiased opinion, his mature judgment, his enlightened conscience . . . [including his vote] ought not to be sacrificed to you, to any man or any set of men living."

Today, lawmakers operate in a volatile climate, with impatient voters regularly ousting incumbents who don't produce as promptly as they might like. People with grievances are the most anxious to shake up the system. But that's all the more reason that Congress needs to deal with issues such as the deficit, the national debt, and the intrusiveness of government. The Tea Party throngs who attended town hall meetings in August 2009, like mine in Lebanon, were not Astroturf, but citizens making important points. But they did not represent all of America or even a majority of Republicans. Pundits are saying our nation is at a cross-roads. I believe it is more like a clover leaf. If activated and motivated to vote, mainstream Americans can steer the country to sensible centrism.

The major concerns running through the country and the world are deficits and national debt. People want all the social services, but are unwilling to pay taxes for them. Greece offered an early example, when years of deficit spending, largely to fund generous benefits, created a debt crisis when the global economic downturn hit in early 2010. Crises in Spain, Portugal, and Ireland followed, with ripples through the European Union and other areas. Another grievance is intrusiveness of government, most notably in this country in the national health-care plan, which requires everybody to have health insurance by 2014 and imposes penalties on businesses that don't comply. The lower federal courts have divided over whether the law is constitutional. The matter is before the Supreme Court.

The vitriol and hatred on all sides is overwhelming. In the political arena, both parties have been pushing purity tests. In November 2009, amid internecine GOP warfare over a New York congressional primary, a group of Republican National Committee members circulated a test to require potential candidates to abide by at least eight of ten conservative principles, or forfeit party financing and endorsement. The principles included opposing bills such as the stimulus, "Obama-style government-run healthcare," card check, and government restrictions on gun ownership.

The same is true on the Democratic side. Zell Miller wrote:

> You cannot agree on just seven of their ten issues, or even nine. All ten must be embraced and ostentatiously hugged to your bosom with slobbering kisses. Remember how the Democrats wouldn't let Governor Bob Casey of Pennsylvania even speak at our national conventions because he was pro-life? Now that was keeping the convention "pure."[2]

As Jim Jeffords wrote shortly after his party switch, "The two political parties are undergoing an ideological purification, which I regret having contributed to."[3]

The way out turns on dealing with the debt and a widespread feeling—which is real—of overreaching by the federal government. Obama's bipartisan commission on the deficit and national debt, officially the National Commission on Fiscal Responsibility and Reform, was right in putting everything on the table. The commission issued its report, titled "The Moment of Truth," in December 2010. The report carried a host of painful recommendations, including raising the retirement age for Social Security, limiting mortgage interest deductions, and cutting defense spending.

But how do we close the chasm in American politics left by the collapse of the political center? How do we recapture that center, from which America must be governed? Coming together on fiscal remedies will get us part of the way there. But any lasting course correction must run through the voting booth. We should consider various strategies and tactics to spur greater participation in elections, and to lessen the parties' lock on the process.

A dozen states have forms of open primaries, virtually unchanged in the past twenty years. Washington's blanket primary, in which voters pick candidates regardless of their party labels, essentially dates to the 1930s. The biggest recent move in this direction is California's Proposition 14, which eliminates parties in the nominating process. All candidates would appear on a single primary ballot. Every registered voter could cast a ballot. The top two vote getters would compete in a runoff. A number of states, including Washington, have adopted variations on this approach. If Pennsylvania had followed such a course, I would not have switched parties.

But California's approach spurs concerns about opening the system disproportionately for the well-known and wealthy, and disenfranchising third parties. Independents generally find it hard to raise money. So California may not offer the precise answer. But it could be a counterforce. The essential point is to have the parties ease off.

The founders did not deal with the electoral process. The Constitution makes no mention of political parties. James Madison, often called the Father of the Constitution and arguably America's first political mastermind, warned in *Federalist* 10 of the evils of faction. He famously wrote in *Federalist* 51, "If men were angels, no government would be necessary."

Still, at its outset this country adopted England's bivalent "either-or" structure, with two competing parties. The system stems ultimately from the ancient Greeks and Hebrews. In the 1720s, the Whigs and Tories crossed the Atlantic and evolved here into Democrats and Republicans. The Tories began as the "court party," later the loyalists. In later forms, they became Federalists and Non-Federalists. The founders eschewed European multiparty systems.

George Washington, a Federalist by instinct, tried to operate in a rigidly nonpartisan manner, with limited success. Now, two centuries of legislating have entrenched and enshrined the interests of Democrats and Republicans at both the state and federal levels through devices such as filing fees and petitions, and have kept out others, which are demeaned as "third" and "fringe" parties. Parties jealously defend the status quo and generally hate reform efforts. It would be tough to break the duopoly of power, and we could never do away with political parties in America, and should not try to.

The solution involves controlling and channeling factions, and increasing candidate and voter participation and ballot access. Sweeping federal legislation is unrealistic. The first hurdle would be getting Congress behind a national reform effort for such approaches as open primaries, in which voters pick candidates regardless of their own party affiliations; blanket primaries, in which voters pick candidates regardless of the candidates' party labels; and top-two primaries, in which voters pick candidates— who may not even state party preferences—and the top two vote getters advance to the general election.

We should advance measures to allow candidates to compete in a general election as independents after losing primary campaigns, as some states now do; increase voting by mail; and permit Election Day registration, early voting, weekend elections, and forty-eight-hour voting. The Motor Voter Act, or National Voter Registration Act of 1993, allowing voter registration while getting a driver's license or social services, was an early move in this vein.

It all begins with everyday citizens. Americans must become more politically active. Democracy is not a spectator sport. It's discouraging that my 2010 primary drew 24 percent turnout, which means the nominee was selected by one-eighth of eligible voters.

For decades, I've been urging voters off the sidelines and onto the playing field, most loudly during my presidential run. As I said following my party switch: for the people who are Republicans that just sit by and allow the Club for Growth and their ilk to continue to dominate the party after they beat Linc Chafee and cost Republican control of the Senate and cost thirty-four federal judges, there ought to be a rebellion; there ought to be an uprising.

With fuller participation, Lieberman would have won his Democratic primary in Connecticut in 2006, and I believe I would have won a Republican primary in Pennsylvania in 2010. If more people would participate, the center would control the parties, which would benefit both Democrats and Republicans—and America.

Christine Todd Whitman called on Republican centrists to become "radical moderates" and sounded a battle cry:

> Until moderates are able to build a robust, grassroots, and financial network that can stand up to the firepower of the far right, they will likely and understandably continue to trim their sails, hoping to avoid the sort of expensive, divisive, and ugly primary challenge Senator Arlen Specter had to beat back in 2004.[4]

We also need to reform the process once we turn from electing to governing. In the last fifteen years, the "world's greatest deliberative body" has degenerated into a do-nothing Senate because of abusive procedural actions taken by both Republican and Democratic majority leaders. The Senate has gridlocked and grown dysfunctional.

A principal foundation of the U.S. Senate's historic stature was the ability of any senator to offer virtually any amendment at any time. The Senate chamber provides a forum for unlimited debate, with the potential to acquaint the people of America and the world with innovative public policy proposals, and then to vote on the issues. That changed in 1993, when majority leaders began using their powers under Senate rules to block amendments. Rules allow the majority leader, through the right of first recognition, to offer a series of amendments to prevent any other senator from proposing one, a process known as "filling the tree." That practice was infrequent until a decade ago but lately has become common, by both parties.

By precluding other senators from offering amendments, the majority leader protects his caucus from taking tough votes. Never mind that senators are sent to Washington and paid to make tough votes. Sometimes after the tree has been filled, senators will hold extensive negotiations to select a limited number of specified amendments on which both sides are willing to vote. In part, this is done to limit the time needed to finish the bill. More often, it's done to eliminate votes on which senators would have to take positions on controversial issues, to deny future campaign opponents fodder for thirty-second TV spots.

The inevitable and understandable consequence of filling the tree has been the filibuster. If a senator cannot offer an amendment, why vote to cut off debate and go to final passage? Senators remain willing to accept the majority's will in rejecting their amendments, but are unwilling to accept being railroaded into wrapping a bill without an opportunity to modify it. That practice has led an indignant, determined minority to deny the 60 votes needed to cut off debate. It came to a head with my calling Reid "tyrannical" in July 2008.

"If the Senate is to function, you have to let pressure off," Coburn said when we talked in his office during my final weeks in the Senate. "And the way you let the pressure off is to debate amendments." Coburn's Web site boasts, "As a senator, Dr. Coburn has offered more amendments than any of his colleagues." Coburn continued:

I think everybody here is a grown-up. And if they lose their amendments, fine; at least they've had a chance to put their say in. And at least they've had a chance to debate what they think are the critical issues. When you don't get the opportunity to do that, it kind of goes back to the word "tyrant."[5]

To stop the practice of filling the tree and to revert to traditional Senate debate and votes, in February 2007 I proposed Senate Resolution 83, a two-sentence amendment to the Senate's standing rules. Despite repeated efforts, the legislation went nowhere.

The House has suffered a parallel decline, through changes in rules governing what amendments can be offered on the floor and how long members can debate. Open rules, which allowed any member to offer a relevant amendment, gave way increasingly to restricted rules and to closed rules, which bar amendments.

While abusing Senate rules has led to gridlock, a decline in comity has inflamed partisanship. Senators have gone to other states to campaign against incumbents of the other party; most notable was Majority Leader Bill Frist's 2004 trip to South Dakota to oppose Minority Leader Tom Daschle. Senators have even opposed their own caucus mates in primary challenges, most flamboyantly DeMint. Such conduct was beyond contemplation in the Senate I joined thirty years ago. Collegiality obviously cannot be maintained when negotiating with a colleague who's working to defeat you, especially one from your own party.

Partisan bickering repulses the American people, as the political class collectively recognized after the January 2011 shootings of Representative Giffords, a federal judge, and seventeen others. It's shameful that it took a massacre to drive the point home. But, for the moment, a breeze of comity wafted through Washington. Above all, we need civility to accomplish anything. Steve and Cokie Roberts, distinguished journalists, put it well in a recent column: "Civility is more than good manners. . . . Civility is a state of mind. It reflects respect for your opponents and for the institutions you serve together. . . . This polarization will make civility in the next Congress more difficult—and more necessary—than ever."[6]

Americans want their senators to work together, and nowhere is that more important than on judicial appointments. The decade from 1995 to 2005 saw Clinton and Bush judicial and executive nominees stymied by the other party's refusal to hold hearings or floor votes. Then, in 2005, the Republican caucus gave serious consideration to invoking the so-called nuclear or constitutional option, to essentially strip the minority of its veto power on judicial nominations. The eleventh-hour compromise by the Gang of 14 established a new standard to eliminate filibusters absent "extraordinary circumstances," with each senator to make his own determination. Regrettably, that standard has not been followed and filibusters continue. Again, the fault rests with both parties.

I proposed a rule change in the 110th and 111th Congresses to keep the 60-vote requirement for cloture, with a condition that senators would have to perform talking filibusters, like Jimmy Stewart in *Mr. Smith Goes to Washington*, not merely present notices of intent to filibuster.

I would also change the rule to cut off debate on judicial and executive branch nominees at 51 votes, as I formally proposed in the 109th Congress. The Senate agenda today is filled with pending judicial and executive nominees, leaving important positions open for months and judicial vacancies in areas facing emergency backlogs. Since even Bork and Thomas did not provoke filibusters, the Senate should be able to do without them on judges and executive officeholders. Senator Henry Cabot Lodge of Massachusetts said in 1893, "To vote without debating is perilous, but to debate and never vote is imbecile."

I would also change the rule requiring thirty hours of post-cloture debate and the rule allowing the secret "hold," which requires cloture to bring the matter to the floor. Requiring a senator to disclose his or her "hold" to the light of day would greatly curtail this abuse. In early 2011, the Senate took some small steps in this direction, but did not get far.

To improve the confirmation process, and especially judicial confirmations, more communication between the executive and legislative branches would go a long way. The process has become so deeply mired in partisanship that a nominee whose views opponents can paint as extreme stands little chance of confirmation.

"It's got to be somebody who was born in an isolation booth, didn't come out until he was old enough to be a judge, and has no paper trail, never made a—never opened his mouth," Bob Dole told me. "And he—or she–might make it, or might not."

I was expressing a similar view in my news conference that caused such a stir the morning after my 2004 election. I do not suggest settling for what Orrin Hatch called "Milquetoast" nominees.[7] But the Senate will no longer be able to confirm polarizing figures, either.

One result of the partisan gotcha climate is that nominees say only as much as they think they must to win confirmation. I told Antonin Scalia he wouldn't advance to chief justice unless he answered questions. We were at a 2003 Constitution Center event in Philadelphia, sitting with Lee Annenberg, widow of former newspaper mogul and ambassador Walter Annenberg. "Lee," I said, turning to Mrs. Annenberg, "you know, a POW gives his name, rank, and serial number. Justice Scalia would only give his name and rank; he wouldn't give his serial number. When they nominate him for chief justice, he's going to be defeated—unless he answers questions."

"Oh, they're not dumb enough to put me up there," Scalia said.

"Oh, yes they are," I said.

In a now-famous 1995 *University of Chicago Law Review* article, future justice Kagan wrote, "When the Senate ceases to engage nominees in meaningful discussion of legal issues, the confirmation process takes on an air of vacuity and farce, and the Senate becomes incapable of either properly evaluating nominees or appropriately educating the public."[8] But at her confirmation hearings in 2010, Kagan continued in the "vacuous" vein she had decried. She declined to answer my questions, even about legal standards, independent of particular cases. In declining to answer one question, she noted that she would return to her solicitor general position if she failed to win confirmation for the high court, and said, "I don't want to count my chickens before I am confirmed."

"You're counting your chickens right now," I replied. "I am one of your chickens, potentially."

As the *Legal Times* reported:

Sen. Arlen Specter (D-Pa.), a perennial wildcard in Supreme Court confirmation hearings, cut short a line of questioning to nominee Elena Kagan today after he said she was not giving him substantive answers.

Specter warned that he was struggling to find a reason not to vote against her.

"You have followed the pattern which has been in vogue since Bork," he said, referring to conventional wisdom that Supreme Court nominees have been hesitant to say much about their legal views after the nomination of the very substantive Judge Robert Bork failed in 1987. "It would be my hope that we could find some place between voting no and having some sort of substantive answers, but I don't know that it would be useful to continue these questions any further."[9]

Paul Kane of the *Washington Post* interviewed me shortly after Kagan's final session ended. "So far it's been a winning hand, but it's not good for the country, court, or Constitution—and certainly not for congressional authority," I said. "I'm giving you a lot of alliteration off the cuff here, Paul."

"You really are!" Kane exclaimed. "This is more Jesse Jackson than I've ever seen from you. Thank you very much."[10]

I told Sheryl Stolberg of the *New York Times* the same day:

She, I think, answered fewer questions than Roberts. Roberts was much more explicit on *stare decisis*, and deference to Congress on fact-finding. Of course he has done exactly the opposite on the bench. . . . She didn't measure up to her own standards . . . . They give purified, prepared pabulum when they come out of the White

House coaching arena. . . . Alito is the same thing. He talked a lot about deference to fact-finding, and then has gone the other way.

For years, Dennis DeConcini and I had pushed a Senate resolution to require nominees to be more responsive. As I said at the Judiciary Committee meeting before voting on Kagan, the time may be ripe to revive that effort.

But we can strike agreements now to surmount at least some of the politics in judicial nominations. Pennsylvania has had a long-standing arrangement to divide nominees between the parties, based on a formula depending on which party controls the Senate and which controls the White House. Under Clinton, when Republicans controlled the Senate, we considered three Democratic nominees for every Republican nominee.

New York has a similar arrangement, going back to Jacob Javits's days in the late 1970s. Chuck Schumer praised that process, saying, "In New York, we are filling every vacancy and I am supporting every nominee. I don't agree with many of them, but we have come to a consensus and an agreement and it will work out well for the people of New York."[11]

I once asked Bob Dole whether, as a general proposition, the president is entitled to more deference than he's getting on judicial nominations. The former majority leader looked out the car window. "Oh, there's a Dole truck, they must be making money. A pineapple truck rolling by." He motioned. A Dole pineapple truck was zipping along a nearby highway overpass. Dole had no connection to the company but had been perennially maligned by critics who assumed he gave his first loyalty to his family business. Eventually, he said:

Well, one way to get that is to spend more time with the Judiciary Committee, if you're president of the United States. You know, have some relationship, instead of just sending up nominees and snarling at each other for six months.

It's going to take an executive president who's willing to spend some time on nominees other than parading them through the photo-op when they're nominated and then every six months say they haven't had a hearing. I mean, I think he has to do that, but that's not going to get them a confirmation. That tends to maybe even polarize it more. So it's got to be quiet, personal.[12]

Dole was the Senate's longest-serving Republican leader, from 1984 to 1996, operating when Republican presidents nominated Rehnquist, Scalia, Kennedy, Souter, Thomas, and Bork to the high court. As to Thomas, he told me:

In that case, there wasn't any consultation. I think they just called to tell us they were going to nominate the guy. And I could understand if they start bringing in members of Congress to consult on every judge, hell, they'd never get one nominated. It's the president's prerogative, so he can nominate, he doesn't have to consult with us. But he should; it would save a lot of headaches later.

Dole said that generally, presidents did not consult him or fellow senators about their Supreme Court nominees.

They generally call you after they're in trouble, of course, and say, "We've got to work on this senator, this senator, this senator," stuff like that. Or, something happened in the committee today, Specter said this, or somebody said this, da da da. So you get the staff to check it out. Ninety percent of the time it wasn't anything. People get uptight at the White House.[13]

Dole may have identified a key roadblock in the confirmation process—presidents' minimal consultation with the Senate. But senators can also foster the dialog, as I did in pressing presidents about their nominees, like my Air Force One discourse to Obama about Kagan. And senators can further ease the process by giving presidents more options in picking nominees. For years, I've pushed a plan for the Senate Judiciary Committee to give the president a list of twenty-five potential Supreme Court nominees that he can review when a vacancy arises. The approach would create a big job for the committee, which in a thoughtful, even torturous way would have to vet scores of prospects in advance. And the senators would have to do much of the work personally, or at least should. As George Watson and John A. Stookey commented in their treatise, *Shaping America: The Politics of Supreme Court Appointments*:

> While all the Senate committee members rely heavily on staff to prepare them for confirmation hearings, some do a considerable amount of the background research themselves. We were told by one of Senator Specter's aides that "He didn't rely on us [his staff] at all. He very much likes to pursue these things himself. And he doesn't like secondary sources either. When I sent him material on flag burning that relied fairly heavily on a standard text, I got a quick note back to provide him with the original sources relied on by the text. He is very much his own counsel."[14]

I don't know which staff member gave that statement, but that was my practice.

By placing a person in a pool of prospective nominees, the Senate would not necessarily be endorsing that person if nominated. The Senate's advice and consent functions are different and distinct, as spelled out in the Constitution's phrase "advice *and* consent."

I initially introduced the measure with Robert Byrd in the mid-1990s. As I told my colleagues from the floor at the time: "The Constitution says the Senate provides advice and consent to the president, and we really ought to get into that business."

My panel concept at one point seemed a cautionary tale about what you wish for. Schumer said I should be number one on such a list of potential nominees. Toomey, then challenging me in the 2004 Republican primary, blasted me on local radio, saying I was the kind of guy who was acceptable to the most liberal Democrat.

Congress should try to stop the Supreme Court from further eroding the constitutional mandate of separation of powers. The Court has been eating Congress's lunch by invalidating legislation through judicial activism after nominees commit under oath in confirmation proceedings to respect congressional fact-finding and precedents. The recent *Citizens United* decision offers a prime example. Ignoring the massive congressional record and reversing recent decisions, Roberts and Alito repudiated their sworn testimony and provided the key votes to permit corporations and unions to secretly pay for political advertising, effectively undermining the basic democratic principle of the power of one person, one vote. Roberts promised to just call balls and strikes. Then he moved the bases.

Congress's response is necessarily limited, respecting judicial independence as the foundation of the rule of law. But Congress could at least require televising the Supreme Court's proceedings, to inform the public about what the Court is doing, since it has the final word on the cutting issues of the day. As Brandeis said, sunlight is the best disinfectant. C-SPAN has been televising House and Senate proceedings for more than twenty years. Televising the Supreme Court would be a big step. The Court rarely even makes transcripts available after its proceedings, and then only for major cases that spark great public interest.

The justices do follow election returns, and the Court does judicially notice societal values as expressed by public opinion. The public ought to know, and respond, to the Court's actions. Televised sessions would increase the public's knowledge and the volume of its responses. The Court, in turn, would weigh those responses when considering which cases to take and how to decide them. Enhanced public scrutiny might also discourage judicial activism and overreaching. FDR assiduously publicized the Court's judicial activism in striking down many pieces of New Deal legislation. Still frustrated, he tried to bull through his Court-packing plan. The plan ultimately failed because of editorials, public opposition, and congressional opposition, but the lesson about activism should be instructive.

Polls show that 85 percent of the American people favor televising the Court when told that a citizen can attend an oral argument for only three minutes in a chamber holding only three hundred people. Great Britain, Canada, and many of our state supreme courts permit television.

Congress has the authority to legislate on this subject, just as Congress decides other administrative matters such as what cases the Court must hear, time limits for decisions, the number of justices, the day the Court convenes, and the number required for a quorum. Television cannot provide a definitive answer, but it could offer significant transparency and insight, and might be the most we can accomplish, given justices' life tenure and judicial independence.

Given the breadth of the Court's authority and the scope of its decisions—so many of which are really public policy choices rather than strictly legal rulings—the public deserves as much access as possible to the Court's proceedings. The more openness and the more opportunity for real public observation, the greater the understanding and trust. As the Supreme Court itself noted in 1986 in *Press-Enterprise Co. v. Superior Court,* "People in an open society do not demand infallibility from their institutions, but it is difficult for them to accept what they are prohibited from observing."

Of course, the Supreme Court could permit television through its own rule, but it has declined to do so. Congress should generally be careful about imposing rules on the Court. With *Bush v. Gore* coming up for argument in 2000, Biden and I wrote the chief justice asking him to televise it, and he wrote us back declining. But the Court did issue an audio recording as soon as the argument was over.

I repeatedly introduced a bill to require the Court to permit television coverage of all its open sessions—unless a majority of justices voted that coverage of a particular case would violate one or more of the parties' due process rights. I would leave that final say to the justices, respecting the Court's authority to make the ultimate decision on constitutional questions. The Judiciary Committee passed the bill 13–6 in April 2010, after earlier passing it 12–6.

Beyond a general policy preference for openness, however, there is a strong argument that the Constitution requires permitting television cameras in the Supreme Court. The Constitution guarantees access to judicial proceedings to the press and the public. In 1980, the Court relied on this tradition when it held in *Richmond Newspapers v. Virginia* that the right of a public trial belongs not just to the accused, but to the press and the public as well. The Court noted that such openness has "long been recognized as an indisputable attribute of an Anglo-American trial."

Further, a strong argument can also be made that forbidding cameras in the Court, while permitting access to print and other media, constitutes discrimination against one type of media in violation of the First Amendment. In recent years, the Supreme Court and lower courts have repeatedly held that treating different media differently is impermissible under the First Amendment, absent an overriding governmental interest.

Anybody can travel to Washington and watch the Court's arguments, which are public—if he has enough free time and enough money, and if there's enough room in the chamber. Recognizing that in modern society most people cannot physically attend trials, the Court specifically addressed the need for media access. Most Americans today get their information from television and through the Internet, which often recycles televised images and footage. Television would provide a level of courtroom access far closer to actually attending than either newspapers or photographs can provide. When television wants to characterize a Court argument, it has to send an artist and rely on his renderings. The TV networks used drawings to report the Supreme Court argument in *Specter v. Dalton* in 1994, when I urged reversal of plans to close the Philadelphia Navy Yard. The approach seemed dated even then.

As technology has improved and television cameras have become smaller and less obtrusive, acceptance of cameras in American courtrooms has grown rapidly, reaching almost every court except the Supreme Court itself. Ironically, it was a Supreme Court decision that helped spur the spread of television cameras in the courts. In *Chandler v. Florida* in 1981, the Court decided that televising criminal proceedings did not inherently interfere with a criminal defendant's constitutional right to a fair trial. Shortly after the *Chandler* decision, the American Bar Association revised its canons to permit judges to authorize televising civil and criminal proceedings. Following those leads, forty-seven states have decided to permit electronic coverage of at least some portion of their judicial proceedings.

In March 1996, the federal Judicial Conference voted to permit each federal court of appeals to "decide for itself whether to permit the taking of photographs and radio and television coverage of appellate arguments." Since that time, two circuit courts have enacted rules permitting television coverage of their arguments. A few years earlier, those two circuits, along with six districts, had participated in a federal experiment with television cameras, bolstering the case that once judges experience cameras in their courtrooms, they no longer oppose the idea.

Some justices vigorously oppose the idea. Justice Kennedy's wife approached me at a social event to tell me what a terrible idea televising the high court was. She didn't want her husband known, because it was too risky. Her concern about security, which others have also voiced, seems vastly overstated. Well-known members of Congress regularly walk in public view throughout the Capitol complex. Other prominent leaders, including presidents, vice presidents, and cabinet officers, all appear in public, with presidents at the extreme mingling with crowds. For justices, such risks are minimal and worth the relatively minor exposure that television coverage would produce.

Even without cameras in the Court, justices have recently burst onto the nation's television screens. Scalia gave extensive interviews for a *60 Minutes* profile in September 2008. All the sitting justices—including Kennedy—gave what C-SPAN bills as "an unprecedented collection of original interviews," which the channel also features on its Web site. Breyer made various national television appearances in 2010 to promote a book. He said it was important for TV viewers to see justices in their robes at the State of the Union address, but he remained concerned that Court coverage would produce ultimately misleading sound bites.[15]

The effort to televise the Courts suffered a severe setback in 2010 with the retirement of Justice Stevens. When I saw Stevens in the Senate barbershop in early July 2003, I asked him about televising the high court, and he told me he was the only vote in favor. Stevens had a history of advocating—and agitating for—a more open Court.

Dole also supported televising the Court. "I think a little fresh air always helps. Maybe some cases," he told me. "When you have the case of *Bush v. Gore*, the public ought to be in on something like that." He chuckled. But Dole acknowledged the justices' resistance.

They like it kind of the way it is, the judges. They don't want anybody to meddle around their business. Picking their nose when
they're on TV and all that stuff . . . Get a special channel on the
Supreme Court or what they're doing. It won't get any advertisers,
but it'd be a public-service type thing.[16]

Reid agreed to include my legislation to televise the Court in the 2010
omnibus appropriations bill, a massive piece of legislation that would
cover most federal spending for the coming year. I talked to House Majority Leader Steny Hoyer, who said he would use his best efforts to keep
the measure in the omnibus in the House-Senate conference. But the
omnibus never passed the Senate. Reid and Durbin said they would press
it in the 112th Congress.

A nother part of the answer on judicial reform involves a more open-
minded approach and more diversity, including looking beyond the
judicial monastery for Supreme Court justices. Mark Hatfield would have
made a fine justice although he was not a lawyer, *because* he wasn't a lawyer. He had been a college professor and a senator, and he offered vast and
varied experience. He was also a cultured and learned man, a Renaissance
man, and knew a lot of law. And he was courteous, hearing everybody
out, displaying a judicial temperament. It's useful to have somebody with
a different point of view on a nine-member Court. To sit on the Supreme
Court, unlike every other court, there's no legal requirement to be a lawyer. But Hatfield never got serious consideration. I was the only one who
was for it. Even Hatfield wasn't for it.

Reagan offered an exception to the usual presidential calculus in seeking a Supreme Court nominee when he looked for a woman shortly into
his first term. Happenstance brought Sandra Day O'Connor to his attention through Barry Goldwater, her principal backer. Goldwater got into a
public spat with Jerry Falwell, who did not care for O'Connor. Goldwater
said he was going to deliver a kick, not specifying the anatomical site,
only that it would be to Falwell's pants. O'Connor hit occasional rough

patches at her Senate hearing. Jeremiah Denton, the former POW and admiral, didn't like her stance on abortion. Judiciary chairman Strom Thurmond, another southern conservative and former military flag officer, gave Denton an extra round of questioning.

On July 4, 2003, I referenced O'Connor's 1981 hearing in a speech at the National Constitution Center, where O'Connor received the Liberty Medal and gave the keynote address. The most memorable element of the program began when those of us onstage were instructed to pull some streamers to open the facade. Instead, a wooden frame composed of two supporting beams and a cross-member, which had been improperly moored, fell on the stage. The frame weighed more than 650 pounds.

As the frame fell, O'Connor screamed, "We're all going to be killed!"

The cross-member hit me in the upper right arm, producing a whopping black-and-blue mark. But no bones were broken, and I was able to stay through the program and play squash later in the afternoon. The frame also injured five others, including Philadelphia mayor John Street. "The frame just missed O'Connor, and created a nationally televised embarrassment," the *Philadelphia Inquirer* reported.[17]

The National Constitution Center symbolizes our nation's past and provides the key for our nation's future. Perhaps among my most significant Senate accomplishments were introducing the 1988 legislation to authorize the Constitution Center and, with Senator Slade Gorton, shepherding through substantial federal funding.

As this book goes to press, many nations around the world are struggling with governance. Our problems of deficit, national debt, partisanship, filibuster, and gridlock are minor compared to the turmoil in Libya, Egypt, Syria, Bahrain, and other countries. The comparison reaffirms Churchill's dictum: "Democracy is the worst form of government except [for] all . . . other form[s]."

Even so, the rise of political extremism in recent decades poses a new, or amplified, threat to the United States. The fringes have displaced tolerance with purity tests and continue purging centrists, with senators cam-

paigning against colleagues and even caucus mates in what sometimes
seems a cannibalistic frenzy. Bob Bennett, Joe Lieberman, Mike Castle—
and nearly Lisa Murkowski—and I are among a growing body count. The
word "extremism" is no longer sufficiently extreme to describe what's going on. The quest for ideological purity is destroying comity and compromise and bringing our government—literally—to a standstill. We escaped
a federal government shutdown at the eleventh hour in April 2011, when
Washington forged a midnight deal to keep the government funded. Im-
passes threaten over the debt ceiling, future budgets, and other matters.

Wisconsin's political confrontation on the cost of collective bargaining
impacting the state's budget deficit is a microcosm of the national political
war. Like other states, Wisconsin lost an outstanding senator in Russell
Feingold, in a Tea Party year. Commenting on Wisconsin's swing to the
right, Feingold noted that elections do have consequences. But he added
that there will be another election in 2012.

That election could provide the answer. It all depends on the electorate. Voters have the power to oust a Congress that passes two-week budget extensions and to defeat governors who indiscriminately slash vital
state appropriations.

The banner adorning the facade of the Constitution Center says it all,
quoting the core of the Constitution:

"We the People."

Notes

One: The New Super Tuesday

1. "The Voters vs. Washington," *CNN Newsroom*, CNN, May 18, 2010.
2. Paul Kane, "Veteran Went Out As He Went In: Fighting," *Washington Post*, May 19, 2010.
3. *Hardball with Chris Matthews*, MSNBC, Feb. 10, 2009.
4. Alexander Burns, "Primary Focus: Whose Clout's at Stake," *Politico*, May 17, 2010.
5. Sasha Issenberg, "Obama Out to Score Big with Prized Demographic: Sports Fans," *Boston Globe*, Oct. 26, 2008.
6. Jason Linkins, "What Is 'Dutch Cleanser,' and Should I Smoke It?" *Huffington Post*, May 18, 2010.
7. David M. Drucker, "Switch Dooms Specter's Last Fight," *Roll Call*, May 19, 2010.
8. Andrew Putz, "The Full Specter," *Philadelphia Magazine*, Nov. 2006.
9. "Top of the Ticket: Democrat Blanche Lincoln Has Trouble Voting in Arkansas. Been in Washington Too Long?" *Los Angeles Times* online, May 19, 2010.
10. Catherine Lucey, "Philly Electricians' Union Boss 'Johnny Doc' Steps Back in the Limelight," *Philadelphia Daily News*, Aug. 16, 2010.
11. *Campbell Brown*, CNN, May 18, 2010.

Two: The Kid from Kansas

1. Edward Rendell, interview with the author, July 30, 1996, Philadelphia, tape-recorded.
2. Richard Fenno, *Learning to Legislate* (Washington: Congressional Quarterly Press, 1991), p. 2.
3. Ibid., p. 14.

Three: Run-a-Dub-Dub, Two Men in a Tub

1. "The Hate Crime Problem," editorial, *Washington Post,* Nov. 18, 1997.
2. George Packer, "The Empty Chamber," *New Yorker,* Aug. 9, 2010.
3. Helen Dewar, "Baker: 'I Am a Slob," *Washington Post,* Nov. 3, 1983.
4. Christine Todd Whitman, *It's My Party, Too* (New York: Penguin Press, 2005), p. 74.
5. Packer, "The Empty Chamber."
6. Sylvia Nolde, interview with the author, June 22, 2010, Washington, D.C.
7. Steve Goldstein, "Specter's Record Inspires Fear—and Loathing—on the Right," *Philadelphia Inquirer,* Feb. 29, 2004.
8. "Senate Shakeup: Historical Views," *The NewsHour with Jim Lehrer,* PBS, May 24, 2001
9. "Arlen Specter: The Contrarian," *Time* magazine, April 14, 2006.
10. Committee on the Judiciary, United States Senate, Confirmation Hearing on the Nomination of John G. Roberts Jr. to be Chief Justice of the United States, 109th Cong. 1st Sess. Sept. 12–15, 2005, p. 387.
11. Tom Coburn, interview with the authors, Dec. 16, 2010, Washington, D.C., tape-recorded.
12. *The Situation Room,* CNN, May 11, 2006.
13. Richard Fenno, *Learning to Legislate* (Washington: Congressional Quarterly Press, 1991), p. 129.
14. Peter DeCoursey, "Specter Succeeds with Tenacity, Ability to Woo Foes," Pennlive.com / *Harrisburg Patriot-News,* Jan. 25, 2004.
15. George F. Will, "A 'Conviction Politician' vs. a Survivor," *Washington Post,* Oct. 30, 1986.
16. E. J. Dionne Jr., "'70s Mode for Pennsylvania Underdog," *New York Times,* Oct. 16, 1986, late city final edition.
17. Juliet Eilperin, *Fight Club Politics: How Partisanship Is Poisoning the House of Representatives* (Lanham, Md.: Rowman & Littlefield, 2006), p. 78.
18. Ibid., p. 87.
19. Charles Krauthammer, "And the Perils of Populism," *Washington Post,* Nov. 8, 1991.
20. Tom Coburn, interview with the authors, Dec. 16, 2010, Washington, D.C., tape-recorded.
21. Sam Brownback, interview with the authors, June 22, 2010, Washington, D.C., tape-recorded.
22. Ibid.
23. Ibid.
24. Mike Duffy, "Popularly Incorrect Bill Maher, Host of Comedy Central's Political Talk Show, Pushed the Right Funny-Bone Buttons," *Detroit Free Press,* June 30, 1996.
25. Lloyd Grove, "Getting a Second Opinion," *Washington Post,* Jan. 27, 1994.
26. Richard Wolf, "Republicans Draw Circles Around Obama Health Plan," *USA Today* online, July 28, 2010.
27. "Dealmaker," editorial, *The Hill,* May 17, 2006.
28. Zell Miller, *A National Party No More: The Conscience of a Conservative Democrat* (Atlanta: Stroud & Hall, 2003), p. 61.
29. Adam Nagourney, "Democrats Reel as Senator Says No to 3rd Term," *New York Times,* Feb. 16, 2010, late edition—final.
30. "Lexington: The Crushing of Arlen Specter," *Economist,* May 22, 2010, p. 38.
31. David Stout, "Defense of Eavesdropping Is Met with Skepticism in Senate," *New York Times,* Feb. 6, 2006.

32. Ibid.
33. Eric Lichtblau, "Bush Would Let Secret Court Sift Wiretap Process," *New York Times*, July 14, 2006.
34. "U.S. Senator Arlen Specter (R-PA) Holds a Hearing on Department of Justice Oversight," *Congressional Quarterly*, FDCH Political Transcripts, July 18, 2006.
35. E. J. Dionne Jr., "Calling Ed Levi," *Washington Post*, Aug. 28, 2007.
36. "Lawmaker: Rove Involved in U.S. Attorney Firing," Associated Press, MSNBC, Aug. 12, 2009.
37. Nell Henderson, "Bernanke: There's No Housing Bubble to Go Bust," *Washington Post*, Oct. 27, 2005.
38. David Leonhardt, "Fed Missed This Bubble. Will It See a New One?" *New York Times*, Jan. 6, 2010.
39. David DeBruyn, interview with the authors, Jan. 14, 2011, Bethesda, Md., tape-recorded.
40. Ibid.

Four: Battle for the Soul of the Republican Party

1. Philip Gourevitch, "Fight on the Right: In Pennsylvania's Republican Primary, Conservatives Test the Party Line," *New Yorker*, Apr. 12, 2004, p. 34.
2. Christine Todd Whitman, *It's My Party, Too* (New York: Penguin Press, 2005), p. 20.
3. *CNN Capital Gang*, CNN, Apr. 3, 2004.
4. Ralph Z. Hallow, "Conservatives Loyal to Liberal Specter," *Washington Times*, Apr. 9, 2004.
5. Douglas Waller, "On the Trail of RINOs," *Time*, Sept. 22, 2003.
6. Dick Polman, "GOP Purists Willing to Sacrifice Their Own to Push Anti-tax Agenda," *Philadelphia Inquirer* online, July 6, 2003.
7. Jeff Miller, "Anti-Specter Ad Lands a Right Hook; GOP Group Called Club for Growth Says Senator Too Liberal. It Backs Toomey," *Allentown Morning Call*, March 30, 2004.
8. Kirk Victor, "All Eyes on Pennsylvania," *National Journal*, Apr. 24, 2004.
9. Matt Bai, "Fight Club," *New York Times*, Aug. 10, 2003.
10. James Dao, "Conservative Takes On Moderate G.O.P. Senator in Pennsylvania," *New York Times*, Apr. 3, 2004.
11. Terence Samuel, "Pennsylvania's Family Feud," *U.S. News & World Report*, Apr. 19, 2004.
12. Bai, "Fight Club."
13. Ibid.
14. Dick Polman, "GOP Purists Willing to Sacrifice Their Own to Push Anti-tax Agenda."
15. Marc Levy, "Toomey Runs with Tea Party, Establishment Support," Associated Press, Oct. 19, 2010.
16. Janet Hook, "GOP's Philosophical Rift Evident in Pennsylvania; Bush Backs the Centrist Incumbent over the Conservative Challenger in a Key Swing State," *Los Angeles Times*, Apr. 18, 2004.
17. Helen Colwell Adams, "Numbers Game," *Lancaster* (PA) *New Era*, Apr. 11, 2004.
18. "The Battle Hymn of the Republicans; How Dick Scaife and a Campaign-Finance Loophole Are Helping to Heat Up a Specter-Toomey Race," *Pittsburgh City Paper*, Apr. 7, 2004.
19. Jeff Miller, "Toomey, Specter May Fight for Same Bucks," *Allentown Morning Call*, Feb. 24, 2003.
20. Carrie Budoff, "Abortion Politics Define Pa. Race," *Philadelphia Inquirer*, Apr. 18, 2004.

21. "GOP Mods Launch a New Round of Ads Against Toomey," *Congress Daily,* Dec. 12, 2003.

22. Janet Hook, "GOP's Philosophical Rift Evident in Pennsylvania."

23. Lara Jakes Jordan, "Labor Contributions Boosting Specter Re-election Bid, Records Show," Associated Press, Nov. 21, 2003.

24. David Keene, "Here's a Conservative Who Is Partial to Sen. Arlen Specter," *The Hill,* May 21, 2003.

25. Alexander Bolton, "Tax Hawks Cooling to Norquist," *The Hill,* Mar. 24, 2004.

26. PoliticsPA.com, Sept. 29, 2003.

27. Peter Jackson, "Poll Shows Toomey Surging As GOP Senate Primary Nears," Associated Press, Apr. 21, 2004.

28. Ben Smith, "The Monday Meeting, a Right-Wing Cabal Ready to Convert N.Y.," *New York Observer,* Feb. 9, 2004.

29. Steve Forbes, "Real Conservatives Prefer Toomey," *Allentown Morning Call,* Apr. 18, 2004.

30. Robert G. Kaiser, "An Enigmatic Heir's Paradoxical World," *Washington Post,* May 3, 1999.

31. David Segal, "Low Road to Splitsville; Right-Wing Publisher's Breakup Is Super-Rich in Tawdry Details," *Washington Post,* Oct. 22, 2007.

32. Ibid.

33. Robert G. Kaiser, "How Scaife's Money Powered a Movement," *Washington Post,* May 2, 1999.

34. "The Battle Hymn of the Republicans."

35. Kaiser, "An Enigmatic Heir's Paradoxical World."

36. Ibid.

37. Ibid.

38. Kaiser, "How Scaife's Money Powered a Movement."

39. Kaiser, "An Enigmatic Heir's Paradoxical World."

40. Kaiser, "How Scaife's Money Powered a Movement."

41. "The Battle Hymn of the Republicans."

42. Rich Lord, "The Righty and the Switch-Hitter," *Pittsburgh City Paper,* Mar. 11, 2004.

43. Jeff Miller, "Bork Backs Toomey for Senate," *Allentown Morning Call,* Jan. 6, 2004.

44. Jackson, "Poll Shows Toomey Surging As GOP Senate Primary Nears."

45. Ralph Z. Hallow, "Specter Rolls Out Bush's Support in Race's Final Days," *Washington Times,* Apr. 26, 2004.

46. John Baer, "Specter, the Warrior, Survives; Conservative Push from Toomey Couldn't Dethrone Feisty 74-Year-Old," *Philadelphia Daily News,* Apr. 28, 2004.

47. Steve Goldstein, "Specter's Close Call Points Up GOP Movement," *Philadelphia Inquirer,* Apr. 29, 2004.

Five: The Toughest Fight

1. Paula Zahn, *Paula Zahn Now,* CNN, Nov. 10, 2004.

2. Charles Hurt, "Conservatives Work to Deflect Specter," *Washington Times,* Dec. 26, 2003.

3. Adam Nagourney, "Senator Ready to Filibuster over Views of Court Pick," *New York Times,* June 21, 2003.

4. Orrin Hatch, 108th Cong., 1st Sess., November 12, 2003, *Congressional Record* p. S14770.

5. Ibid., p. S14550.

6. Chris Mondics, "Foes on Right, Left Await Specter's Vote on Federal Judge," *Philadelphia Inquirer,* July 21, 2003.

7. Helen Dewar, "Appeals Court Nominee Again Blocked; Senate Action Renews Angry Exchanges over Charges of Anti-Catholic Bias," *Washington Post,* Aug.1, 2003.

8. Mondics, "Foes on Right, Left Await Specter's Vote on Federal Judge."

9. Nomination of William H. Pryor Jr., Senate Committee on the Judiciary, June 11, 2003, p. 135.

10. Ibid., pp. 142–43.

11. Ibid., pp. 153–56.

12. Robin Toner, "Bias Claims Anger Demos; Ad Portrays Them as Anti-Catholic," *New Orleans Times-Picayune,* July 27, 2003.

13. Patrick Leahy, Senate Judiciary Committee meeting, 108th Cong., 1st Sess., October 2, 2003, official transcript, pp. 58–59.

14. Dewar, "Appeals Court Nominee Again Blocked."

15. Harry Reid with Mark Warren, *The Good Fight: Hard Lessons from Searchlight to Washington* (New York: G. P. Putnam's Sons, 2008), p. 203.

16. Hurt, "Conservatives Work to Deflect Specter."

17. "Bush Launches Second-Term Agenda Detailing His Priorities," *Fox Special Report with Brit Hume,* Fox News, Nov. 4, 2004.

18. *This Week,* ABC News, Nov. 4, 2004.

19. Carl Hulse, "Abortion Remark by G.O.P. Senator Puts Heat on Peers," *New York Times,* Nov. 5, 2004.

20. "All Circuits Are Busy, Sen. Specter," *The Hill,* Nov. 18, 2004, p. 8.

21. Steve Goldstein, "Specter Presses Campaign for Chairmanship," *Philadelphia Inquirer,* Nov. 10, 2004.

22. Senator Arlen Specter with Frank J. Scaturro, *Never Give In* (New York: Thomas Dunne Books, 2008), p. 48.

23. Paul Kane, "Hatch's Backing Boosts Specter," *Roll Call,* Nov. 17, 2004.

24. "Karl Rove Discusses President Bush's Election Victory," *Meet the Press,* NBC News, Nov. 7, 2004.

25. Specter with Scaturro, *Never Give In,* p. 48.

26. David Brog, interview with the author, July 31, 2010, Washington, D.C.

27. Specter with Scaturro, *Never Give In,* p. 49.

28. David Keene, "In Defense of Sen. Specter," *The Hill,* Nov. 15, 2004.

29. Steve Goldstein, "Specter Wins Panel's Backing," *Philadelphia Inquirer,* Nov. 19, 2004.

30. David Stout, "Frist Sees Hurdles for Specter," *New York Times,* Nov. 15, 2004.

31. "Republican Opponents Ramp Up Efforts to Deny Arlen Specter the Chairmanship of the Senate Judiciary Committee," *CBS Evening News,* Nov. 16, 2004.

32. "U.S. Senators Orrin Hatch and Arlen Specter Hold a News Conference," CQ Transcriptions, Nov. 18, 2004.

33. Goldstein, "Specter Wins Panel's Backing."

34. Specter with Scaturro, *Never Give In,* p. 163.

35. Major Garrett, "Judges: More to That Deal Than Meets the Eye?" Fox News Channel, in *The Hotline,* May 27, 2005.

36. Ibid.

37. Steve Goldstein, "Specter: Filibuster Deal Lesser of Undesirables; He Won't Say How He Would Have Voted but Notes That the Compromise Could Enhance the Judiciary Committee's role," *Philadelphia Inquirer*, May 25, 2005.
38. "Samuel Chase," *An American Experience*, PBS online.

Six: Manifest Injustice

1. Patrick Leahy, *Fox News Sunday*, Sept. 2, 2007.
2. William Yardley, "Craig Defends Decision to Stay in Senate and Attacks Romney," *New York Times*, Oct. 16, 2007.
3. Associated Press, "Senator Admits Use of an Escort Service," *New York Times*, July 10, 2007.
4. Carl Hulse, "Rising Pressure from G.O.P. Led Senator to Quit," *New York Times*, Sept. 2, 2007.
5. David Catanese, "John Ensign, Citing 'Consequences to Sin,' Announces Retirement," *Politico*, Mar. 7, 2011.
6. Yardley, "Craig Defends Decision to Stay in Senate and Attacks Romney."
7. Jeffrey Toobin, "Casualties of Justice," *New Yorker*, Jan. 3, 2011, p. 38.
8. Ibid.
9. Ibid.
10. Elaine Scoliono, "Washington at Work," *New York Times*, Apr. 5, 1990.
11. Ibid.
12. Christine Todd Whitman, *It's My Party, Too* (New York: Penguin Press, 2005), p. 113.
13. Peter Nicholas, "Santorum Expects Lott to Keep Post," *Philadelphia Inquirer*, Dec. 18, 2002.
14. Robert Dole, "Announcement of Intent to Resign from the U.S. Senate," 104th Cong., Sept. 7, 1995, *Congressional Record*, p. S12799.
15. David Durbenberger, interview with the authors, Sept. 30, 2010, Washington, D.C., tape-recorded.
16. Ibid.
17. Ibid.
18. "Senate Leader Confesses He Detests Washington," United Press International, Mar. 30, 1982.

Seven: Stimulus

1. "1 Year Later, How's the Financial System Overhaul?" *Morning Edition*, National Public Radio, Sept. 16, 2009.
2. Gardiner Harris, "Specter, a Fulcrum of the Stimulus Bill, Pulls Off a Coup for Health Money," *New York Times*, Feb. 14, 2009.
3. Ibid.
4. "Economic Stimulus Package," Andrea Mitchell interview with Senator Arlen Specter, Feb. 2, 2009.
5. Interview with Ray Suarez, *NewsHour with Jim Lehrer*, PBS, February 5, 2009.
6. Ibid.

7. Liz Sidoti, "Obama Asks Democrats to Quickly Pass Stimulus Plan," Associated Press, Feb. 6, 2009.

8. "The Big Talker," Michael Smerconish, WPHT, Feb. 9, 2009.

9. Lisa Murkowski, interview with the authors, Dec. 2, 2010, Washington, D.C., tape-recorded.

10. Reuters, "Unauthorized Flight Costs Ohio Governor," *New York Times*, Oct. 11, 1996.

11. Richard Durbin, interview with the authors, Dec. 2, 2010, Washington, D.C., tape-recorded.

12. Joseph Lieberman, interview with the authors, Dec. 16, 2010, Washington, D.C., tape-recorded.

13. Shailagh Murray and Paul Kane, "Congress Reaches Stimulus Accord," *Washington Post*, Feb. 12, 2009.

14. Richard Durbin, interview with the authors, Dec. 2, 2010.

15. Carl Hulse and David M. Herszenhorn, "Pared-Down Bill," *New York Times*, Feb. 7, 2009.

16. Scott Hoeflich, interview with the author, July 21, 2010, Washington, D.C., tape-recorded.

17. Charles Babington, "Capital Culture: Mystery of the Old Clock Persists," Associated Press, Aug. 17, 2010.

18. "Media Stakeout with Senate Leaders," Federal News Service, Feb. 6, 2009, 8:05 p.m.

19. Carl Hulse and David M. Herszenhorn, "Bank Bailout Is Potent Issue for Fall Races," *New York Times*, July 11, 2010.

20. *Lehigh Valley Ramblings*, blog by Bernie O'Hare, Mar. 31, 2009.

21. Kate Schramm, interview with the author, Washington, D.C., Oct. 11, 2010.

22. Ben Pershing, "Kennedy Makes Brief Appearance for Stimulus Vote," *Washington Post* online, Feb. 9, 2009.

23. G. Terry Madonna, "With Moderate Out, Partisan Lines Are Drawn," *Centre* (PA) *Daily Times*, May 22, 2010.

24. *Anderson Cooper*, CNN interview with Dana Bash, Feb. 10, 2009.

25. *American Morning with John Roberts*, CNN, Feb. 11, 2009.

26. Arlen Specter interview with Mackenzie Carpenter, *Pittsburgh Post-Gazette*, Feb. 12, 2009, tape-recorded.

27. Scott Hoeflich, e-mail to the author, Oct. 13, 2010.

28. Ibid.

29. Arlen Specter, radio interview with Bill O'Reilly, Feb. 12, 2010.

30. Scott Hoeflich, e-mail to the author, Oct. 13, 2010.

31. Harris, "Specter, a Fulcrum of the Stimulus Bill, Pulls Off a Coup for Health Money."

32. Sewell Chan, "In Study, 2 Economists Say Intervention Helped Avert a 2nd Depression," *New York Times*, July 28, 2010.

33. Michael Grunwald, "How the Stimulus Is Changing America," *Time*, Aug. 26, 2010.

34. Thomas Fitzgerald, "Conservative Pat Toomey Woos Moderates in Senate Campaign," *Philadelphia Inquirer* online, July 18, 2010.

35. Gail Russell Chaddock, "GOP Centrists Give Obama a Majority—Barely," *Christian Science Monitor*, Feb. 10, 2009.

Eight: Too Candid

1. Aaron Blake, "Specter and the Left Begin to Make Nice," *The Hill*, Apr. 30, 2009, p. 8.

2. Robert Casey, interview with the authors, Dec. 1, 2010, Washington, D. C., tape-recorded.

3. James O'Toole and Timothy McNulty, "Specter Stuns Senate by Switching Parties," *Pittsburgh Post-Gazette*, Apr. 29, 2009.

4. Aaron Blake, "Dems Press Specter to Switch Sides," *The Hill*, Mar. 17, 2009.

5. Josh Drobynk, "Specter Hints at Showcasing His 'Independent' Side," *Allentown Morning Call*, Mar. 19, 2009.

6. Dick Polman, "The American Debate: Time for Specter to Join a New Party," *Philadelphia Inquirer*, Philly.com, Mar. 8, 2009.

7. Dan Simpson, "Switch Sides, Sen. Specter," *Pittsburgh Post-Gazette*, post-gazette.com, Apr. 22, 2009.

8. Sally Kalson, "Abandon Ship, Arlen," *Pittsburgh Post-Gazette*, Feb. 15, 2009.

9. Harry Reid with Mark Warren, *The Good Fight: Hard Lessons from Searchlight to Washington* (New York: G. P. Putnam's Sons, 2008), p. 6.

10. James M. Jeffords, *My Declaration of Independence* (New York: Simon & Schuster, 2001), p. 83.

11. Reid with Warren, *The Good Fight*, p. 74.

12. Carl Hulse and Adam Nagourney, "Specter Switches Parties," *New York Times*, Apr. 29, 2009, Late edition–final.

13. Janet Hook and James Oliphant, "Sen. Arlen Specter Switches Parties," *Los Angeles Times*, Apr. 29, 2009.

14. Jared Allen, "House Dems Emboldened by Specter's Party Switch," *The Hill*, Apr. 29, 2009, p. 4.

15. Michael O'Brien, "Bloggers: Right Furious, Left Wary and Doubtful," *The Hill*, Apr. 29, 2009, p. 1.

16. Scott Boos, interview with the author, Sept. 9, 2010, Washington, D.C., tape-recorded.

17. Robert Casey, interview with the authors, Dec. 1, 2010, Washington, D.C., tape-recorded.

18. Emily Heil and Elizabeth Brotherton, "Heard on the Hill," *Roll Call*, April 29, 2009.

19. Alexander Bolton, "Defection Reshapes Senate," *The Hill*, Apr. 29, 2009, p. 1.

20. Robert Casey, interview with the authors, Dec. 1, 2010.

21. Joseph Lieberman, interview with the authors, Dec. 16, 2010, Washington, D.C., tape-recorded.

22. J. Taylor Rushing, "Snowe, Collins Warn the Party It Must Wake Up," *The Hill*, Apr. 29, 2009, p. 1.

23. *CQ* Staff, "Reaction to Specter Decision from Republicans, Democrats," CQ Today Online News—Congressional Affairs, Apr. 28, 2009, 4:09 p.m.

24. O'Brien, "Bloggers: Right Furious, Left Wary and Doubtful."

25. Susan Page, Ken Dilanian, and John Fritze, "The Senate's Magic Number: 60," *USA Today*, Apr. 29, 2009.

26. Dan Balz, "Will GOP Sleep Through Wake-up Call?" *Washington Post*, Apr. 29, 209.

27. Paul Kane, "On First Day as a Democrat, Specter (Again) Bucks His Party," *Washington Post*, Apr. 30, 2009.

28. Mark Leibovich, "He Flipped!," *New York Times*, May 3, 2009.

29. Senator Harry Reid, "Media Stakeout with Senate Majority Leader Harry Reid," Federal News Service, Apr. 28, 2009.

30. Scott Kraus, John Micek, and Brain Callaway, "Specter Splits," *Allentown Morning Call*, Apr. 29, 2009.

31. Daphne Retter, "Specter of Doom for GOP—Republican Senator in Switch to Dems," *New York Post*, Apr. 29, 2009.

32. Page, Dilanian, and Fritze, "The Senate's Magic Number: 60."

33. White House event, Arlen Specter Becomes Democrat, Apr. 29, 2009.

34. O'Toole and McNulty, "Specter Stuns Senate by Switching Parties."

35. Robert J. Dole, interview with the author, October 8, 2010, Washington, D.C.

36. David Durenberger, interview with the authors, Sept. 30, 2010, Washington, D.C., tape-recorded.

37. Scott Boos, interview with the author, Sept. 9, 2009, Washington, D.C., tape-recorded.

38. Ibid.

39. Alexander Bolton, "Top Dems Rebel on Specter," *The Hill,* Apr. 30, 2009, p. 1.

40. "GOP May Soon Be Gaining Some Party-Switchers," *St. Louis Post-Dispatch,* Oct. 16, 1994.

41. "PA: Specter Says Support for Coleman Was Mistaken," *Frontrunner,* May 6, 2009.

42. Scott Hoeflich, interview with the author, Washington, D.C., Oct. 20, 2010, tape-recorded.

43. "Son of Specter," editorial, *Wall Street Journal,* July 16, 2010.

44. Richard Fenno, *Learning to Legislate* (Washington: Congressional Quarterly Press, 1991), pp. 156–57.

45. Matt Bai, "Voter Insurrection Turns Mainstream, Creating New Laws of Politics," *New York Times,* May 20, 2010.

46. Leibovich, "He Flipped!"

47. Liaquat Ahamed, *The Lords of Finance: The Bankers Who Broke the World* (New York: Penguin, 2009), p. 222.

48. Alexander Bolton, "Specter Receives Warm Reception from Dems," *The Hill,* May 6, 2009, p. 4.

49. John Stanton, "Specter Will Be Junior Democrat on Committees," *Roll Call,* May 5, 2009.

50. Paul Kane, "Party Switch Costs Specter His Seniority on Senate Committees," *Washington Post,* May 6, 2009.

51. Kimberly Hefling, "New Democrat Specter Loses Committee Seniority," Associated Press, May 6, 2009.

52. Scott Hoeflich, interview with the author, Oct. 19, 2009, Washington, D.C., tape-recorded.

53. "GOP Gleeful with Specter's Demotion," *White House Bulletin,* May 6, 2009.

54. Wolf Blitzer interview of Harry Reid, *The Situation Room with Wolf Blitzer,* CNN, May 6, 2009.

55. "Indecision '96 Won't Be Easier on Dems," Knight-Ridder Newspapers, Aug. 27, 1996.

Nine: God's Going to Stand Before You

1. John Fritze, Susan Page, and Richard Wolf, "A 16-Month Drama, with 8 Key Moments," *USA Today,* Mar. 26, 2010.

2. David M. Herszenhorn and Robert Pear, "Senate Lays Groundwork for a Final Health Care Vote," *New York Times,* Dec. 23, 2009.

3. John Fritze, Page, and Wolf, "A 16-Month Drama, with 8 Key Moments."

4. Howard Kurtz, "Journalists, Left Out of the Debate; Few Americans Seem to Hear Health Care Facts," *Washington Post,* Aug. 24, 2009.

5. John Fritze, Page, and Wolf, "A 16-Month Drama, with 8 Key Moments."

6. Ibid.

7. Bob MacGuffie, "Rocking the Town Halls—Best Practices / A Political Action Memo," *Right Principles*, first reported by *Think Progress*, July 31, 2009.

8. Brian Beutler, "Tea Party Town Hall Strategy: 'Rattle Them,' 'Stand Up and Shout,'" *Talking Points Memo*, Aug. 3, 2009.

9. Scott Hoeflich, interview with the author, Sept. 13, 2010, Washington, D.C., tape-recorded.

10. Ian Urbina and Katharine Q. Seelye, "Senator Goes Face to Face with Dissent," *New York Times*, Aug. 12, 2009.

11. Ibid.

12. Andrew Putz, eds., "The Full Specter," *Philadelphia Magazine*, Nov. 2006.

13. Daniel Newhauser, "Members Are Not Dodging Town Halls," *CQ-Roll Call*, June 21, 2010.

14. Mike Madden, "You're a Socialist, Fascist Pig!," Salon.com, Aug. 14, 2009.

15. Jeff Zeleny, "After Displays of Rage, Skipping Town Halls," *New York Times*, June 7, 2010.

16. Mike Faher, "Johnstown Grad Seeks Congressional Seat," *Johnstown Tribune-Democrat*, Aug. 27, 2009.

17. Peggy Noonan, "The Town Hall Revolt, One Year Later," *Wall Street Journal*, July 9, 2010.

18. Robert Pear and David M. Herszenhorn, "Congress Sends White House Landmark Health Overhaul," *New York Times*, Mar. 22, 2010.

19. David M. Herszenhorn and Robert Pear, "Health Vote Is Done, but Partisan Debate Rages On," *New York Times*, Mar. 23, 2010.

20. Andrea Johnson, "Conservatism: Infamous Town-Hall Woman Is All About.com it," *Lebanon* (PA) *Daily News*, Nov. 1, 2009.

Ten: Red Meat

1. Jeanne Cummings, "New Hope for Stalled Labor Bill," Politico.com, Apr. 29, 2009.

2. Steven Greenhouse, "Democrats Drop Key Part of Bill to Assist Unions," *New York Times*, July 17, 2009.

3. Ibid.

4. Eileen Connelly, interview with the authors, Nov. 5, 2010, Philadelphia, tape-recorded.

5. Ibid.

6. Ibid.

7. Shira Toepliz, "Labor Has Tough Choice in Pa.," *Roll Call*, June 3, 2009.

8. Ibid.

9. William K. Stevens, "Official Calls In Press and Kills Himself," *New York Times*, Jan. 23, 1987.

10. Chris Nicholas, telephone interview with the author, May 7, 2011, tape-recorded.

11. Stan Caldwell, telephone interview with the author, Sept. 8, 2010.

12. Cummings, "New Hope for Stalled Labor Bill."

13. Michael O'Brien, "Hoffa Met with Specter on Monday," *The Hill*, Apr. 28, 2009.

14. Cummings, "New Hope for Stalled Labor Bill."

15. Greenhouse, "Democrats Drop Key Part of Bill to Assist Unions."
16. Kevin Bogardus and Sean J. Miller, "Unions Taking On Dems Who Do Not Toe Labor Line," *The Hill*, Mar. 11, 2010.
17. Eileen Connelly, interview with the authors, Nov. 5, 2010.
18. Bogardus and Miller, "Unions Taking On Dems Who Do Not Toe Labor Line."
19. Toepliz, "Labor Has Tough Choice in Pa."
20. Bogardus and Miller, "Unions Taking On Dems Who Do Not Toe Labor Line."
21. Mike Oscar, telephone interview with the author from Philadelphia, Dec. 7, 2010.

Eleven: Fatally Flawed

1. John Bradley, "Why Is Joe Sestak Surging over Arlen Specter? The Answer in One Day of Campaigning," "Political Hotsheet," CBS News, May 17, 2010.
2. Alexander Bolton, "Defection Reshapes Senate," *The Hill*, Apr. 29, 2009.
3. Adam Nagourney, "Specter, After Shifting Parties, Faces Fire from Both Sides," *New York Times*, May 12, 2010.
4. "Rendell: Sestak 'Lost a Lot of Credibility' by Not Saying He'd Support Specter," May 17, 2010, pa2010.com.
5. Nagourney, "Specter, After Shifting Parties, Faces Fire from Both Sides."
6. Stan Caldwell, telephone interview with the author, Sept. 8, 2010.
7. Paul Carpenter, "It Is Ungentlemanly to Say 'Lady,'" *Allentown Morning Call*, Jan. 27, 2010.
8. Andrew Malcolm, "Specter May Be Haunted by Exchange with Bachmann," *Los Angeles Times*, home edition, Jan. 24, 2010.
9. Eric Roper, "Audio: Sen. Arlen Specter Tells Bachmann to 'Act Like a Lady,'" StarTribune.com, Jan. 21, 2010.
10. Carpenter, "It Is Ungentlemanly to Say 'Lady.'"
11. Ibid.
12. "The Joe Sestak 'Question'—Anatomy of an Interview That Spread Like Wildfire," *Larry Kane Report* online, May 28, 2010.
13. Colby Itkowitz, "Ex-President Clinton to Stump for Sestak," *Morning Call*, Aug. 4, 2010.
14. Jonathan Martin and Glenn Thrush, "Obama Steers Clear of Shaky Specter," *Politico*, May 17, 2010.
15. Nagourney, "Specter, After Shifting Parties, Faces Fire from Both Sides."

Twelve: Cold Rain

1. Candy Crowley, *Anderson Cooper 360 Degrees*, CNN, May 18, 2010, 11 p.m.
2. Scott Hoeflich, interview with the author, July 16, 2010, Washington, D.C., tape-recorded.
3. Michael Sokolove, "Joe Sestak, the 60th Democrat," *New York Times*, Aug. 18, 2010.
4. G. Terry Madonna and Michael L. Young, "Arlen Specter's Perfect Storm," pa2010.com, May 19, 2010.

Thirteen: The Aftermath

1. Kate Kelly, interview with the author, July 16, 2010, Washington, D.C., tape-recorded.
2. Dan Eggen, "Small Conservative Organization a Big Thorn in the GOP's Side; Club for Growth Has Influenced Races in Several States," *Washington Post,* May 20, 2010.
3. G. Terry Madonna and Michael L. Young, "Arlen Specter's Perfect Storm," pa2010.com, May 19, 2010.
4. Katharine Q. Seelye, "Specter Legacy Is Study of the Perils of a Switch," *New York Times,* May 23, 2010.
5. "Rendell: Sestak Affair 'Hard-Knuckle Politics,'" Associated Press, May 30, 2010.
6. "Much Ado About Mr. Sestak," editorial, *Washington Post,* May 30, 2010.
7. Sean Sullivan, "OCE Complaints Spike After Sestak Flap," *National Journal's Hotline,* July 20, 2010.
8. Colby Itkowitz, "Clinton: I Didn't Try to Get Sestak Out of Race," *Allentown Morning Call,* Aug. 13, 2010.
9. Letter from RNC Chairman Michael Steele to Attorney General Eric Holder, Aug. 18, 2010. Mark Preston, "RNC Asks DOJ for Investigation of Sestak Affair," CNN.com, Aug. 18, 2010.
10. Dick Polman, "In the Dark," Philly.com, July 28, 2010.
11. T.W. Farnam and Dan Eggen, "Outside Spending up Sharply for Midterms," *Washington Post,* Oct. 4, 2010.
12. Peter Baker, "Tide Turns, Starkly," *New York Times,* Nov. 3, 2010.
13. Brian Lamb, Susan Swain, and Mark Farkas, eds. *The Supreme Court: A C-SPAN Book Featuring the Justices in Their Own Words* (Philadelphia: Public Affairs, 2010).
14. "Taxpayers Pay for Cut Boasts," *Pittsburgh Tribune-Review,* Aug. 15, 2010.
15. Tom Shales, "After King's Mannerly CNN Reign, Barbarians Might Storm the Gates," *Washington Post,* July 6, 2010.
16. John F. Harris and Jim VandeHei, "The Age of Rage," *Politico* online, July 23, 2010.
17. Michael Smerconish, "The Media's Black-and-White World," *Washington Post,* June 11, 2010.
18. Michael Shear, "Ailes Tells Fox Anchors to 'Tone It Down,'" *New York Times,* Jan. 11, 2011.
19. Lisa Murkowski, interview with the authors, Dec. 2, 2010, Washington, D.C., tape-recorded.
20. Ibid.
21. Ibid.
22. Ibid.
23. Ibid.
24. Robert Casey, interview with the authors, Dec. 1, 2010, Washington, D.C., tape-recorded.
25. Ibid.
26. Ibid.

Epilogue: The Way Out

1. "Sen. Patrick Leahy Holds a Hearing on the Elena Kagan Nomination," June 30, 2010, *CQ* Transcriptions.
2. Zell Miller, *A National Party No More: The Conscience of a Conservative Democrat* (Atlanta: Stroud & Hall, 2003), p. 14.

3. James M. Jeffords, *My Declaration of Impendence* (New York: Simon & Schuster, 2001), p. 130.
4. Christine Todd Whitman, *It's My Party, Too* (New York: Penguin Press, 2005), p. 230.
5. Tom Coburn, interview with the authors, Dec. 16, 2010, Washington, D.C., tape-recorded.
6. Steve Roberts and Cokie Roberts, "We Need Civility," *Pottstown* (PA) *Mercury,* PottsMerc.com, Nov. 23, 2010.
7. Orrin Hatch, 108th Cong., 1st Sess., Nov. 12, 2003, *Congressional Record,* p. S14550.
8. Elena Kagan, *University of Chicago Law Review* 62 (1995), p. 919.
9. David Ingram, "Specter Unhappy with Kagan's Answers," *Legal Times Blog,* June 30, 2010.
10. Interview with Paul Kane of the *Washington Post,* July 1, 2010, tape-recorded.
11. Charles Schumer, Senate Judiciary Committee meeting, 108th Cong., 1st Sess., Oct. 2, 2003, official transcript, p. 77.
12. Robert J. Dole, interview with the author, Feb. 17, 2004, driving through eastern Pennsylvania, tape-recorded.
13. Ibid.
14. George Watson and John A. Stookey, *Shaping America: The Politics of Supreme Court Appointments* (New York: HarperCollins College Publishers, 1995), p. 140.
15. Mark Sherman, "Justice Not Sold on Having Cameras in the High Court," *Grand Rapids Press,* Oct. 10, 2010, p. 2.
16. Robert J. Dole, interview with the author, Feb. 17, 2004.
17. Joseph Tanfani, "Frame Fall Blamed on Builder," *Philadelphia Inquirer,* Aug. 1, 2003.

Index